10/88

GOLDEN GIRL

GOLDEN GIRL

*The Story of
Jessica Savitch*

Alanna Nash

E. P. DUTTON NEW YORK

Published in the United States by E. P. Dutton,
a division of NAL Penguin Inc.,
2 Park Avenue, New York, N.Y. 10016.

Published simultaneously in Canada by
Fitzhenry and Whiteside, Limited, Toronto.

Library of Congress Cataloging-in-Publication Data
Nash, Alanna.
The golden girl.
1. Savitch, Jessica. 2. Journalists—United States—
Biography. 3. Television personalities—United States—
Biography. I. Title.
PN4874.S297N37 1988   070'.92'4 [B]   88-18921
ISBN: 0-525-24667-3

Designed by REM Studio
1 3 5 7 9 10 8 6 4 2

First Edition

For Bob

In 1984, five of the ten Miss America finalists said they planned to become television news anchors. For some of those young women, an early role model was probably a mesmerizing blonde named Jessica Savitch who illuminated the network airwaves for a time in the late seventies and early eighties like no one before or since. She made the word "anchorwoman" something different: She made it magic.

As someone who never wanted to be a Miss America contestant, but who was fascinated by the anchorwoman role model, I wondered what it would be like to live Jessica's life, an existence that seemed so desirable and perfect, the ideal wedding of beauty and brains.

I discovered, in research that would be in many ways like a two-year television apprenticeship, that the story of Jessica Savitch is a fairy tale. More so, it is a cautionary tale. It is, in the words of her most intimate friend, Ron Kershaw, the story of "someone who drove herself beyond the limits of anyone, and then didn't know how to stop it, to turn it off, and just be at peace for a while. It is the story of the little girl who flew too close to the sun, and her wings melted."

It is that, and it is more. But most of all, it is a nightmare, hung in the fragile balance of truth and illusion that is television.

Contents

Preface   xiii
Acknowledgments   xvii
Prologue   1

1. The Family   *3*
2. "An Engine Inside of Her": The School Years   *33*
3. A Great Magnetism: CBS, Houston,
    and Ron Kershaw   *71*
4. The Fourth Largest Market: Philadelphia   *128*
5. Famous   *165*
6. To the Network: NBC and Washington   *205*
7. Jessica Savitch-Payne   *233*
8. Nightmare   *269*
9. The Spiral: New York   *285*
    Epilogue   *330*

Sixteen pages of photographs follow page 170.

Preface

On the surface, Jessica Savitch was a commercial for the American Dream. Beautiful, blonde, a network news anchorwoman by the time she was thirty, she was the stuff of fantasy, a cool but vulnerable vision who wafted into 15 million households each night and proved herself "a goddess for the McLuhan age," as writer Michael Mallowe was to observe. "Edward R. Murrow had told it like it was—lyrical words from a leathery mug. But Savitch fed our fantasies of how it should be—Brie and Beaujolais in a penthouse on Central Park."

Savitch appeared to have it all—even wide appeal to both sexes. She was named the fourth most trusted anchor in America, over Charles Kuralt, Tom Brokaw, Peter Jennings, and Ted Koppel in a 1982 *TV Guide* public opinion survey. Men wanted to know what lay behind her frosty countenance and her radiant smile. And women adored her, seeing her as something of a double role model—a brilliant journalistic pioneer as well as a Grace Kelly for the eighties.

Then in October 1983, the newswoman became a news item. Bucks County, Pennsylvania: a horrible, watery death in a freak accident. Now Jessica Savitch, who had once been in contention as the first woman to anchor a weekday evening newscast, with full admission to the hallowed circle of Rather, Brokaw, and Jennings, would be only a footnote in broadcast history.

But, as *Time* magazine said, "Jessica Savitch left resonances." As a journalist, or as a correspondent gathering the news in the field, Savitch never had been able to equal her strength as a news reader. Yet as a focused manipulator of the medium, she was almost without peer. Millions of viewers remembered her as someone who had seemed to reach across the television to speak directly to *them*.

"She was phenomenal—about the best I've ever seen," says NBC correspondent John Palmer. "Twenty minutes or so into her newscast, she'd usually go for a little kick, or a little bite. And she would smile and lean forward, or tilt her head to the side. My father found her so captivating that he would sit there and wait for that. Even if the bite wasn't funny, he loved that smile. And as far as television was concerned, that was the highlight of his week."

Savitch managed to communicate the paradox of vulnerability beneath authority. Her audience came to care about her in a way they did not care about Barbara Walters, John Chancellor, or Walter Cronkite. To young women, especially, she was one of their own who had struggled—and triumphed—in a man's world.

Within three years of signing with NBC, however, Savitch lost that winning exuberance. In tight close-up, the camera, which had worshiped her, turned into a cruel lover. The real Jessica Savitch had begun showing through the image intended for public view. Where she once had projected vulnerability and authority, she now projected vulnerability and danger, a seething sort of discontent at first, and then a wild despair. Soon a nation would know she was a woman with troubles, and secrets.

By that time, Savitch, whom *Newsweek* had dubbed "NBC's Golden Girl," had lost much of her luster, at least with the NBC brass. She no longer appeared as a correspondent for "Nightly News," only as a weekend anchor and as the presenter of the "NBC News Digest," the 60-second news capsules. Finally, in 1983, she lost her Saturday night anchor slot to Connie Chung. Something had gone terribly wrong.

I wanted to know why Savitch's star had set. Newspaper articles carried only the barest of facts—about a divorce after less than a year, a quick new marriage, the loss of a baby, and, after only five months, a new tragedy with her second husband. How could one person survive such a series of events? To what extent might she have had a hand in courting them?

In some ways, my quest for the answers to the Savitch enigma began as a journey of self-exploration. I was thirty-six when I started research for this book, the age Jessica had been when she died. Was there actually a personality profile of the journalist in general and the broadcast journalist in particular? Did Jessica seek fame as a panacea for a host of psychological ills? What did her rapid rise at the network say about the way the industry was changing, with the primacy of the performer over the journalist? What were the real ingredients behind our national fantasy of her?

Soon after I began my work, what unfolded was a horror story. Almost everything Jessica Savitch appeared to be, she was not. Wholesomely sexy, savvy, and well-prepared on camera, Jessica was something altogether different when the red light went out— lost, unable to manage the stark reality of everyday life. Why?

Most of the information in this book comes from interviews I conducted with Savitch's friends, colleagues, bosses, teachers, doctors, lovers, secretaries, neighbors and clergymen, spanning the entire length of her life. The majority of the more than three hundred people I interviewed talked on the record. Others spoke for background, meaning I could use their information, but I could not attribute it to them. Though I talked with one of Jessica's uncles and three of her cousins, her immediate family declined to be interviewed, pending the resolution of their suit for wrongful death against the Commonwealth of Pennsylvania. That suit was settled in January 1988, as this book was completed.

I never met Jessica Savitch. When her point of view is offered it is mainly through the recollections of her friends. The quoted dialogue I use comes directly from the primary sources as they remembered it. And while I found a consulting psychiatrist to help me interpret or confirm certain of Jessica's behavioral patterns, whatever observations I have made about her psychological motivations have been based on conversations with several of the psychiatrists she saw in the last seven years of her life. Not all of these are mentioned by name in the text, and the fact that a psychiatrist's name appears in these pages does not mean that he assisted me in my research.

"The ideal subject of a biography," said *Time* magazine in 1984, "is someone who has succeeded at something, but at a pretty stiff price. The story of such a person inspires both envy and the soothing balm of pity." Few people measure up to those criteria as well as Jessica Savitch. She is the perfect, cruel metaphor.

Acknowledgments

J essica Savitch was a woman everyone recognized but nobody knew. To those people who thought they knew her well, she handed out only tiny pieces of herself and of the woman she had created. Only by assembling those pieces—culled from literally hundreds of sources—could anyone hope to understand what drove her in her quest for national recognition.

I am extraordinarily indebted to everyone who shared his recollections of Jessica, and whose name appears as such in the text. I am equally grateful to those who spoke for background or "not for attribution," and whose names I cannot credit.

In addition, my professional and personal thanks go to: Chris Albertson; Holly Atkinson; Johnny Bazzano; Jamie Blaine and Jim Dugan of *The Kennett Paper*; Richard Bond; Bonnie Borton, John Lippincott and Sharon Murphy of Ithaca College; Jean Carper; Martha Carr; Edward Carson; Ann Caslin; Jean Caslin; the late Richard Caslin; Mary Castle; Teresa Cavanaugh; Nada Chandler;

ACKNOWLEDGMENTS

Mary Ann Childers; Faith Childs; John A. Clement 3rd; John Cochran; Emilie Knud-Hansen Coleman; Mort Crim; Judith Crist; Jill Croston; Rachel M. Dach; Janet Deckman; Muriel Dobbin; Joan Durham and family; Judy Farinet; Debi Faubion; Julius and Reisel Fischbein; Jane Fitts; Melissa Forsythe; Rosalie Fox; George Fridrich; Roberto Fucigna; Clara Gatti; Eleanor Gochenaur; Gladys and Ray Gochnauer; Connie Goffredi and Janet West of the Columbia University Graduate School of Journalism; Susan Goren of New York University; Jane Hall; Bob and Janet Hayes; Catharine Heinz of Broadcast Pioneers Library; Richie Heinze of the Manahawkin, New Jersey *Times-Beacon*; Judith Adler Hennessee; Britt Hilander; Carolyn Hodges; Kristin Hubbard; Edie Huggins; Bob Iler; Henry Kisor of the *Chicago Sun-Times.*

Also: Thomas H. Kreneck; John A. Lack; Tony Lame; Jim Lee; Susan Ludel; Clayton L. Magruder; Jeanne Martinet; Marsha Mercer; Nancy Merrill; Maxine Mesinger of the *Houston Chronicle;* Caren N. Mitchel of Women in Communications, Inc.; Daniel J. Moriarty; Scott Newell; Peat O'Neil of the *Washington Post*; Robert Page of the *Chicago Sun-Times*; Maralyn Lois Polak of the *Philadelphia Inquirer*; Charles Quinn; Brenda Radcliffe; Martin and Jo Rand; Peter Ross Range; Betty Jane Reed; Ronda Robinson; Ann Rogers; Howard Rosenberg of the *Los Angeles Times*; Leah Rozen; Howard Sacks; the late Gloria Safier; Frank Scheidt; John Schultz; Margaret Shannon; Eric Silverman; Betty and Fred Sinclair; Susan Standley; Liz Smith; Sara M. Stalkus; Wayne Stevens of CKWW; Bob Stewart and Jim Holland; Charlotte Tharp; Edna B. Timmerman; Edward Tivnan; Lea Thompson; Becky Trachtman of American Women in Radio and Television, Inc.; Stanley Tretick; Linda Upton and Cynthia Hazeltyne; the staff of the Vanderbilt University Television News Archive; Diana Walker; Mary Walton of the *Philadelphia Inquirer*; Carol Wendel; James Whalen, president of Ithaca College; Art Wiese; Mary Alice Williams; Christy Wise; Don Woodman; Hugh C. Wright, Jr.; Lorrie Yapczenski; and Karen Anne Zupko.

A number of people without whom I never would have understood my subject gave unselfishly to this project time and time again. They include: Steve Berger; Lelia M. Bright; Tony Busch; Carl Cochran; Jered Dawaliby; Marc Koslow; and Barry Swartz.

And, doubtless, there would have been no book had it not been for the following people: Wendy Pannier Johnston, who drove me through every square mile of the Delaware Valley, set up numerous interviews in Kennett Square, and helped me understand Jessica's early years; Lilyan Wilder, who provided video tapes, interviews with Jessica's friends, and tea and sympathy when the going got rough; Judy F. May, who offered friendship and moral support beyond all measure; Florence King, who believed in the project long before any publisher did; and my parents, Allan and Emily Kay Nash, who lovingly aided me every step of the way.

My very special thanks to Diane Caslin Alexander, who transcribed hundreds of hours of taped interviews, pored through countless books and articles, and, in general, loaned her life to the good of this project for well over a year.

And finally, I cannot adequately express my thanks to Joyce Engelson, my editor; Charlotte Sheedy, my agent; and to Sara Blackburn, a genius with a blue pencil who facilitated the work on the manuscript in record time and became a valued friend in the process. All three gave the book more time and consideration than any writer could ever hope for.

Prologue

On October 23, 1983, Jessica Savitch was spending the day doing something generally out of character: She was enjoying herself. It was a Sunday, and she and her new boyfriend, Martin Fischbein, a thirty-four-year-old executive with the *New York Post,* had driven one and one-half hours from Manhattan to New Hope, Pennsylvania, a fashionable country retreat and artists' colony. There they had planned to spend an idyllic autumn afternoon browsing in the antique shops and galleries, and discovering whatever else the sleepy little town had to offer. *The Great Weekend Escape Book,* which lay on the car seat, suggested a stroll along the grassy towpath that followed the Delaware Canal. "Imagine yourself living here when mules pulled coal barges up and down the 60-mile canal . . . overhanging trees reflected in its mirrorlike surface," the guidebook beckoned.

But it had rained too hard for a leisurely walk, and sometime after five P.M., Jessica and Martin showed up early for their six-

thirty dinner reservation at the 190-year-old Chez Odette, a romantic, cozy inn off South River Road, in back of the canal. At
seven-fifteen, when she and Fischbein got up to leave, it was already dark outside. A light fog had begun to settle on the canal,
which had been dry most of the summer but had filled with water
during the rainy weekend.

Jessica hardly went anywhere without her blue-eyed Siberian
husky, Chewy, and today was no exception. When she and Martin
walked to their rented blue Oldsmobile station wagon, Jessica
apparently crawled in back with the dog. Fischbein got behind the
wheel, buckled his seat belt, and began to ease out of the parking
space. To reach the exit, he needed to turn south, go past the front
end of the restaurant, and cross the bridge that spans the canal.
But whether he became disoriented in the hard rain, or believed
he could take a shortcut out of the back of the parking area onto
the road, Martin drove north out of the gravel lot and up a wide
dirt incline onto the towpath, ignoring two twelve-by-eighteen-
inch signs that read Motor Vehicles Prohibited.

According to New Hope Police Chief Walter J. Everett, Fischbein may have swerved to avoid a parked car, and veered too far
to the left. Whatever the reason, the car flipped over and plunged
fifteen feet into the muddy canal, coming to rest upside down in
three feet of mud and four feet of water. The mud effectively sealed
the doors, turning the automobile into a death trap.

"It's reasonable to assume Jessica Savitch made some attempt
to get out and Martin Fischbein did not," Bucks County Coroner
Thomas Rosko said later. According to the rescue squad, Jessica
ended life as she began it, in the fetal position, her feet drawn
under her, and her back to the door. She died only sixty miles from
where she was born.

1

The Family

At night, the slender trees that line the side-walks of downtown Kennett Square, Pennsylvania, come alive with thousands of tiny white lights, turning what is already a picture-perfect village, with its proud Victorian architecture and converted row house shops, into something out of a fairy tale. To a child with even the slightest imagination, the town could easily be a place of magic and wonder. "When I was a little girl in the 1950s," Jessica would write in *Anchorwoman*, "I wanted to be a princess . . . living happily ever after with her Prince Charming."

It was here that Jessica spent the first thirteen years of her life. To most of Jessica's peers, the little hamlet, with a population of 3,700, seemed a mix of Norman Rockwell, Thornton Wilder, and "Leave It to Beaver." It was Main Street, U.S.A.

"Kennett Square was an amazing place to grow up in, because you were so isolated," remembers Damon Sinclair, an independent filmmaker who now lives in nearby Chadds Ford. "You were thirty miles southwest of Philadelphia, but you could have been almost anywhere in the middle of America. It was an entity unto itself.

"Of course, in the fifties, it was probably pretty pure and sweet all over America," he continues. "But in Kennett, I think you grew up with an overwhelming sense of security and well-being, because you knew everybody, and everybody knew you. If you walked into Voorhees' Hardware and said, 'Gee, Mr. Leach, I'm looking for something for Dad for Christmas,' he'd say, 'You know, he was in here the other day, and he was admiring this pen knife.' That's the kind of town it was."

Predictably, the cultural revolution of the sixties came and went without Kennett Square taking much note of it. The lives of the townspeople continued to revolve around work and home, the Rotary and Lions clubs, Little League, scouting, and the various religious affiliations, predominately Quaker. With few exceptions, the people who lived in Kennett also worked in Kennett. Children went through grades 1–12 at the Kennett Consolidated School, where the teachers usually had taught their parents before them.

"To a certain extent, everybody knows your business in Kennett," says Damon Sinclair. "And while it's a comfortable place for a child to grow up in, a lot of the people are pretty Puritanical and petty. There's a consensus of thinking about things in a small town like Kennett, a sort of Presbyterianism. It's a fair, Christian approach to life, but it's also slightly judgmental about people who don't quite fit in. And it can get pretty spooky."

In the early 1930s, Kennett Square was a community where English and Irish Quakers, Scotch-Irish Presbyterians, Irish and Italian Catholics, and a thriving population of blacks, who had first made homes in the town in the early 1800s, coexisted in harmony. The town could boast of two Friends meeting houses, two Baptist churches, one Catholic church, one Presbyterian church, and one African Methodist Episcopal church. But there was only a smattering of Jewish families, and no synagogue or Jewish cemetery.

Benjamin Yussavitch, Jessica's paternal grandfather, was born in 1899 in the Bessarabia region of Russia, near the Romanian border. He came to America around 1912, through the efforts of his older sister, Gisa. The eldest of six children of a grain merchant and miller, Gisa immigrated to America sometime around the turn of the century. Both her parents were dead, and although she knew no English when she arrived, she began going to school and went to work before she was a teenager. Eventually, she married a well-to-do Philadelphia wholesale dry goods salesman named Harry Wiseman.

In time, Gisa and Harry brought over her five siblings. Of the boys, first came Theodore, who arrived by cattleboat, and then Joseph, and Benjamin, the youngest. The Wisemans taught them English. Somewhere along the line, probably in immigration, they simplified the family name of Yussavitch. But though they became Americanized rather quickly—Gisa now called herself "Gussie"—they held fast to their Jewish religion. And Ben never shed his thick Yiddish accent, which sometimes made him difficult to understand.

According to Gussie's daughter, Beatrice Marker, Ben and Ted went to work for Harry Wiseman as traveling salesmen, calling on retail accounts. One such trip led Ben to Youngstown, Ohio, where he met Lillian Dinaberg, a strikingly pretty blonde sixteen-year-old. They married a short time later, around 1921.

Lillian Savitch had a lot in common with her husband. Her granddaughter Dorothy Savitch believes that she was born to a Jewish family in a part of the Soviet Union that is now Poland, and that she came to the United States as a small child. Like her husband, Lillian spoke with a heavy Yiddish accent, and like him, she possessed a tremendous drive to succeed and a strong sense of independence. In a long-ago photograph of the Savitch clan gathered at what appears to be a wedding reception, Ben and Lil stand out like hired guests brought in to lend class to the event. Immaculately dressed and well-groomed, they radiate confidence and poise.

In the late teens or early 1920s, both Ben and Ted moved from Philadelphia to Coatesville, Pennsylvania, where Ben settled down in a house on Sixth Avenue, near Main Street. It was here that he brought his young bride. The children came quickly and close together—Leon, who was nicknamed "Sonny"; Rachel, usually called Rae or "Sissy"; David, or "Buddy"; and then Emmanuel, who answered to either Manny or "Junior." The Savitches actively reared their children in the Jewish faith, and Ted and Ben joined with others to help build the Beth Israel synagogue.

"Like many Jewish families coming over here, they kept a lot of orthodoxy," says Leon's daughter, Dorothy. "They may have

5

even kept a kosher household at some point. But eventually there were a lot of ways that broke down."

By 1923, Ted had gone into the pawnshop business, while Ben opened a menswear shop in the black section of town, on what was then Boxtown Avenue, now South First. But Coatesville had only one industry—steel. And when the Lukens steel factory all but shut down during the Depression, "The town was absolutely busted," as one old-time resident puts it.

About 1932, Ben closed the Coatesville store and opened one in Kennett Square, some fifteen miles away. He called it The Triangle Shop and offered low-cost, or distressed, clothing for men, women, and children. At first the store, located at 106 North Union, was modest. But Ben soon found he'd tapped into a growing market: the local workers, whose needs were not being met by the other clothing stores in town.

Molly Melchoir had a tailor shop next door, and remembers that Ben commuted to Kennett each day with his helper, Dominic Scamuffa. "Benny had an old Dodge that was so rusty that I don't know how he got back to Coatesville each night," she recalls. "But he was very sociable, and that place just blossomed. They had a wonderful business."

Scamuffa, now the immediate past president of the Coatesville city council, recalls that if the business didn't come to Ben, then Ben went to the business. "Once or twice a week," he says, "Ben would load up his wares and go different places and peddle work clothes to the men as they came out of the stone quarries and lime plants. Ben had good PR," he says. "Very, very good."

Always dapper, Ben Savitch was gregarious, outgoing, and eternally optimistic. His granddaughter Dorothy says she understands how he could have sold anything to anybody. "My grandfather was very charming," she explains. "He liked to tell stories, and he liked to make stuff up."

To the other merchants in town, Ben was known as an aggressive merchandiser. If so, Ben was also generous, and several of the older residents of Kennett Square still speak of his kindness. "He was very good with the poor people," says Anna Basilio. "During the Depression, we would [pay him only] a little a week—maybe twenty-five cents—and he would never ask for nothing."

As the business continued to prosper, Ben moved his store to State Street, in the heart of the town's shopping district. And next door Lil opened a high-quality ladies' specialty shop, carrying expensive brand-name merchandise. She called it Adelle's and billed it as "the Fashion Center of Kennett Square."

"I don't know whether the store really ever made money or not," says Bill Lipschultz, who grew up with the Savitch children in Coatesville. "But you couldn't tell from the Savitches, because they always had their best foot forward. They always put on a great front.

"You have to understand," he continues, "that the Savitches were always a leader family. They made the balls, and they rolled them, too. They just *shone.* And Lil *really* put on a show for everybody. She liked to have people appreciate her, and she had to be the center. But the whole family could make you feel inferior. They were so sharp, and they were always having a good time and going somewhere. *Nobody* was going to get ahead of them."

Ben died in 1980. "They had a lot of fights and walk-outs," says Dorothy Savitch, "but overall, I think they had a very happy marriage."

Beatrice Marker, Ben's niece, concurs. "They really had a terrific marriage, in that their values were the same," she says. "When they celebrated their fiftieth wedding anniversary, Uncle Ben presented Aunt Lil with a gift and said, 'This has been a fifty-year love affair.' And I remember thinking that was true. Their life-style, too, was fine for them. Whether it would be for anybody else doesn't matter."

Despite her apparent love of attention, Lil, like her husband, displayed a warm and giving nature. Several of the women who worked in her shop remember her as a magnanimous employer, and a nice person, even if "Ben was more outgoing and friendly than Lillian," according to Margaret Rigler, who worked at Adelle's for a time in the sixties.

"I remember Lil as always having parties," says Betty Sinclair, who lived across the street from the Savitches after they bought a handsome stone house at 234 Lafayette Street. "She gave elaborate gifts, too, especially at Christmastime. In order to be friendly with the gentiles, she really had to knock herself out.

"Lil had a maid who came in every day," she goes on, "and I remember that while Ben and Lil had an umbrella and table out in the backyard, nobody but the maid ever used it—she'd go out and have lunch there. Because Lil didn't have time to go home and

7

sit down for lunch. She was always working. She was all business, but it was good business. She had a style about her—she was a very good-looking woman."

Other people in the town are far less warm in their recollections.

"When the Savitches first moved here from Coatesville, they lived up on Miller's Hill," says one man, who can trace his ancestors back to the founding of Kennett. "But then when they got pretty successful, they bought that beautiful, spacious home on Lafayette Street. That house was considered to be one of the finest homes in Kennett, and my mother resented it when Lil bought it. She always taught us never to draw a line between race, color, or creed. But Lil pushed her weight around, and a lot of people didn't like it."

Anti-Semitism demanded that the Savitches know their place. "When you talk about the typical aggressive Jewish woman, that was Lil Savitch," remembers one Kennett woman who grew up with the Savitch children. "She was flashy. This was really a funny town to grow up in, because you had your wealthy Quakers, your Italian mushroom growers, and then the few of us [of other Protestant faiths] in between. But there were very few Jewish people, and they were not accepted anywhere back in those days. They couldn't have joined the country club if they'd wanted to, for example. And the fact that the Savitches owned several stores didn't elevate them to any position of respect. Because whatever [respect] they gained, they jeopardized by their behavior. They were just promoting themselves all the time. They had no inhibitions."

Charlotte Kanofsky, widow of Burton Kanofsky, who went into the family hardware business with his twin, Alan, remembers what it was like to be a Jew in Kennett Square during the late forties.

"My husband had lived here since he was a kid," she begins, "and I was from Massachusetts. I didn't know how to drive, and you could only get delicatessen or kosher foods in Wilmington. So on Sundays, the Jewish men in Kennett Square would take turns driving to Wilmington to get the rye breads and bagels and fishes, and then deliver them to all the Jewish people in town. But we're talking forty years ago, and at that time about the only Jews were my husband, his brothers, and the Savitches. Then later some others came in. But there never were too many of us here. Everybody was so provincial, and so bigoted. If your family didn't come

8

over on the Mayflower . . . well, it's a very narrow-minded town."

Lil Savitch and Charlotte Kanofsky might have been expected to become friends, or at least to feel an occasional bond of cultural identity. But Mrs. Kanofsky found the Savitches something of an embarrassment.

"They were obnoxious," she says. "Especially Lil. She was always bragging about this kid, or that kid, or how much money they made last week, or the fortune they spent on that car. I'm outgoing, but I'm not of that school. I don't brag, and I don't like people like that. They bother me. I knew [those stories] weren't true. She had a very vivid imagination."

Ben and Lil didn't seem to have much interest in socializing beyond their own immediate circle, either. Richard Taylor, whose father published the town's newspaper *The Kennett News and Advertiser,* recalls that for all of Ben's vitality in the store, he kept a low profile in community affairs. He was not active in the Chamber of Commerce or the merchants' association, preferring to go along on his own.

Another Jewish resident of the town points out that Ben and Lil weren't active in Jewish affairs, either. "They just weren't interested," he says, "and I don't know why. But what people say is true. Lil was always talking big, even if she backed a lot of it up. Sometimes they were so flamboyant it *was* an embarrassment. And Ben was as bad as she was. It was hard to beat Lil, but Ben was right in there."

But if Ben and Lil felt they didn't fit in and had no real standing in the community, they had achieved their primary goal, which was to establish themselves as successful, hardworking people, to arrange for a retirement of leisure and security, and to provide opportunities for their offspring. While they thought it was important to make a good living, they projected their real ambitions onto their children, who they hoped would make a contribution to the world, distinguish themselves in the professions, and honor their name. Rae, as the only daughter, was counted upon to marry well and to be a respected member of the community. The three sons, however, were expected to study law, go into medicine, or carry on the family business. And all the children were instructed to marry and rear their children within the Jewish faith.

But things were not to turn out exactly as the parents planned.

"Rae, or Sissy, was a knockout," says Betty Sinclair. "She

wasn't pretty, but she had a lot of style when she walked. But she was terribly spoiled, and she was snippy. She had to go to Philadelphia to find friends. Eventually, she married a wealthy Jewish man at one of the big hotels in Philly, and the marriage didn't work out, because she was so spoiled. I remember her sashaying up the street, flaunting her furs. And this was during the war, when people didn't have things like that."

"No doubt about it," says another Kennett woman. "Sissy was a bitch. Nobody liked her."

"That's right," says Charlotte Kanofsky. "She thought she was going to be somebody famous—the second Greta Garbo."

A member of the Savitch family agrees. Saul Savitch, Ted's son and Ben's nephew, shakes his head and sighs. "We weren't very fond of Rae," he says. "She was a pain in the butt. But, of course, she was the only girl, and they just spoiled her. That guy she married was a real character, too. I think the marriage was annulled, and then she married somebody else that Aunt Lil and Uncle Ben didn't like very much. But Sissy wasn't the kind of Savitch that the boys were. We called her a three-dollar bill."

The parents took much greater pride in Leon and Emmanuel, both of whom became lawyers, and both of whom got their degrees from Harvard. Leon, class of '48, became a superior court judge in the state of California. And Manny, class of '51, became a partner in an old established San Diego law firm. Sissy, whom Bill Lipschultz describes as "so gorgeous she made Elizabeth Taylor look like a frog," also moved west.

That left David, or "Buddy," the second son, and the third and next to last child, who would become Jessica's father, the person whose memory seemed to dictate much of her future and her fate. Born in Coatesville on November 19, 1925, David Savitch stood apart from his family from the beginning. "My father always said that Buddy was the best-looking of the family," says Leon's daughter, Dorothy Savitch. Taller than Ben, at 5' 10", David had dark blond hair, fair skin, and blue eyes. According to the recollections of the Kennett merchants, as an adult, David was slightly stocky but nicely built, and wore glasses. He had one other distinguishing feature—he lisped, although to what extent is up for question.

Photographs of David show him to be classically handsome and fine-featured, but the Savitches considered him deficient in another area. Saul Savitch puts it delicately. "I don't think he was the brightest one in the family," he says. And Grace Merrick, a former teacher at the Kennett Consolidated School, implies the same. "David was a fine boy, very pleasant and anxious to learn," she says. "All the boys were avid pupils. But Manny was very brilliant."

Were the Savitches confusing intelligence with ambition? "I knew Buddy for thirty years, and I never heard him say what he wanted out of life," Bill Lipschultz says. "I don't think he really *did* want anything out of life. The Savitch boys had everything going their way. They were all good-looking, they were energetic, and they had great personalities, except for Buddy. The truth of the matter is that Buddy never distinguished himself at anything. You couldn't pick out anything wrong with him, and you couldn't pick out anything great about him. He was just a nice guy."

"Buddy never seemed to be like the rest of the family," says one of his contemporaries. "He was quiet and subdued, and the rest of the family was more outgoing and noisy. He wasn't as gregarious as they were. And of all the children, he was the nicest, and the most sensitive. Where the others were a little more flamboyant, he was conservative. He was a gentleman, with very fine manners. And he always seemed to be by himself."

As an adult, Jessica would tell her friends Lonnie Reed and Louise Schwing that her father had gone to Harvard like his brothers, but David Savitch is not listed in the Harvard alumni directory. Furthermore, his cousins, friends, and teachers vividly recall that he went into the navy shortly after graduating from Kennett Consolidated School in 1943. He was based in Corona, California, where he became a pharmacist's mate and, by some accounts, also worked in radiology. When he got out of the service, according to Dorothy Savitch, Ben and Lil wanted him to go to medical school.

But a year or so into his military duty, David had become ill with glomerulonephritis, a disease of the kidneys. The condition is almost always caused by streptococcal infection, usually strep throat, and there is some suggestion that David had originally contracted it in childhood. Often, the victim's first symptoms are puffiness of the face and eyelids.

With proper care, most patients recover from the disease after a period of weeks or months. But approximately 5 percent of those who do not fully recover lapse into a latent or subacute phase. The

11

latent stage of the disease can last for months or even years, and may develop into chronic nephritis, which permanently damages the kidneys. But in the subacute phase, the patient is most certainly headed for the advanced stage, which slowly, over months and possibly years, leads to the serious uremic stage.

In 1945, after fifteen months of service, David Savitch received a medical discharge from the navy. During his illness, he had fallen in love with Florence Goldberger, a navy nurse who, according to Molly Lipshultz (Bill's wife), had been assigned to care for him. Florence was seven years older than he and had attained the rank of lieutenant junior grade. Since David was an enlisted man and Florence an officer—"He had to salute her," Jessica would later say—they weren't allowed to date. But David was certain he wanted to marry her.

Like David, Florence was born and grew up in Pennsylvania, the child of immigrant parents. Her father, Edward Goldberger, was born in Satoraljaujhely, Hungary, in 1885. While Edward's son, Bernard, reports that the exact year of his father's immigration is unknown, he probably came over shortly before the turn of the century.

Florence's father chose to settle in Philadelphia, where he went to work in the clothing industry. In 1907, at twenty-two, he was learning to be a cutter at the A. B. Kirschbaum Company, a sweatshop located at the corner of South Broad and Carpenter streets. There he met a seventeen-year-old worker named Aldamira "Mamie" Spadoni, a Catholic woman who had come to America in 1901 from Senigallia, Italy. They married in 1909 and had three children, Albert, Bernard—who today uses the surname of Spadoni—and Florence.

Edward supported his family through a variety of jobs, the last as a manager of a small Philadelphia dairy. According to Doris Haber, Florence's best friend, the Goldbergers lived in South Philadelphia, which was typically populated by Italians and poor Jewish immigrants. "It's Society Hill now, but it wasn't then," she says with a laugh. Mrs. Haber says Florence took her nurse's training in a hospital in Philadelphia and then went into the navy.

When nineteen-year-old David Savitch came home and informed his parents of his intention to marry the slender, dark-haired nurse, Ben and Lil were not pleased. The way they saw it, Florence Goldberger had four strikes against her: She was certainly not of the Savitch family's economic level. She was too old for their son. Judging from her photograph, she was not as good-looking as David, and she seemed to pay no attention to clothing or style. But the fourth strike was the most serious. Florence Goldberger was only half Jewish, and by Jewish law that meant she was not Jewish at all. Her mother was Catholic, and Florence herself had been reared in the Roman Catholic faith.

Years before, both Manny and Rae had expressed interest in dating gentiles, and Lil had put her foot down. According to Kennett native Ann Lynch, David had dated her girlfriend, "But his family broke up the romance because he was Jewish and she wasn't. Which was fine, because if the relationship had been strong enough, they would have done something about it."

This time, however, David defied his parents. During the summer of 1945, he went back to California, and on September 6, he married Florence Goldberger. The ceremony was performed in Riverside by a judge of the Justice's Court. When they applied for the license, David, who was several months shy of his twentieth birthday, lied about his age, saying he was twenty-one. He listed his occupation as student. Florence gave her father's place of birth as Philadelphia, not Hungary, her age as twenty-seven.

"We were pretty old-fashioned people," says Saul Savitch. "My brother married a gentile girl, too, and for a while my parents were just sick. But I always told Florence she was nice enough to be Jewish, because she was one heck of a wife and mother."

Beatrice Marker, Ben's niece, doesn't think the fact that Florence was gentile posed a real problem to the family. Dorothy Savitch agrees, but adds that she didn't learn that Florence wasn't Jewish until after Jessica's death. "My family had omitted telling me that," she says.

Florence omitted telling people that herself. In fact, Doris Haber, her best friend since 1949, didn't know it until 1982, when she read Mary Walton's profile of Jessica in the *Philadelphia Inquirer*. The subject upsets her even today. "I can't tell you how close I've been to them," says Mrs. Haber. "To me, she's my friend, and she's Jewish. If she's not . . . well, I still don't think there's any truth to that. That was something we just took for granted."

The exact opposite of the Jew who passes for gentile, Florence Goldberger was a gentile who assimilated into the Jewish culture, performing so flawlessly that for thirty-three years she had fooled her friend, who was married to the community's lay rabbi. She had also convinced her husband's old friends. "It was many, many years before we found out that Florence wasn't even raised Jewish," Molly Lipschulz says.

Why was Florence so protective of her secret? And why did she marry a man she knew was so ill, a man who she knew had a good chance of dying when he was still young? "She had been told his days were numbered when she married him," Charlotte Kanofsky confirms.

The very model of frugality—"A real no-frills person," as one man describes her—Florence was neither a gold digger nor was she interested in pursuing an upscale life-style. To the contrary, she was modest, quiet, and liked to stay comfortably in the background. A woman who had been accustomed first to the regimen of working-class existence and then to the discipline of military life, she had little interest in upward mobility. As Molly Lipshultz says, "She doesn't need any kudos, and she doesn't need any glamour. Florence isn't showy."

According to Jessica's friends, Florence was a woman who had difficulty expressing her love in the usual demonstrative ways, by touching, kissing, or hugging. But she apparently loved David Savitch with everything that was in her. If marrying him meant losing her identity to his, or allowing his religious beliefs to eclipse everything she'd been brought up to believe, she was ready.

Bill Lipschultz says that David's friends wondered what it was that drew him and Florence together. "Nobody ever figured it out," he says. "They really didn't match. As far as I'm concerned, she's a nice person, but she would match with very few people. It looked like Florence was always afraid to talk to you. For that reason, my guess would be that Ben and Lil didn't think too much of her, because she just didn't have that old zip. In other words, if you weren't really sharp, and you weren't going to Harvard, you weren't much. It may have some significance that they got married out in California, and that Lil didn't do a big wedding."

Just what David saw in Florence may be something as simple as a patient falling in love with his nurse, or a frightened man hungering for the company of someone who might be able to save him. But it would not be unreasonable to assume that David Savitch wanted a mate who was totally unlike his mother—and father—someone who was the opposite of image-driven, of outgoing, of ambitious, someone who appreciated him as he was and would not constantly press him to achieve the trappings of success.

Soon after the wedding, David brought Florence home to Kennett Square. Medical school was now apparently out of the question, and since David's brothers were studying for their law degrees, Ben and Lil suggested that Buddy—a name David now detested, according to Saul, for its diminutive, ineffectual connotation—go into the family business. He did. At first, he worked alongside his father in the Triangle; eventually his parents would give him a store of his own to manage, one that carried a higher class of men's fashions. The store would be named not "David's," not even "Buddy's," but "Benny's."

In contrast to the stately old home on Lafayette Street, in the finest part of Kennett, David eventually took his wife to live in a new brick bungalow at 812 Taylor Street, in the southeast quadrant of town.

"I think you'd have to classify it as 'the other side of the tracks,'" says one longtime resident who knew David in high school. "Certainly it was not where I would have expected Dave Savitch to live. But then I think the other children were treated better than Dave was. You had the feeling that the Savitches didn't waste their efforts on Dave, because he had either chosen a different path or a different wife."

By all accounts, David was no businessman. "He wasn't great with the customers," says Bill Lipschultz. "In other words, he didn't beat his brains out. You wanted a shirt, he sold you a shirt. He wasn't very successful at it, and he never smiled. He just wasn't happy. Maybe the rest of the family looked at him and said, 'Hey, what are you doing? You got a haberdashery store—you're just nothing.' But it wasn't true. Buddy was all right."

"I never thought David had any personality, at least not in the store," says Betty Sinclair. "He wasn't very friendly, and his store wouldn't have gone at all if his father hadn't come over and helped him. You'd go in, and he wouldn't smile or say much. But Benny would always smile, and Lil did, too."

At home, David was apparently a different man.

"David Savitch was really one neat guy," says Betty Bogle, the Savitches' neighbor, who lived directly across the road at 807

Taylor Street. "He would always grin, no matter what. Everybody liked him."

Molly Lipshultz agrees. "Buddy always looked like he was satisfied. I only saw him pleasant and smiling."

And Florence worked to keep him that way, doing what she could to alleviate the pressure and the strain. According to her friend Doris Haber, she took special pains to watch his diet, since nephritis patients pass albumin, a form of protein, in the urine. "He could eat the stuffing, but not the turkey," Mrs. Haber explains, and Florence was always trying to tempt him with the right foods.

"Because Buddy was not well, I guess, Florence tended to baby him," says Charlotte Kanofsky, who lived directly across the street. "He didn't strike me as being too forceful, and I don't remember him fixing things, for example. But the retail business is a killer, with terrible, long hours on your feet. So I always felt sort of sorry for Buddy. You could forget him very fast."

In 1945, Ben's eldest sister, Gussie, who had brought all the Savitch children to America, died. She had been a brave woman, an adventurer, and in a way, a pioneer. And she had been the caretaker of the family when the parents were gone. A year later, Ben saw Gussie's daughter, Beatrice Marker, at the unveiling of Gussie's gravestone.

"Uncle Ben told me that Florence was pregnant," Beatrice remembers. "This would be the first person born in the family after my mother's death, and in keeping with the Jewish heritage, Buddy had promised Uncle Ben that the child would be named after her."

Gussie's real name had been Gisa. The baby was given an English equivalent, Jessica.

Jessica Beth, as the parents named the baby, was born at the Delaware Hospital in Wilmington on Saturday, February 1, 1947. In years to come, her birthday would sometimes erroneously be reported as February 2, or the year changed to 1948, the latter mainly because Jessica was determined to become a network correspondent before she was thirty and thought she'd better build in extra time.

From almost the moment Jessica arrived in the world, it was clear that she took after the Savitch side of the family. Green-eyed, and blonde like Lil, she had her father's full lower lip and many of her grandfather's features, including a square jaw, and a twinkling quality that came to their faces when they smiled.

But Jessica had one other characteristic that bound her almost exclusively to her father: She lisped. When she began talking, Jessica was to recount, she told people her name was "Jethica Thavitch." As an adult, she would say that she also had a stuttering problem. While a lisp is generally caused by the misplacement of the tongue, or the structure of the teeth or jaw, stuttering is seen as a manifestation of a disorder in the physiological, psychological, or neurological functioning.

However, like most of the Savitches, Jessica was an outgoing, confident child. Later, she would tell one of her doctors that she had been toilet trained at twenty-six months, and that she learned to read and talk at an early age. And, apparently, she had few inhibitions.

"My father was a home movie buff," she told Maralyn Lois Polak of the *Philadelphia Inquirer* in 1975. "All my early memories are probably 'technically augmented.' I can still picture myself in Kennett Square, running up to the camera, lifting up my dress, showing the ruffles on the back of my panties."

Jessica learned early where to direct her attention for the most return. She saw that she could please her father by performing for him, and that she would be rewarded with cuddling and affection.

"My sense," says one of her psychiatrists, "is that they were very close. There was expectation, and teasing, as well as little temper flare-ups. She was his first child, and his darling, and those things are like any love affair, with all kinds of ups and downs. But nothing outside of anything you would expect with any father and daughter."

To Jessica, David Savitch was the most important person in the world. The only problem was that she never seemed to have enough time with him, since he worked six days and two nights a week and then played poker on Tuesday night. So Jessica would make frequent trips down to the store. "She used to sit on the front steps there and wait for her daddy," says Frank Virgilio, once David's employee and today the store's owner. "She'd come in and jerk around like a little girl does, impatient, you know."

Jessica and her father had their rituals. In the spring, David would drive her around Chester County and show her the budding trees and flowers, stopping to pick four-leaf clovers. They would often end up at Longwood Gardens, the famous aboretum just outside of Kennett Square that Pierre Samuel du Pont, the grandson of the founder of the Du Pont Company, of Wilmington, developed in 1906. The name of du Pont was to be found all around Kennett, for the renowned family had put a generous share of its chemical fortune into the area's institutions.

When Jessica was not quite two, and her head full of blonde curls, David Savitch met a young couple, Doris and Charlie Haber, when they got caught in the rain one day on their way to see Charlotte Kanofsky. The Habers had just moved to town with their four-month-old baby, and David invited them over.

"Jessica answered the door," Mrs. Haber remembers. "She was so precious and gorgeous. She looked like a little Shirley Temple doll. I remember she jumped up and down and said, 'My mommy's pregnant!' "

The new baby, named Stephanie, arrived on December 12, 1948, only twenty-two months after Jessica. According to Charlotte Kanofsky, the child was premature, and there was much concern over her well-being. If Jessica was her father's child, Stephanie was her mother's, resembling Florence in coloring and personality. And she would grow up to enter the helping professions, teaching special education, working with children who had learning disabilities. As a child, she was as quiet as Jessica was outgoing, as content to hang back as Jessica was to introduce herself to strangers. When Jessica was about four, and Stephanie two, the family sat for a formal portrait. In it, Jessica, looking as radiant and beautiful as any child out of the movies, stands in the middle, facing her father, who stares warily at the camera. On the right side of the picture, detached from the others, sit Florence and Stephanie, the child on the arm of her mother's chair. At first, mother and daughter seem not to belong with the others, as if photographs of two different families had simply been mucilaged together. Stephanie and her mother both appear sober and unsmiling, like losers in some vital, primal contest. "Florence never looked happy," says one Kennett woman. "I never saw her smile."

There is nothing to suggest how Jessica reacted to having a new baby in the house—particularly one who needed extra attention—except for one recollection of Doris Haber: "I saw Jessica take a bite out of Stephanie when she was three," Mrs. Haber says. "She was a real little monkey, very strong minded." As the years went on, the closeness between the sisters either got lost or never quite developed.

"Stephanie was more like a natural child," Betty Bogle says. "They didn't push her the way they did Jessica. They pushed that kid into everything."

Jessica knew in retrospect that the eldest child is always the "boy," regardless of the child's actual sex. "If there is a boy and a girl," she told journalist Judith Adler Hennessee in 1979, "the girl gets to be loved and petted just for being, or because she is pretty. But the boy has to be more. He has to accomplish, to do. With three daughters, the youngest is the girl. I was not pushed, but I was expected to achieve. Not to have done well wouldn't have been tolerated. It just wasn't a possibility. [We had] a total disbelief in failure."

From the recollections of the townspeople, Jessica was not only the first grandchild, but Lil's favorite, a fact that would forever haunt Jessica's image of herself. Lil intended for her to amount to something dazzling in life, to be a real Savitch, special. And as if in preparation for the station Jessica was expected to attain, Lil treated her like a young princess, showering her with gifts.

"I remember Lil coming into the store and saying, 'I'm here to buy clothes for *my Jessica*!'" Mary Leto, owner of the Town Shop, says. "I'll never forget the way she'd say it, with such a loving feeling."

Carmela Cordivano, at Connor's Drug Store, recalls the same. "Lil always favored Jessica more," she says. "She was always buying her things. But then Jessica was very lovable and sociable, and, of course, really bright."

It was decided that Jessica would enter pre-school early. In 1951, at the age of four, she was enrolled at the Heess Scott Kindergarten, a small, private school in downtown Kennett Square. The two women who ran it could only accommodate twenty-five students, and Sara Heess remembers Jessica well.

"Jessica was, of course, a very attractive little blonde girl," she begins. "But she was outstanding in the fact that she was so wholesome, so well-balanced and composed, and yet so 'with it.' She was interested in everything. She was very easily trained and well-disciplined, just going along with whatever was expected of her. I'd say she was a model child, completely balanced in every way. We were very fond of her."

The following year, when the Savitches attempted to enroll

Jessica at the Kennett Consolidated School, they were told that she was too young to enter first grade. Her birthday fell just one day short of Pennsylvania's age requirement. The family then enrolled her in a private school in Wilmington, where age restriction wasn't enforced. Several family friends and neighbors say that Jessica was enrolled at Tower Hill, the toniest of Wilmington's four private schools. Others believe it was Tatnall. But no school in the area has a record of her attendance. Her father drove her to Wilmington every morning of that year.

In kindergarten, Jessica had blended well with the other children. But in private school, most of her classmates were from wealthy blueblood families, predominately WASP. She felt uncomfortable, as if she didn't fit in, and had a difficult time making friends. Years later, she would tell her psychiatrist that she had felt such pressure to do so that she had invented a fake girlfriend named Jenny.

Jessica's girlfriend wasn't an imaginary playmate, an invented companion, as in the *Harvey* syndrome. Instead, as her doctor explains, "Jenny was someone Jessica invented for her family because she was embarrassed to tell her mother that no one played with her. This way, she thought that she would appear normal. All of that, including the fact that she was sent off to school fairly early, gives you a sense of the standards that she held, and the perfectionism and compulsiveness."

The incident, Jessica told her psychiatrist, was her earliest recollection.

Luckily, the neighborhood offered plenty of children to play with in the afternoons, and photographs attest to the fact that Jessica often spent time with the Kanofsky kids.

"It was a fairly mundane childhood," her friend Mary Manilla says, "and Jessica spent a lot of time fantasizing. She was also very competitive." And when she found she could manipulate the other children by throwing temper tantrums if she didn't get her way, she took advantage of it. In years to come, Stephanie would tell one of Jessica's suitors that when they were children and played games, "It wasn't worth the aggravation if Jessica didn't win. So they'd just give it to her."

One day, Jessica picked a fight with the wrong person when she attempted to defend the Savitch pride. "A little boy in the neighborhood beat up my sister," she said in the Polak interview, "and I went looking for him and beat him up. Then he smashed me in the face with a baseball bat." The nose was broken and disfigured, a condition Jessica would not have corrected for thirty years.

According to Dr. Jack Sheen, the Los Angeles plastic surgeon who performed the operation, the trauma, which was possibly aggravated by a much later accident in 1983, resulted in a deviated septum, a decrease in the nasal airway that left Jessica with only 30 to 40 percent of normal breathing capacity. In addition, it severely diminished her sense of smell, which in turn affected her ability to taste certain flavors.

"The tongue picks up the taste of sweet, sour, salty, or bitter," Sheen explains, "so she could certainly discern those. But all the subtle flavors are appreciated by the ability to smell the food. She had none of that, because the organ of olfaction is located in the nasal airway high up, between the eyes. And when it is obstructed, and no air circulates, you can't smell anything." The injury may have contributed to what Jessica's friends refer to as her notoriously poor eating habits. By the time she reached her twenties, she often subsisted on nothing more than one saltine or apple a day.

In 1953, after one year in Wilmington, Jessica entered second grade at the nearby Kennett Consolidated School. She could walk to school with her best friend, Faith Ann Thomas (now McCormick), who was only a month younger than she was and lived two houses up and across the street.

The girls had several things in common apart from their age. Both were the eldest children in their families, both were exceptionally bright, and both had strong, determined personalities. Jessica discovered early on that she couldn't boss Faith around the way she could the other children, and she came to respect her, to accept her as an equal. "She and Jessica were very close, almost like sisters," remembers Charlotte Kanofsky. Faith's father, Ed Thomas, says, "Jessie was as cute and nice a little girl as you would ever want to meet. We loved her like she was our own."

The private school experience had made Jessica acutely aware of how her Jewishness could be a stigma, as well as a source of pride. In 1955, when Ray and Gladys Gochnauer moved into the modest development of two- and three-bedroom homes, Jessica came over and introduced herself. "She said, 'You know I'm Jewish,' " Gochnauer remembers. "And I said, 'That's okay, I'm Dutch.' "

The fact that Jessica was Jewish, and attended synagogue and Hebrew school regularly, apparently did not pose any threat to her friendship with Faith, either. The girls spent Jewish holidays in the Savitch home, and Christmas and Easter, when they'd hunt for eggs, in the Thomas household. On their cheerful street lined with flowering dogwoods, oaks, and maples, Jessica and Faith forged the essence of American, small-town childhood: sledding on the steep hill in the winter, playing dress-up in their mothers' skirts and high heels, selling poppies and nut cups to raise money for the Junior Legion, going off to Girl Scout camp, and riding in the town's Fourth of July parade.

Ed Thomas says the girls were also "great for putting on their own shows," which they would write, produce, and star in together, drafting the smaller children for supporting roles. "They'd tell the little ones where to stand, what to say, and when to say it, and then they'd go around the neighborhood and invite everybody to the performance," Thomas remembers.

Faith's mother would hang a curtain on the clothesline on the back patio, and Jessica's elderly next-door neighbor, Mr. Kendig, would come over and play the piano. Sometimes Faith and Jessica would fabricate plots and story lines; sometimes they would simply sing and dance, Jessica showing off the new steps she learned at her ballet and tap lessons. The audience sat on the bank in the Thomases' backyard and bought penny candy and lemonade from the impromptu refreshment stand.

Once the Savitches got a television set in 1954, the back-porch theatre productions fell off sharply. The girls were entranced by the novelty and the entertainment of TV, becoming faithful supporters of the "Mickey Mouse Club" and imitating the Mousketeers in skits of their own. "Jessica was always Annette," says Faith, "because Annette was the best-looking."

Jessica also liked the "Camel News Caravan," not because she was interested in the news, but because of the presence of John Cameron Swayze. "We thought it was a really neat name," Faith remembers. "We were hung up on it." On excursions in the car, the girls would sit close together in the backseat, giggling and repeating the name over and over until they were too tired to say it again.

When the family first got a television, Jessica would often turn down the sound because it interfered with her conversations with her father, and because, Doris Haber says, she couldn't stand to hear the announcer's voice. In time, though, Jessica noticed how much her father liked the news programs, and in particular, Edward R. Murrow's classic CBS documentary on migrant workers, "Harvest of Shame." It occurred to her that an ongoing discussion of news events might be something she could share exclusively with her father, without intervention from Stephanie or their mother.

As a young child, Jessica had seemed to love her mother very much. But as she got older, she began to devalue Florence, who had given up her nursing career when she married and had little life outside the home and family. Florence was also a strict disciplinarian, and her daughter thought she was harshly rigid about time, duty, and obedience. In contrast to her father, who laughed all the time when he was at home, her mother, Jessica thought, had almost no sense of humor. "Jessica certainly didn't see her mother as a model for identification, for emulating," one of her psychiatrists says. "That was very much oriented toward her father."

"When I was growing up," Jessica said in an address to national Girl Scout leaders in 1981, "I was educated from books you don't see around elementary schools anymore—books featuring Mother, Daddy, Dick and Jane. Daddy was always depicted going to work, or to a sporting event, or on some other interesting jaunt into the vast reaches of that mysteriously exciting world outside. But Mother was always placed in the kitchen. And should she inadvertently make it to some other part of the house—or, perish the thought, the *lawn*—she always wore an apron or carried a spatula, so you could see where she *truly* belonged. Dick was prepared to grow up like Daddy, into Daddy's various roles. And I was prepared to be Jane. The books, and the world around me, with its narrow list of role models for women, made it apparent that I had few choices."

The feminist sensibility these words display came later to Jessica. And so Jessica studied her *Weekly Reader* to learn about Dwight D. Eisenhower, Jimmy Hoffa, and racial desegregation, easing the topics into the dinner table conversation as a way of winning David Savitch's approval. "I guess I started 'doing the news' at that time," she would say later.

23

Soon, Jessica was sharing her new hobby with Faith. "I noticed they would talk about things that you wouldn't expect girls that age to be thinking about," says Ed Thomas. "I'd say, 'I wonder who they've been talking to?' It was amazing, some of the things that Jessie would say had happened in the world."

If Jessica's troubled future could have been predicted during these years, no one seems to have noticed. To Anne Marie De Wire (now Williams), who was in her grade at Kennett Consolidated School, she was "always laughing, and she had an impish sense of humor, an infectious giggle."

To Ken Wendel, who taught her seventh-grade social studies, "Jessica was always happy and smiling. She could come in when you would be 'down' or busy, and she would brighten your day. Jessica struck me as a very normal kid."

As Jessica grew older, Lil continued to treat her like a princess, taking her to New York on buying trips, paying for her private dancing lessons, and bringing her expensive, unusual presents, such as jeweled sweaters and jeweled lipstick cases—things other girls her age didn't have. The constant present buying was an ongoing source of irritation to Florence, who wanted her children to grow up with the same values she had and to keep their feet planted firmly in reality. But Lil wanted Jessica to have the best, to be privileged. And she wanted things to fall into place for her. When Jessica was required to sell fifty boxes of Girl Scout cookies, Lil bought forty-nine, freezing them and "foisting them off on neighborhood kids all year long," Jessica would remember.

At times, Florence and Lil's differences would erupt into full conflict, but Florence was largely without allies. Her brother, Bernard, lived in nearby West Chester, Pennsylvania, but her parents, who lived in Tuckerton, New Jersey, near the seashore, seldom came to visit. Even when they did, her mother, Mamie—Jessica called her Nana—was no match for the dynamic Lil. "She was very Italian, very somber and strange," says Charlotte Kanofsky. "You have a picture of the old Italians, sitting on their doorstep with the kerchief on their head? That's this grandmother."

Barry Swartz, one of Jessica's high school boyfriends, says: "I'm sure Jessica was flat-out embarrassed of Nana, as most of us were of our grandmothers. Here we were trying to be the most sophisticated people in the world, and her grandmother was just a very nice first-generation immigrant-type lady, and that wasn't what her other grandmother was. One grandmother would be dressed to the teeth, with the furs and such, and the other would be in floppy mules and flower print housecoats. If I had to contrast the two households [Nana's vs. Ben and Lil's], I'd think Jessica's feeling was, 'I ain't gonna get stuck in Nana's household if I can help it.' "

"Florence was a very level-headed woman, but with Lil around she didn't have a chance," says Betty Bogle. "I remember seeing Jessica in [Lil's] shop one time, and Lil was telling her, 'You're going to do this, and that, and you're going to make money, money, money.' I knew then that the kid was in for it."

The pressure must have been intense. Both Ben and Lil had taught their granddaughter by example, and for them image clearly was more important than reality. It was not only money that Lil stressed to her granddaughter, but the importance of mingling with the right people and ingratiating herself to those who could help her advance in life. Lil made Jessica see that hard work, a degree of style, and knowing a few well-placed people would carry her a long way. She continually held up the California contingent of the family as models of accomplishment.

As a result, says one of Jessica's psychiatrists, "She had a sense of pride about the California uncles and aunt, and how uniquely successful they were, but she also felt that she didn't live up to them, as if that were a romanticized, royal side of the family that she was disengaged from. She placed them above her as a child, and then later as an adult, perhaps because they were in the professions, and she wasn't."

It is probable that Jessica, as smart as she was, picked up on her grandparents' feeling that David was somehow inferior to the rest of the family, and wondered if, by extension, her own worth was also in question. As a child, then, she may have felt that she had to be outstanding and distinguish herself not only for her own sake, but for that of her father as well. "She had to live up to an awful lot in her mind," the same doctor says.

At this stage, Lil emphasized, the best way for Jessica to be a success in life was to concentrate on maturing into the perfect young lady, polite and friendly to all. The boys and girls in Jessica's class liked her sufficiently to elect her homeroom representative, and for a brief time, she "dated" a boy whose grandfather was a du Pont.

Betty Bogle, who lived across the street from the Savitches, was also assistant troop leader for Jessica in Brownies, Girl Scouts, and Junior Legion, an organization that taught the girls the virtues of American patriotism. Bogle says she took a special interest in the child, mainly because she was concerned about the way Jessica was being molded. She shared Charlotte Kanofsky's view that Jessica was "always like a little actress—always on." And she thought the Jessica her teachers saw was not necessarily the real one.

"I felt sorry for the girl," Bogle remembers. "It was like she never had time to be a child. They were always taking her somewhere to show her off, to be in presentations of one kind or another. I think she had every lesson going. Jessica struck me as a very unhappy child. I don't think she ever knew what she wanted, because she never had a chance to find out for herself. She was just pushed beyond knowing who she was."

The Savitches' third child, Lori, was born on April 27, 1956, when Jessica was nine. Lori, Jessica soon discovered, was more like her—more like a Savitch—than Stephanie. And Jessica would look out for her.

By the late fifties, the Savitch family appeared to be a happy, settled unit. "[David] was also very good with Lori," remembers one of Jessica's friends. "Nothing was ever too much trouble. He would bring the baby down to our house in the evenings and talk to my father, entertaining her all the while, and then carry her wherever she wanted to go. He was a good family man."

As well as running Benny's, David was now helping his father at Ben's newest men's store, Don Gregor, in Newark, Delaware. And he had accumulated enough money to buy a typical Eisenhower-era "dream house," in New Garden, four miles outside of Kennett. The house was new, and had been built on spec; in many ways it was similar to the one Ben and Lil had bought at 104 Country Club Drive in Newark, following a brief, and by some accounts disastrous, move to California near the start of the decade.

The community of New Garden—largely a middle-class pocket surrounded by mushroom farms—still didn't have the prestige of Lafayette Street, but it was a definite step up from Taylor Street. The Savitch home, at 62 Heatherly Lane, was a one-floor, red brick affair, with a large yard, an attached garage, and three bedrooms—ordinary by today's standards, but stylish for the time.

According to Al and Louise Walker, who bought the house from the Savitches and still live there today, Jessica and Stephanie shared an enormous room. Jessica was growing up. Her blonde hair had faded to dark brown, the same color as Ben's.

Jessica could no longer run over to Faith Thomas's house whenever she liked, but she found a new best friend in Linda Kilmer (now Schroeder), who lived next door. From the day the Savitches moved in, Linda realized that Jessica was different. "She had everything planned out," says Linda. "She knew exactly what she wanted, and she was very competitive, in a friendly sense. Some people found her bossy, and we had our conflicts, of course. But with me it was more like, 'You're coming along with me, and we're going to do this well.' In fact, she got me in with the so-called popular group, which was what Jessica always wanted to be in with. Sometimes I thought, 'Oh, Jessica, let's not push so hard,' but she always wanted to rise above where she was. And she always told me I should strive for more and better."

The Savitches assimilated Linda into the family, taking her on short trips with them. David taught her how to swim. Linda and Jessica spent the last years before their teens in typical girlhood fashion, playing croquet "endlessly" in the summers and ganging up on the younger kids in the neighborhood, particularly Stephanie. "Sometimes Stephanie was deserving, but most of the time she wasn't," Linda says. "There was always a lot of competition between them, even though they were so different."

Some of the most exciting moments in the Savitch household occurred when Jessica received packages from her Aunt Rae out in California. Usually these contained clothes that were "much more sophisticated" than anything Lil carried at Adelle's. "I can remember orange pants in particular," Linda says. "Jessica was very fond of those orange pants. I'm not sure her mother was so fond of them. They were a little tight. But Jessica was crazy about her Aunt Rae. She pictured herself growing up to be just like her."

In contrast to others' memories of Florence as cool and aloof, Linda thought her a caring person, someone who would stop her work in the middle of the day to load up the kids and take them swimming. "But she made us behave," she says. "She would stop the car if we were fighting. And I remember once we were having difficulty with some crafts project. My mother would have just taken it over and done it herself, but Mrs. Savitch said, 'No, you're going to learn how to do it, so you'll know how.' I respected her. She was strong."

Linda's memories of Jessica's father are more vivid. "He was a wonderful man," she says. As he had done earlier with Jessica and Faith, David drew the girls into discussions about current events, soliciting their opinions and encouraging them to form their own ideas. "I wouldn't say he was an intellectual," Linda says, "but they had a wall of books in their den, and I know he used to read a lot of them—that they weren't there just for show. I particularly remember him reading *The Brothers Karamazov*. And Jessica had her wall of books, too."

According to Linda, David Savitch was a man who was happy just being with his wife and children.

The Savitches had been living in New Garden for only about three years when David's health began to deteriorate steadily. It was now fourteen years since he had been hospitalized for glomerulonephritis, and he had been in the chronic phase—with headaches, weakness from anemia, shortness of breath, and intermittent swelling of the ankles—since 1956. Now he was moving toward the uremic stage, where doctors relied on laboratory tests to determine the degree of kidney function. If output fell to 10 percent of normal, uremia would likely follow.

Bill Lipschultz had played poker with David every week since he got out of the navy. He had always known vaguely that David was ill, "but I didn't know what nephritis was. I thought it was nasal congestion!" At the end of 1958, Lipschultz started noticing that David looked pale, and that his patience was easily strained. Then a golfing experience, during which David displayed a particularly uncharacteristic lack of consideration, convinced him that "Maybe Buddy really *is* sick."

Sometime around Jessica's twelfth birthday, she and her father had one of what Jessica would later call their "Sunday Syndrome" fights. On Sundays she often would fight with members of the family and end up packing her things and pedaling off on her bicycle until hunger or darkness caught up with her. This time when Jessica ran away, she hid in a field near her house. When it got dark, and she was still not home, her father came looking for her in his car, driving up and down the road, shining his lights across the fields. Jessica saw him, but she refused to give him the satisfaction of finding her. After several hours of combing the New

Garden countryside and calling his daughter's name on the night air, David became panicky. But Jessica still would not reveal her hiding place. When she finally did come out of the field, "Her father was very angry with her," says one of her boyfriends. "He told her she'd never amount to anything. And it absolutely stunned her. She never got it out of her mind."

"The story of her running away was a vignette that she and I used a lot to show the depth of her feelings," says one of Jessica's psychiatrists. "She let her father keep searching so that he would suffer and feel bad. It was almost a suicidal thing, like, 'Look how bad he made me feel. I'm punishing him.' And that kind of sadomasochistic, ambivalent relationship then became a paradigm for all of Jessica's relationships with men. Because she never ever had a chance to work it out in that childhood model with her father."

In April 1959, David started telling friends the truth about his health: His renal insufficiency had been acute since February. During one of his frequent conversations with Albert Lipschultz, who was Bill's brother and ran the family-owned Kennett Auto Parts store down the street from Benny's, David said, "Well, Al, I may not ever see you again. I'm going into the hospital, and I don't ever expect to come out."

"I thought he looked fine," Lipschultz recalls. "I said, 'You're kidding.' But he said, 'No, Al, I'm serious.'"

As the illness progressed, David "suffered horribly, but he never complained," one of his relatives remembers. Jessica spent a lot of time reading about her father's disease, studying how she could make him more comfortable when he got home. But in the early hours of Monday, May 11, 1959, the day after Mother's Day, David Savitch died of uremic pericarditis at Wilmington's Memorial Hospital. He was thirty-three.

In the early 1970s, Jessica would meet a television reporter named Ron Kershaw, who would become the second most important man in her life. One day they were talking about their fathers, and Jessica dissolved into tears. She explained that despite his five-week hospitalization and his final seven-day bout with uremic pericarditis, she hadn't been told how ill her father was, and worse, that her mother never directly told her that he had died. The terrible, smothering realization that he was never coming back crept in when the house began to fill with out-of-town mourners.

Jessica ran crying out of the house and into the backyard, where her mother caught up with her and chastised her for weeping. Jessica didn't grieve or accept the truth of his death until a year later, she told Kershaw, when she and Stephanie pulled the black drape away from his gravestone at the unveiling. There was her father's name, she said, staring back at her from the cold marble.

"There was always a haunted aspect to Jessica," says Kershaw. "And I think it has to do with the way the family handled the father's dying. They never discussed it with her, and she never got to talk about her feelings of desertion, of betrayal. Emotionally, on a number of levels, she was fixed at that moment, when she lost her father and her entire way of life. I don't think she ever felt secure again. It screwed up her life for good."

The story would be a convenient way to account for much of the emotional path Jessica would later follow, except for one detail: It seems not to have been true. According to both family and friends, after David had been in the hospital a short time, Jessica knew he was seriously ill. Linda Kilmer remembers her talking about it. "Jessica always got a new dress, or something new, for a party," she says. "And I remember one party in particular where she said she wasn't going to have anything new anymore, that her father was very sick. Not long after that, she came over to the house in tears. She said he was dying."

Jessica was also at the hospital for the final moments of David's life.

"I had been to the hospital once to see Buddy," Saul Savitch says, "and he looked bad. I could tell he was suffering. Not too long after that, I was playing golf one day, and the caddy manager came out and said, 'Your Uncle Ben called. He's in terrible shape. Your cousin is dying.' So I went to the hospital and the kids were there. I remember Jessica wore braces on her teeth.

"It was a pretty sad situation. Florence had tears in her eyes. She was standing on one side of the bed holding Buddy's hand, and I stood on the other side, holding the other hand. His eyes were way back, and he had tubes coming out of him everywhere. Florence said, 'He won't live very long at all.' In a little while, I got a phone call from someone wanting to know how Buddy was doing. When I came back, he had already died. And I remember them taking Jessica in [to the room], and I remember her walking out. She cried like a baby."

That afternoon, Doris Haber drove Jessica around town, and out to the Pyle Bi-Lo Market that she and her husband managed in nearby West Grove. "She was really terribly upset," Mrs. Haber says. "I can still hear her. She said, 'I'm going to grow up and do something in research so people won't have to die like that.' "

The following day, services were held at the Chandler Funeral Home, at Delaware Avenue and Jefferson Street in Wilmington. "They had an open casket," Charlotte Kanofsky says. "Florence went up to the coffin and bent over and said, 'Good-bye, Buddy.' And then she kissed him. I'll never forget that. Never."

David Savitch was buried in the Jewish Community Cemetery off Foulk Road, on the edge of Wilmington. Afterward, the family sat *shivah* at home. Florence, unschooled in certain Jewish customs, wanted to do things right. She called Doris Haber and asked if her husband, the lay rabbi of the community, would come over and cover the mirrors, a custom that is not explicit in Jewish law. Although it had never occurred to Mrs. Haber that Florence might not be Jewish, that she relied on guides for the Jewish homemaker, instead of years of accumulated experience, "I couldn't see any reason why they asked for that. Because most Jewish families don't even want it. It's a very Orthodox custom."

Saul Savitch remembers being in the home on at least two days of *shivah,* and that "Jessica was there, and I thought she handled it pretty well." Jane Rupert, one of Jessica's seventh-grade teachers, says that the death upset everyone at school, "Because, of course, Jessica was upset."

Why, then, did Jessica tell Ron Kershaw such a different version of the truth? Perhaps she suffered such shock that she had virtually blocked out many of the events of that awful week. In the deepest psychological sense, she didn't want the events to have been true, or to have been told to her. Or perhaps by then she had told the unveiling story so many times that she had come to believe it herself. But the more likely explanation is that the story had already become an ingredient in the larger-than-life persona she would invent for herself in the years following her father's death. There would come to be as many versions of Jessica Savitch as there were people to listen to them.

"All I can tell you," says David Buda, who worked as Jessica's personal manager in the last months of her life, "is that by reading her childhood diaries [which she gave him], I know that she perceived her father's death as being directed *at her,* and that she took it as a personal rejection. It made her distrustful of human relationships in general. And once Jessica had success in television, she was convinced that people loved the woman on TV, but that basically there was no hope of her being loved for herself, or ever being happy."

A year after David Savitch's death, the family gathered for the unveiling of the gravestone. Afterward, Ben and Lil held a reception at their house in Newark. Frank Virgilio, who attended, reports that it was elaborate and elegant. But no matter what hold David's parents had had on him in life, in death he belonged to his wife and children. The stone carried the prideful claim:

BELOVED HUSBAND AND FATHER

DAVID SAVITCH

1925–1959

"Her father's death was a tremendously formative event in Jessica's life," her psychiatrist says. "She never had a chance to resolve her anger, her feelings of sadomasochism, or for that matter, the teasing aspect of their relationship, because she was still a very little girl when he died. And her guilt made her feel that she was noxious and deadly to anybody she came in contact with, that she was just no good."

Jessica had lost the parent whose warmth and approval she had courted and counted on. She was still Lil's princess, but that was a province her mother could not accept.

For months after the death, Jessica would dream about her father coming back and about what they would say to each other to take away the pain. Sometimes as she lay in bed before she fell asleep, she thought she saw him in the shadows the trees threw against her bedroom wall. In the years to come, she would look for him in almost every man she met. And she would spend the rest of her short life trying to please him.

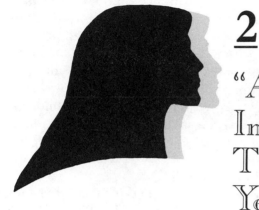

2

"An Engine Inside of Her": The School Years

Almost immediately after David Savitch died, his widow began talking about moving to New Jersey. She told Doris Haber that it was devastating for her to go past the store, because she could still see her husband standing there in the doorway with his hands on his hips, the way he did when things weren't busy.

Jessica, too, was having a hard time. When she returned to school, her classmates noticed that she was different, quieter, and that she walked around with her head down. "I think she thought her grief had to be secondary to everybody else's," Anne Marie De Wire says, journeying back twenty-eight years in her mind. "She felt that because Lori was a baby, Stephanie was younger, and her mother was so young to be widowed, everybody else's needs superseded hers. When she came back to school, she was transformed."

Now that David was gone, Ben tried to become a substitute

33

father to the children. Clearly, he and Lil intended to take a much more active role in rearing the girls than most grandparents. That was precisely what Florence hoped to avoid.

"I think Florence's way to get out of it was to move to New Jersey, to be near her own parents," says Betty Bogle. "But it was too late for Jessica. The harm was already done."

According to Linda Kilmer, David Savitch didn't leave much life insurance, which had been difficult to obtain because of his illness. But he had carried mortgage insurance on the house, and after a year or so, Florence put it on the market. Meanwhile, Ben sold David's partnership in the store to Frank Virgilio, telling him he was giving half of the sale price to Florence. At the end of 1960, halfway through Jessica's freshman year of high school, Florence asserted her independence from her husband's family in a way she could not have done when he was alive: She packed up the children and moved to Margate, New Jersey, a small residential and resort community five miles west of Atlantic City.

"She left here with practically no money," says Betty Sinclair. "The Savitches didn't treat her very well."

According to others, however, Florence made it clear that she had no intention of accepting charity. "She absolutely cut off all the Savitches," says Saul, who had taken care of David's funeral arrangements. "I don't know what happened, but she took a dislike to somebody, and that was it."

At first, Jessica was shattered by the move. "I felt like Dorothy in *The Wizard of Oz*," she was to write in her autobiography, "swept away by the tornado to a strange land. Everything familiar to me was gone: My father, my home, my school, my community, my friends, and even, in a way, my mother, who resumed the nursing career she had abandoned when she married."

Through the years, Florence would work at a succession of nursing jobs, at Atlantic City Hospital, at Shore Memorial Hospital in Somers Point, at the Children's Seashore Home, and at the Atlantic County Vocational School in May's Landing. Although Jessica would in time tell the press that Florence was her inspiration—"My mother showed me by example that it was not only OK to work, it was expected"—privately she expressed shame that Florence had to work to support the family. She had been the first one in her circle to lose a parent, and none of the mothers of her friends went out to work. That Florence did made Jessica feel isolated, a misfit.

Now her father's death meant not only a dreadful emotional loss and a disruption in her locale and routine, but a major change in Jessica's social position. Margate is a suburban community populated chiefly by Jewish and Italian professionals and their families. In contrast to the affluent homes of many of Jessica's new classmates, the new Savitch home was a lower-middle-class frame bungalow on a tiny lot. Mustard-colored with a brick-veneer façade, it is the house in which Mrs. Savitch still lives. Florence had the front bedroom, Stephanie and Lori shared the back, and Jessica had the room in the middle to herself. "It's a small house, probably no larger than eleven hundred square feet," says one of Jessica's friends. "But neat as a pin."

The Margate house was a distinct comedown from Jessica's environment in Kennett Square, and according to one of her boyfriends at the time, she was angry at her father for dying and changing things, for making them the "poor relations" of the Savitch clan. Still, she wrote to a Kennett Square friend during this period that she felt a great sense of responsibility to somehow compensate the family for losing him, and on Valentine's Day, she went out and bought heart-shaped boxes of candy for her mother and sisters because her father had always done so.

Jessica continued to receive frequent packages of expensive clothes from Lil ("Florence would just go nuts when those boxes would arrive," boyfriend Barry Swartz remembers), but she felt dowdy and out of place with her more affluent classmates at Atlantic City High School. Today, her school contemporaries invariably remember her as an exceedingly well-dressed teenager, and two still joke about the fact that one of her nicknames was "Natalie Attired." Photographs of her taken during the time show her as the very model of teenage fashion, dressed in tailored Villager blouses and, for formal portraits, pearls—a far cry from the image of herself that she would painfully remember.

"When they moved to Margate," says Lew Katz, a friend from the latter period of her life, "Jessica felt she just couldn't compete economically with the other middle-class Jewish kids who lived there. After Jessica died, Florence told me that when they first came to Atlantic City, Jessica went out and got a job in a dress store. Florence said, 'One night, I happened to walk by this shop, and I looked in the window, and there was Jessica mopping the floor.' She said, 'My heart went out to her, because she hadn't told me about it, and because she was just working so hard.' " But

Jessica didn't know her mother was there, Katz says, and instead of knocking on the window, Florence just watched her daughter through the pane. They never discussed it, and Florence never told her what she knew.

Jessica was soon to receive still another blow. About four months after the family's move to New Jersey, Edward Goldberger, Florence's father, died in nearby Tuckerton at the age of seventy-five. Florence had lost her husband and her father in the span of twenty-two months. The death was more tragic than it appeared, for at 12:30 on the afternoon of March 23, 1961, Edward Goldberger had walked into his garage, closed the door, and started his car. New Jersey State Police ruled the death suicide by carbon monoxide poisoning. Shortly after Goldberger's death, his widow, Mamie, came to the Savitch home in Margate to live. She shared a bedroom with Florence.

Florence's brother, Bernard Spadoni—who says he took his mother's maiden name because he feared that it would otherwise die out—reports that Jessica and her grandfather had been close. The only substantiation is a neighbor's recollection that Jessica often came to see him when she moved to New Jersey, and her acknowledgment to him in *Anchorwoman*: "Edward Goldberger: For loving memories."

Exactly when Jessica learned the circumstances of her grandfather's death is unknown. None of the friends from any period of her life remembers hearing about it. In 1982, however, Jessica told a friend she planned to write to her mother about "Eddie's suicide," and "suicide in the family." If she knew about it in 1961, the suicide was bound to have reinforced the sense of abandonment she was still experiencing from her father's death and her mother's return to work. It would also have deepened her sense of shame.

In the early sixties, when Jessica was just settling into the area, Atlantic City, once the spectacular "Playground of the World," was "teeter-tottering between being a great place to live and becoming a lousy place to live," says Herb Dudnick, a former NBC producer who grew up there.

In its halcyon days, the seven-mile island, with its mild summer climate and celebrated Boardwalk, had been the most prominent and accessible resort area in the Northeast. The ocean beach was magnificent, the Boardwalk hotels elegant and luxurious, and the city's famous amusement piers offered everything from concerts to art shows and high-diving horses. The Miss America Pageant was held in the cavernous Atlantic City Convention Hall, and the town was clean and friendly. There was little street crime to speak of, though, as Dudnick says, "It's always been a Mafia town. Anybody who says the Mafia just walked in during the last ten years is crazy."

By the 1960s, however, Atlantic City had long begun to fray around the edges. When air travel became commonplace, well-to-do vacationers began bypassing the Jersey shore for more exotic locales. As tourism slowed, the town plummeted into long-term decline, eventually driving many of the grand hotels that fronted the Boardwalk into bankruptcy.

In the early 1970s, far more serious problems washed ashore in Atlantic City. The population, which had hovered around 66,000 in the late 1930s, had fallen to 40,000. In the summer, unemployment ranged from 15 to 18 percent, jumping to 26 percent in the winter. A sizable portion of the residents, especially blacks, who made up nearly half of the population, lived in dilapidated ghettos, often in conditions bordering on squalor. The coming of legalized gambling in the mid-seventies, which has turned the city into the Las Vegas of the eastern seaboard, has done almost nothing to alleviate these circumstances.

There is something bleak and tawdry about Atlantic City today. The town is a captive of the casino-hotels, and the vacationers are, too. It is a rare visitor who ventures beyond the casino itself, with its lively restaurants and glitzy shops.

The 1960s were still transition years for Atlantic City. In the summer, a million people came to visit, almost everybody got working papers at fourteen, and nearly a dozen movie theatres showed a new picture every week.

Atlantic City High School was huge and cliquish. A three-story, 1922 neo-Gothic castle with a crenellated clock tower, it was the largest high school in New Jersey, accommodating 3,200 students—Jews, Italians, Catholics, blacks, Chinese—who socialized as groups in fraternities, sororities, teams, and clubs.

"It broke down basically by religion," says one Jewish member of the class of 1963, "although that's not to say that you didn't have friends out of those groups."

When Jessica first left Kennett Square, she had written to her classmates back home about how lonely she was. But by the following summers, when Linda Kilmer and Anne Marie De Wire visited her in Margate, she had begun to find her niche. She'd made a number of new friends, joined a Jewish sorority, Delta Omega Beta (DOBS), and had taken up water skiing, largely through her friendship with Jeff Greenhawt, a plumpish classmate who was to become almost like a brother. During Jessica's freshman year, Jeff Greenhawt watched out for his new friend, and in time, she would watch out for him. Sometimes they double-dated, Jessica usually going out with a dark-haired boy named Steve Labov, or a big, strapping redhead, Steve Altman. Mostly, however, she and Jeff, who lived only three blocks apart, traveled in a predominately Jewish clique of neighborhood kids who attended school functions together and got together on the weekends for a movie and a sandwich.

In Jessica's sophomore year, the clique began hanging out at the home of Eleanor "Rusty" Nicholl, a Catholic girl who lived with her divorced mother, Helen, in Margate. Unlike Jessica's Jewish friends, Rusty's plans for the future were concentrated on marriage and motherhood, but she and Jessica found common ground. Both came from single-parent homes, and both had a quick and lively sense of humor. In time, Rusty would become Jessica's only close high school girlfriend. As she had done with Faith Thomas, Jessica would take Rusty to synagogue with her, and accompany her to mass.

Rusty's mother, whom Jessica called "Auntie Helen," was every teenager's fantasy of what a parent should be. Kind, understanding, and generous, she turned her home into a twenty-four-hour open house for all of Rusty's friends, making herself available as a sounding board to anyone who had a problem considered too severe to talk over at home. The routine called for dating couples to spend Friday evenings at the Nicholls' house, and Saturday nights at the movies, with a swing back by Rusty's for cake and milk.

"It was a place to go whether Rusty was here or not," Helen Nicholl explains. The one house rule banned liquor on the premises, but nobody seemed to mind. This was the last generation of high school innocents. None of the group smoked or drank to any extent ("Although we did screw around a little bit," says one), and drug use had not yet found its way into the middle-class homes of Atlantic City. "We were not wild and crazy kids," Rusty Nicholl says. "The worst thing Jessica and I ever did was cut school once a year to go Christmas shopping."

In April 1962, the spring of her sophomore year, Jessica began dating a senior named Steve Berger. Tall, thin, and sporting a dark crew cut, Berger was something of a school celebrity. He had his own radio show on WOND-AM, a 1,000-watt Top 40 station in nearby Pleasantville, New Jersey. The kids at school thought he was weird because he wasn't interested in football and was high-strung, but they respected him, too.

"The radio station consumed my life," remembers Berger, now vice-president of radio for Nationwide Communications in Columbus, Ohio. "So the big date was like, 'Hey, why don't we go over to WOND?' I took her out there and showed her around a little bit, and then I said, 'You have a nice voice. You should do this, too.'" Jessica liked the idea, and recorded several weather intros for Berger's shift. When he played them back for her, she was, as she put it, "intoxicated."

"After I heard my voice," she would say on a television talk show in 1983, "I just knew that was what I wanted to do. It was *mystical.* I went home and turned on the radio, and I said, 'Mother, listen to this!' And she said, 'What?' I said, 'That's *me!*' And she said, 'Well, it doesn't sound like you.' But I thought it was *wonderful.* I knew then that I wanted to go into broadcasting."

Berger thought Jessica, with her long neck, her diagonal Russian eyebrows, and poised manner, seemed more elegant than other girls her age. One day he set up his Rolleiflex and posed her in the dining room of his parents' apartment. Jessica was sensitive about the noticeable acne scars on her chin and jawline, so Berger lit her in a way to minimize them. The camera caught her in a look that teetered between child and femme fatale, with her dark hair teased into an upsweep.

In the next months the two would be together constantly, going to band concerts at the Steel Pier, sitting on the rock jetty in Longport, and attending the senior prom. Berger worked with her in an effort to tame her lisp, showed her how to run a tape recorder, and helped her understand the use of different types of microphones. He was also in love with her, he says, though the relationship was strictly chaste.

The following fall, Jessica and Jeff Greenhawt went to the station's owner, Howard L. Green, and asked about becoming the first regular co-hosts of a Saturday morning youth program, "Teen Corner." Green liked the novelty of putting a girl on the air—he had two women on his FM station, but one was a British announcer and the other read poetry—and he liked the idea that Jessica and Jeff were already a natural team. They got the job. The station stood on stilts in the salt marsh on Old Turnpike Road, and they called it "The Jukebox in the Swamp."

"When I look back on it," says Greenhawt, now part-owner of several Florida radio stations, "it was very exciting, because we were actually on the air at a professional, commercial radio station. But Jessica was a lot better at it than I was."

The format of the hour-long show called for the teenage hosts to moderate reports from area high school correspondents, to interview one or two adult guests, and to introduce records in between. On the surface, "Teen Corner" didn't demand much of its hosts, but Jessica and Jeff also wrote the program, and they would arrive at the little "saltbox," as they called it, three hours before air time to put the show together.

Steve Berger says that from the day he first met her, Jessica spoke in a somewhat mannered, affected way. Before long, she would hit upon the formal announcing style she would employ for her entire career: hyper-correct enunciation—with a broad, finishing-school "a" sound—delivered in hurried, breathy cadence.

"It was fascinating to watch Jessica perfect her on-air presence," says Jeff Greenhawt. "She was very warm and caring to people she knew, and she had a terrific sense of humor. But her on-air persona was much straighter than she was. At WOND, the approach was much looser and more entertainment-oriented than reading hard news. But Jessica used to study Pauline Frederick [NBC's famed United Nations correspondent] a lot for writing and presentation."

Howard Green took notice of Jessica's progress. "She was a very tenacious, very ambitious, and very knowledgeable gal," he remembers, "many years beyond her age of fifteen."

In time, Green thought Jessica was ready for a show of her own, and offered her the twelve-to-eight Sunday airshift, making her the only female disc jockey in the area. On "Teen Corner," an engineer had been in charge of setting levels, cueing records, and playing commercials, and all Jeff and Jessica had to do was talk. Now she would have sole responsibility for everything that went out over the air.

Aside from worrying about what she was going to say, she had to run the audio board and take the transmitter readings. She also had to know how to play commercials on the cartridge machines, and for those commercials still on reel-to-reel, she had tó thread the tape machine, cue it up, and back it off the right number of turns so the sound would begin precisely when she pushed the button. One tape machine took two seconds to start, while one particular turntable took ten seconds. That meant that if Jessica were reading copy, she had to put a dot next to the word that came approximately ten seconds before the end of the commercial, so that there was no dead air between segments. Here is where she would also get her first experience delivering news every half hour in a "rip 'n' read" newscast—tearing copy off the Associated Press wire service machine and reading it cold on the air. As an adult she would joke about the time she read, "The President said today— continued on the next page—" and went right on talking.

While station manager Mike Elliott liked her spunk and attitude—"She was extremely personable, and as long as she was convinced it would work, she'd give anything a try"—he thought Jessica was "terrible" as a disc jockey. "What I lack in talent," she said with a sheepish smile, "I make up for in ambition and drive."

Jessica was making a name for herself, and even achieving a small amount of financial independence. WOND's teen disc jockeys earned only the minimum wage of $1.25 an hour—Jeff's check for one pay period was $33.55—but they often picked up an extra $60 to $90 a week emceeing record hops. In addition, Howard Green encouraged them to go out and find sponsors for their show, paying them a percentage of the commercials used on the air. Jessica was also working a few hours a week at a souvenir stand called Irene's, baby-sitting for neighborhood children for a dollar an hour, and, in the mornings, running the switchboard at the Coronet Motel, near the Boardwalk. But the station was the thing. "WOND became my center," she wrote in her autobiography, "taking the place of all I had lost. At last I felt as though I belonged."

"Jessica was surprised as hell when things started happening for her," Steve Berger remembers, "because her sense of self-worth was all screwed up. She thought she was an 'ugly duckling.' After she had a little success on the radio, she talked about how proud her father would have been of her."

A former WOND disc jockey recalls that when he first told Jessica she ought to think about becoming a reporter—that she needed to be out and involved with the public, and not stuck in a little studio in a swamp in New Jersey—she balked. "In her mind," he says, "news was not where you were going to be a personality, where you were going to be a star. I explained to her that as a reporter, she could get into places I couldn't, that she had an entree almost anywhere. She finally said okay, she'd try it."

Jessica delivered her first spot news report for the station on November 22, 1963, the day John F. Kennedy was killed. The event was especially emotional for her because she had met Kennedy in 1960, when the President-elect visited Wilmington. As the president of "Dem-Teens," she had presented him with flowers at the New Castle Airport in Delaware. Now she was being called upon to deliver the news of his death to the senior assembly. Howard Green asked her to give a telephone beeper report of teen reaction. The sixteen-year-old began: "I am ashamed for my country."

The next year, the station sent her out to cover two other news events—President Lyndon Johnson's address before the United Auto Workers in March 1964 and his return to Atlantic City that August for the Democratic National Convention. In 1978, she would tell newspaper reporter Arthur Wiese, then of the *Houston Post,* that when Johnson landed in Atlantic City for the convention, "I remember the President bounding off his plane and rushing right up to greet [NBC reporter] Nancy Dickerson. I heard him say, 'Hi, Nancy,' and I knew that was what I wanted to do with my life."

A letter Jessica wrote to a friend after Johnson's first visit suggests that she had already made up her mind about her life's work. She described the thrill of covering a national political event, rubbing elbows with the national press corps, and being noticed by Johnson and by Robert Kennedy. "It was really that event—and not the Nancy Dickerson episode—that made Jessica decide she wanted to be a journalist, and particularly a television journalist," Jeff Greenhawt says.

Now Jessica was fixated on getting thin. Ray Freeman, a WOND disc jockey, had said he thought she was "just a tad chubby," and she knew the TV camera made anyone look ten to twenty pounds heavier than he really was. Rusty Nicholl remembers, "No matter who was there, Jessica would lay on my living room floor with her feet tucked under the sofa, and do a hundred sit-ups."

Mrs. Nicholl worried about her. "I always thought there was a certain lonesomeness to Jessica," she says. "Her life seemed to be segmented—this part was for these people, and another part would be for somebody else. She surrounded herself more with acquaintances than real, loving friends. And I had the feeling she kept a lot of her important feelings secret, that there were so many things about her that she just didn't tell anyone. She lived in her own little world."

From the time that Jessica began dating Steve Berger, it was general knowledge that the two were going steady; she kept his ring when he went off to college in Philadelphia in the fall of 1962. Berger came home every weekend to do his air shift at WOND, but while he was in Philadelphia, Rusty noticed that Jessica would sometimes leave school in the afternoons with Steve Altman, and that he often came by later to pick her up.

"She denied that they were dating," Rusty says, "but it was more than just somebody giving her a ride home. Everybody saw them in the hall together. Still, nobody said, 'What a bitch!' They just said, 'Oh, that's Jessica. If you want to be with her, you've got to realize she's going to be dating three other people, too. You've got to take her on her terms.' " It was a pattern Jessica would cling to for the rest of her life, including the time during which she was married.

Steve Berger wasn't oblivious to the situation. "I was this geeky-looking kid on the radio, and here was this very attractive woman who was interested in me," Berger recounts. "For that reason, I was willing to take an inordinate amount of shit from her. But one day, I just said, 'That's it.' Jessica was for Jessica, only and always Jessica. Never anyone else. It wasn't that she was so wrapped up in her work. She was too wrapped up in Jessica. I can recall being terribly sick one time, with fever, chills, and the whole works. And she kept saying, 'Well, what about our date? Can't we go out?' I didn't need that in my life."

So one Friday in April 1963, a year after they started dating, Berger came home to end the relationship. He told Jessica that afternoon. "I'll never forget it," he says. "She called me up on the phone that night, and tried to be conciliatory. I said, 'No, there's no way we can work this out. You and I are just not going to make it, period.' And the last thing she said to me was, 'I'll get even with you for this!'

"Since then I've known other women who lost their fathers young," says Berger. "They become self-destructive so that other people will leave them. Jessica was a story she was telling herself. Those kinds of women decide the aura they want, and then they build it. She was good at it, too, because people bought it. Jessica's biggest talent was to create the persona that you saw on television. And the fall from grace to middle-class America was probably what drove her to be a star."

Because her father's last illness had begun in April, Jessica was convinced that the month held bad tidings for her, a superstition she would carry into adulthood. Now, at sixteen, in the melodrama every teenager knows, she played the Bobby Darin record "I'll Remember April" until no one around her could stand it any longer. The record had come out in 1959, the year her father died.

Two weeks after the breakup, Jessica began seeing Barry Swartz, who was a year ahead of her in school; she had first met him on a double date. "She started that 'April is the cruelest month' stuff with me, too," says Swartz, now a plastic surgeon in San Antonio. "One of the first things we did was make a pilgrimage to her father's grave. She said, 'I have to be the best, because my father told me to always be the best.' Actually, I doubt very much if a father tells a twelve-year-old that."

Indeed, those words sound more as if they might have come from Ben and Lil than from David—unless Jessica was rewriting that awful moment when he told her she would not amount to anything. "I don't think I'll ever resign myself to the fact that my father is dead," she later told Swartz. "I don't think I even want to."

In short order, Jessica and Barry were an item, even though Barry had grown up on the wrong side of the tracks. His father ran a "very unsuccessful" secondhand furniture store; the family lived with Barry's grandparents; and there was a great deal of domestic turmoil. The family vehicle, he remembers with embarrassment, was a pickup truck.

Jessica seemed to be crazy about Barry—a tribute to her character and judgment after years of being drilled by Lil in the arts of upward mobility. When he went away for pre-med at Dickinson, in Carlisle, Pennsylvania, she wrote to him every day, often baking brownies for him and sending him little gifts. Her candor about her feelings toward him at the time is both touching and troubling. She told him she had been brought up to think that no one was good enough for her, but she now knew that was wrong; not only was Barry good to her, but she thought he had the proper appearance and personality to impress the right people. Besides, she told him, he was Jewish, and he loved her.

Ben and Lil, who frequently drove the two-hour trip to Margate, were alarmed that Barry came from such an impoverished background, even if he did plan to become a doctor. Lil, in particular, tried to make Jessica see the error of her ways, arranging invitations for her to attend debutante parties and trying to steer her in the direction of the more affluent and the more prestigious.

Jessica was both resentful and flattered by it all. "I'll be a damn du Pont or die trying," she said, tongue in cheek. But not long after she gave a speech on the du Pont family for history class, she told Barry she had met the young Irene du Pont at a Wilmington gathering. Irene, who was making her debut in a few months at the Holly Ball, had been rude to Jessica until she discovered that she was related to Ben and Lil, who were respected in the community. "If I have to be related to someone in order for her to be civil to me," Jessica told Barry, "then she can take her goddamned Holly Ball and shove it sideways."

Barry dreaded Jessica's trips to visit her grandparents. "Wilmington was Never-Never Land," he says. "She'd come back from there with her cape flowing. It was, 'Last week I was with the du Ponts, and this week I'm Anastasia.' I never knew what to believe. But I'll bet half of that stuff never happened."

Until the beginning of her senior year, Jessica had believed that she and Barry had always stopped their lovemaking before things got too far out of hand—her hymen was still intact, and she was technically still a virgin. But then she told him she'd discovered she'd "broken the seal" with a Tampax long ago, and that what she'd assumed had been just "fooling around" had really been "going all the way." They had committed "a mortal sin," she said, and she didn't want them sleeping together again until they were married.

Thus when Jessica traveled the three hundred miles to visit Barry at Dickinson College, he was surprised to learn that she'd now started drinking Singapore slings and Asti spumanti, and that she no longer had any reservations about their sex life. "She was just doing whatever to try to act cool," he says. "We'd get a bottle of wine and hide out in a motel and come out maybe three times a weekend." Over the next year and a half, Jessica would experience three genuine pregnancy scares, the third one seeming so serious that she finally went for a test.

"I would have married her," Barry explains. But Jessica had already formulated her life's plan—college at Emerson or Ithaca, graduate school at New York University, a job in communications in either Philadelphia or New York, and *then* marriage to Barry. The order was important. The pregnancy test turned out negative, but Jessica asked Barry to line up an abortionist, "just in case."

"There were a lot of different Jessicas," Barry says. "I usually say, 'Which one do you want to hear about?' Because there was this hard, nasty, son-of-a-gun lady who was going in one direction, and underneath it all, there was a scared kid who wanted to curl up and be left alone.

"She would say, 'I wish you were here, so that I could lay my head on your shoulder and cry and hear you tell me that it will be all right.' But then she'd say, 'But that is weakness, and above all, I must never be weak.' She was a very vulnerable person," Barry says, "but she didn't want anyone else in the world to know."

Jessica's senior year was turning out to be the most hectic time of her life, and her psychology teacher, Carolyn Stierhem (now La Mountain), worried that she was "too hyper. Jessica had a single-mindedness that was rare as hen's teeth for a high school student," she says. "There was no question about what Jessica wanted to do, but I was a little concerned that she didn't feel as though she had achieved anything if she were not number one—and number one in bold letters and neon lights. I saw a feeling of almost panic come across her face when she talked about trying to get to the top."

Jessica's letters to friends began to consist of only two topics: her radio career and her health, particularly her continued insistence on jeopardizing her well-being with chronic dieting and lack of sleep. In one sixteen-month period, she wrote more than fifty letters to Barry Swartz in which she detailed an injury or an illness—everything from malnutrition to mononucleosis, from anemia to fainting to hyperthyroidism—even migraine headaches and a breast lump. Just how many of these conditions might have been imagined is impossible to know, since Jessica had a tendency to make things more sensational than they were. But according to a surgeon in Somers Point, New Jersey, her most improbable story, which described the draining of a benign cyst on her left breast, was indeed true.

In October 1963, the sixteen-year-old began making references to Barry about having other frequent bouts of crying, unexplained depression, and taking tranquilizers. Finally, she told him that her general practitioner had recommended that she see a psychiatrist, and that she was currently under the care of one in Wilmington. Jessica would see the doctor when she visited Ben and Lil. She complained to Barry that none of the moments of her life approached reality.

From the late 1970s until shortly before her death, the adult Jessica was to see four psychiatrists in three different cities. The intensity and length of her treatment was different with each one, from semi-regular office visits to telephone consultations as often as three times a day in times of crisis.

At least two of these psychiatrists thought she showed features of borderline personality disorder, which the *DSM-III* (the American Psychiatric Association's desk reference) defines as "a pervasive pattern of instability of mood, interpersonal relationships and self-image."

"Jessica was terribly afraid of being abandoned," one of these psychiatrists comments. "But the only way she could see [anyone] as being valued fully was if they were negative about her. That meant they were honest and telling the truth, because that confirmed her own negative views. And she thought anyone who was absorbed by her, and laudatory of her, was obviously missing something. Therefore, she devalued that person. They weren't worth her time."

After some months, Jessica told Barry that she thought her problem was trying too hard to get somewhere, instead of turning to herself and being happy in the here and now. Barry says he was amazed at her new insight, but to this day, he believes the Wilmington psychiatrist was another figment of her imagination, a teenage cry for help.

Part of Jessica's stress during this time came from a conflict with her mother and grandparents over her choice of college. For the past two years, she had had her heart set on attending either Emerson or Ithaca, primarily because both were well known for their communications departments. The chances for her acceptance were good. She told Barry that her Scholastic Aptitude Test (SAT) scores were 653 in English and 566 in math. Her spelling was atrocious, but she demonstrated an uncommon command of the language, an excellent vocabulary, and a flair for creative writing. (A love poem she'd written for Barry had won her $25 in a *Senior Scholastic* contest.) With all her activities, she had maintained a high B average all through high school, with C's only in chemistry and typing.

Ben and Lil had always been proud that Jessica had done so well on the radio, but now that she was maturing into a young woman, they hoped she would go on and do what her father had not—become a doctor or lawyer. Communications was "no place for a lady," they told her, and offered to send her to any school in the country if she would change her mind. Ben sat her down for one of their "beauty and the beast talks," as he called them, and added the additional carrot of a year in Europe as a graduation present.

Jessica thanked her grandparents, but explained that she wanted to go to college right away, to Ithaca. She would major in communications. She would apply for every scholarship she could. That was that.

Florence wasn't keen on Ithaca, either. The college was a seven-hour drive from Margate, and she complained that Jessica would be too far from home. Florence wanted her to go to Montclair State College and become an English teacher.

"Montclair State College!" Jessica exclaimed to Barry. "What chance would I have of meeting the right people there? I hate to hurt my mother, but I don't know how I can avoid it."

Florence tried to explain that becoming a teacher would give Jessica the tools to become a real person, and not someone who lived in a dream world. After all, how many women had succeeded in broadcast journalism?

"It wasn't that my mother didn't think that I could do the job," Jessica would tell television interviewer Ponchitta Pierce years later, "but that the job wouldn't be there for me to do. All she kept thinking was, 'You're not going to come back on our doorstep, are you, Jessica, dear, and cost us a lot of money when we have two other little girls growing up?'"

In the end, Jessica got her way, and $2,000 in scholarships—

$1,500 from state and national veterans' organizations "because my father died from a condition that was aggravated during his service in the navy," she explained to Barry, and $500 from Ithaca College, which granted her an early acceptance. She went up for a visit, and came back all aglow, telling Barry and Rusty she'd done a half-hour shift on the campus radio station. "I impressed the hell out of them!" she said. "There are only five girls in communications, but I'll be student director by my junior year or die trying."

When Jessica arrived at Ithaca in September 1964, she was shocked to find that her dorm, Williams Hall, was not one of the new modern buildings she'd toured during her visit to the South Hill campus, but an old, two-story frame house at 130 East Buffalo Street, in the heart of downtown.

"It's horrible," Jessica told Barry Swartz. "I'm either going to have it condemned or get state slum aid." But the radio and TV studios were right next door, with a cafeteria and post office nearby.

Soon she was coping well with the onslaught of college life, although she hadn't much tolerance for the hazing that lower classmen were expected to put up with during orientation. When an upperclassman asked her, "How low are you, Freshman?" Jessica threw her jacket over her shoulder and shot him a grin. "Sky high," she yelled, "and still climbing!"

In her quiet moments, Jessica confided to Barry that most of her behavior was just a bluff, that while she knew people thought she was poised, talented, and even fearless, she was really scared to death. And that she was always lonely, too—even with him.

"She was very insecure about this move to a whole new world," Barry remembers. "Of course, I was insanely jealous. She had to know that she was really pretty, and that she was about as hip as they came. I said, 'I don't know what you're worrying about. In no time, guys will be falling all over you. You won't be able to move without someone wanting to do everything for you.'"

Indeed, within days of arriving on campus, she had been asked to run for student council, she was getting along well with her roommates—a situation that would change as time went on—and making friends with Judy Girard, another radio-TV major. Now that she'd fixed up the room—putting leopard bedspreads on the old college beds and hanging Barry's pictures on the walls—Jessica

49

felt practically at home. "And guess what?" she told Barry. "I got three letters from my mother! Maybe she really does love me."

Jessica would express the same feeling a few months later, when she told him that she couldn't believe how proud her mother was of her grades. But she told Barry that her relationship with Florence had been strained, that they seemed to argue about everything, including Jessica's wanting to bleach her hair blonde. She did it anyway.

Whether she was fully conscious of it, Jessica had taken the first step toward the creation of herself as a media personality. Except for other cosmetic changes that would appear throughout the years, by the time she graduated from Ithaca in 1968, the transformation would be nearly complete.

To many of the students who passed through Ithaca College in 1964–1968, the era would be one of tremendous social unrest and upheaval: the Vietnam War, the continuing struggle for civil rights, the public burning of draft cards, the rise of the counterculture, student demonstrations. Jessica would let her hair grow long and straight and wear the expensive wardrobe of miniskirts and sweaters that Lil would send in the mail, but she was not a child of the sixties. Her need for achievement, for validation, was too great for her to sustain any real concern for anything else, even her own personal maturity. Her college years would be only a holding period, a necessary formality before she could enter the competitive world of professional broadcasting.

Now she embarked on succeeding in local radio. Howard Green had suggested that she take a shift at WOND's sister station, WENY, in nearby Elmira, New York. And WTKO, a commercial station in Ithaca, had agreed to talk to her about a job in production. But the bulk of her work would be for WICB-AM-FM, the campus station, managed entirely by students. She told Barry during her first fall at Ithaca that she didn't think she'd have much competition in becoming the college's top female announcer.

According to Jessica's version of what happened next, in *Anchorwoman,* she was blackballed from the campus station because she persisted in pursuing the position of on-air announcer at a time when it was reserved for men only, and then punished when she broke the barrier. The story was, in truth, more complicated than that. Jessica wanted a deejay shift on the campus AM station, and with her WOND experience, naturally assumed she would get one. She got insulted when John von Soosten, the student manager, required her to audition for the spot. She ran through it quickly, and was later flabbergasted to learn she had not been selected, although another freshman, a male, had. That left her no choice but to try the campus FM station, which broadcast to a smaller audience and was generally thought to be less prestigious. There, out of the estimated 125 radio-TV majors—only five of whom were women—she told Barry she was named assistant news director. It was a particular coup for a female freshman, she said, and a position that frequently sent her out in the field as a reporter. In addition, she was given a Friday evening FM air shift, "Music of the Masters," which propelled her to make a frantic call to Barry for a list of classical composers.

But it was still the AM exposure she wanted. Finally, she managed to get on the station once a week, using the air name of "Jill Jackson" to co-host a women's show, "Town Talk," with her sophomore roommate, Dee Adamczyk. Clearly, she was working steadily on campus radio, if not in the positions she desired.

As she had done at WOND, Jessica soon began spending virtually all of her time at the studios, eschewing the usual college social activities, refusing the flirtations of the boys from Cornell, and forming few close friendships with women, who she believed were jealous of her. She was adamant that nothing would interfere with her goal, and told a would-be suitor, "I'm here to become a success in communications."

In November of that year, Jessica was elated to obtain an exclusive interview with the popular folk singing group, Peter, Paul and Mary. She told Barry that she was the "golden girl" of WICB and that it was the first time Florence had been proud of anything she did in broadcasting, but that she was resented and disliked at the station because she was progressing too quickly. The truth was that she still craved the AM disc jockey spot, and that her fellow students despised her for her relentless ambition.

The following month, Jessica decided to go after a job as a WICB newscaster. While station regulations allowed her to work as a program *announcer,* according to Marvin Diskin, a professor in the department at the time, it was still a sad fact that only the male students—and the upperclass students, at that—were allowed to deliver a newscast. Not to be outdone twice, Jessica protested, citing her work as a "rip 'n' read" newscaster at WOND, and won

51

a 15-minute, state and local news shift twice a week. She also wangled an "up-tempo personality" show, for which she would interview folk singers Bob Dylan (who would continually address her as "little girl") and Miriam Makeba.

But a couple of days before she was to begin her news show, an uproar ensued when several members of the staff complained that Jessica, who would be the first woman newscaster in WICB history, was in clear violation of station policy. They wanted her off.

Indignant and distraught, Jessica sought the advice of Professor Diskin. "First of all, Jessica is the one who coined the phrase, 'There's no place for broads in broadcasting,'" advice she had attributed to him in *Anchorwoman,* says Diskin, now on the faculty at Purdue. "That was not my line. But I did say, 'Jessica, here's the reality. You want a career in broadcast news, and at this time, other than Nancy Dickerson and Pauline Frederick, there are very few women in that position. The traditional approach for a woman is to work your way in through a secretarial position. Learn to take shorthand. Learn to type ninety words per minute. But unfortunately, no matter how bright or how good you are, it's almost impossible to break into this male-dominated business.'"

Jessica refused to buckle, taking her case to Rudy Paolangeli, another faculty member who served as the station's primary adviser. She won, and on February 17, 1965, went on the air with her first solo newscast.

"When she was confronted with an obstacle," says Diskin, "Jessica went at it head-on. I can't tell you specifically how she achieved her victory, but she did it, and she opened the way for women at Ithaca College."

The incident was a wonderful example of perseverance and fortitude. But alas, the second half of the story as recounted in *Anchorwoman,* in which Jessica was barred from the station for failing to shut down the transmitter, appears to be a fabrication.

By this time, Jessica was also involved in ICB-TV, the college cable channel that served the Ithaca community. In October, she had signed on as a floor manager for the upcoming election night coverage, where she would stand between the cameras and cue the talent when the command came over her headset. The director was Tony Busch, a senior, who, aside from his dark crew cut, bore a startling resemblance to David Savitch, right down to his glasses,

his imposing girth—195 pounds at 6′ 1″—and the way he pronounced certain words. Tony had seen Jessica around the department. He thought of her as the sort of young woman who wore far
too much makeup—the right amount for appearing on camera,
maybe, but not for street wear.

The first day Jessica showed up for crew, Tony, a precise,
fastidious boy from a disciplined Catholic background, was appalled at her appearance. She wore a wrinkled, man's white shirt,
and wheat-colored Levi's that looked as if they'd been slept in. He
watched her for a moment from the control booth, and then pulled
the mouthpiece on his headset into place. "Pardon me," he said
over the set. "Did you just get up? I would suggest you go back
home and change your clothes. When you're ready to conduct
business, you are more than welcome to come back."

Busch, now the chief operating officer of a video production
house in East Rochester, New York, laughs out loud when he tells
the story. "She went storming out of there," he says, remembering. "She looked like hell."

In short order, Jessica returned to the studio in a fresh, crisp
outfit. She had a defiant swagger about her, a sign of wounded
pride. But Jessica respected people who stood their ground. Those
who knew her best continually refer to the fact that if anyone
seemed too eager to let her have her way, she could turn on him
in a heartbeat. Tony admired her for coming back. Minutes later,
when he was scanning the monitors in the booth, the camera
inadvertently caught her in its viewfinder and he noticed how
photogenic she was, with her high cheekbones and her keen, Slavic
eyes. She radiated intensity and intelligence, he thought.

Later, Tony took Jessica aside and said he was sorry if he'd
been too harsh. Would she be interested in sharing the talent
duties on election night? She said yes. Don Alhart would sit at the
anchor desk, and Jessica would record the Tompkins County vote
tallies on the blackboard behind him. She would be the only
woman on the set, and one of only two freshmen on the crew. It
would be her first real exposure on camera.

On election night, even the crew commented on how striking
Jessica looked in her little black dress, with her hair, now a becoming ash blonde, flipped up in arrogant twists on the sides. Whenever she stepped forward to write the numbers on the blackboard,
the crew saw something extraordinary in the monitor. The camera

seemed mesmerized by her, intensifying her already powerful physiognomy into a riveting on-air presence.

That presence had remarkably few flaws. At times, Jessica turned her mouth down at the corners in a kind of creeping sneer that conveyed disdain, a mannerism Marvin Diskin would help her overcome. But there was no denying that she possessed a singular gift for communication, even if the cool figure on the screen was, underneath it all, a frazzled jangle of nerves—so much so that halfway through the election night coverage, when Jessica again stepped before the camera to tally the votes, she managed to let the blackboard tumble down on top of her.

In the weeks to come, Tony Busch would find other shows for Jessica to work, so impressed was he with her "inbred talent" and her professional approach to production. Tony also suspected he was falling in love—trouble, for he was already pinned to another girl. He was now calling Jessica by her middle name, Beth. The first time he did it, Jessica was taken aback. "That's what my father called me," she said.

Tony gave up his girlfriend and committed himself to Jessica. "At times, she was a very calculating and impossible person to live with," he recounts. "But at other times, she was an extremely warm individual. For as long as she lived, all I ever had to do was to ask her to do something, and she would do it with no reservations. Of course, not too many people saw that side of her. But I saw her as a very loving person who didn't know how to love, because the high price of loving was too expensive in relation to the objectives of her life. It was a terrible tragedy. As time went on, she buried the real Beth, and rode through life high on the electronic image."

Despite a part-time career as a cameraman, Tony, the son of a salesman for Armour and Company, the beef packager, put aside many of his ambitions to help Jessica realize hers. He arranged to have her make a demonstration tape in Rochester, where he had begun working with a producer named Bill Schwing, who headed the Empire Sports Network. By March 1965, using the new demo tape, Tony had gotten her two commercials in Rochester. The tapings paid $100 for each commercial minute, and Tony would see to every detail—from arranging the bookings to handling the billings—without taking a fee, even buying Jessica her own lavalier, or pin-on microphone, and painting it white to blend with her outfits. "She had the talent," he says. "All I did was open the door and hold her hand."

Now that she was making TV commercials, Jessica, who was not quite five feet five inches, was convinced she needed to lose more weight, and began taking diet pills to get down to 102 pounds. She regimented her intake to only one meal a day and often refused to eat at all unless someone accompanied her to the cafeteria. She also began to resort to staying up all night to catch up on her studies, using Benzedrine tablets to keep herself awake.

"Beth was constantly concerned about failing, about losing her position," Tony says. "In my estimation, it was not a healthy drive. It was an obsession. She was absolutely possessed. I think she was very afraid and uncomfortable with her personal side, and perhaps that's why she was so consumed by her television life. She felt she could control it, and she could communicate with a camera better than she could with a person. Looking back, I doubt if any love relationship of hers would have been successful. But I always very much hoped so."

Jessica tried to keep her relationship with Tony quiet. She was, for all practical purposes, pinned to Barry, to whom she continued to write daily letters with the ritual signature of, "For always and forever in love, Jessica." But by the spring of 1965, she was both deeply involved with Tony ("Obviously, we had the kind of healthy relationship that any twenty-one-year-old guy and eighteen-year-old girl would have") and inviting Barry to visit her on campus, sleeping with him at Snyder's Tourist Home on Tioga Street, close to her dorm. During the first part of April, Jessica was telling Barry about her passionate longings to spend the summer by his side, saying she was so lonely that she often cried herself to sleep. But barely a week later, the love affair was over.

"She just outgrew me," Barry says. "She was the one to actually break off the relationship, but I had wanted her to do that for a long time. Jessica was basically a very good person. But her center had somehow gotten terribly screwed up. And I didn't know how to straighten it out."

That summer, wearing Tony's pin—he belonged not to a social club, but to Alpha Epsilon Rho, the national honorary broadcasting fraternity—Jessica went home to work at WOND and invited him to Margate to meet her family and friends.

Tony's personality was an irresistible mix of protective, take-charge attitude and teddy bear affection, and Florence and the girls warmed to him from the start. But whenever Jessica visited his house in Rochester, it was clear that she and his mother would never be friends. Mrs. Busch wanted an old-fashioned girl for her son, and she reacted to Jessica's quick temper with hostility, accusing her of bossing her around in her own home. But "Flossie," as Jessica had taken to calling her mother, seemed to light up with Tony in the house, fixing him special homemade pizza muffins until he threatened to pop. Florence and Tony, with their shared Catholic background, understood each other in an unspoken way. "Tony's too good for you," she told Jessica.

Having graduated from Ithaca, Tony went to work for an advertising company in the little town of Newark, New York, and arranged to be paid, after four months' labor, with a diamond engagement ring. "Jessica's grandparents went into orbit," he remembers, "one, because they sized you up by how much money you had in your pocket—and, of course, I had exactly none—and two, because I was a Christian, and Jessica had announced she planned to convert to Catholicism. She'd even begun study classes."

Tony had been to temple with Jessica on the anniversary of her father's death, but she told him she had begun to grow dissatisfied with Judaism, that she no longer felt comfortable as a Jew. That summer, Ben and Lil had come over to Atlantic City, staying at the Deauville Hotel on the Boardwalk. Tony and Jessica met them at the pool.

"I was lying on a deck chair between her grandmother and grandfather, watching Jessica dive off the board," Tony says. "There was a rather rotund woman sitting on the other side of Lil, and she noticed Beth wearing my Saint Christopher's medal around her neck. All of a sudden, the woman turned to Lil and said, 'My, what a nice son you have, but the *shiksa* he's going with—too bad!' " Tony turned in time to watch the blood drain out of Lillian Savitch's elegant face.

In her sophomore year, Jessica asked Tony if he might help her find more work making commercials. He told her she would need to join AFTRA, the television and radio artists' union, and that he would put out a few feelers to his friends Mike Verno and Ann Rogers, both of whom ran advertising agencies in the Rochester area.

Over the next three years, Jessica would make some fifty commercials, mostly for regional grocery stores and banks, as well as industrial filmstrips for R. T. French, the mustard company,

Bausch and Lomb, and Kodak. Often, she supplied only voice-overs, where her voice was heard but she was not seen on camera. But being on-camera was what Jessica wanted most of all. In time, she would live to be on camera.

When Tony took Jessica to meet Ann Rogers, a/k/a Joan Starkweather, the strong, diminutive woman in her mid-thirties had already lost count of the thousands of young women she had auditioned for commercial and modeling work in her career. She had started in the business the year Jessica was born, and since that time, a veritable pink-collar ghetto had passed through her door, girls willing to work seven days a week, willing to work nights, willing to work first thing in the morning, willing to sacrifice every shred of personal life to achieve and accomplish, to see their faces smiling back from the little screen. What was so upsetting to Rogers was that so often she would "see them unwind, see things come apart inside, hear springs begin to go," wires start to snap. She had seen young women focus so intently on the work that they seemed to have virtually nothing left of themselves. It was a syndrome, and once it swung into motion, the damage was almost irrevocable.

Now Rogers would turn her attention to the thin blonde in the black headband. "Quite frankly," Rogers remembers, "she didn't stand out off-camera. You would not think she was a knockout if you saw her somewhere." And, indeed, throughout her life, Jessica would impress many strangers as someone who had almost no sense of herself as an attractive, sexual person. "She was very masculine that way," says a woman who met her in the last three months of her life. "I was really surprised. It was like she was an eight-year-old boy."

Nevertheless, from the first time Rogers put her in front of a camera, she recognized that Jessica had a natural instinct for performance. Rogers, who also produced all her own commercials, coached Jessica on how to look into the lens, to treat the camera as if she were talking to one person, not the thousands who might be watching the final product. And when she ran Jessica's first piece of film through the projector, she couldn't believe the transformation. In person, Jessica was flat-chested and almost birdlike; privately, she would joke about her padded bras and her "hat rack" figure. But the camera kept these secrets and gave her a healthy glow, a streamlined sensuality. "She was really so exciting," Rogers says.

One day, Jessica came over to the WHEC-TV studios in Rochester to watch the post-production work for one of her commercials—the transferring of the "A" and "B" rolls of film onto videotape, a process of alternating segments of the original film, which can, for instance, produce dissolves and fades. "When she walked into the control room," Rogers remembers, "the crew said hello to her, and as we were about to begin, she stood against the wall in the back of the room. They started to run the commercial, and suddenly, the director and the crew, looking at her on the monitors, broke into whistles. One of them said, 'Wow, who is *she*!' They went on and on about her, like, 'Oh, my God, this vision!' But never once did they connect the girl on camera with the girl who was propped up against the wall."

The camera, then, was clearly Jessica's love object. Standing in the back of the darkened control room that day, she, too, must have realized the attraction, and may have contemplated what it was that allowed her to throw this romantic glamour around herself when she looked into the camera. Was she recapturing that perfect security of the past again as the star of her father's home movies? She would write to the dead man on his birthday, and for as long as she lived, every time Jessica faced a camera, she would perform for David Savitch, acting out their private, long-ago rituals of cameras and current events. It was a moment when all was forgiven, when he was hers, and hers alone, a reunion in the dark recesses of fantasy, where everything would always be all right.

"She was always so frightened before she went on camera," says David Buda, who later became her manager. "But then when she finally got in front of it, she was fine."

"Ordinarily, I'm very shy, except on camera," Jessica would tell Maralyn Lois Polak in 1975. "I'm probably more real, more at ease, better adjusted in my work than in any part of my life. I'm happier, more comfortable, better able to cope. I even move better. Privately, I'm very emotional, insecure, unsure, overly sensitive to criticism, very high strung, nervous. But these things don't affect my job performance."

During her years at Ithaca College, Jessica made some twenty commercials with Rogers, earning $50 to $75 for each. She achieved her biggest exposure in some half-dozen television spots for the local Dodge dealer. Pamela Austin had made a huge hit as the rodeo-riding national Dodge Girl, sparking the creation of regional Dodge Girls throughout the country. Jessica would later note on her résumé that she had led the Dodge Rebellion for Upstate New York ("Regional Dodge Girl—Commercials, Television/Radio"), but Ann Rogers says it never got beyond the talking stage.

Instead, Rogers says, Jessica became famous in the region as the first local woman to play an ongoing character in commercials, when Rogers wrote a series of Culver Dodge scripts around the "Perils of Pauline," paralleling the hair-raising stunts that Austin appeared to perform in the national spots. One particular commercial called for Joe Barnett, the local dealer, to jump a shiny new Dodge on horseback.

Jessica loved to tell the story of how her horse jumped over the Dodge but the dealer's didn't, catching its hoof on the car.

Ann Rogers remembers the day well. Jessica was decked out in white go-go boots and a red cowgirl outfit. "She was brave beyond belief," she says. "She would do anything. You'd say, 'Do you ride a horse, Jess?' And she'd say, 'Oh, yeah!' Well, she got on the horse, and she was doing the best she could to hold it together. She didn't jump the car, because I wouldn't allow it. But somehow during the sequence, the horse ran off with her. It was very scary, because Jessie wasn't able to bring it under control. But Joe got to her and stopped it. To this day," Rogers says, "I never met anybody like Jess. She was very disarming."

As the commercial work picked up, Jessica found herself commuting the hundred miles to Rochester more and more frequently. Often, the call came at the last minute, and she would have to improvise quick transportation—getting cars, or hooking up with rides.

"She was very creative in facilitating," says Rogers. "She always seemed to have somebody there working out the problem for her, primarily men. And she would come anytime. It didn't matter if there was a snowstorm or if she had to miss a dozen classes. I'm sure that money was not the motivation. It was like she had an engine inside of her, and nothing could deter her from where she was going and what she was going to do."

By now it was apparent that Jessica needed a car of her own, and sometime during her sophomore year, Ben and Lil bought her a new Chevrolet Chevelle. Jessica called the little car "Gazelle Chevelle," and talked to it as if it were alive, darting around the ribbons of roads that lined Ithaca's scenic gorges.

Now that she was a sophomore, Jessica was eligible to be

admitted to Alpha Epsilon Rho. But that winter, when the fraternity announced its new members, her name was not among them.

"The guys blackballed her," says Tony. "She called me one night absolutely hysterical. I got on the phone to Don Alhart, who was the president, and told him I thought they were being unfair."

The fraternity reconsidered, and Jessica went on to become its corresponding secretary. Now she was more determined than ever to show the boys at Ithaca College just exactly what she could do. She thought of Bill Schwing, and wondered if he could use her services on the sports and special events shows he ran out of Rochester.

"That first day, when Tony brought her up to our bowling show," Schwing says, "I knew she was a natural. She just had a presence on camera that very few people have. She needed a lot of help in some aspects, but in others, she was about as good the first time I took her on a shoot as she was the day she died."

Schwing especially liked Jessica's voice, which ranged from medium-high to low and stayed compact, without much variance. He saw that no matter how excited she got, the bass quality of her voice didn't change, which made it ideal for microphone transmission. And so the easygoing Schwing began giving Jessica freelance work in her sophomore year, using her as on-camera and voice-over talent as well as for on-line production jobs. Occasionally, she also helped write scripts. The association would extend beyond Jessica's college years, and would provide her with an extraordinary internship, an opportunity to learn professional television production from the ground up.

"From that first day I met her until she graduated from school, I always knew she would be whatever she wanted to be," Schwing says. "When you gave her a project, you didn't have to worry about it again. The only thing was, she needed a lot of patting on the back, and sometimes she could be a little flaky. If there was a four-lane highway with no cars on it, a sidewalk with a doggie turd on it, and another sidewalk with a crocodile on it, she'd walk up the side where the dog turd was and *just miss it* by jumping onto the walk with the crocodile."

"In Jessica's case," says Schwing's director, Don Friedman, "Bill was a true mentor. He worked with her to help her learn to dress, and he coached her with her speech. By the time she came to do a show with me, she was ready. But she had a number of mechanical things to overcome, and I would not have wanted her if Bill had not said, 'Trust me, let's use her.' "

With Tony Busch and Bill Schwing, Jessica began to form the nucleus of the kind of support group she would gather about her all her life—people who would run interference for her problems, who would facilitate the advancement of her career, and who could offer her the sense of security she hadn't been able to find with Florence and the girls.

By the middle of her sophomore year, Jessica was spending almost more time in Rochester than she was in Ithaca ("I spent college in my car," she would tell *TV Guide* in 1979), often staying with Tony Busch and his parents when the shoots lasted several days. But her relationship with Mrs. Busch was becoming increasingly strained, and it was only a matter of time before she began camping at the Schwings' house. Bill's wife, Louise, found Jessica to be "a nice kid. I liked her, even though she had an arrogance about her, and was very untrusting of women. But we became very good friends. My parents thought I was crazy to let a teenage girl be around my husband that much."

Jessica had no romantic designs on Bill Schwing. Twelve years her senior, he thought she saw him as something of an "older brother." Schwing realized that Jessica needed camaraderie and that "She seemed to get an awful lot out of family-type relationships."

Schwing suggested that Jessica might be able to get a summer relief position at WBBF, Rochester's top rock and roll station. He offered to speak to program director Jack Palvino about the possibility of her becoming the station's first and only female disc jockey.

"Jessica was totally wrapped up in broadcasting," says Palvino, now general manager of Rochester's WVOR-FM. "I knew she'd succeed, because it was the focus of her life. She had a fire burning inside her." Without hesitation, Palvino put Jessica on the air for the summer. Since the male jocks were called "Busy Bees," after the double-B call letters ("WBBF—Home of the Busy Bees— Give Them a Buzz"), Palvino dubbed his new air personality "Jessica, the Honeybee." She never used her surname on the air.

In 1966, AM radio was king, and format rock and roll, with its regular rotation of Simon and Garfunkel, the Byrds, and the Beatles, was every teenager's guide to romance, redemption, and self-

61

recognition. It offered a pipeline to everything mystical and important, the very be-all of "cool." And to be a teenage disc jockey in the late 1960s, with the American fixation on youth and popular culture, seemed like unimaginable ecstasy.

"WBBF was hot stuff in those days," says George Palmer, a freelance engineer who often worked with Bill Schwing. "Outside of Buffalo, it was *the* rock and roll station. So for Jessica to get on the air there was a spectacular coup, because that was a real male-oriented station, in a male-oriented market. And in no time at all, she was real well known, because with all the colleges in the area, there were a lot of young people who listened to the radio. Everybody in town knew who she was."

In years to come, she would talk about the experience with television interviewers Nancy Merrill and Don Alhart:

> I got this job doing eight hours straight on the air, and they sent me out to do live remotes at supermarket openings in a trailer, which they called the Beemobile. The Beemobile was a large glass-enclosed box, with a large greenish-yellow thing on the top which was supposed to look like a beehive. I would hand out black-and-yellow "bees" and play records. But it was so hot in there that you had a choice: You could either put on the air conditioning, or you could play the records. But you couldn't do both, because there wasn't enough power. . . .
>
> There were all sorts of perils in the Beemobile. The kids would come around and rock the van back and forth, for example. But the good part of it was that I paid for my education and I had the opportunity to do sports and news.

Nick Nickson, WBBF's music director at the time, stands behind the desk at his current job as public relations director for Rochester's WHAM, pulling out playlists from the summer of 1966. "Actually, Jessica only had a four-hour shift," he says. Nickson flips out a playlist with Jessica's picture at the bottom. In a photograph of startling presence, Jessica, wearing a black, off-the-shoulder top, sits behind a WBBF microphone and tilts her right shoulder toward the side of the frame. She conveys a look of confident ease, and even wearing a headset, she seems as beautiful as any young movie star of the day, her eyes sparkling and opened wide, her skin creamy and pure. She is a teen goddess of unending allure, her fingertips caressing the microphone, and her full lips parted seductively in mid-sentence.

"Jessica was very different from the usual college girl," Nickson says. "She had moxie. We were all pretty proud of her, because here we were number one, and we were still being innovative. We'd had women announcers, but they did women's programs. Jessica was the first deejay. And we thought she was nice to have around, even though she wasn't exactly the warmest person in the world."

An air check from the time shows Jessica's speech to be frequently swallowed and rushed, even for manic rock and roll radio. But there was no denying her appeal, the melody of her inflection, nor the fact that she was able to stay on top of the hectic format.

At the end of her first summer at WBBF, Jessica was rewarded with a regular Saturday shift from three to seven as part of the WBBF "Million Dollar Weekend." During the summer, when the Schwings pointed out that it made no sense for her to drive back and forth to Rochester from Ithaca, Jessica moved in with them. In the fall, now that she had the Saturday show, the Schwings invited her to stay over on the weekends, which she would do throughout her junior and senior years. Bill thought it was a good idea for her to pay room and board—"Twenty dollars a month, I think; it was just a pittance"—but if Jessica forgot, Louise wouldn't ask her for it.

Solid and traditional, the Schwings represented a way of life that Jessica had not known since before her father's death, a way of life she hungered for to the marrow of her bones, but rejected for herself for fear it would thwart her rise to the top. The Schwings would become the first of three important surrogate families she would attach herself to in the next ten years.

On Saturdays, before her radio show, Jessica began dropping by the Holy Angels School, a Catholic boarding school for troubled girls. Some were children who simply could not function within the traditional family unit, or who had been placed there by families who could no longer care for them in the home.

"The girls loved her," says Tony Busch. "She'd play records with them, and they would talk, and she'd even roller skate with them. I think Beth really felt that she wanted to give something of herself, and that she received satisfaction from it. And the Sisters of Charity who ran the place—these sweet, wonderful nuns who wore the black-and-white habits and big silver hearts around their necks—thought Jessica was just the greatest thing since, well, coffee, I guess."

The Schwings found Jessica endearing, exasperating, and complex.

"We treated her like one of the kids," Louise says. "I did her laundry, and I cleaned her room, because we just had to close the door. She was sort of a slob, frankly. But she was basically a generous person. I mentioned one day that I needed a hair dryer, and she went out and got one for me, even though she had very little money. She *hated* not having money. But she couldn't manage it at all. She told me she wanted to be 'somebody,' and to have people pay her way. That was her big dream in life."

Louise remembers the time in the summer when Florence drove up to Rochester with Stephanie and Lori and stayed at a motel in nearby Henrietta, New York. Florence invited Louise and the children over for a swim, and when the two women were alone, Florence spoke her mind.

"Louise, I would just like to thank you very much for helping my daughter," she said. "I know she needs it."

"When I think back now," Louise offers, "Jessica desperately needed help. I think she was calling out for it, but I didn't really hear it."

By the winter of her junior year, Jessica's impossible schedule and personal rigidity finally caught up with her. The only way she could obtain unlimited class cuts, necessary for the sometimes daily commuting, was to stay on the Dean's List. The pouches that had hung beneath her eyes since childhood now began to resemble bird's eggs, and she was downing iron pills four at a time. On top of it all, one of her fallopian tubes had somehow become blocked, paralyzing her with such pain during her periods that she would have to take to her bed. She was also on prescription medication for her skin.

"She came into WHEC one day to do a commercial for us," says Ann Rogers, "and she was covered with tiny red hives, all over her face and down her neck. I remember saying, 'Oh, my God, are you all right?' And she said, in a sort of wispy, slowed down voice,

'Yeah, yeah. Everything's okay.' And she put some makeup on and went out to the camera, and I swear to you, she looked fantastic. You would never have known she had hives. But I always felt she was under a tremendous amount of internal pressure. And I saw her many times when she was a pretty sick girl, and very frail."

"She couldn't sit still for ten minutes," Louise Schwing remembers, "and she would chatter on in that awful, nervous way. By then she was very thin because she wouldn't eat a proper meal. And she would bite her nails until they would honest-to-God bleed. I'd have to slap her hand and say, 'Jess, don't *do* that!' It was terrible."

From there, Jessica spiraled into the first of six intense and traumatic episodes that would mark her last two years of college.

"During her junior year, Jessica was a student in one of my relatively large psychology classes," remembers Martin Rand, then of Ithaca College. "At that time, I was also the 'campus shrink.' And one day, someone brought Jessica over to my office and said, 'Here, she's a mess.' And she was. She had simply stressed out. She was incoherent to the point that I wouldn't have wanted her to go on the air, or trusted her to make a decision."

Jessica and the psychologist spent an hour talking that first day, and when she started to leave, Rand, a tall, athletic man with a powerful presence, mentioned that he and his wife, Jo, a nurse with a Ph.D. in higher education administration, lived halfway between Ithaca and Rochester, in Willard, New York. He invited her to stop by on her commutes.

"She was a very bright, very competent person who was trying to do too much too soon, and was pushing herself just too damned hard to get there," Rand says, lighting his pipe. "It seemed to me that she needed a place to simply hang out and let her hair down, a chance to take the mask off and be whoever she was." And so, after spending Saturday nights with the Schwings in Rochester, Jessica would head out toward Ithaca, sleeping over Sundays—and sometimes Friday nights on her way north—at the Rands'.

The Rand home, a large, friendly house on placid Seneca Lake, was a veritable community shelter for an eclectic mix of students and academics, artists and bohemians, and anyone with no place to go for the holidays. Martin Rand offered magnificent meals of fish fresh from the lake, exotic vegetables, an assortment of wines, and, on some nights, two varieties of pie. Jo Rand, with her quiet, dignified air, was warm and caring. The house was a haven from the pressures of college and of life.

"Even if you were screwed up, nobody here looked at you that way," says the Rands' son, Craig. "It was like, 'Come on in! You're okay!' And actually, Jessica was far from the most screwed-up person around here."

Like the Schwings, the Rands became one of Jessica's surrogate families. But if Bill Schwing saw himself as an "older brother" to Jessica, Martin Rand was something else.

As one of the visitors to the house at the time recalls, "Dr. Rand always had this sort of arrogance, this godlike image of himself. So if Jessica had a need for the Rands, the Rands also had a need for Jessica. They always had guests there—always—and people who were a little bit in awe of them. There's no question that it all played well into the father image that Jessica wanted."

"It was never construed as a professional relationship," Rand says. Yet his importance to Jessica would be assured by the mere existence of his favorite hobby: Dr. Rand loved to take home movies. In a dozen scenes from the treasured old reels, Jessica appears as intimately assimilated into the family as if she had been born to it—washing Jo's hair in the kitchen sink; baking a "Get Well" cake with the Rands' daughter, Debbi; handling the speedboat as Martin Rand, up on skis, glides across the mirrored surface of Seneca Lake; and sitting in the living room in her nightie, painting her fingernails, her hair in curlers. Even when she protests the camera's rude interruption, she looks happy, clearly a part of something she considers safe and secure.

"I think Jess needed an extended family for several reasons, but one overwhelming one," Rand offers. "She somehow felt that she couldn't be dependent on her mother, because even then, Jess saw her mother as not really fully able to take care of herself. In many ways, Jess probably tried to take over her father's role as far as she could. But here at our house, she could be the dependent one, be the child rather than the super-adult."

As the stress of her work began to overwhelm her, Jessica became more difficult to be around, even when she visited in Tony's home. Mark Busch, Tony's brother, was perplexed. "I thought she was troubled, almost two people," he says. "She'd be a nice, normal girl, and then something small would happen, like maybe she wouldn't get her way, and she'd just fly into a rage. She was like a wire pulled tight and ready to snap."

"We had a lot of blowups, or disagreements," Tony confirms. "And they were quite intense. They were battles that battlers would be proud of. She was putting some heavy demands on me, wanting me to move out of my parents' house, for example. I tried to explain to her that there wasn't enough money for that, and then she said, 'Why don't you go live at the Y?' But it seemed that if you said no to something, she took it as an automatic challenge. At other times, she would get so worked up about things, like, 'Why can't you come and get me! You don't love me! You don't care! Help me!' and lay a guilt trip on me."

Finally, Tony realized the relationship was never going to be calm and settled, and that it was damaging for both of them. He feared that somehow he was responsible for Jessica's not eating and for her general nervousness. He also knew that he would expect her to fill the role of a traditional, supportive wife, and that it was beyond her capability to do so. To make matters worse, his friends had told him they had seen Jessica with other men.

"I think Florence and I had something very basic in common," Tony says. "We both gave Jessica all the love she would take."

The conflict came to a head after Tony was drafted into the army in 1967, during Jessica's junior year. He came back from basic training, and "When I got home, Jessica was at my parents' house. I was telling the family all about this military stuff, and I showed them one of the exercises they made us do, which was the Gorilla Stomp, where you jump down into a deep knee bend, and then jump up and beat your chest and growl. I thought it was kind of humorous, and so did my parents. We were laughing and having a big time. But Jessica thought it was very humiliating for the army to put me in that situation, and she was extremely upset that I would even do this. To make a long story short, she tried to get me not to go back, and, of course, I had to go back."

When it came time to go to the airport, she broke out in hives in the car. And then she threw up in the terminal.

"It was possessiveness, more than anything else," Tony goes on. "She just worked herself up so much over it that she wound up getting sick. But how can you rationalize with a person like that? That's when I started to realize that there was no way to make the situation succeed, as much as I wanted to. And it just became obvious that she was consumed by this career goal, and nothing but."

A few months later, Tony ended the romance, although he and Jessica would continue to be friends for the remainder of her life. "I think we always had a deep respect for each other," he says. "That never really ended. But there was only one way she could have stopped that intense drive, and that was by dying."

Jessica told the Rands that she and Tony had split over their differing views about sex, "that Tony wanted more than Jessica was willing to give," as Rand puts it. Tony, ever the gentleman, says delicately only that "She was extremely warm. She didn't have any hangups in that area." Rand thought Jessica was "asexual," with no particular interest or pleasure in sex. "It was something that we would talk about from time to time," Rand says, "and I clearly came away with the impression that she was not someone who particularly liked sex. In fact, both during her college years and four or five years later, I came away [with the feeling] that she strongly didn't like it, but realized that sometimes she had to do it."

Jo Rand got the same impression: "She felt that sex was just dues that she had to pay."

When Jessica was about to enter her senior year at Ithaca, Bill Schwing had a new idea for a teen dance program called "It's Happening Now," a Rochester version of "American Bandstand," with WBBF's Jack Palvino as the host. The plan was that Jessica would co-produce the show with Jeffrey Wheat, a producer-director at WXXI, Rochester's public television station. Jessica telephoned him for a meeting.

"It was really a funny situation," recalls Wheat, now a cinematographer in California, "because, for whatever reasons, when we got together I didn't want to look at her, and she was very shy to look at me. There was just a tremendous attraction."

Within weeks of that meeting, Jessica was mentioning Wheat at the close of her air shift: "I'd like to dedicate my show to one who's so far away but still listening, maybe. Jeff, this is for you."

The son of a realtor, Jeff Wheat had interrupted his schooling to pursue a career in TV production and had advanced quickly at the local level. "We had fun," Wheat says. "We did things together, and went away a lot—skiing trips in the winter, visits to her grandparents in Wilmington—and we kept big scrapbooks of photographs to document all our activities."

But Jessica was also moody, he remembers, and goes on to describe a recurring dream that she had during these months. "Each time, an old woman came to her and asked if she wanted to see the future. Jessica said yes and a curtain opened up, and a series of photographs were presented like slides. One of the pictures had Jessica working in news in New York, and another one showed her in Philadelphia. As the dreams progressed Jessica said, 'I want to see more.' And the voice said, 'No. I can't show you any more.' And Jessica asked, 'Why?' And the voice said, 'Because it's not nice. It's not good.' She pressed her about it, and the woman told her that she was not going to live to be an old lady. She told her she would be very successful, but that she was going to have a short and unhappy life.

"Jessica would tell me about each of these dreams, and we would try to figure out what all the pictures meant. One of the images was of a group of people on a lake. She described them to me, and we didn't recognize any of them. About three weeks later, she and I happened to be at Dr. Rand's house, spending the weekend, and we went out to the end of the dock. I looked over at Jessica, and she had gone absolutely white. I said, 'What's the matter? And she said, 'Turn around.' And there was the picture, or image, from her dream. All of the people she had described were there."

Jessica would continue to be fascinated by dreams and so-called psychic phenomena. But she rarely spoke of religion, or mentioned her own religious upbringing. "It was a long, long time before we ever knew she was Jewish," says Martin Rand. "I suppose she could have been trying to feel us out about our attitudes toward Jewish people, but I don't think she considered herself religious, period, at least not during that stage of her life. She used to refer to God as 'Sky Chief.' I got a kick out of that."

At this point, it was not unusual for Jessica to get up at three or four o'clock in the morning to drive to Rochester for early shoots. Exhaustion was no longer the exception, but the norm. The crying jags occurred more frequently now, and when her car spun out of control on the ice on her way to the Rands', Jo Rand remembers that although Jessica was uninjured, a gas station attendant found her "roaming around in the snow . . . she had just regressed. She was saying, 'Where am I? Where am I going?' "

"She was in the infirmary a lot," Jeff says, "because there were occasions when she was more than exhausted. You'd start into a conversation, and she would begin talking about things that didn't figure in at all. She'd just be blithering about something. When these episodes occurred, I tried to do what I could. She used to love to be held and rocked, for example, so she would sit on my lap, and oftentimes, she would even suck her thumb. She just needed reassurance. And when she was really overtired, she would stutter. She was very sad, very frustrated, and very confused."

Jessica would alternate such incidents with periods of buoyancy and apparent well-being, and she managed to keep her grades up. But one day, Jeff got scared. "We were talking on the phone, and she was literally out of control. I didn't know if she was going to kill herself. I kept her on the line and went to another phone and called Dr. Rand, and I said, 'Get up to her dorm.' "

"Jessica would often have these periods where she would just talk crazy gibberish for a few days at a time," Louise Schwing says. "But this one time, she came to the house with Dr. Rand, and she was totally hysterical. I mean, really, really gone. And I sat on the couch with her for hours, just holding her. She cried, and cried, and cried. And to this day, I still really don't know why, except that everything had caught up with her. But she said, 'I never wanted you to see me this way.' "

In May 1968, when Jessica graduated from Ithaca College, she gathered the old forces around her. Florence and the girls came up from Margate, Ben and Lil from Wilmington, and Rusty Nicholl from Philadelphia, where she was now working as a medical secretary. The Schwings came down from Rochester, and Jeff Wheat was there with his camera. His snapshots capture a radiant Jessica in mortarboard and gown, holding up the diploma she had worked so hard to get. Ben and Lil stood on one side of her, and Florence on the other.

"Florence and the grandparents hardly spoke at the graduation," Louise Schwing remembers.

3

A Great
Magnetism:
CBS, Houston,
and Ron Kershaw

Jessica continued her radio and commercial work in Rochester that summer after graduation, living part of the time with the Schwings and part-time with Jeff Wheat. When fall came, she went home to Margate and sent résumés to two dozen radio and TV stations in New York, all three networks, and several production houses in Los Angeles. While she waited for replies, she and Jeff commuted for visits every few weeks.

Jeff had been a familiar figure in the Savitch household for some time now, and on one of his trips to Margate, he and Jessica had spoken to Florence about getting married. Jessica wanted her mother's approval, and she wanted Jeff to ask for it in the old-fashioned way. Florence, whom Jeff found to be "a little cold, reserved, but a nice, generous lady, with a funny cackle of a laugh," gave the couple her blessing, and during one of Jessica's visits to Rochester, they ordered an engagement ring. Meanwhile, Jeff says, the résumés were starting to gain attention. Jessica told him that

Merv Griffin had offered her a production job in California and that she was deciding whether to take it.

"One weekend," Jeff remembers, "I got out of work, picked up the ring, and drove long hours to get down to Margate. But when I went to give it to her, Jessica said, 'Right now isn't a good time. I don't want to take it just yet. I'm really confused about my life and my career. I don't even know which coast I'm going to be on.'

"I was upset, because I thought we'd made a commitment to each other," Jeff says. "But I took the ring and went back to Rochester. And then one weekend she said, 'Look, if you've still got the ring, let's get married.' And I looked at her, and I realized that she was really confused, so I said the same thing to her that she had said to me—'This isn't the right time. I want to marry you, and I love you, but you're not sure what you want. And I don't want [a wedding] to be a way out of making a decision.' And that was the last time that we got into the ring business."

Jessica told friends that she had decided against the Merv Griffin job, and that she was holding out to see what other positions were available, particularly on the news end of the business. Aside from her youth, the common complaint Jessica received on job interviews, she was to say years later, in a speech accepting an award as Business Woman of the Year, was that women's voices were not authoritative enough to deliver news. "If a male broadcaster said, 'Good evening, a fire destroyed Washington today,' the audience would have said, 'How terrible.' But if I had come on and said, 'Good evening, this is Jessica Savitch, a fire destroyed Washington today,' the audience would have said, 'I don't believe that . . . and I won't believe it until a man tells me so.'"

But the twenty-one-year-old job applicant had the good sense to send a résumé and picture to Joan Showalter, the head of personnel for CBS. As it turned out, that decision brought her one of the few lucky breaks of her life.

A Virginia expatriate, Joan Showalter balanced what Jessica later described in *Anchorwoman* as "the gracious characteristics of the Southern belle" with the steely resolve of a woman who was fully prepared to protect her considerable bastion of power in one of Manhattan's biggest corporate labyrinths. As the highly influential head of personnel, she oversaw the hirings and firings of the corporation's broadcast division, publishing division, and record division. For more than two decades, CBS employees have been familiar with her air of contained strength and confidence, from her hairstyle—a short, no-nonsense kind of bob—to her austere, all-business style of dress.

Joan Showalter was not a woman to cross. Her job demanded that she supervise every area—benefits, raises, transfers, reorganizations—that vitally affected each of the sprawling corporation's employees, and she insisted on exercising her mandate. Many executives inevitably collided with her authority, for if she resented it when department heads wanted to wield their own power, they resented not being free to do their own hiring, that Showalter could force them to comply with company rules and standards.

Joan Showalter was about forty on the day in 1968 when Jessica Savitch arrived for her appointment at 51 West 52nd Street—the CBS corporate headquarters, known as Black Rock. Showalter had "responded warmly" to Jessica's letter, and talking with the personnel director that day, Jessica realized that if in the past she had disregarded women and counted exclusively on men for her ascent, she had been too quick to do so. Now the combination of ambition, fragility, and vulnerability that had compelled so many men to help her elicited the protection of a powerful woman with no husband or children to look after. Showalter was also impressed with Jessica's willingness to work hard, and with her refusal to be denied a chance to break into professional broadcast journalism.

"Jessica was one out of fourteen thousand who had written letters for interviews," Showalter told journalist Judith Adler Hennessee for a *Ms.* article in 1979. "But she so stood out in her résumé, her preparation of materials, and her delivery that I knew she was a high achiever. She had a projection of strength, even though people told her she was too attractive—that she'd play around too much. So her looks worked against her, she had no journalism degree, and it was almost impossible for her to be taken seriously in any capacity. But I knew as soon as she hit the door that she had talent. I told her not to give up, that she would be a network correspondent by the time she was thirty."

Steve Berger had been Jessica's first sponsor, and Bill Schwing had been her first mentor, but Joan Showalter would become her first truly powerful ally. Although there were no appropriate jobs available at CBS at the time, Showalter promptly took her on as temporary vacation relief. After two weeks, she moved her into the promotion department as an assistant, and then in July 1969, made her an administrative assistant for the network. At $92.50 a week, Jessica would "float" from department to department. Whenever her temporary boss protested that Jessica had no secretarial skills, Showalter would plug her in somewhere else. Sometimes her duties were so menial that she would be reduced to going to the Chinese laundry to pick up an anchorman's shirts, or ordering three-drawer file cabinets for such executives as Fred Silverman, then the director of CBS's daytime programs. Silverman sometimes took time out to talk to the new apprentice. Years later, they would meet again. He would become the president of NBC a year after Jessica's arrival there in 1977.

During her early tenure at CBS, when there was often no specific job for her to perform elsewhere, Showalter would put Jessica to work answering the phone in the personnel department.

"When I would call her," remembers Rusty Nicholl, "Jessica would answer the phone with, 'Joan Showalter's office.' And I'd say, 'Jessica?' And she'd say, 'No, just a minute please.' And then she'd come back and say, 'Jessica Savitch.' I'd say, '*God,* that girl sounds just *like* you!' And I know damn well that *was* Jessica, because there aren't that many people with that voice. But she wanted me to think there was somebody beneath her answering the phone for her. It's sort of funny, but that's the way she was, from high school on."

Rusty accepted Jessica's need for such subterfuge and deception and wrote it off to "a wonderful imagination." But she never really knew what to expect from her old friend.

Jessica was lonely in the city, and she was becoming more and more frustrated in her job at CBS. Every afternoon at half past four she would go up to personnel and talk with Joan Showalter, who was now a confidante. It was impossible for Jessica to start out on the air in New York City, Showalter told her, but sooner or later, she said, she would find a way to ease her into the WCBS radio newsroom. "NewsRadio 88," as the station was called, was the top of the line in all-news radio programming. With a WCBS credit on her résumé, Jessica would be able to walk into a station in almost any of the smaller markets and at least get a starting job. Showalter counseled Jessica to be patient.

Meanwhile, Jessica had been carrying on a voluminous correspondence with the Rands. She told them that she had landed a number of freelance production and modeling jobs, and that she was also going to New York University at night, working toward a master of fine arts degree in cinematography. She also mentioned the offer to work with Merv Griffin, telling them that Lillian was urging her to accept it. The Griffin story was apparently another invention by the young woman who was so desperate to be recognized as special by the world, for in 1982, when Jessica appeared on Merv Griffin's talk show to promote her book, she turned to the host with an impish grin. "By the way, I've got to tell you something," she began. "I'm really glad to be here tonight, because I couldn't get a job as a production assistant on your show twelve years ago." The audience tittered with laughter. "I came in to the receptionist and I said, 'Look, I'm a journalism major. I've got a master's degree in political science. Let me be a production assistant on the Merv Griffin Show.' And she said, 'Honey, you're in line right after me!' "

Jessica's letters to the Rands were troubling signs that her difficulty in accepting the realities of daily life and her grandiosity were now becoming more pronounced. Instead of describing her frustrations as an entry-level worker, she regaled the couple with stories about her importance at the network, her secretary, her trips to exotic destinations—London, Nice, Barbados—and her famous and successful boyfriends, including an unnamed soap opera star.

Martin Rand, sitting in the comfortable living room of his upstate New York house, thumbs through the letters and tosses them aside. "It's certainly my impression that Jessica was not sleeping with these guys," he observes, "but that she was being used by them because she looked awfully good on the arm, and because she put on a good front."

"She told me," says Dick John, the man who would soon become her boss in Houston, "that when she was really down and out in New York, she made a substantial part of her living by serving as an escort for gay men. They'd be invited to social affairs or parties where they couldn't take their boyfriends, and they simply needed a female companion. I don't think it was an agency, where they had her picture up on the wall and a guy would pick her out. But she'd go out on dates with them for a fee. She never had the feeling there was anything morally wrong or reprehensible about their life-style, and she was very clear in her mind about that."

In the spring of 1969, Tony Busch, Jessica's old boyfriend from Ithaca, was in New York on business and happened to cross the street at 51st and Broadway. There, coming toward him in the crosswalk, was Jessica, wearing sunglasses. "She had her nose up in the air," Tony remembers. "I said, 'Hey, babe,' or something crude and familiar like that to get her attention. And before she ever looked, she started to swat me with her attaché case." Tony took her arm to block the assault, and then Jessica recognized him and broke into a smile. They went somewhere to talk.

"I told her I was engaged," Tony says, "and we talked a little bit about old times. But she seemed to me like a frightened young girl in a fast-moving world. She wanted to stop running and just be herself."

When Jessica first arrived in New York, she lived not at a rundown women's hotel on East 36th Street, as she would later tell friends, but at the Barbizon Hotel for Women, the renowned dormitory at 63rd and Lexington populated largely by young models, secretaries, and artists who had come to the city to seek their fortunes. During the spring of 1969, she moved to a brownstone at 34-41 71st Street, in Jackson Heights, Queens. Sparsely furnished, the walk-up apartment opened into a large living room, with a long hall leading to two bedrooms, a kitchen, and bath. "It was cute," says one of Jessica's infrequent visitors. "And the neighborhood seemed nice."

Jeff Wheat, meanwhile, was alternating his time between Rochester and New York, working for a record company in the city, returning to his old job at the television station, and going back to college. Jessica asked the Rands not to tell Jeff about the racy New York escapades she was reporting to them if they happened to see him. After a time, Jeff moved in with her in Jackson Heights.

"I don't think we broadcast that too much," he says, "because she was concerned about what her mother thought about things." But Jessica was comfortable enough to invite Jo Rand to stay at the apartment when she was in town, and, on one occasion, the couple invited the Schwings, who had just moved down to Princeton Junction, New Jersey, to come to dinner.

Jessica's feelings about family life were now more ambivalent than ever. Stephanie was getting married in the fall, and though

Jessica, performing her second maid of honor duty of the year (Rusty Nicholl had married Robert Wilson in the summer of 1969), had given her sister a luncheon, she told Louise she was disappointed that Stephanie was marrying when she was so young, that she was not doing more with her life. "It wasn't what she'd planned for her family," Louise says. Jessica's feelings about women who subverted their youth in marriage extended beyond her family. Four years before, she had learned that Linda Kilmer, her childhood friend from New Garden, had become engaged. "She wrote me this really long letter saying she thought it was a mistake," Linda remembers, "and we should go on and do better things." The wedding ended their friendship, Linda adds.

Bill Schwing was now in the city, working for a company called Transmedia, which "cleared time," or arranged to place syndicated programming on television stations throughout the country, and he began to call on Jessica for freelance work. The year at CBS had brought her a number of valuable contacts—the importance of which Ben and Lil continued to emphasize—but Jessica feared that the experience had stultified both her intellectual and her creative energies, and she hungered to be in the thick of a real production again.

At this point Jessica was vacillating between broadcast management and performance, and Bill tailored her assignments around honing her production skills. One such job involved a three- or four-camera production for a demonstration tape of a young Philadelphia opera singer. Jessica was to produce the tape and then supervise the editing. "It was really kind of a lackluster thing," recalls George Palmer, the freelance engineer for Schwing, "because of the budget that we had. The people who commissioned it weren't all that pleased with it, and Jessica ended up taking the rap."

But when she was given far greater responsibility, as the line producer for the Miss Black America Pageant at New York's Felt Forum in 1970, Jessica earned the respect of everyone involved. "She seemed to enjoy it," says Bill Schwing, "and it was a lot for her to do. She had to know the content of the program, where it fit, and what time each segment was supposed to come in. She used a few swear words like we all do, and got angry a few times, but it came off very well. And it was a pretty good credit for a twenty-three-year-old."

Jessica thought so, too, and told the Rands that she was especially proud because her sister Lori had worked as the cue card clerk.

By now, Jessica was juggling her job at CBS, her freelance talent and production work, her occasional modeling assignments—one involved a trip to Puerto Rico in May 1970—and her domestic life with Jeff. She never seemed in danger of overloading the way she had at Ithaca, but Jeff worried about her health, and he found himself having to force her to eat. At home, at night, Jessica would talk with him about her work, about Joan Showalter, and about her plans for the future. But he was distressed that she rarely made time for her personal side. It was now three years into their relationship, but he could seldom find the person he had fallen in love with.

"It's not that I wanted to get married and start a family," he says. "But her career came before everything—before sleep, before play. Finally, she rationalized that she didn't have time for past friendships. She was only interested in the present and the future, and if you weren't part of either one of those, then she didn't have time for you. And she put it exactly that way."

And so the relationship was over.

"It was a pretty abrupt parting," remembers Jeff's friend, George Palmer. "Jeff took it real well at the time. But I think he realized that she was several people rolled into one. She was the fun-loving person, and the driven person. And I think there became a third person, and that was the cool professional."

Clearly that was the image Jessica was now trying to project to the Rands. Over the next few months, she told them in great detail about her courtship by an advertising executive named Howard Marks. She had met him during her college days, when Marks came to Rochester to test market a British product called Smoker's Tooth Powder and needed talent to record the local dealer tags ("Available at Sears Roebuck") for his radio spots. Marks, who had his own company, was impressed with both Jessica's energy and her work, and invited the teenager to look him up if she ever came to New York.

In March 1969 Jessica called him, and Marks, who was eighteen years her senior, took her to dinner. Soon she was telling the Rands that Marks was giving her gifts of precious jewelry and had offered to buy her a car.

December 1987: Howard Marks, listening on the phone to a description of the long-ago letters, lets out a choking sound.

"Holy smokes! None of it is true," he says. "She came to New York and I gave her a few freelance jobs, and in addition I introduced her to just about everybody in the business who could audition her for radio and television voice-overs. And, as a result of that, she got a little bit of a start."

Q: The letters talk about your new movie company . . .

MARKS: I never had a movie company, old or new.

Q: About a diamond and emerald pendant . . .

MARKS: I never bought anybody a diamond and emerald pendant. I might buy you one, but you would be the first. These are not exaggerations of the truth. They're total fabrications! She was enough of a success that people should have been impressed with the truth. I genuinely liked her. She was a really good person, and a grateful person if you did anything for her. I never had any hints of any fantasy stories, or that she was making up a life with me as her boyfriend.

Q: She didn't express personal interest in you, apart from the job opportunities?

MARKS: Well, that's a little awkward, but the answer is yes. She was extremely attractive.

Q: Do you think she pursued you?

MARKS: It's hard to tell. She certainly couldn't have been more warm and affectionate. But she never asked me for anything. By my standards, she was a genuine, wholesome kind of person. I don't think coming on to somebody is unwholesome. But my own analysis is that she was so lonely that she was embarrassed not to make up this romantic life. And I think that's all it was.

Sharon Sakson, a television producer who got to know Jessica well in the last years of her life, remembers a discussion along similar lines. "At times, I thought that TV was too hard on her," Sakson observes. "I'd say, 'You always look so perfect and thin. Go back into modeling.' And she'd say, 'No, because men took advantage of me.' When she first went into it, she said, she didn't know what it would be about. She thought the first guy really loved her, but then she found out they all expected her to sleep with them. She said, 'With broadcasting, I can really use my mind.' But it seems like Jessica was on a collision course to destroy herself no matter what she went into. She was telling me what a horror her life in modeling was, but I know her life in TV was just as much of a horror as that."

Sometime late in 1969, Marvin Friedman, the news director at WCBS Radio, found himself in need of an administrative assistant. Her duties would include putting together work schedules, keeping track of vacation requests, collecting time sheets, running down listener requests, and keeping logs and files—whatever it took to keep the office running smoothly.

"Jessica was introduced to me as someone who I should very seriously consider hiring," remembers Friedman, now in public relations in New York City. "She obviously had someone in her corner. From what I've read—because I really don't know—it probably was Joan Showalter. And since I had the opening and needed a person anyway, I saw no reason not to."

The job was strictly administrative and logistic, and Jessica took her place at a small desk in the WCBS newsroom. This was her first real exposure to a professional news operation, and she had much to learn about the way it worked. She remained quiet and unobtrusive, concentrating on doing her job well and blending in with the staff. Few of her fellow workers got to know her. Lou Adler, an anchorman and reporter, hardly noticed her at all, recalling her today only as "very attractive and reserved." And Jerry Nachman, then a reporter and until recently the news director at WRC-TV in Washington, remembers her mostly as being "awfully coiffed and tailored, very poised."

"Even though she didn't talk to a lot of people," says Nachman, "it was pretty clear she was overqualified and uncomfortable in her job. I really didn't know her. But if you spent ten minutes with her, you realized that she was being underutilized, and that she was being frustrated by one or two gate-keepers who were being arbitrary. There's a lot of social Darwinism in broadcasting, because in order to do really well, you need a series of promotions. And what happens is, people get hired and go, 'I made it to CBS in New York! I work at Black Rock! Now what?' For a lot of people, the second job never comes."

Specifically, Jessica made it clear early on that she had journalistic ambitions, but "The existing management seemed uninterested in allowing her to proceed," as Nachman terms it. At one point, Ed Joyce, head of the CBS Radio Group, had interviewed Jessica for a desk assistant's job. But Joyce, known around CBS as "The Velvet Scythe," had turned her down, saying her journalism background wasn't strong enough. According to Ron Kershaw, the man who would become her closest friend, Joyce also told Jessica that because she was a woman, she had no future on the air. Both rejections were traumatic for her, she would later recount. CBS had long been regarded as the best news-gathering agency in the world, and its patron saint, Edward R. Murrow, had been David Savitch's favorite journalist.

From the experience with Ed Joyce, Jessica rallied to ask Marvin Friedman how she might move closer to achieving her goal of getting on the air, or at least being able to take a writer's test. She was thwarted here, too.

"Jessica knew she was not going to work her way up from this job to a reporter's job," Friedman says, "and I told her that right out. Our policy at the time was to hire professional people with professional experience. And I did not—and still don't—consider college or disc jockey work as experience for a news writer or reporter. But I said, 'If you want to take a crack at writing a news program, I'd be happy to look at it for you.' And I recall seeing maybe one or two [scripts] in all the time she worked for me." Jessica obviously had ambition, Friedman thought, and he figured she would be there as long as it took her to find something else. "Those were mutually acceptable terms."

Jessica could look to Joan Showalter for protection and encouragement, but she had no real allies close by, no one to help her refine her skills. She had met a young woman, Mary Pangalos (now Manilla), a former *Newsday* reporter who now worked on both the radio and TV side of the operation. Mary had taken Jessica aside and tried to explain to her "the game that was being played— that everybody wanted everyone else to fail," but she was usually out on the street on assignment.

If she wanted to be one of the best, Jessica decided, she needed tutoring *from* the best, and approached Charles Osgood, then the anchorman for the "Six to Nine Show." Osgood told Jessica that if she wanted to come in before six A.M., she was welcome to sit with him while he wrote copy. From Osgood, Jessica would say, she learned the importance of writing clear, concise, and punchy news copy. For practice, he told her to take three wire-service versions of a story and rewrite them as one, shaping the facts—including the basics of journalistic reporting, who, what, when, where, why, and how—into her own style. "He gave me a lot of valuable pointers," Jessica would write in her book. "Shorter is always better; a sentence that reads well might not speak well; sometimes a perfectly constructed sentence will have four esses in a row; think it out in your mouth; write for the audience's ear."

But Jessica also needed someone who worked at covering the news to let her in on the realities of the business. She found him in Ed Bradley, the "60 Minutes" journalist who was then still a local reporter on the WCBS Radio staff. They felt a kinship together, Jessica would say, a black man and a white female, "struggling to make our way in an industry that was still largely a bastion of white males."

When Jessica had interviewed Miriam Makeba, the South African folk singer, for her college station, she had told Barry, "I really felt ashamed of the fact that, for the most part, I cannot stand the American Negro." She later told Louise Schwing that she couldn't see how any white person could ever get romantically involved with a black. But in the winter of 1970, she found herself falling in love with Ed Bradley. "You've got to understand," says Mary Manilla, "Ed is a stellar person. He didn't know whether he was black, green, or purple, and you didn't either. He was just Ed Bradley. Frankly, I always thought that was one of the great and best romances of her life." And, indeed, years later, when Jessica was laughing with a lover, "Suddenly," the man recounts, "for some reason, I asked her what had been the biggest turn on of her life. And she said it had been with Ed Bradley. She was rather poetic about it, actually. She said, 'It was seeing his nude body on the beach, glistening in the moonlight.' " (Ed Bradley ignored two requests to be interviewed for this book.)

At first, she told the Rands, and then later, other friends that the affair was somewhat erratic. Then, after a summer that included their spending time together on Cape Cod, she told them it had turned serious, and that she worried about Joan Showalter finding out about the relationship. Jessica was certain she would disapprove.

In early 1971, CBS announced that it intended to cut back 15 percent of its employees in all divisions. Jessica told the Rands that she wasn't worried because she had protectors in high corporate places. Still, it seemed clear that she was not about to advance beyond a clerical position at WCBS. If she intended to become a network television correspondent by thirty, she needed to get on with it. She was now twenty-four.

As head of recruitment for CBS, Joan Showalter was in an excellent position to help Jessica obtain interviews with the news directors of the network affiliates and CBS owned-and-operated stations throughout the country. According to what Showalter told journalist Judith Adler Hennessee, she thought Jessica might do well to go to Boston or Baltimore. But perhaps the western market would give her a chance to pursue a different kind of development, reporting for and about people outside of the eastern corridor, whose life-styles and attitudes differed from anything she had been exposed to before. Showalter thought of St. Louis or Houston. Near the end of April 1971, she and Jessica sat down together and produced a résumé. Then Showalter arranged for Jessica to have a professional photograph made, and coerced WCBS-TV into preparing an audition tape of her reading the news.

Since the ten-pound, high-band dubs were expensive, Jessica first sent prospective employers the résumé and photo, with a note that the audition tape was available on request. The letters went out on official CBS stationery.

In addition to trying the CBS affiliates, Jessica mailed a résumé to Donald H. McGannon, head of the Westinghouse, or Group W, stations. McGannon passed it along to Joel Chaseman, program vice-president in charge of news. Chaseman, based in New York, telephoned her and said he'd like to see the audition tape. Jessica lugged the heavy dub over to his Park Avenue office on her lunch hour, and the two sat down and ran it together.

The audition, which still exists, opens with Jessica, wearing a navy top with a red, white, and blue scarf rolled tight and looped at the neckline, sitting behind a desk. Her hair is long, but pulled back and clasped behind her head. Her face is noticeably pock-marked. A technician stands in the foreground with a slate board, and a voice-over supplies, "WCBS Studio Audition, Jessica Savitch, Take One." The technician steps aside, and Jessica, poised, but frightened, takes a big gulp and begins to read from the Tele-

PrompTer: "Fire Base Six under North Vietnamese siege; peace talks again underway in Paris; and Off-Track Betting gets off to a modest start. Now, the details . . ."

Jessica had worked on her five-minute script for three weeks, and it turned out to be an impressive balance of hard news, feature, and commentary. But sitting nervously with Joel Chaseman, Jessica thought that Ed Bradley's comment—"It looks like you're just trying to get through it"—was accurate. "*Think* about what you're saying," he had told her, according to *Anchorwoman*. The smile that would in time endear her to millions of viewers had yet to be developed, and her eyes, which appeared more liquid than intense, seemed sad. Nevertheless, by the time Jessica got to her last story, a commentary on President Nixon's chastising his student hecklers, she read with such conviction that Chaseman sat up in his chair.

"When it was over," Jessica was to write, "he turned the lights on, looked at me wincingly, and said, 'That was really horrible. However,' he hurried to add, 'you do have a definite presence on screen. If you work on your delivery, I predict you'll make a name for yourself one of these days.' "

Chaseman, now president of the Post-Newsweek stations in Washington, smiles as he reads the description in *Anchorwoman*. "Did I really say that?" he laughs. "I have absolutely no recollection of the tape, but I remember her. I thought she had genuine star quality. There are only two other people I've seen who have that type of star quality—Barbra Streisand and Woody Allen. I said to Jessica, 'Stop screwing around with networks, and go to a station and go to work.' Because she was a very compelling personality. And I saw that she could be a powerful manipulator of the tube."

With Joel Chaseman, Jessica would begin to form a new network of powerful male friends whom she would call on for advice at every step of her career. They saw her as she saw herself—a dazzling young television star in the making. Some of them would come to her aid simply because she was personable and talented and deserved to get ahead. Others were flattered that she would think them wily enough to plan a strategy, and would rise to the occasion rather than lose her good esteem. Still others wanted to protect her, to shield her vulnerability from the harsh reality of the business, where a hiring or firing hinged on a ratings point or an unexpected change of the guard.

It was spring of 1971, and Ed Bradley was leaving CBS to do

freelance reporting in Paris, and later Saigon. In the weeks before his departure, Jessica began to fly around the country on job interviews. An early stop was St. Louis, where Bob Schaefer, the news director of the CBS owned-and-operated station, KMOX-TV, had agreed to talk to her. The assistant news director was Tom Becherer, now of CONUS Communications.

"One morning," Becherer recalls, "Bob said, 'I've got to go to lunch with somebody's bimbo from New York, so you're going with me.' It was a sunny afternoon, and we went to the Crest House. I remember that day well, because I was remarkably taken with her, even though she had no experience as a reporter. She was so open, so eager. And when we got back from lunch, I said to Bob, 'Jesus, if you don't have a job, create one! This lady's going to be something else.' And he said, 'I'm not hiring anybody's bimbo. Let her go get some experience, and then she can come back.' I never did know who Jessica's angel might be," Becherer continues, "but it was somebody who had enough clout to get her out to talk to the news directors at the O and O's."

Down in Houston, Dick John, news director of the CBS affiliate KHOU-TV, had a different reaction to the photo and résumé. He took them up to Dean Borba, the general manager, and told him he wanted to bring Jessica Savitch down to talk. "There was definitely something about the picture," says Borba, "but the CBS letterhead obviously made me want to read the thing. I figured gee, this is somebody with a job in the Big Apple. They ought to be pretty good."

That May, when Dick John went to meet her at the Houston Intercontinental Airport, Jessica, jittery with nerves, lost her New York composure and threw up in a nearby ladies room. The flight had been unusually bumpy, and she was dressed in a smashing brown suede pants suit that was far too heavy for Houston's muggy climate.

The incident had been humiliating, but on the drive down the airport's circular garage, Jessica threw up for the second time—this time in John's car—spoiling her beautiful suede suit. "I felt so sorry for her—I wish I had a picture of it," he says. "She was just absolutely drenched, she was so hot, and so sick." But Jessica would later tell him there had been another reason for her nausea. "She'd attended a wild party in New York the night before," he says, "full of booze and drugs and uppers and downers."

Despite this awful beginning, Jessica appeared to the newsroom staff as an altogether thrilling, exotic creature. "The minute I saw her in that brown suede pants suit, I thought, 'Oh, damn, what have we got us here!'" remembers Carl Cochran, a former KHOU staff writer and producer. "I'd never been out of Texas to speak of, and here comes this vision. It was like, 'My *God*, I've never seen anyone like that in person!'" Nor was Jessica's star quality lost on the management, which was looking for two eye-catching reporters; come fall, the station's six o'clock news would expand to an hour.

The week after her trip to Houston, Dick John called and offered Jessica a job at $135 a week. She was torn, and telephoned most of her advisers to solicit their opinions. Joan Showalter said if she were serious, this was the opportunity. Jessica agonized briefly about whether she should decide to go to Paris with Ed Bradley, Mary Manilla remembers. "She said that Ed picked her up in his arms and said, 'Jessica, this is what you've worked for all your life. You'll take it, and you'll be great. You've got to do it!'"

The staff of WCBS gave her a going away party. Bob Gordon, then a salesman for the station, was there.

"We were standing around, and I said, 'So, Jessica, what is it you're going to be doing?' And she said, 'I'm going to Houston. I'm going to be a TV reporter.' I sort of laughed. She was a gorgeous girl, and very sharp, but her lisp was so noticeable that you'd never think she'd make a career on the air. I said, 'No, no, what are you really going to do?' And she said, 'That's what I'm going to do.'"

As her departure neared, she had a series of conversations with Joan Showalter. The two had become very close, and Showalter took great pride in her protegée. If past behavior was predictive of future strength, Showalter told her, Jessica had everything going for her. She had applied herself long and hard to achieve her goals, she was serious about journalism, and her looks were infinitely superior. She would be whatever she wanted, and she would be wildly successful. In no time, reporters would be lining up to profile her for magazine and newspaper stories. But when that happened, Showalter said, there was one thing she must always remember: Never, ever, talk about your private life.

When Jessica moved to Houston that June, she had two worries. The first was that she'd never actually covered a news story professionally before, a fact she'd neglected to mention to Dick John and Dean Borba. The second was that she considered Texas—with its endless flat terrain, blistering climate, "kicker" culture, and "Howdy y'all" vernacular—the most foreign place this side of the moon. In 1971, Houston was still a rough-and-tumble town, not the sprawling urban metropolis it is today. Not only did Jessica have no friends there, but, "I didn't even know anyone who *knew* anyone who had been there," she would tell a reporter seven years later. "It was frightening."

For a time, she stayed at the Ramada Inn two blocks from the station on busy Allen Parkway. But she soon had company: Joan Showalter came to visit from New York.

"I thought it was strange that she had this maternal sort of chaperone staying in the room there with her," Dick John remembers. "I couldn't figure out why she was here."

From cameraman John Shaw's perspective, "Joan fed Jessica's ego, and she fed her dream. She made her believe it, and Jessica talked about it to everybody. She had an exact outline of how she was going to make it."

Indeed, on her first day at KHOU, when Jessica tagged along with reporter Judd McIlvain to watch him cover a story at the Manned Spacecraft Center, she announced her ambitions. "We were just chatting in the van on the way out there," he remembers, "and I asked her what she wanted to do in journalism. She said, 'My plans are to be a network anchor. I'm going to replace Walter Cronkite.' I said, 'Oh, good,' you know. It seemed so unrealistic. But she said, 'No, no, I think it'll probably take me about five years.' " She would repeat her intentions to John N. Davenport, a reporter for KPRC, the NBC affiliate, in the months to come. "I rolled my eyes to the ceiling," he says. "She had supreme confidence."

In the beginning, Jessica had to bluff about her journalistic skills. "Dick John told us that she'd had some experience," recalls the forthright Ron Stone, then an anchor at the station. "It was obvious that she'd lied—that she didn't have any experience at all in television news. But the thing that amazed us was that once you told her how to do something, you didn't have to tell her again. And the third time she did something," he adds smiling, "she did it better than you. I liked her for that."

One day, before Jessica ever went on the air, Dean Borba

suggested that she think about changing her name. "I said, 'You know, Savitch is a hard, Slavic name,' " he remembers. "Before we launch you into this thing, it might be easier if you . . ." Borba, sitting in the kitchen of his Northern California home, breaks into a laugh. "That's as far as I got, because oh, God, her eyes just lit up! She said, 'As much as I want this job, I would never do that! How could I face my dad?' "

Dean Borba says that Jessica had an innate sense of the events that constituted news, but that "there were certain basics we had to teach her." From there, Dick John began to train her in the premise of local news—that it was not just news that happened in one's own town, but any news that directly affected the people who lived there. A television station was judged overall by the quality of its news operation, John told her, and the way to attract viewers was to build a reputation for getting on the big stories early, sticking close, and wrapping up last.

KHOU, with its red neon call letters proudly displayed on the microwave relay tower in back of the long, low station, had attained a certain degree of notoriety ten years earlier when Hurricane Carla roared through Galveston along the Gulf Coast, killing twelve people. The station's news director and anchor at the time was a young Texan named Dan Rather, and Rather's firsthand coverage of the storm and its aftermath led to his breaking in at the parent network.

Under Rather's direction, the station motto had been "Nothing's too big for us!," and he had engaged in such ambitious feats as sending news teams to cover the Texas delegation at the national political conventions. A well-circulated photo from the time, according to Borba, shows a tenacious Rather, supported by several crewmen, suspended horizontally above the throng of reporters gathered around John F. Kennedy. As a result of such all-out efforts, Rather had lifted KHOU's ratings from third to first—over Channel 2, KPRC, the strong NBC affiliate, and ABC's KTRK, Channel 13.

In 1971, however, KHOU had slipped to second place, behind KPRC, and, by some accounts, was threatening to drop to third. For a time in the late sixties, KHOU had hung on to the top spot by producing almost sheer entertainment; the news personalities had engaged in a lively, "pick and scratch" kind of banter on the set. But then the anchor defected to another station, and KHOU's competitors, particularly KPRC, began beefing up their equipment and their reporting staffs, building two to three times the manpower of KHOU. When Dick John came to the station in 1967, "We were kind of comparable to the New York Mets," he says. "Channel 11 became famous because we were so bad." To compound things, KHOU's owner, Corinthian Broadcasting, with stations in Tulsa, Sacramento, Fort Wayne, and Indianapolis, was known as "the cheapest operation in the country," as John terms it, sucking money out of Houston to nourish the other stations in the fold.

KHOU had long subscribed to the theory that local TV news is tabloid journalism of the highest sort. Dan Rather had leaned heavily on explicit footage of Houston's fires, auto accidents, murders, and other catastrophes. Dick John had tried to back off from this emphasis, even though crime and violence were proven ratings builders. In the news shop, they called such stories "the fuzz and the wuz," referring to the police and the dead bodies. Local reporters had a sort of cowboy mentality about covering the news, and rarely were they denied access to any situation, often walking directly into the scene of a murder, for example, along with the police.

Houston in the early seventies was basically still a spot news town. In-depth and enterprise reporting, along with special series, had yet really to take root in the industry as a whole. And in those days before "sat-cams," live reports, and electronic news gathering (ENG), everyone shot film, which had to be processed, and which meant the chances of one station getting a report on before its opposition were slim. In some respects, says former KHOU cameraman Jaroslav Vodehnal, Houston was a non-competitive news town. If a photographer ran out of film at a news conference, someone from another station would likely give him a fresh 400-foot canister.

"Local TV news was still kind of in its infancy," says Randy Covington, formerly of KHOU, and now the news director at KYW in Philadelphia. "News reporting tended to be fairly quick, run-and-gone stuff. But Houston was an incredible mix of cultures and standards then, the old Texas and the new Texas, and minorities [blacks and Mexican-Americans] were having an enormous impact on the political scene."

As it turned out, Jessica could not have picked a better place to start her television career. The city was an upbeat place with a boomtown mentality, still being discovered by an influx of people from the North and East who were eager to latch on to the prosperity brought by Houston's petrochemical enterprises.

"Jessica encapsulates the Houston ethic," observes Thomas H. Krenick, special projects coordinator of the Houston Metropolitan Research Center and archivist of a collection of KHOU news film from the 1970s. "It's a town of promotion, where the day after tomorrow has always been more important than today. People admired Jessica's hustle, because they were all hustlers. This has always been a place where things are inflated—where disasters are inflated, where money is inflated, and where dreams are inflated. Jessica fit right in. Houston is the end of the rainbow, or the beginning of it. Everything is 'going to be.'"

Because KHOU was a non-union station, Jessica, as one of its six reporters, was expected, like the rest of the staff, to double up on duties and be prepared to do whatever it took to get a story on the air. In case a photographer wasn't available, she would have to know how to shoot some of her own stories with a silent 16mm Bell & Howell Filmo camera. She would also have to be able to edit film, write a script, and, if needed, narrate the assembled package in voice-over.

As Dennis Murphy, then a Channel 11 reporter with Jessica and now an NBC correspondent, puts it, "KHOU in those days was Charlie Brown's All-Stars."

According to Dick John, Murphy was of particular help to Jessica when she first came to the station. She also sought out Ron Stone, who tutored her in interview technique, showing her how to segue from one question to another in easy flow. But out in the field, the photographers were astounded at how little she knew about putting together a story.

"She literally knew nothing," recalls cameraman John Shaw. "Everybody who went out with her [on assignment] had to tell her exactly what to do. I remember saying, 'Well, you interviewed the guy. Now you've got to do a stand-up,'" a reporter's on-camera transition or summation of the facts. Cameraman Wally Athey was equally patient with Jessica, instructing her to, "Stand this way and turn your shoulder to me," or volunteering, "That stand-up doesn't sound too good. Let's do it again." On the way back to the station, both cameramen would refine the learning process for her.

Since Jessica had never worked with pictures before, they helped her formulate the finished stories in her mind, suggesting how the writing might fit around the images, and how the pieces should cut together.

As time went on, Jessica began to grasp the concept of writing descriptive phrases to match the video frame-for-frame, and turning out a concise, professional news story. But while she had learned to distill the information in her script, according to Athey, she still had trouble presenting the material in a stand-up—an expensive dilemma when shooting film, which, unlike videotape, cannot be erased and reused.

"One day," remembers John Shaw, "she was really having a hard time with her stand-up. I said, 'You might want to try what Ron Stone does.'" Stone had come up with an ingenious technique of tape recording his stand-ups and then playing them back in his earpiece on camera, repeating the words just a second behind the prerecorded material. It took tremendous concentration, but once perfected, it made for a smooth delivery and excellent eye contact with the camera, "like you really knew what the hell you were talking about," says Judd McIlvain, who also had learned it from Stone and mentioned it to Jessica.

"Everybody helped her, no matter what," says John Shaw. "There wasn't a day when we didn't walk out of that station saying, 'We did it again!' You know, changing chicken shit into chicken salad. And she would laugh along with the rest of us."

Jessica was convinced, however, that two of the station's cameramen, Bob Wolf and Don Benskin, both renegade cowboy types who prided themselves on their footage of some of the most dangerous news events of the decade, resented working with a woman, and that they did nothing to hide their feelings. She was determined that they weren't going to get the best of her, or prevent her from effectively covering her assignments. Eager to prove herself the equal of any reporter on the staff, she told Dick John that both Wolf and Benskin tried to trip her up on stories, and played practical jokes on her in front of interview subjects.

Cameraman John Shaw defends Wolf and Benskin, saying he believes they only meant to indoctrinate Jessica into the realities of the business with good-natured teasing.

Benskin, wearing jeans, a Western belt buckle, and boots, also denies that he and Jessica ever had problems. "I don't think I ever tried to screw her over. She may have felt that way, because she was a woman. But the fact is she would screw up enough [on her own], even though she was a good female reporter. I got along with her real well. She looked good, and she smelled good," he adds smiling. For all his flexing of muscle, Benskin's real objection to Jessica seems to have been that he regarded women to be in need of special protection and didn't want to be distracted from his job by looking out for her safety.

Bob Wolf, now a marshall with the City of Houston, was KHOU's "cop shop" man for fifteen years. In that time, he likes to brag, "I've probably seen five thousand people shot, stabbed, killed in airplane crashes, drowned, burned, hanged, and mass murdered." He spent so much time with the police that he considered himself almost one of their number, riding around in the black-and-whites with them at night, and getting tipped off for an exclusive whenever a raid was in the works. With a disdain for non-Texans as obvious as the San Jacinto Monument, Wolf was a one-man band, shooting his footage and filing stories, too. He ran around doing whatever he liked, chasing police and fire trucks, shooting random mayhem and violence, living in his own world and writing off the rest as irrelevant. On the big stories, however, the station would also dispatch a reporter. And the intrusion of someone else on his beat—particularly a 108-pound female from New York City—was not to be suffered long.

"He had a car with fifteen thousand radios [police scanners] in it," says Don Benskin, his protegé, "and he liked showing that shit off, and who he was." Wolf, who had been Dan Rather's photographer on Hurricane Carla, had greeted each new KHOU employee with the same warning: "I was here before you got here, and I'll be here after you leave."

A number of Wolf's former co-workers regard him as a Damon Runyon character with a heart of gold. But Dick John is less romantic. "Bob Wolf did everything he could to make Jessica's life impossible, like making her look at people with meat cleavers through the tops of their heads," he says. "She'd never seen anything like that before."

Wolf admits he may have been a little harsh. One day he got a call that there was a "floater" in the Houston Ship Channel.

"A floater is somebody who drowns," he explains in a beefy drawl. "Gas forms in the stomach, and it bloats, and that's what brings 'em back up to the surface most of the time. They become putrid, and they've been known to pop. And maybe I was a little sadistic, but I figured, well, that's a good place for her to see it. You know, you play pranks on a cub, and I considered her someone who hadn't paid her dues, and a female, and probably had no business in journalism anyway. I probably told her that she should be home making babies instead of doing that, because in those days, a lot of the cameramen were pretty chauvinistic."

When they got to the Ship Channel, Wolf says, "Being the sweet, kind gentleman that I am, I told her to stay at the top of the embankment, and not to climb down. But she was very insistent that she get right in the big, fat middle of it. So when they brought the floater out, and the wind changed, she got a good whiff of it. That odor permeates your clothes and everything else. She never did get sick, but she was very queasy. So that was her introduction to covering the police beat. To the best of my recollection, that was her first floater, too."

Jessica ended up earning Wolf's respect. "She was a good reporter to work with after that," he says, "because she listened to what I told her. She was a feisty little lady, and she wanted to be perfect, and she was very demanding about that perfection. She turned out to be a pretty good gal."

"In the 1970s, when blacks and women were new to the industry," says Bob Nicholas, a black reporter formerly of KHOU, and now at KPRC, "the two were looked upon as stepchildren. [The feeling was] we're allowing you in the door, but only for a while, and you must learn your place. Jessica had a drive that intimidated men. They were not accustomed to seeing that in a woman, and they didn't like it that she knew what she wanted."

After Jessica had been in Houston several weeks, she moved to a one-bedroom apartment at Allen House, about two miles from the station on West Dallas. The apartment was clean, motel-modern, and furnished, and the rent was $169 a month, reasonable at the time. Jessica would say later that her mother made a pilgrimage to help her get settled, and now she had more permanent company—a black feline she would name Sveltie.

Since she stayed at the station some fourteen hours a day, the apartment was only someplace to sleep. "I don't think she was real happy," observes Judd McIlvain, whose desk was behind hers in the newsroom. "The rest of us would go home at night to family or people we knew, and she didn't do that. Her whole life was tied to the station, and she didn't dare be away from it. She was afraid she'd miss the big story that would take her to New York."

That meant she wanted to be assigned all the important stories, hoping one might be of such national interest as to be aired on the "CBS Evening News" with Walter Cronkite.

One morning, a train carrying eight cars of explosive chemicals derailed at the Santa Fe tracks on Mykawa Road in southeast Houston. A tankcar had exploded, resulting in what Don Benskin remembers as only a smoldering fire. The station sent one reporter to the scene, and Jessica and Benskin were assigned elsewhere, to "another dog-meat story," as he recalls.

"We were going out the Gulf Freeway," he says, "when we heard that they'd had another explosion at Mykawa Road. We were biting at the bit to get out there, so we told the station, 'Oh, we're close by,' when we really weren't. We could see the smoke on the horizon, and we were excited that we were finally going to get to do what looked like the lead story of the day. I was driving like crazy, and Savitch was hanging out the car window, yelling 'Get out of the way!' at every son of a bitch on the road."

When they got to the scene, Benskin drove past a roadblock, leaving the guard standing and staring with his hands on his hips. By this time, KHOU photographers Wally Athey and Ron Cutchall were already filming on one side of the tracks, and Bob Wolf was shooting at large. The fire was now making a roaring sound, "like sucking the air." Benskin picked a spot about one hundred yards down the tracks and he began to ready his equipment as Jessica practiced her stand-up.

"She hadn't said over two words when the damn tankcars exploded," he remembers. "I was carrying an Auricon [sound camera], and this thing just blew me smooth off my feet, like somebody picked me off and threw me in the ditch. Jessica was standing in front of me, with her back to the thing, so it must have blown her down, too. But when I got up, it had knocked the camera off me, and I grabbed a silent camera and shot the mushroom cloud. Debris was falling all around. For a second, it was so hot that you thought your flesh would burn off. I heard Savitch scream, and I turned around to see her running down the road with her hands in the air."

"It would scare the fool out of you," Bob Wolf admits. But

when Jessica regained her composure, she filed a report that all the photographers—particularly Wolf and Wally Athey—would applaud. By the time Benskin caught up with her, she was sitting in a patrol car, slightly dazed. A photographer for the fire department had been killed, a number of people were taken to the hospital, and a cameraman for another station was severely burned.

As Jessica began editing her story, word came that the network wanted a feed for its evening news. The newsroom tuned in to hear the announcer say, "CBS News with Walter Cronkite . . . Dan Rather at the White House . . . Jessica Savitch in Houston . . ."

Jessica was enormously proud of her performance at Mykawa Road, and now she hungered for more network exposure, hoping, as Judd McIlvain surmised, that someone high up in the CBS news division would discover her and bring her back to New York. She was insistent that she appear on camera in every story she covered, and if she somehow didn't, she would want to go out back of the station and shoot a stand-up in front of what would jokingly be called the "Jessica Savitch Everywhere Bush." She also lobbied to do double closes, shooting one for the local broadcast ("This is Jessica Savitch . . . Newswatch 11") and another for CBS News. "She would always try to get on the feed no matter what—any story, any story," says John Shaw.

In the meantime, Jessica was trying to do whatever she could to impress the local management.

"She hadn't been there any time," remembers McIlvain, "when she started getting all this mail. She would show it to everybody, saying, 'Look, I got fifty letters this week!' Well, none of us got mail like that," he says. "So one day I just started looking at it. I said, 'Gee, Jess, do you realize that all your fans live right in your neighborhood? This stuff has all been postmarked right around your house!' And she looked at me sort of funny, and she said, 'No, I didn't know that.' The next week when she got a bunch of mail, she pointed out to me that it came from all over. You couldn't beat her for drive and determination. But I always accused her of going out on the weekends and mailing herself fan letters. If Jess thought it would raise her image in people's eyes, I'm sure she'd do it."

Throughout her KHOU tenure, Jessica experimented with whatever she could think of that might elicit the most viewer response. One day she amazed the Houston journalism community by wearing the briefest of what were then termed hot pants to cover an air show at Ellington Air Force Base, standing on the ladder—or the wing, according to Dick John and Wally Athey—of a jet fighter. Judd McIlvain was flabbergasted: "There was no way you had any idea of what she said in the stand-up, and you probably didn't even see the plane." KHOU sports reporter Ron Franklin remembers taking her aside and asking, "Jess, what are you doing?" And Jessica turned around and winked. "Franklin," she said, "whatever it takes to get ahead. If they like my legs, then they like me."

Aside from the fact that Jessica first struck some of the people in the newsroom as unbearably egotistical ("It was like you wanted to say, 'Humility, sweetheart, humility. You've got to make that a part of your vocabulary or it's going to be a rough road,'" recalls Franklin), several of the reporters resented having to scramble to keep the rookie from showing them up. For the first time anyone could remember, the newsroom was competitive. People now had to *ask* for stories.

"Dick [John] had an assignment board," recalls Dean Borba, "and Jessica would go in and put her name on it before anybody else got there. She'd figure out what she wanted, and then she'd do her homework and fight for assignments. I remember Dick telling me about it. He'd say, 'I can't keep ahead of her half the time.'"

A native of Tulsa, the cherub-faced Dick John had started out his on-air career at WKY-TV in Oklahoma City, where his co-anchor was Frank McGee, later a top draw for NBC. John went on to become a writer for "Today" show newscaster Frank Blair, and to anchor NBC radio newscasts. Today he is a media consultant. "Whenever a good assignment came up and she didn't get it, she'd come storming into my office and cry and cry," says John. "I'd hand her another handkerchief until finally she'd taken all that I had, and she ended up buying me a big box of the best there was—Irish linen. The guys were afraid of her. They thought, 'My God, she's going to take my job!' No doubt about it, she added a spice to that operation that it had never seen. It was like, 'You guys either lead or get out of my way.'"

John Shaw remarks that she would "absolutely go crazy" if she didn't get what she wanted. The episodes earned her the nickname of "Jessica Savage."

One morning, Steve Edwards, who anchored and produced the weekend news, and thus acted as assignment editor for the broadcast, found himself with a slow news day.

"I said, 'Look, Jessica, there's not a lot going on. Why don't you go over to the big shoe show in town? You can have fun with it—two hundred thousand pairs of shoes have descended upon Houston," remembers Edwards, now a talk show host at KABC-TV in Los Angeles. "She demurred about it, but she did it, because there wasn't anything else."

But shortly afterwards, Judd McIlvain, the station's preeminent street reporter, called in to say he wanted to do a story on the aftermath of the Corpus Christi flood. He had already arranged for a helicopter, he told Edwards, and enlisted photographer Billy George. "I said, 'Great! You got it!' " Edwards recalls, "and Judd went down to Corpus."

At four o'clock, Edwards sat down with the staff to line up the six o'clock news. "I said, 'Okay, we're going to open with Judd McIlvain and the flood aftermath story, and then we're going to—', and Jessica said, 'We're going to open with *what?*' " Edwards says. "I said, 'Judd went down to Corpus to do a flood story.' Well, she got very, very upset. She said, 'You sent *me* to the *shoe show* and you sent *him* down *there?*'

"She began to yell that I had no respect for her, or for her ability to do a real story. This went on to the point that I had to take her out of the newsroom and into an editing room, because she was just screaming and crying."

The way Judd McIlvain remembers it, Jessica tore her fingernails until they bled, and became so agitated that Edwards had to slap her to bring her under control.

"I can't imagine that I slapped her," Edwards corrects, "but I guess the part about the fingernails is true. I remember holding her wrists to stop whatever she was doing, and saying, 'Calm down, calm down, Jessica! This is not important! Your whole life is not being summed up in the assignment of stories here today.' She was extremely bright, a terrific iconoclast, but she was a complex person with stronger drives and needs than a lot of other people around her in a fairly needy business. Sometimes people had difficulty understanding that."

"She really was amazing," says Ron Stone, "because here she was twenty-four years old, had never worked in news before, and was in there fighting and scratching with the rest of us, who were fairly decent folks for the state of the art at the time. Of course, if you're any good in this business, that's the way you ought to act. She was a natural for television. But we knew she was a little crazy. You never knew when she was going to throw one of those fits."

Jessica also engaged in several emotional tirades with the engineering crew. The most famous incident occurred one night when she was in the studio narrating a news story. The pieces she attempted were often ambitious and creative, involving not only the usual "A" and "B" rolls of film, but sometimes a "C" roll as well. Her nemesis was an engineer who had butchered her stories more times than anyone cared to remember—punching in an audio "cart" [cartridge] too late under the silent film, for example, and making Jessica look bad on the air.

"The level of technology at that time was very low," Dick John recounts, "and the guys tried their dead-level best on all eight points to make it come out smooth. But this particular night, the engineer jumped one reel over the other—took video from one chain instead of audio, and audio from a chain that was nothing but a lot of Jessica saying, 'Goddamn it, can't you get it right out here?' And it went on the air that way. She went charging into the control room screaming like an absolute banshee. I don't know what she did to the poor guy," John says, a bemused expression on his face, "but she had to be pulled off of him. He was terrified. And it totally disrupted the entire news program and the program that followed."

Such outbursts tended to alienate Jessica from much of the newsroom. One reporter dismissed her as "a drama junkie." Bob Nicholas, for instance, thought she had serious emotional problems. "I always saw her as a frustrated little girl who missed out on something at a very early age in life, although I never knew what it was." But according to Steve Edwards, she was also enormously generous. Sometimes he would use her apartment to take a nap between long shifts, and so would other members of the staff. "That's the kind of friend she was," Edwards says. "If I had said, 'Look, I have to move my whole family in for the next six weeks,' that would have been all right with her."

When Jessica first moved to Allen House, another KHOU news personality came over to the apartment one day, and was somewhat taken aback when she offered him marijuana. "She had a bag of it in her freezer," he says, chuckling. "I'm somebody who never gets offered this stuff, so I laughed, and she laughed too, and that was it. But at the time, I think probably everybody was into it. Houston was very much a happening place."

Certainly marijuana use was common in the KHOU newsroom, and Dick John knew it. "Jess and [producer] Carl Cochran smoked pot all the time," John says, "used it wildly. And Carl was notorious."

Cochran, now the executive producer of corporate television for Pacific Bell, confirms the description. But, he says, Jessica was "absolutely" familiar with regular marijuana use before she got to Houston.

"Frankly, that was one of the reasons that Jessica and I hit it off," he explains. "Jessica's and my drug use was at the exact same level during the Houston period. Grass was pretty prevalent at KHOU, and Jessica was in no way bringing up the rear. We were smoking tons of it. She got about sixty percent of her supply from people at the station, infused with sources that she would meet on the job. After a while, even in the Houston years, the strata in which Jessica was able to function were high enough that she could get pretty much anything she wanted, including cocaine. But we used it only recreationally, just an exploratory touch of coke now and then."

And at all three stations, the news photographers—characteristically more hedonistic than their reporter counterparts— were especially known for their large marijuana consumption.

"Yeah, sure," says Don Benskin. "Jessica did some weed here, but I don't think she dealt in drugs more than anybody [else]. Pot, especially, was big at that time. She got some at the station, and there were other people who could get drugs for her if she needed them." Benskin stares at the ceiling. "I'm glad I didn't have any type of affair with her," he adds. "I think I would have fallen in love with her. And that would have been disastrous."

Cameraman John Shaw, probably the most artistic of the KHOU staff photographers, also had been drawn to Jessica. "She was so striking when she first came to the station," he remembers. Since Shaw was living at the time with the woman who would eventually become his wife, he did his best not to imagine himself romantically involved with the new reporter, and concentrated purely on their work product. But he couldn't help but talk about

Jessica at home, and his girlfriend, Ellen, became convinced that he and Jessica were having an affair. She kicked him out of the house, and he went to stay at Jessica's.

"It was purely platonic," Shaw explains. "In the back of my mind, I would have liked to have made it otherwise. I mean, I was in the girl's apartment," he adds with a laugh. "I was infatuated with her, but then I wasn't, because she wasn't that beautiful. Everybody always comes up to me and says, 'Jeez, she was a really beautiful girl!' And I say, 'No, she really wasn't.' She must have had a fantastic makeup artist at NBC, because when you saw her in the morning when she woke up . . . well, she had lots of pockmarks. If you took her clothes off, she was just skin and bones. And really hyper all the time."

After three weeks, Shaw moved back home. In the interim, he and Jessica had gone out to dinner a lot, and gone for drives, just to talk. He was surprised when she told him that wherever she'd lived, she'd had few girlfriends, forming friendships almost exclusively with men.

From their talks, Shaw thought that Jessica "had a problem with her father," one that carried over into her other male/female relationships. "The first or second night I moved in," he says, "she went into her room, and I heard her on the phone through the wall. She was just crying and crying. I later found out she was talking to Ed Bradley, who was her mentor and her lover at the same time."

John Shaw remembers that just before he moved out—others would date their meeting in 1972—Jessica had begun dating a reporter for KTRK, the local ABC affiliate. His name was Ron Kershaw, and after David Savitch, he would come to be the most important man in her life. She would become his all-consuming romantic passion. Years later, friends on both sides remember their troubled confusion at how dark and complicated—how symbiotic—the alliance could be. "It was the most intense relationship I was ever around," says Kershaw's friend, journalist Dick Williams, and others were alarmed at the control and dominance the two would alternately wield over each other. For both Ron and Jessica, it would be more than love, more than hate, but obsession, a way to escape from, but repeat, the past. "It was," as their mutual friend Sharon Sakson would say, "one of the relationships of the century."

William Ronald Kershaw was about four years older than Jessica and had grown up in the shadow of the Smoky Mountains, in Asheville, North Carolina. Now the news director at the CBS owned-and-operated WBBM-TV in Chicago, he is a moody, reflective man who seldom talks about his childhood to anyone, skillfully diverting conversation away from discussion of his family. Rarely, he has alluded to a youth of grinding poverty. Sharon Sakson remembers his telling her that he spent his boyhood on a chicken farm, and that he had been reared by his grandparents. While Jessica perceived herself as having been abandoned by both parents, Ron was much more intimate with rejection. "He ended up being raised by his grandparents because his daddy abandoned him and his mama couldn't support him," says Dick Williams. "He was very bitter about his parents."

The experience made Kershaw a bona fide hillbilly, "a hellraiser," and he was proud of it. But he was also looking for a ticket out of his particular Southern circumstance, and he found it, in 1961, with the air force. There, a friend recounts, he took a high school equivalency test—his basic education had come from the oral tradition, music, visual images, and art—and served as a cryptographic specialist, working in codes and communications while assigned to the Middle East and Southeast Asia.

The air force, Dick Williams says, provided Kershaw with medical and dental treatment for the first time in his life. His Houston colleagues would be shocked at how bad his teeth were— "I just couldn't believe he was on TV like that," says Dick John— and at how many of his upper teeth were simply missing, a factor that dictated what he could and could not eat.

Kershaw began his professional journalism career in 1968, when he interned as a news aide at the *Washington Post,* working on the foreign news desk. A year later, he arrived in Houston and entered television news, becoming one of KTRK's jack of all trades—photographer, reporter, producer, editor, and anchorman—at $500 a month, learning to report, he says, by inventing it as he went along. Somewhere along the way he married and had two children, a daughter, Lee Ann, and a son, Ronald Byrne, known as Beau. Kershaw and others insist that he and his wife, Claudia, were already separated by the time he met Jessica Savitch; the marriage, he says, was "a childhood mistake." Other former colleagues, including his boss at the time, Walt Hawver, KTRK's news director, say he left his family for her. The Kershaws were divorced in March 1972.

In the mid-seventies and throughout the eighties, when he drifted into the management side of the business, Kershaw would be regarded as a gifted news director, a television guru with almost magical powers, sought after by top affiliates and networks alike. He would become the perfect metaphor for the creative, crazed mystic who loved the medium, lived for it, who viewed it as the most fascinating, compelling, and powerful instrument ever, and who intuitively understood its capabilities and potential almost better than anyone else. Some have called him the best producer in the history of television.

"He's a genius," says Sharon Sakson, echoing the opinion of a variety of others. "He knows exactly the power of images, words and sound, and how they should match for maximum impact. His gut feeling was always right. He's a very erratic leader, because he's so emotional and so intense on the job. And if you worked for him, you suffered, because he always had a vision of what a thing should be, and he loved perfection. He was always looking for it. But his life was full of disappointments. He had such expectations of the world, that things would be good. And he could never find that they were."

Exactly how the Houston journalism community regarded Kershaw in the early seventies is open to debate. The record shows that he was, in many ways, the station's top gun reporter, winning several awards for his spot news, documentaries, and 30-minute reports on racial conflict and on the Houston medical beat. Several of his competitors recall him at the time as simply "a very bright guy." Another says he was "not a heavyweight journalist, and not anywhere near Jessica's caliber as a reporter," although he had a knack for making routine stories interesting—a quality for which Jessica also would be known during her Houston years. "Ron was a tough reporter, a good writer, and terribly dull on the air," says one of his friends. "Ron is genuine. He's not an actor. You really have to be a bit of an actor to sell yourself on local television."

Dick John agrees. "Ron was a good, solid reporter, but he had no star quality. And when it became knowledge that he and she were an item, there was no contest. He was 'Jessica Savitch's boyfriend.' "

Kershaw had, of course, taken note of Jessica as a competitor.

She had caught his eye from the beginning. He liked her passion, and her intensity. And he thought she might be able to tap into his own passion, to draw it out in a positive way. To many, Kershaw came across as an angry man with an icy veneer, a guarded, antisocial figure who refused to play political games to get ahead, whose high standards in journalism and in life prevented him from stroking people or soothing ruffled feathers. But underneath a sometimes frightening exterior was a sensitive, introspective man, "an incredible romantic," in the words of one of his co-workers. A loner, certain like Jessica that he would die young, he was slow to trust and make friends, spending most of his free time in seclusion. He seldom slept, staying up all night drinking, using drugs, and listening to rock and roll, which he regarded as the real art and poetry of his generation.

"Kersh would get into these mystic states and have these brilliant visions," says one of his friends. "Then he'd drag in late the next day and say, 'Boy, have I got an idea for a piece!' And he would. Where most of us read our information, Ron is one of those people who just absorbs it. He's one of the most remarkable people I've ever known."

One day not long after Jessica arrived in Houston, the TV stations got a call that the transmitter for the city's leftist Pacifica radio station, KPFT, had been bombed. Kershaw covered it for KTRK, and Jessica for KHOU. "Their studios were on the third floor of a loftlike building," remembers Kershaw, "and basically, she went up ahead of me, wiggling her ass the whole way. I probably wouldn't have even needed that, because I was attracted to her anyway. So I asked her out, to a Traffic concert." Kershaw recalls with some cynicism that years later Jessica would refer to it in *Anchorwoman* as a Yes concert, perhaps for the sake of some wordplay that followed.

Unlike most of the men to whom Jessica was attracted, Ron Kershaw had no social position, no money, and no real prestige. He was not even overtly handsome, although aside from his hellish teeth, he was attractive: His reddish hair, cleft chin, and sad eyes fell together in a compelling way, while his full lips turned down at the corners and were set in a perpetual, melancholy look. There seemed to be something slightly dangerous about him.

Jessica liked Kershaw's strength and fiery idealism, and she considered him the best reporter in Houston. She would also write in *Anchorwoman* that "much of what I believed about my mission in the industry" was formulated with him, that "we saw ourselves as innovative reporters in an emerging field . . . he taught me a lot about how television is more than just a radio story with some pictures added."

Jessica realized that Kershaw knew when television worked and when it didn't, and because his praise was slow in coming and difficult to earn, she would, in time, value his judgment above that of all others. She would work to please him the way she had strived to please David Savitch. And she would allow him behind the façade she put on for the world, and show him her vulnerable self. Because of the large space between his two front teeth, she would call him "Rabbit," or frequently "Rab." And because she was his Jessica Beth, "one determined, skinny little motherfucker, the toughest little princess you've ever seen in your life," he would call her "Brat."

"Television is a child's medium, it's magic," says Kershaw. "That's why she loved it, and that's why she gloried in it. We grew up on the ideal of what it could be, on Murrow and Howdy Doody, and the whole thing was ours to play with. I think that when we were together was the first time she could be the 'little girl.' She was one hundred percent life, and she had the ability to light up where she stood. I liked the little girl, because I was missing a childhood myself. We were friends, lovers, and sister and brother. And I think she associated me with her father. He lived in books, he loved the Civil War, he loved Sir Walter Scott, and he loved Edward R. Murrow—all the things I do. I said to her that if there was any way that I could give her five minutes with her father, I would move heaven and earth—exchange my life to do it—just so he could tell her he was proud of her. Because that's all she wanted, his approval."

There would be another important factor in their relationship. Jessica would tell Carl Cochran, her chief confidant during the Houston years, that Kershaw had unlocked a new sexual energy in her, that "she was unable to experience that plateau of sexual intimacy with anybody the way she could with Ron," he recalls. "That was one of the thrills she would always try to recapture with other men." And, indeed, when passion flared, they did not deny it. Judd McIlvain was embarrassed to walk into the news director's office one quiet Sunday afternoon and discover Jessica and Ron making love on Dick John's couch.

Before long, Kershaw would catch Jessica in little lies—things that didn't matter especially, but which confused him about the honesty of their relationship. For a while, he tried to look at it as "the cuteness of a child," because he found she would lie automatically, even about something seemingly noble, such as giving money to the poor—"No, I didn't do that!" Then Kershaw discovered that the lying was linked to something else.

"When we first started going together," he remembers, "one of our first arguments concerned a theory she had about how she could control her life. Control was very important to her. And she told me she put her life in little boxes, like drawers in a jewelry box. She thought she could keep her career in one drawer, and the two of us in another, and her family in still another. That way, she genuinely believed that she could have it all. That was the key. I disagreed with it, and we fought about it. But she was a very brilliant producer of 'Jessica Savitch.' She wanted you to think she was extremely simple, and to take whatever version she chose to present in that particular time and place. She posed an enigma for anyone who wanted the solution to the little boxes—how they all added up to the real Jessica."

As an example, despite her feelings for Ron Kershaw, Jessica couldn't stop thinking about Ed Bradley. Before leaving for Europe and on his stateside trips, he flew down to see her several times, John Shaw recalls, and Shaw invited them over to his and Ellen's house. On one visit, Bradley stayed for a week, and John and Ellen drove them down to Galveston to sightsee. A black man and a white woman—especially a blonde woman—were not easily tolerated in the South in the early 1970s, and Shaw remembers that "We couldn't go to many restaurants, although it helped that it was two couples."

A few of Jessica's Houston colleagues openly disapproved of the relationship with Bradley. Dick John had seen him picking Jessica up in front of the station on two occasions. But when Dean Borba caught them kissing in Jessica's car, he "went ape," as John remembers it. "Dean called me upstairs and said, 'Dick, we've got to do something!' I said, 'I haven't the remotest idea what you're talking about.' And Dean said, 'Yes, you have.' So I called her in and said, 'Jess, why in the Sam Hill are you trying to get away with a relationship like this? You'll not only ruin yourself, but you're going to cause me a hell of a lot of trouble.' "

John remembers that at first she was belligerent, wanting to know why she couldn't continue to see Bradley.

"I asked her where he lived, and she said he worked for CBS, but when he was down here, he lived with her. I said, 'Bless your heart. You're a nice, sweet kid. But the first squawk about this to the company, and you're gone. It's that simple. That might fly in New York, but it won't in Houston, Texas.' So from that point on, Bradley stayed behind the log, and didn't pick her up. She left him at the apartment when he came into town."

Ed Bradley's trips to Houston were far less troublesome to KHOU management than they were to Ron Kershaw. Already deeply in love with Jessica, Kershaw was resentful of anyone in her past, and worse, it was now obvious to him that Jessica had not left Bradley behind when her CBS days were over. The very mention of his name would fill Kershaw with rage, and Jessica, by several accounts, sometimes fanned the flames.

"We're not talking about a vulnerable, quiet little mouse here," says one of her friends. "We're talking about someone who, in an argument, would give as good as she got. She was a slapper, and a hitter when she was angry, and she would tug, and tussle, and punch, and pull hair, and kick and scratch and gouge. You bet."

Jessica began turning up for work with an occasional black eye and bruises. When the photographers questioned her about them—Don Benskin had noticed marks on her neck—she made excuses. But when another woman, staff artist Cholla Runnels, inquired, Jessica confessed that she and Ron had fought, although she refused to go into any detail.

"Their fisticuffs, and the situations that required applying salve to Jessica's physical and emotional wounds, were primarily predicated on the Ed Bradley situation," offers Carl Cochran. "But often when two people arise in conflict, there will be a surface nature of the argument, with something else going on underneath. Whatever it was, they got locked into a pattern where Ron would dish out physical abuse, and Jessica, by conveying a tolerance for it, allowed it to go on."

Kershaw, sitting and drinking in a hotel bar in Chicago in early 1987, explains it this way: "She did almost as much as anybody could to me—as much as I did to her, probably—and we still loved each other like nothing else on this earth. She drove me crazy, and I drove her crazy, too. But we were both already crazy to begin with. I think Jessica picked fights with me to make it *so bad* that she would have reason to hate me. Then she could justify leaving me. But she would always come back."

One of Ron's closest friends concurs. "He could be a mean son of a bitch when he wanted," the man says, "but in my view, he and Jessica acted out roles. They played little games that would lead to certain confrontations. And if I knew more about sexual psychology and gratification, I would say that one of the reasons they did that was because it gave them pleasure, that making up was better than breaking up."

In September, three months after Jessica had arrived in Houston, Steve Edwards vacated his weekend anchor chair to host a talk show. Management announced that they would hire two people from within the ranks to replace him, one for Saturday night, and another for Sunday. Through the week, Dick John would continue to anchor the six o'clock news with his dog, Errol Flynn, at his feet, and Ron Stone would anchor the ten o'clock broadcast. Jessica would later say that she was so certain she wouldn't get the spot ("I had ruled myself out because I'd been socialized to think a woman couldn't have it—I didn't even know if I wanted it") that the night of the auditions, she went home, only to get a call from Dick John, who was asking her to return. She went back, she told Maralyn Lois Polak of the *Philadelphia Inquirer,* in a severely tailored suit.

"I'd never seen a woman doing a news show," she would say. "I figured if I wanted them to listen to what I was saying rather than how I looked, I'd try my best to look like a man. So I toned down my looks—no makeup, hair pulled straight back, mannish jacket and turtleneck. I looked very young and *was* very young, so I tried to look more authoritative. Then I finally realized that was silly. 'I'm capable. I don't have to be somebody else. I don't have to be a man.' "

But at the time, she would say, "If I could have worn a tie, I would have."

The audition tape, everyone agreed, was terrible. But what Jessica didn't know was that she was a shoo-in for the job anyway. "I was told that in order for the thing to look fair, we would hold auditions," says Dick John. "But it didn't matter. I knew where I wanted her to be. In this business, you look for people who attract people on the other end of the tube, who somehow rivet you with the sense that they're talking only to you, if only subconsciously. And she was *it*. She had a great magnetism, and a great sense of what TV is about. Men liked her because she was pretty and sharp, and women liked her because they thought she had a handle on things, and because she was going places. You couldn't beat that combination with a stick. Still, I couldn't tell her, 'You've won already, relax and enjoy this,' but she had."

John assigned Jessica to the Sunday night shift, with newscasts at six and ten. Bob Nicholas got the Saturday spot. The newscasts would make history: Nicholas was the first black anchor in the market, and Jessica the first anchorwoman in the South. To Jessica, the job's real importance was that she would be seen by nearly two million people, in the fifteenth largest market in the country, and that she would be featured in *TV Guide*, just as Joan Showalter had predicted. "Dick John made Jessica the way Sam Phillips made Elvis," says reporter Dennis Murphy. "Everyone else just shined her up, and unfortunately, screwed her up a little."

In time, Jessica would come to trust the camera the way she would nothing else. "It was almost as if there were a missing part of her life that the camera filled," her friend Josh Howell would say. "It was just her and the camera, and there was no reason to be on-guard." But there were no TelePrompTers at KHOU in 1971, and her first night on the job, Jessica was so nervous that she "twitched like a jack rabbit caught in somebody's headlights," as a staff member would recall. Bob Nicholas, watching in the studio, noticed her hands "going absolutely bananas. And one of her legs was just—" He makes a pumping motion. "She was an absolute wreck. But she was almost two totally different people on-camera and off. On camera she was the person she always wanted to be—under control, and in complete charge of her destiny. That's what made her convincing."

Because her writing skills were still somewhat pedestrian, Carl Cochran, who produced the show, wrote her script, including the lead-ins to the packaged pieces. That first night, at the end of the six o'clock report, Cochran came running out of the booth to congratulate her.

"We were obviously euphoric that it had worked," he remembers, "and we were walking down the hall when I looked down and saw her hand. She was carrying her script, and there were two rivulets of blood running down the side of the page. I said, 'Goddamn, what the hell is that?' She was totally unaware of what was going on, but she had been so nervous during the show that she had literally gouged her nails through her fingers. Later, it was something that she would do with some regularity."

The viewing audience loved her. "I took a call from one guy who said he absolutely could not stand me," she told the *Houston Chronicle* at the time, clearly elated. "He didn't want a woman telling him anything. He hated me so much, in fact, he even called back to tell me again after the ten o'clock report."

But the paper's TV-radio editor, Ann Hodges, raved, "I can't think of any recent TV news development—including the innovation of hour-long formats—that has generated more viewer excitement than Channel 11's new weekend anchor team."

And indeed, in short order, Jessica began receiving the amount of fan mail she had earlier described to Judd McIlvain, as well as requests to speak to various groups in the community. To top it off, a local disc jockey began singing, "I've never been to heaven, but I've seen Jessica on Channel 11."

"She just took Houston over," says Dick John.

The joyful management began to believe that KHOU might actually regain some of its ratings points. And Jessica reveled in the fact that she had won the admiration of her colleagues. "She was better than the rest of us at the business of television, and that's all there is to it," anchor Ron Stone concedes.

Jessica, in the quest for perfection that Lil had bred in her long ago, still was not satisfied with her performance. To make it to the network, she would need to be extraordinary, to expand every possibility for advancement. She talked Dean Borba into paying for a speech coach to help her overcome her lisp, and she consulted a local plastic surgeon about performing dermabrasion on her old acne scars. "She was certain the scars would block her career," the physician remembers. He discouraged her, saying he couldn't promise sufficient improvement to warrant either the procedure or the inevitable line of demarcation and enlargement of the pores.

But Ron Kershaw, who taught Jessica the elements of a good, well-paced newscast, told her he knew what would improve her performance more than anything. Her on-camera smile was weak, or at best, tentative. Kershaw saw that it could be luminous. "I said, 'You've got to show teeth.' Teeth is vulnerability in primates, whether you're a chimp or Dan Rather. A lot of people appear to be vulnerable, but she not only knew she should be, she was," he continues. "We planned it, but when she smiled at the end of a report, that was her. She wanted people to like her, and she needed the approval. The times when she lit up that screen were perhaps the only times in her life that she was genuinely happy. She only existed electronically."

Still, the moments before broadcast were a nightmare. Steve Edwards says: "I still have this image of Jessica running down the hall into the studio, pulling the curlers out of her hair, screaming, dropping things all over the place, thirty seconds to air, yelling, 'I'm never going to get on!' Four-letter words all over the place, and then hitting the air with, 'Hello, I'm Jessica Savitch,' as if she'd been perfectly calm all day long."

That extraordinary power of concentration would serve her well throughout most of the rest of her life. No matter what fracas was going on around her, when the red light came on, she became a public trust. It was more important to her than anything else. "She really did have an astonishing ability to be what she ought to be in one situation, and to be something totally different in another—whatever was warranted," says Dick John. "You're talking about a unique individual, driven by the devil, really. With all kinds of devils to deal with."

Jessica was now beginning to make friends around Houston, but as it turned out, there was an old one in town that she didn't know about. Barry Swartz, her high school boyfriend, had just begun his general surgery residency at the Baylor College of Medicine, under the famous cardiovascular surgeon, Dr. Michael De-Bakey. One night, he turned on the television and was astounded to see Jessica. They had had no contact since her Ithaca days.

"I called her up and we had lunch at the hospital cafeteria," he recounts. "It was an amazing scene. Here's big Dr. Swartz, with his beeper, his scrub suit, and his shoes covered with blood, and there was Jessica, with her beeper, her tape recorder, and her press passes, both of us showing off how well we'd done." After that, when Jessica became ill and needed a doctor, she would call him on occasion. "I really cared for her back then," he says. "But it was strange. She was a different person than I'd known in Atlantic City."

Now that Lil was no longer buying her clothes, Jessica sometimes took on a tacky look at work. But, always dressed in slacks,
she was also ready for whatever story came up, whether it meant
trudging around a turkey farm or conducting an interview at
NASA. Her hair in those days was usually arranged in one of three
ways, the traditional Texas helmetlike upsweep, a longish flip, or
simply pulled back and held with yarn.

From the time she'd joined the KHOU staff, Jessica had
refused to be assigned a regular beat so that she might be available
to cover the breaking news of the day. A list of her stories from
October 15 to November 9, 1971, shows her filing reports on
shoplifting, women in the maritime, Ralph Nader, an oil spill and
fire in the Gulf of Mexico, drugs in schools, and a two-day EPA
conference. At other times, she did a feature on the closing of the
brothel that would inspire the Broadway hit *The Best Little Whore-
house in Texas,* as well as a short prison documentary. But she
generally left what little investigative work the station was doing
to reporters with better skills.

She did cover more than her share of Texas politics, including
the 1972 gubernatorial race. During the Democratic primary, she
traveled with candidates Ben Barnes, who was being touted as the
next Democratic candidate for president, and Frances "Sissy"
Farenthold, a lawyer, state representative, and later head of the
National Women's Political Caucus.

Farenthold, the first woman to run for statewide office in
nearly fifty years, would become something of a role model for
Jessica, not only because she "demonstrated to me that it is possible to be simultaneously aggressive and feminine," but for her
personal code of ethics. Both Jessica and Ron Kershaw, who covered the campaign for his station, were struck by the fact that
Farenthold, a pro-abortion Catholic in a Southern Baptist, male-
chauvinist state, came "that close" to getting the nomination, and
would have gotten it, as Kershaw says, "if she had given in on any
issue. But the day she announced her concession—with me on one
side of her holding the mike, and Jess on the other—she said,
'I was told how to demogogue safely in this state, but I refused
to do it. Because it is just as important how one gets to an office,
as having that office.' If Jess and I ever did any kind of project
together," Kershaw says, "we would remember that, and talk
about it."

In the fall of 1971, Jessica, who often covered the court house, became intrigued with the Houston mayoral contest between Louie Welch and Fred Hofheinz. Welch was seeking an unprecedented fifth consecutive term, and his challenger was the thirty-three-year-old son of Roy Hofheinz, a liberal Democrat who had served as mayor of Houston from 1953 to 1957. The senior Hofheinz was a flamboyant, powerful, and enormously wealthy figure, but also a humanitarian: During his administration, he saw to it that a number of Houston's public facilities and downtown lunch counters were racially integrated.

The junior Hofheinz lost his 1971 election in a runoff, but everyone knew it was only a matter of time before the office was his. On election night, when firemen were escorting Mayor Welch from his campaign headquarters to his car, Jessica moved in for an interview. "The raw tape showed Jessica moving forward, with the firemen pushing the mayor through the crowd," remembers Judd McIlvain. "Jessica tried to squeeze in, but one of the fireman pushed her back as they came through." With that, McIlvain says, "She took the microphone and whopped the guy over the head. But she swung with a bigger stroke than she meant to, and she almost hit the mayor, too!"

The incident was the first of several that would divide the Houston media into two camps—those who resented Jessica for what they called "showboating," or generating publicity for herself at the expense of the story and creating news where there was none—and those who viewed her as a gutsy, no-nonsense reporter who would stop at nothing to get her story.

"She wasn't deep, and she wasn't profound," says a reporter for a competing station, "but if three reporters banged through that door, and they all had notepads out, she could out-hustle them all. She was good." And if Carl Cochran believed that "for all her professionalism, she was obsessed with style over substance," Ron Franklin says she was not afraid to ask a tough question, and that she had always done her homework.

"It was jealousy," says Bob Nicholas. "Because the reporters then had been in the market a long time, and they'd always covered the stories the same way with the same group, all agreeing on how it was going to be done. If one guy walked away, they all did. But here came Jessica, saying, 'I'm not taking no comment for an answer. I'm going to make you answer me.' She would always take the extra step, and as long as she was there, they'd stick around.

I saw it on three or four occasions. When Jessica walked away, then they disappeared."

During the mayoral race, Jessica had gotten to know the wife of Fred Hofheinz, the former Elizabeth Winfrey, who went by the name of "Mac," and now they would begin a friendship that provoked considerable comment. The tall, thin redhead had been a socially prominent sorority girl majoring in philosophy when she met Fred Hofheinz, then a handsome, slightly built law student, at the University of Texas in the late fifties. When Mac and Fred married, they returned to Houston, had two children, and settled down on a secluded, piney twelve-acre estate in the Tanglewood section of town, beside Buffalo Bayou. The house was complete with swimming pool and servants' quarters in the rear. In some ways, Houstonians considered the couple the local equivalent of the young Jack and Jackie Kennedy, cultured and full of promise, the bright young comers. But "We all understood that there were problems in the marriage," says Arthur Wiese, formerly with the *Houston Post.* Mac Hofheinz, by all accounts, was estranged, outspoken, and bored to tears. The press called her the "Martha Mitchell of Tanglewood."

Asked today about Jessica, Fred Hofheinz explains that "I wasn't the friend. Mac was the friend." But, he says, his wife, from whom he's been separated for many years, does not wish to talk about her days as Jessica's confidante. "She is concerned that she not say anything that would be offensive to the record."

Mac was eight years older than Jessica, and the young reporter was flattered that so prominent and charming a local woman sought her friendship. The lonely Mac admired Jessica's vibrancy and accomplishments, and Jessica was drawn to Mac's restlessness and affluent life-style. Besides, who better to tutor her on the complexities of the Houston political system than Fred Hofheinz? "You live with the local television stations when you're a hotshot urban politician," he says in retrospect. "They're the most important people around."

Nonetheless, according to Dick John, the reporters and photographers at KHOU were taken aback when Mac Hofheinz began actually accompanying Jessica on her stories. Fred Hofheinz recalls that "Mac went with Jessica in a lot of instances where the two of them would even block doors to make sure they could get their target."

John N. Davenport remembers that "Many of us thought it was passing curious that she would treat her job as a kind of social thing, like, 'Let's all go cover fires together!' and 'Isn't this fun!' I considered it a rather amateurish way to look at journalism. And the firms I've worked for wouldn't have allowed it."

Soon "Everybody just took it for granted [that Mac would go on stories]," says John Shaw. "It was a strange relationship."

Despite a widespread campaign that featured many unsubstantiated rumors, Fred Hofheinz was elected mayor of Houston in 1973 at the age of thirty-five. He was, in the estimation of some, one of the best mayors in the history of the city. He won the election by a narrow margin, but he had galvanized the black community and went on from there to redefine Houston politics. After having been outnumbered for many years, progressives and liberals finally came to power.

But in 1977, when Hofheinz was eligible to run for a third term of office, the rumors caught up with him. That summer, a Harris County grand jury investigated a spring drug raid during which a public official was allegedly arrested and later released. While Hofheinz was never formally named as the subject of the investigation, he accused the grand jury foreman of connecting him to the case. The grand jury disbanded after failing to find any evidence of criminal acts by "a high city official," but a juror implied to the *Houston Post* that, indeed, "there was an attempt to use the jury as a political tool" against Hofheinz.

The days leading up to those events were no doubt trying ones for both Hofheinz and his wife, who began spending more time with Jessica. Carl Cochran believes the relationship between the women was based on genuine emotional give and take.

"Jessica was just starting her professionalism, not knowing anyone in town, and Mac was totally isolated," Cochran explains. "There was no warmth between Fred and Mac, and yet she had to remain isolated in the Hofheinz shell so she couldn't do any damage. So here we have two people basically functioning in isolation who found that it was safe for them to run around together. Suddenly Mac had a person with whom she could associate on a regular basis without arousing any suspicions, because it would appear to the world to be just a relationship between two professionals—a political wife and a journalist, who were friends. That relationship went through a lot of bumpy periods, but primarily it continued to reinforce itself and repeat itself, because they offered each other support. It was safe companionship for both of them."

If Mac Hofheinz was a "safe" companion, Carl Cochran was another. A self-avowed homosexual, Cochran says his friendship with Jessica was "an ideal world for both of us. She could make those male identities that were so important to her, and achieve male peer group support, and yet not have the sexual conflict that tainted so many of her other male relationships. We found in each other a camaraderie that pushed all the buttons that needed pushing, but did not have that destructive sexual pressure."

In February 1972, Jessica was assigned to cover the jury trial of Texas House Speaker Gus Mutscher and his two top political aides, accused of conspiring to accept a bribe in return for granting legislative favors. Jessica, KHOU photographer Ron Cutchall, and staff artist Cholla Runnels were sent to Abilene, some three hundred miles northwest, to file field reports as part of a continuing series. If found guilty, Mutscher, married to former Miss America Donna Axum, would become the highest-ranking official in the state of Texas ever to be convicted of a felony. Most of the news organizations in the state sent representatives.

The judge for the case, J. Neil Daniel, described in the Abilene *Reporter-News* as a "country boy," was not used to a standing room only crowd in his courtroom, and he was particularly unaccustomed to tolerating women in pants suits, even if it was the dead of winter in the age of miniskirts. That posed a particular problem for Jessica, who didn't own a dress. Furthermore, it looked as if the trial might last several weeks. But the judge made it clear: Any woman who entered the Taylor County courthouse wearing trousers would be barred from the proceedings.

"We were incensed," remembers Cholla Runnels. "The temperature had dipped to below thirty-two degrees, and here we had to go to this country store and get these little farm dresses." Mac Hofheinz came to Jessica's rescue, flying in a dress to her specifications. "Jessica said, 'By golly, if the judge wants me to go back where women are supposed to act like women, get me a long dress, as pioneer-looking as possible!' " Runnels recalls. To further prove her point, she filed a tongue-in-cheek report for the six o'clock news, standing on the Abilene courthouse steps in slacks ("Women who do not comply rapidly find their pants-suited figures out on the street") and appearing to change into her long dress—presto!—in the wink of an eye.

Female reporters were still such a rarity that when Jessica filmed the arrival of Mutscher and his wife at the courthouse, a photographer for the Abilene *Reporter-News* snapped pictures of her in action, and the paper ran them on page one. "Who said CameraMAN?" the cutline read. "Jessica Savitch, of KHOU, Houston . . . demonstrates the changing image of newsmen . . . er . . . newspeople."

The trial dragged on. Out of desperation for something to do at night, the press corps, most of whom were in their middle twenties, formed a "glee club," meeting in one another's motel rooms to drink and sing.

"There was an enormous amount of camaraderie in this group," says Arthur Wiese. "We'd start about eight o'clock, when the sidewalks were rolled up, and sing until midnight. There was something about the chemistry of the people and the moment that allowed us all to have a great deal of fun. But Jessica didn't seem to fit in, or want to fit in. We kept needling her to come, and finally she showed up one night, and sat through about an hour of it. I don't think we ever got her to sing, but she laughed a little bit, which was very unusual for her to do around a group of people. Normally, it was just that sardonic little smile."

Often, Jessica would go back to her room at night and telephone Ron Kershaw in Houston. On several occasions, their conversations became so heated that Cholla Runnels, in the room next door, heard Jessica screaming through the wall. "One night it went on for about three hours," she remembers. "She was using language like you never heard. She'd say, 'What the blank-blank do you think I'm doing up here?' And, 'I have a job to do, I'm not just screwing around!' "

Jessica invited Mac Hofheinz to come to Abilene to keep her company. The press delegation thought it was "very odd that the wife of Fred Hofheinz would come three hundred miles to sit through the proceedings of a bribery case where she didn't know anyone involved," says Wiese. But Mac's presence was particularly distressing for Cholla Runnels. The station had been alotted only two seats in the courtroom, and since Mac wanted to sit with Jessica, Cholla was expected to crouch under a table to make her courtroom sketches.

"We talked it over, and I said I'd try, because I wanted to accommodate Jessica," she says, "but I sure didn't like it very much, and I couldn't see well enough. I went along until one day when Mac turned around to me and told me to run down and get her coat. I said, 'Hey, wait a minute, that's it.' I told Jessica, 'I've put up with Mac long enough.. I either get my own seat, or I'm complaining to the station.' " And so, she says, Mac went home.

On March 15, 1972, the jury returned its verdict: It found Texas House Speaker Gus Mutscher and his aides guilty of conspiring to accept a bribe. Judge Daniel handed down five-year, probated prison terms. The press scurried to surround Mutscher as deputy sheriffs attempted to escort the speaker and his wife to their car. But when Jessica's photographer, Ron Cutchall, stuck his camera in the middle of the wolf pack, Deputy Sheriff David Dalbert allegedly shoved him—by some accounts Dalbert only hit the lens cover of the camera in the crush—to get out of the way. Jessica would later say that she asked Dalbert to move because he was blocking the camera, at which point the deputy placed his hand over the lens.

Whatever the circumstance, Jessica, replaying her moment at Welch headquarters, hauled off and clubbed the deputy with her microphone, by her own report, on the head and arm.

"That's not right," Dalbert told the Abilene paper ten years later. "I still remember it like it was yesterday. She hit me on the arm, not over the head. But it still hurt . . . it swelled up and turned blue." Dalbert denied that he shoved anyone or tried to grab a camera, claiming that Jessica, whom he called a "heathen," had assaulted him purely for publicity. In 1981, he said, he pointed Jessica out on TV to his children. "My kids say, 'That's the woman who hit Daddy!' "

Cholla Runnels says Jessica did indeed first warn the deputy to remove his hand from the camera lens, and that when he refused, she "rapped his knuckles with the microphone—I mean really got him! She always took care of her crew when we were out with her." But both Frank Healer, then of WBAP-TV, and Sandy Test, who covered the trial for the Texas State Network, agreed with Dalbert's version of the melee, which ended with Donna Mutscher swinging her purse at newsmen, and the wife of Mutscher aide Rush McGinty accidentally kicking Jessica in the shins. Healer said he was embarrased both by Jessica's physical attack and her "string of fifteen-letter words," adding that it gave all the news media a black eye. Test concurred.

Jessica was briefly detained, and the incident—plus a photograph—made the Associated Press wire service. Among some members of the press, at least, Jessica began looking like a cult figure, especially to women just breaking into the business. Cynthia Griffin, then the "weathergirl" at KTRE in Lufkin, Texas, says that "during the off-the-air times, many of us at the station would watch to see Jessica in action."

Meanwhile, Jessica's relationship with Ron Kershaw continued to boil over into her work life. "She was difficult to live with when she and Kershaw got into their matches," offers Ron Stone. "One day she and Ron Cutchall, the cameraman, were out somewhere on a story, and Jess got mad at Ron Kershaw and threw a fit and locked herself in the bathroom at a filling station. Cutchall called in on the radio and said, 'You've got to come over here. She's in there kicking and screaming and won't come out.' I think it was Dick John who went over and settled her down. And as I recall, she went about doing her story that day as if nothing ever happened. Best I can figure, she and Kershaw either screwed all the time or fought all the time. I don't think there was any in-between."

Dick John was usually the person Jessica called whenever things got out of hand. Bob Nicholas thought they had something of a father-daughter relationship, since Dick was eighteen years older than she, but that they had also "married each other in a strange, but healthy, way." Jessica was a bomb waiting to explode, he says, and Dick John was the only person who could get her under control.

During the time Jessica worked at KHOU, John says, she telephoned him at home "between a half dozen and a dozen times" to say that Ron Kershaw had just left, and that, as she told him, he had turned into a monster. Usually the calls came in the small hours of the morning, and Jessica would be sobbing.

"My wife would get me out of bed, and I'd go over to the apartment to get Jessica patched up," he remembers. "I've seen her with both eyes black and blue, and all up and down. She was lucky she didn't suffer a broken cheekbone, because he'd really punch her out." John recalls that she often took time off from work to recover.

"I'd say, 'Fine. When the cosmetics are right, and you're right, come on back.' Then I'd send word up and down the line that Jessica was either on assignment or not feeling well. But she would not walk away [from the relationship]. Some people have a deep-seated need to do penance, and I think maybe that's what it was. If it had become public that Ron Kershaw from [Channel] 13 was beating up Jessica Savitch at [Channel] 11, it would have been cataclysmic."

Sometimes Jessica would complain to the Hofheinzes. "I don't understand [that relationship] at all, and never did," says Fred Hofheinz. "Jessica was a hot little chick, and Kershaw was possessive, and sullen, and wasn't exactly Mr. Personality. He was the last guy in the world you'd match up with her."

They fought for a myriad of reasons. The most basic was that they knew each other so well—and had given the other such power—that they felt threatened by their very intimacy and their vulnerability to each other. The slightest comment could escalate into a rage, followed by a shattering night of terror. "We did horrible things to each other," Kershaw says, breaking down.

After the rage had passed, he would sit in his apartment, play his records, and cry aloud: "Oh, Brat, I'm sorry I did that. It was the evil craziness in me. I'm a good Rabbit sometimes."

"She could be unbelievably forgiving to him," says one of her friends. "He would beat the shit out of her, but then after she calmed down, she'd tell him, 'All of us carry twelve-year-olds around inside of us. It was the twelve-year-old Rabbit who couldn't understand the twelve-year-old abandoned Brat. And the twelve-year-old Brat who couldn't help but hurt the twelve-year-old Rabbit.' It was incredible."

Dick Williams understood why Jessica would never be able to give Kershaw up. "Aside from this magnetism they had for each other, no two people needed each other more," he observes. "But we're talking about this crazy thing called television. And Kersh knew that 'Jessica Savitch, television anchorwoman' was an illusion. And he knew how to preserve the illusion. She *knew* that he knew that, and that he knew how to keep her on top, so she had to have him. His advice was always the best advice she got."

On July 13, 1972, Jessica and Ron got into difficulty of another kind. The episode had begun the day before, when two men from Washington—an Ethiopian citizen on a student visa and a man

119

identified as "a father of a big family"—commandeered National
Airlines Flight 496 during a run from Miami to New York. They
demanded $500,000 and two parachutes, and planned, once these
were obtained, to jump out over Mexico and disappear. The
money was provided on a stop in Philadelphia, where the hijackers
released the 113 passengers and switched aircraft, taking four
stewardesses hostage, in addition to the pilot and flight engineer.

After several stops, including one in Dallas early on the morning of July 13, the hijackers forced the plane down at the unlikely
Dow Chemical Company commuter strip at Lake Jackson, Texas,
some fifty miles south of Houston, near Freeport. The big 727
barely managed to come to a stop before it overshot the tiny
5,000-foot runway, blowing four tires in the process. The hijackers
then pushed the now-injured pilot and the flight engineer from the
plane, and held the stewardesses at gunpoint for nearly eight
hours. Law enforcement officers and newspeople swarmed to the
scene.

Jessica, hoping for another lead story, was one of the first
media people to arrive at the little airstrip, taking her place with
the rest of the press at a hangar a quarter of a mile from the plane.
But by the time Ron Kershaw and his KTRK photographer, Greg
Moore, drove to the site, Brazoria County sheriffs, Lake Jackson
volunteer firemen, and Department of Public Safety (DPS) officers
had barricaded the entrance to the airport, refusing to admit additional reporters to the premises. Kershaw, who was driving,
steered deliberately around the roadblock, only to be stopped
again. Greg Moore, on the passenger side, got out to negotiate,
while Kershaw's colleague, Allen Pengelly, who had helicoptered
in earlier, came running with his camera. The story, still on file at
KTRK, shows the ensuing scuffle, which began when a DPS officer
reached inside the automobile and tried to wrestle Kershaw's silent
Bell & Howell Filmo from his hands. Kershaw held on, and the
officer then pulled him from the car.

At this point, Jessica, wearing sunglasses and a pink and white
pants suit, charged into the fray, shrieking for the officer to let him
go, at the same time capturing the event with her microphone.
Kershaw, cut on the chin, and the officer, still scuffling, then fell
into a shallow drainage ditch. They were rolling around in the dirt
when the furious Jessica went to Kershaw's aid, swiftly kicking the
downed officer twice in the kidney region. When it was over, Jes-

sica, Ron, and Greg Moore were arrested and taken to the Lake Jackson police station, where Moore was charged with failure to obey a police officer, and Ron and Jessica with assault. The three spent several hours in jail until their stations bailed them out; by that time, the hostages had been released and the hijackers had surrendered. Charges against the journalists were dismissed five days later.

It was an event that would cement Jessica's reputation within the local media as something of a loose cannon. Again, as in the Gus Mutscher situation, she had become the news she was there to report, at the expense of full coverage for her own station. At six o'clock, Jessica went on the KHOU set and calmly related the events of the hijacking. But KTRK had the hijacking *and* the scuffle. Dick John, a sinking feeling in his stomach, switched channels to see his star reporter playing a prominent role in his competitor's lead story. "That foot belongs to Jessica Savitch," Ron Kershaw, sitting on the anchor desk, said in his voice-over narration. "Always one to stand up for freedom of the press." The episode earned Jessica a three-day suspension from KHOU—the first time a reporter had received such censuring in the history of the station—as well as an FBI file.

During one of the several periods when Dick John and his wife were separated ("we've been married, divorced, and married"), John asked Jessica on a date. "She knew that I liked her, that I had a real strong attraction to her," he says, sitting in the lounge at the old Ramada Inn where Jessica had stayed sixteen years before. "And she liked me." He stops to think it over, takes a sip of his drink, and the words just slip out: "In a very special way, I loved her."

That first night, he remembers, they went to a restaurant on Westheimer, where they enjoyed "a wonderful dinner and a lot of wine," and later went dancing at a Greek taverna. "She went wild out there on the floor," he recalls, smiling. "And I wasn't prepared to keep up with her, except I tried. We had a hell of a time. People just vacated the floor." When her date took her back to Allen House, Jessica invited him in.

"We sat down, and she was smoking a funny cigarette of some kind, when all of a sudden, she just keeled over," he says. "But then she stood up and tried to walk into another room, and fell right through the glass-top coffee table." John, frightened that she

121

had badly cut herself, rushed to pick her up. But Jessica, miraculously unharmed, had passed out. The news director carried her into her bedroom, removed her shoes and outer clothing, and tucked her into bed. Then he left. For years, the episode puzzled him. He was never certain that she hadn't faked the fainting—"It wasn't enough wine for her to pass out"—and he wondered how she'd managed to fall through a table.

Some time later, Jessica was in her apartment with Ron Kershaw. The two had lit candles and incense, done some cocaine, as Jessica would later tell a friend, and had made love. Still unclothed, Ron and Jessica began to chase each other through the apartment. Somehow, she fell backwards and again went down on the glass-top table, this time cutting her back and her upper arms. "It wasn't so bad that she couldn't administer to herself," Carl Cochran remembers. "But exactly how it happened is a throw of the dice."

Both incidents may have been nothing more than Jessica's heedlessness, her general disregard for caution. Earlier in the year, for instance, she had apparently suffered a drug overdose, necessitating an ambulance. But she was also preoccupied. In September, she had told the Rands that she was starting her "great paper and videotape blitz" of all the networks, stations, and bureaus in which she'd like to work. The "big move," she said, was still being engineered by Joan Showalter, with whom she was constantly on the telephone.

But by this time, Jessica was getting plenty of offers on her own. Recently, she'd gotten a call from Tom Becherer, who had tried to persuade his boss to hire her in St. Louis the year before. Now Becherer was the news director at Baltimore's WJZ, a Group W station, and he hoped he could lure her back east.

"In those days," says Becherer, "Westinghouse had five-year contracts. And I attempted to sell Jessica on this over the telephone. But she felt her career was about to take off, and she resisted. I was schmoozing her something fierce, and trying to make her feel this was the greatest opportunity of a lifetime. And she said, 'But Tom, five years! In five years I'll be thirty years old!'"

Thirty, of course, was Jessica's target age for making it to the network. She couldn't afford to get tied up that long in Baltimore. Nevertheless, Becherer thought he'd convinced her to come. He was drafting the contract when he got a phone call from the program vice-president in charge of news for Westinghouse Broadcasting, Joel Chaseman—the man to whom Jessica had shown the horrible CBS audition tape a year and a half before, who had spotted her "star quality." Becherer didn't get many calls from the important executive, and he was, as it puts it, "shaking in my boots."

"You've been talking to Jessica Savitch," Chaseman said.

"Yeah, I've got great news! I got her to agree to a five-year contract! She's coming to Baltimore!"

"Get out of it," Chaseman said. "They need her in Philadelphia more than you need her in Baltimore. And they won't even talk to her until you get out of the picture."

Some time before, Jim Topping, the handsome, collegiate-looking news director for KDKA, Group W's Pittsburgh station, had breezed through Houston on a talent hunt. Westinghouse had assigned Topping and several other news directors to tour the country and evaluate reporters and anchor people, so that when the company needed new talent to come into the system, they knew where to find it.

Like others of his ilk, Topping would come to town, check into a hotel, and watch local news programs. "This was before three-quarter-inch tapes—they were two-inch tapes at the time—so we didn't travel with portable tape machines, just wrote up little cards and sent them into the central office." Topping flipped on KHOU and saw Jessica Savitch. He liked her.

When Topping got back to Pittsburgh, he mentioned Jessica to his boss, program manager Dave Salzman, a twenty-eight-year-old whiz kid on his way up. But before Salzman could pursue the recommendation, he had left KDKA to become program director at the Westinghouse flagship station, KYW, the NBC affiliate in Philadelphia, where he'd been brought in as a "fixer." In the last year, WPVI, the ABC affiliate, had hired an anchor named Larry Kane who had, in the words of Jim Topping, "blown everybody out of the water." KYW fell from first to second place in the market, and everybody was worried.

Dave Salzman remembered what Jim Topping had said about Jessica Savitch, and he called her to see if she might be interested in coming to Philadelphia. Jessica told him she'd send him a tape. She was positively glowing when she hung up the phone. Philadelphia was the fourth largest market in the country, and a giant step closer to a network job. And there was an added incentive: validation. Philadelphia television served both Kennett Square and South Jersey. Everyone from home would see her.

The problem was that as a Westinghouse station, KYW would demand a five-year contract. When Dave Salzman called back and asked Jessica to come up to talk, she naturally turned to Kershaw for advice. They had talked of marriage, and what affected one would affect the other. One day, they planned to leave structured television and go off to do creative projects of their own. Kershaw told her to hold out, no matter what they proposed, for at least a second offer. "Make 'em come kiss your ass," he said. Jessica promised not to sign anything until she checked with him. She said she was really using the free plane ticket to visit her mother.

Before she left for Philadelphia, Jessica went to see Dean Borba—who to this day cannot remember if he had a contract with her—and told him she'd had offers from other markets. Borba was hardly surprised. She was extraordinarily talented, and she'd been working for a pittance: He was currently paying her $9,800 a year—her salary of $135 a week, plus a fee for anchoring. (She had asked for a $1,000 raise, and the New York office had refused.)

"I said, 'Jessica, who's talking to you?' " Borba recalls. She told him Westinghouse. Borba hated to see her go, but he knew it was futile to try to get her to stay. For the moment, at least, he would act as her agent. He was familiar with Westinghouse contracts. He warned her what they would entail, and told her what clauses she should try to get stricken if possible. "She said, 'How much do you think I should ask for?' " he remembers. They discussed $20,000, more than twice what she was making at KHOU.

"Whatever you do," Borba said, "don't fence yourself in at the top. If you happen to hit it big, and you get an offer from a network, you don't want a contract that throttles you from moving when the moment's right. If a network says they want you, it's because they have an opening, and it might not exist in two years when your contract expires."

But when Jessica got on the plane to come back to Houston, she had forgotten all that advice. All she knew was that she had signed a five-year contract at $17,000 a year. Salzman had been vague about her anchoring duties—she really had been signed as a reporter—but Jessica knew an anchoring job was in the bag. And in Jessica's "Wouldn't it be nice, therefore it is!" way of thinking, Ron had a job in Philadelphia, too.

"She fuckin' *lied*!" Ron Kershaw bellows in a Chicago apartment in 1987. "She told me she wouldn't sign a deal, she came back, she said she didn't sign a deal, and that she *knew* that the ABC station would give me a job, and that we'd go live in a gingerbread house in Philadelphia and be very happy. Hey!" Kershaw shouts, pacing the floor, "what kind of variance of the truth is *that*? Give me a fuckin' break! But she *allowed it to happen*. Selling her soul, taking the low road because her insecurity drove her to do it. Five fuckin' years for that kind of money, for a megastar! People went to Botany Bay with better deals than that! They should have paid *tons* for her, and they would today."

In years to come, people would say Kershaw was jealous of Jessica's success, that he didn't want to see women advance in the industry, even though he would go on to hire some of the best in the business. "That was her cliché remark," he counters. "She should never have left Houston. That was Jessica Savitch's stupidity, her rank ambitiousness, to try to climb the ladder, because she was too afraid to sit back and wait for things to come to her. They victimized her, because they're petty motherfuckers. They fucked up her life, and mine. And she brought it on us."

Kershaw would eventually see if WPVI, the Philadelphia ABC affiliate that was, like KTRK, owned by Capital Cities, would give him a job. But in the days immediately following Jessica's return, no amount of consolation would tame him. Jessica insisted that she had gotten a verbal promise to be released from her contract should a bigger job come along, or even if she wasn't happy. Kershaw laughed in her face. Worse, he told her, this incessant lying had jeopardized their future. How could he trust a woman who lied to him all the time? It drove him nuts. For a while, he did not even want to see her.

Jessica ached with indecision. Years later, she would talk about it to her friend Lonnie Reed. "It was so sad," Reed says, "because she had worked so hard. She was really moving in her career, and yet this new job was going to take her away from this man she thought she loved, and who was, in many ways, bad for her. So she really wasn't excited about her new job opportunity at all. She saw it as, 'Oh, God, I'm actually going to get what I dreamed about, and it's not going to make me happy.' That was always her worst nightmare."

Now, some four weeks after the second incident with the glass-top table, Jessica reached for a razor blade and cut an inch-and-a-half-long gash on her neck. From there, she turned the blade to one wrist and then the other.

"I always felt that particular attempt was more a cry for sympathy than anything else," says Carl Cochran. "The neck wound was superficial, but she did a little better job on her wrists than she intended to. It was a real mess, very grim. But even if there had been no medical treatment, I don't think she would have died. If you looked at the treatment involved, you could characterize it as a suicide attempt, yes. But if you delved into the motivation, I don't think there was real intent for death."

The word went through the newsroom like a hurricane. "It was like, Jesus Christ! Jess tried to kill herself!" Ron Stone remembers. But soon Jessica was back at work, wearing long-sleeve blouses to cover the bandages on her wrists, and tying her scarves a little more fully at the neck.

Before long Cochran found he could joke with her about it. "It was almost like she had self-inflicted marks on her wrists and corresponding marks on the backs of her arms from going through the table. I said, 'Oh, fine, you had to have a matched set. You weren't content to have any patch of skin on your body without a scratch or a bandage,'" he recounts. "And we would laugh." In years to come, Jessica would tell new friends that she had tried to commit suicide in Houston. But by then, the story had a practiced, breezy tone.

Jessica was to begin her new duties on Monday, November 13, 1972. Barely two years ago, she had been collecting time sheets at WCBS.

Steve Edwards and his wife gave her a going-away party. She arrived with Kershaw, but the tension was high between them. Kershaw sat there as long as he could, drinking and listening to people wish Jessica well, reliving the time she did this, the time she did that. Laughing. Finally, a mild altercation. Kershaw left on foot, in the rain.

"I knew walking back from Steve Edwards's party what would happen when we left Houston," he says today. "I didn't know about Joel Chaseman or Dave Salzman, but I knew what would happen. I just didn't know how hard it would be."

Later, he had a dream, he would tell her, "a nightmare, in which the two of us were on this road walking. It was cold and foggy, a grey kind of light. I remember calling to her, but she couldn't hear. I tried running, but my legs were like cement—they would hardly move. I had this deep panic—this terror—to protect her from what seemed a sinister place and presence. But she just floated away into the mist, like she was sleepwalking." He woke up, he says, "sweating with night fever."

On her last day at the station, Jessica looked around the newsroom one last time. By the time she saw Dick John, she was misty-eyed. John reached out to hug her. "You guys sure are different," she told him, tears trickling down her face. "But I'm glad I met you."

Houston was over. "She always had trouble enjoying the moment," as Lonnie Reed would say. "She was always living on the next page."

4

The Fourth Largest Market: Philadelphia

Jessica arrived in Philadelphia without Ron Kershaw, who stayed on in Houston, trying to make sense of it all. They would talk on the phone at night, but the conversations almost always turned into painful arguments. When Jessica would tell him how much she missed him—and his children, Beau and Lee Ann—Kershaw was alternately heartbroken and furious.

"You should have thought of that before you left!" he would reply in a caustic tone. Then Jessica would begin to cry and beg him to come to Philadelphia, saying she wasn't sure she had what it took to survive in such a large market by herself. Ron would say that first she'd nailed his feet to the deck, then jumped overboard and yelled to him that she was drowning. Soon the screaming would start. It would go on for half the night.

During the day, there were different pressures. Each morning, when Jessica showed up at KYW, a brown brick fortress at 5th and Market streets on Independence Mall East, she was nervous and apprehensive, fully aware that she had to prove herself all over again to a new audience, a whole new set of fellow reporters, and a new management team that hadn't been there long itself: Jim Topping, who had spotted her down in Houston, had come from Pittsburgh to take on the news director duties, and Alan Bell, formerly with Group W in Baltimore, had only recently been installed as the general manager. Things were still in a state of flux as Topping, Bell, and Dave Salzman, the program director who had hired her, figured out how to bump WPVI, the ABC affiliate, from number one.

The first order of business had been to introduce an early weekday broadcast, "Newswatch 5:30," anchored by Mort Crim, the straightforward, pleasant newsman just up from WHAS, the CBS affiliate in Louisville. It would be an innovation if they could lock in a news audience at 5:30 and roll it over to the six o'clock "Eyewitness News" show, the bastion of Vince Leonard, dean of the Philadelphia anchormen—then they might have a chance to outflank their competitor.

Jessica might have been expected to try to fit in gracefully until she learned her way and impressed her new employers. Instead, she came to work sporting fringed, Western clothing, and her hair teased in the familiar Texas style. Nevertheless, veteran KYW reporter Malcolm Poindexter remembers her as flexible and easygoing, at least in the beginning. When she finally got on the air with a short feature about recycling garbage, she told the Rands that "two days a week, I come in and do an in-depth story—as 'in-depth' as superficiality can be." On the other three days, she said, she would report to work and have her hair and makeup done, and appear on the eleven o'clock news as the station's New Jersey correspondent to "read things that are written for me."

Later, Jessica would joke that for years, in the minutes before airtime, she was forced to elbow her way into KYW's first-floor lavatory and share its mirror with the blue-haired ladies who attended the "Mike Douglas Show," taped on the station's premises. She would have to slather on her makeup and lacquer her hair under their admiring, persistent gaze, and found the experience so unpleasant that she fought for and eventually won a makeup mirror of her own.

As for going on the air and reading material that someone else had written for her, KYW was indeed a union shop, with editors—

"producers" in today's language—preparing the scripts, as Carl Cochran had done for her in Houston. But Jessica was not above checking out facts, nor was she above making sure that she understood everything she read on the air. Shortly after she arrived in Philadelphia, she was preparing her Sunday night newscast and found she needed clarification on a story. She walked upstairs to KYW-AM, the 50,000-watt radio station which had broadcast an all-news format since September 1965.

Karen Fox, the news correlator, responsible for gathering breaking news, remembers her as "the only TV reporter who ever came in person to check out a story." This time, Jessica asked for an editor named Dave Neal, who had started his career in New Jersey and was generally regarded in the building as the specialist on that state. Born David Gomberg, the forty-seven-year-old Neal was a former shoe salesman who had drifted into the business in the days when shtick was everything. Neal was a much-loved individual; gruff and menacing on the outside, he was a loving husband and father, and in the words of one of his colleagues, "a big, beautiful hush puppy." He also considered himself a feminist. Now he looked up from his desk to see what appeared to him to be a refugee from "Hee Haw."

"Somebody told me you're a nice guy and you'd help me out," Jessica said.

"I turned around to everybody and said, 'My God! Look at this!'" Neal remembers. "'This little *shiksa* has come to Philadelphia wearing cowboy boots with horseshit on the heels.'"

Jessica informed the garrulous Neal that she was not a *shiksa* at all. "Oh yeah?" Neal shot back, raising his bushy eyebrows. "Then we've gotta make a JAP [Jewish American Princess] out of you."

The standards of television reporting in Philadelphia differed greatly from those in Houston. From the initial demonstration of both her reporting and reading skills, most of Jessica's Channel 3 colleagues regarded her as inexperienced, even as little more than a trainee—not quite ready for the fourth largest market.

"When she first came, she was really not very good," recalls Mort Crim, now at WDIV-TV in Detroit. "She still had a very noticeable lisp. But you could see that the potential was there."

Jessica was turning heads just the same. Bill Mandel, then a writer for the *Philadephia Bulletin,* remembers standing outside

KYW talking with a friend the first week she arrived in town. A KYW news car pulled up, and "this beautiful young woman" got out with her crew. Mandel, two years younger than Jessica, introduced himself, and welcomed her to the Delaware Valley's journalistic community. Jessica flashed him a smile that nearly knocked him down.

Back in Houston, Ron Kershaw was aggravating himself about whom Jessica was meeting, and just exactly what she was doing with her time. She assured him that she wasn't seeing anyone, that she spent most of her evenings at the station. Kershaw began to call her at KYW to check up on her. The reporters' cubbyholes were small and close together, and most of the newsroom heard everything that went on. Vince Leonard, born Homer Leonard Venske, who had been at KYW since 1958, was astounded to experience these sessions, which were not infrequent. "She would be sitting there quietly one moment, and the next she would virtually explode. There would be *a lot* of crying, a lot of emotion."

Soon, Kershaw came for a visit, and since Jessica was staying with friends until she found an apartment, he checked into a hotel. There he and Jessica would repeat their frenzied cycle of fighting and loving. One moment they would agree that the relationship could never work, and the next they would pledge to marry. Finally, they faced the realization that they did not seem to be able to function without each other. Jessica said she would forgive Ron for his physical assaults if he would forgive her for signing the Westinghouse contract. They became engaged on Christmas Day, 1972, and planned a spring wedding. Jessica wore his ring.

When Kershaw got back to Houston, he told Walt Hawver, his news director, that he intended to move to Philadelphia. Hawver and his wife had often had Ron and Jessica over to dinner, and Hawver remembers asking him if he were sure he was making the right decision. "But he was very much in love. Just starry-eyed."

Hawver, a respected figure in the Capital Cities chain, told Kershaw he would call Mel Kampmann, the news director at WPVI in Philadelphia, Capital Cities' flagship station, and tell him that one of his best people was moving to town and ought to stay in the company. When Kershaw called Kampmann himself to confirm, the story goes, Kampmann said he knew about him, and that he would find a place for him in the shop. Jessica told the Rands that she thought she and Ron would "live happily ever after," and in

131

anticipation of their new life together, rented a garden apartment, number 623, at 4000 Gypsy Lane in southwest Philadelphia.

So it was that Ron Kershaw moved to Philadelphia, reasonably assured of a job. But when Mel Kampmann discovered that Kershaw's girlfriend was Jessica Savitch of Channel 3, he immediately withdrew his offer, explaining that he couldn't have an employee who was dating the competition. Furthermore, Kershaw reports, Kampmann said he doubted that anyone in the market would give Kershaw a job once they learned of the relationship, no matter how good he was.

As Kershaw left the station, Kampmann's words rang like echoes in his ears. In that one terrible moment he knew that his relationship with Jessica would never be the same. It meant the end of everything they had planned, everything they had shared, and the beginning of what Kershaw would refer to as his "unending night fever," a slow motion spiraling toward immeasurable grief and loss. In her heart, Jessica knew it too. She told the Rands that she spent every moment trying to work out an alternative, even though she was sure there wasn't one.

To Ron, however, Jessica tried to minimize the impact. She told him she was certain she would be able to do something, and approached Dave Salzman about Kershaw working at KYW. In 1980, the husband and wife team of Don Farmer and Chris Curle would make history co-anchoring on the Cable News Network, but in 1973 such a practice was strictly against the rules of most companies. At Westinghouse, the policy was especially stringent. Salzman said no.

From there, Jessica tried Bob Morse, the news director at Philadelphia's CBS owned-and-operated station, WCAU. Morse liked Jessica. He, too, had tried to hire her before she signed with KYW. But Morse told her he didn't need Kershaw, and what's more, that he didn't think Kershaw's tape was very good. Now, despite the Westinghouse policy, Jessica picked up the phone and told Joel Chaseman she was putting Ron's tape in the mail. A few days later, Chaseman called back. "That's the best produced audition tape I've ever seen," he told her. "But I don't like the reporter."

In the days to come, neither Ron nor Jessica could bring themselves to mention the topic. Kershaw felt as if his limbs were frozen, as if he were a man three times his age. He could not move, could not speak, without extreme effort. Finally, one evening on Gypsy Lane, wearing a Snoopy shirt her father had given her long ago, Jessica turned to Kershaw and told him she could not stand the guilt any longer. A fight ensued, and when it was over, the Snoopy shirt was in tatters.

"I was so bad to her," Kershaw says, choking back tears. "I don't know why, except it was so important for me to be something in her eyes, and no matter what I did, I couldn't make up for failing her in Philadelphia. It meant so much to me that she respect me, and yet the people she respected more rejected me. I don't know why they wouldn't give me a job. I could have helped them. I could have made money for them. I would have worked myself to death for them, just to be in the same ballpark that she wanted to play in. I loved her so," he says, his head in his hands, "but it drove me crazy. It just kept going on, over and over, in my mind." Until her death, Kershaw never went into a clothing store without searching for a Snoopy shirt for his Jessica Beth.

In early 1973, Jessica was promoted to weekend anchor, just as Dave Salzman had implied when he had hired her away from Houston. The management troika agreed that it was a good idea. Two years earlier—the year Jessica went to Texas—the Federal Communications Commission had handed down a ruling prohibiting discrimination in the hiring and promotion of women in broadcasting. Stations now had to file affirmative action plans for women as a requirement for license renewal. Only months after Jessica assumed her anchor chair, the Philadelphia chapter of the National Organization for Women (NOW) would attempt to win serious recognition from the news media, particularly TV. KYW management would invite members of the local chapter to meet with the entire news staff—anchors, reporters, and producers. NOW wanted more coverage for their own activities, their representatives said, but they also wanted more women in visible reporting and anchor roles.

As it was, the station already had several female reporters on staff, but none had a truly high profile, and none was a bona fide star. Certainly not Trudy Haynes, the black woman who had been the first female in all of Philadelphia TV news. Haynes was considered a bit too old for that, and far too staid. Orien Reid was livelier; she, too, was black, but hardly considered a breakthrough personality. A third, Marciarose Shestack was "enormously popular with other Marciarose types, which is to say she had a very narrow but definable appeal to the affluent, the literate, the sophisticated, and the middle-aged," says then station manager Alan Bell.

That left Jessica Savitch—young, bright, and hip.

Alan Bell saw how it all could fit together. "Jessica's real appeal was not to men," says Bell, now with Lorimar Telepictures in Culver City, California. "Her fans were young professional women and young blue-collar women—people who writhed with the injustice of being kicked around just because they happened to be born female. They rooted for someone who appeared to be doing a man's job."

There was another plus to putting Jessica on the weekend anchor desk. KYW, the station of choice for the sophisticated, intelligent, and serious-minded, traditionally appealed to the middle class, the upper-middle class, and the wealthy Philadelphia Main Line residents over fifty. It desperately needed a news personality who could attract the middle-majority and the eighteen- to forty-nine-year-olds. That share of the market generally watched WPVI, the station's major competitor.

Before the year was up, Alan Bell would begin to groom Jessica for an even more important role in the organization. Bell, a Harvard man who was witty and esoteric, had big plans for Jessica Savitch. He saw that she had a magic way before the camera, that "She was able to take something that really wasn't there in life, and push it through the machinery and come out a totally different being."

In the weeks to come, Jessica told the Rands that the turmoil with Ron had almost paralyzed her. There was so much yet to absorb in her new work situation that she was now trying to think only of herself, and not the relationship. At home at night, she and Ron were "trying not to step on each other," she told them. "Sometimes it is so good, and when it's not, it's hell. I'm just taking it day by day and holding on."

While Jessica was at work, Ron would be alone in the apartment with the cat. Sveltie sensed his frustration and anger and quickly grew afraid of him.

But shortly, Jessica would install another person in the apartment—Carl Cochran, her producer and friend from Houston. While the KHOU staff was fully aware that Carl had moved to Philadelphia and taken up residence with her, except for one brief mention to Jim Topping, Jessica never talked about Carl around KYW. In the analogy that she had laid out for Kershaw, Carl Cochran occupied his own secret drawer of her life. Back in Houston, it had been obvious to all that Cochran adored her, that "He would have done absolutely anything under the sun for her," as Ron Franklin remembers. Cochran had been almost as anxious for Jessica to succeed as she was herself. Now, she would call upon him for all manner of propping up, from help in the creation of her pieces to taking care of the chores around the apartment.

Since Kershaw was often gloomy and sullen, and Jessica so completely dependent on him for emotional support and well-being, Cochran, who had moved to Philadelphia "with every intention of doing some writing," found himself devoting more and more time to buoying Jessica's spirits. Often that meant sharing her growing indulgence for drugs. At the time they lived on Gypsy Lane, Cochran says, their consumption of marijuana stayed at the same high recreational level they had reached in Houston. But now their occasional, exploratory use of cocaine had progressed to the frequent recreational level as well.

Neither was worried about it. News magazines reported that cocaine was not physically addictive, and that it was only somewhat psychologically addictive. Today, researchers know that even with non-addicts, cocaine use changes the brain chemistry, producing exaggerated lows and false highs, as well as feelings of aggression, anxiety, and paranoia. The drug also attacks bone marrow and muscle fiber, suppresses sex hormones, and impairs the immune system. It also constricts the blood vessels, thus starving the entire body of proper nutrition.

"Cocaine use is a four-step process," explains Cochran, who sought treatment for substance abuse several years ago. "First you do it because it's hip and it's fun. Then you do it because of the energy it gives you. After that, you do it just to maintain that energy level and to avoid the dreaded fall-off and despair. And then in the last stage—which I believe Jessica was in at the time she died—you continue to use it as a combatant to irrational paranoia."

By the time they lived on Gypsy Lane, Cochran says, Jessica was at step two, enamored of cocaine for the energy it gave her, "since she was prone to work herself into a stupor." Soon, Cochran realized that the drug use was having a disastrous effect on both of them. Despite having made great headway in his writing, he would have to put it aside to tend to Jessica's disintegrating personal life. "By the time I got to Philadelphia," he says, "her emotional needs were such that resolution required almost twenty-four-hour a day attention."

While Cochran attempted to take care of Jessica at home, Dave Neal had become her protector at work. She was happy that Neal, with whom she was beginning to have an almost familial bond, had recently moved over to the television side of the operation, first as assignment editor and then as assistant news director under Jim Topping. What she didn't know was that Alan Bell had "assigned" Neal to her, that he had made Neal her "rabbi," someone who could help mold her until Bell called her into play to take KYW back up to the top. At times, Neal's first order of business was holding Jessica together for the duration of the day.

Now that Jessica was anchoring, and beginning to achieve a reputation around town, she decided Kershaw was right: She wasn't being paid enough money. She was irritable in the newsroom, drawing flack from her colleagues, and getting into battles. Part of her discontent came from the realization that she needed to improve herself—to take speech lessons, for example—and that she didn't have the money to do it. When she first appeared on the anchor desk, word had gone around the building that she had no personality on the air, that "she looked like a military news reader from the Argentinian Army." She was terrified that unless she made some improvements immediately, she would be tossed out of the market, perhaps never to get her shot at the network.

Dave Neal was now ensconced in the assistant news director's seat, with only a sliding glass partition separating his office from that of Jim Topping. One day Neal was working at his desk when he heard Jessica screaming at Topping that she needed more money. As she left Topping's office, Neal motioned for her to come in.

"I said, 'Look, you're in there fighting for a lousy fifty bucks a week. By the time they take the taxes out, you're only going to get twenty. Don't go in there and ask for money. Go in and say you want them to send you for speech lessons. Go in and say you want to get your hair done, a new wardrobe. They'll be happy to help you improve yourself, because you'll be better on the air." Neal saw a look of recognition flicker across her face. "Quit acting like a *shiksa*!" he told her, waving a finger in her face, and bringing it to rest on the end of her nose. "Think Jewish!"

Because Neal figured, "She's an anchorwoman—she ought to look like a movie star," the cosmetic changes came first. Jessica had been extremely self-conscious about a chipped tooth, and Neal arranged for a dentist to cap "three or four" in front. Next came a wardrobe for air. Initially, Jessica struck a deal with Jones of New York, which supplied not only the clothing, but because she was insecure about what tops went with which bottoms, also a master coordinating chart. In time, Neal would set her up with the Blum Store in Bala Cynwyd, where owner Rita Rappaport would dress her in "ice cream shades—peaches and pale greens—and blouses, or sweaters, with blazers, and scarves to accent her eyes." Rita would eventually become a close friend, but Jessica joked about the look in private, calling herself "the Human Barbie Doll—dress me up, put on my eyelashes, and send me on the set."

The change that would draw the most viewer mail by far was Jessica's new hairstyle. Bill Mandel, the *Philadelphia Bulletin* writer who had now become a friend, suggested that she go to a stylist named Barry Leonard. Leonard, whose sign read, Barry Leonard, Crimper, ran the "only unisex, hip barbershop in town," as Mandel puts it. "He looked kind of like George Hamilton," he says. "The clients would be arranged in a circle, and then he would dance around the circle cutting, while assistants would blow dry and roll."

Leonard went to work. Jessica's hair had a kinky texture which needed smoothing for TV so that the light would reflect off of it, not refract. And he saw that she needed to darken her "all different varieties of blond," since television lights tend to make hair look lighter than it actually is. Finally, he knew that her schedule was such that she needed a style she could manage herself, without weekly trips to the shop. The result was a distinctive bob, but, as he says, "with a little different feeling to it," parted on the left-hand side, coming down and turning under. The hairstyle caught on. Soon little imitation Jessicas could be seen along the streets of Philadelphia and its suburbs.

Despite these improvements, Jessica kept insisting that what she really wanted was speech lessons. Jim Topping argued that there was only one coach worth going to, Lilyan Wilder, but Wilder was in New York. Aside from the time the commuting would take away from Jessica's duties, Wilder charged $50 an hour, and usually suggested two-hour sessions for people who came only once a week. Jessica insisted she would make up the time, if the station would pay the fee. Topping gave in.

Each week Jessica would drive to the 30th Street train station and take the Metroliner to New York. Then she would catch a cab to the East Side, where Wilder ran an office/studio out of her apartment. A petite, dynamic woman in her late forties at the time, Wilder was exacting and meticulous. She had been a Broadway and television actress, had studied with Lee Strasberg, and had taught voice and articulation at the Strasberg Theater Institute. Since 1969, she had been consulted by television stations from across the country, all wanting help with news personalities who needed to speak more clearly or who lacked certain on-camera presence. Soon she was recognized as the foremost speech consultant of her kind. None of her students would ally themselves as closely to her as Jessica Savitch.

"Jessica used her lisp as a kind of excuse to come to me," says Wilder, sitting in the studio of her Manhattan apartment, where Jessica's photograph stands in a frame on the table. "Her lisp, which was more of a tight-jawed lisp than a lateral lisp, was actually not that bad, but she had a nasality, a kind of 'aah' sound instead of an 'ah' sound. What she really came to me for was to develop the confidence she needed to be in front of a camera, and to deal with the mechanics of television. More than anything else, we worked on her delivery techniques and her presence."

At the beginning of each session, the two would review a tape of Jessica's most recent broadcast, analyzing how well she had brought out the content, the substance, and the depth of the stories, how she had presented whatever humor or tragedy the story carried, and how she had handled changes of thought. Wilder gave her a series of exercises to help her become what she calls "being private in public," to free her personality and her naturalness so that she might react spontaneously in a self-confident and commanding way. The idea was for her to allow herself to *be* herself with millions of people watching.

One of Wilder's exercises involved reading a TelePrompTer. "Whenever a person focuses on the TelePrompTer or the script," Wilder says, "it gives him a kind of vapid, sing-songy way of speaking, and a glazed look across the eyes. I taught Jessica the technique of imagining the camera as a real person, someone that she knows and is eager to share this information with."

The idea when reading a script, Wilder told her, was to give the first thought or sentence to the person she imagined she was speaking to, along with the beginning of the second sentence. Then she should look down at the material, and look up again to give the person the end of the thought.

"What was amazing to me," says Wilder, "is that she came back in a week and *knew* it! I was floored, because I had been doing this for *years* with people, and it would take them quite a while. I said, 'Jessica, how did you do it?' And she said, 'You told me to do it, so I did it.' "

Wilder would say that of all her students, Jessica applied herself the most. What she didn't know was that Jessica had been looking for such a passageway for the last two years. Long ago, when Jessica was making commercials in Rochester, Ann Rogers had first taught her to imagine the camera as a real person. But with news reporting, and scripts and TelePrompTers to consider, she had lost that vital connection. Now she found a way to regain it. Not only did Wilder instruct her to visualize the camera as a person she could get a response from, she also taught her student to "actually look into his eyes, to re-create a moment, to discourse with him about what you're talking about," as Wilder put it.

For the first few weeks after she began the sessions with Wilder, Jessica laid down a rule at KYW: Whenever she was reading the news, there was to be no sound or movement in the studio, no technicians walking across the room, and no kibbitzing. The studio must be secured, and only the camera and floor men allowed inside. She was determined that her performance would be an intense, uninterrupted experience between her and the camera. Perhaps she'd found her way back to David Savitch.

Jessica had already started thinking about the next step of her career. KYW was an NBC affiliate, but her ambition to be hired by a network still focused on the more prestigious CBS. To that end, she was frequently on the telephone to Joan Showalter, and now she also occasionally called Bob Morse, the news director at WCAU, and invited him to dinner. Since WCAU was CBS owned-and-operated, she hoped he knew the comings and goings of the various network correspondents. She was eager to hear about any job openings.

Jessica also kept up her contact with Westinghouse news executive Joel Chaseman, who would offer advice on the phone from New York and, whenever he was in Philadelphia, companionship over a meal and a movie. One particular chilly night, they walked around after the show, talking and munching on popcorn. Jessica spoke about her discontent.

"She wasn't yet established in Philadelphia, and didn't feel comfortable there," he remembers. "But Jessica always struck me as the kind of person who was never really satisfied. Every time she got to a goal, she found there wasn't much there for her. She was always searching, trying to be perfect. I don't think she ever had a month or two, or certainly not longer, of sustained enjoyment or fulfillment. She was always chasing a horizon, and it was always receding in front of her."

Jessica usually kept the existence of such meetings secret from Ron Kershaw, in part because he was jealous of even her most platonic relationships, and also because he had little patience with her constant quest for a network job. "Those letters—CBS, NBC, ABC—mean so much to you," he would taunt. "Why can't you just concentrate on doing good work?" But getting to the network was almost all that she thought of. Now, at twenty-six, she had started rolling back her age by a year. That way, if KYW did insist on holding her to her five-year contract, she could still say she had made it to the network before she was thirty.

She was getting noticed. As KYW's weekday anchors, Mort Crim and Vince Leonard received the major share of public exposure, but with her new hairstyle and wardrobe and the increased visibility she enjoyed as both a reporter and weekend anchor, Jessica was now recognized as part of the KYW news team. Soon, a New Jersey man named Jim Knapp set up "the Jessica Savitch Fan Club International." And Ida McGinniss, who ran a booking agency called The Speakers Bureau and represented several other KYW news personalities, began slating luncheon appearances for her at $150 a session. Carl Cochran wrote her speeches, and often even drove her to the dates. Because off-camera public speaking terrified her, and because she seemed wooden at the podium, Jessica began taking acting lessons. Within a year, Maury Levy of *Philadelphia* magazine would write that with the exception of her colleague Mort Crim, she was "probably the most honest, believable television news person in town."

As Jessica's star began to rise in Philadelphia, Ron Kershaw became increasingly anxious. Frozen out of the Philadelphia market, he was now beginning to explore work in other cities. He and Jessica agreed that if he found work elsewhere, they would buy a house between the two cities and commute to their jobs. But so far, he had had no luck, and the tension between them was mounting.

"I was so bitter about having made this move and her being so stupid as to have signed that deal," he says, "that it was like the Original Sin. If she got up from the table and bumped it and spilled my milk, the argument that would ensue would eventually get back to, 'Why did you tell that fuckin' lie?' I could not let it pass."

Kershaw had reason to be jealous. Now, away from both the apartment and the station, Jessica was beginning to keep a diverse array of company, forming relationships that would be tucked away in the most secluded compartments of her life.

One night when Ron was away on a job interview, she attended a party in Philadelphia. There, she struck up a conversation with a man in his early thirties who had been indicted on a federal charge involving fraudulent stock market tradings. For the next several months they would continue to see each other, although almost never in public.

Interviewed for this book with the understanding that he could speak freely without attribution, he explains today: "Here she was, trying to climb the ladder [of success], and there I was, embroiled in not exactly shady, but certainly unsavory activities. I was destitute, and I was facing prison, so in the interest of her career, dating was prohibited. She would never have taken a chance on my going to the station to meet her. I was a secret part of her life."

In the beginning, he recalls, the relationship was purely physical, to the extent that "there was almost no conversation the first couple of times." Aside from a shared interest in marijuana and cocaine ("I was into it fairly heavy, and the stuff she had was always the best available"), the attraction was based on what each represented to the outside world. He was enthralled with her celebrity, and "I think she liked the scoundrel in me, or what she thought I was. I represented a great 'letting go.' There was nothing she had to be ashamed of, because I was already coming from shame in my own life. I was the last person she would have to impress with her ethics or morals."

141

As the affair progressed, the sensual aspect of the relationship quickly diminished. He found that when they were together, Jessica just wanted "to get high and talk." Mostly, she wanted to talk about spiritualism and metaphysics. She told him she often wondered why she had been born, what place she had in the scheme of things, and what lessons she needed to learn in her time on earth. She said she felt like an impostor in her profession, that the others—Mort and Vince—deserved to be there, but she did not. "When are they going to catch me?" she asked him. "When are they going to know that I really don't belong?"

"The transformation from the time she was straight and the time she was high was really amazing," he says. "It was like we would go up into the balcony and watch her life, the same way you go up in the balcony for an overview of a theater. She would be almost like a little girl again. I remember asking her if she felt she were doing something important in the women's movement, because that's the way people were beginning to talk about her. But she said no, she was really only interested in being the leader of her family—to take the place of her father.

"There was a lot of self-disgust at times, but I think those moments were absolutely real—that that was the real Jessie, wishing that she could somehow be more conscious of her life. Of course, it took drugs to get her to that. Then she would have to put on the costume, and go back and be 'Jessica Savitch' again."

By this time, the hot-tempered Jessica that her colleagues had known in Houston was beginning to emerge in Philadelphia. Vince Leonard had seen enough outbursts in the newsroom that when *Philadelphia Bulletin* columnist Rex Polier criticized her in print as "just a charming, talking head" who conveyed no sense of authority or knowledge as an anchor, Leonard removed that section of the station's paper in the hope that Jessica wouldn't see it.

"I was just protecting myself," he offers with a laugh. Leonard, now of KPNX-TV in Phoenix, turns serious. "I'm sure she had some mental problems," he says. "No doubt about it."

The summer of 1973, Jessica went down to Atlantic City to do a story about the throngs of Philadelphians who headed there each day to the beach. Her soundman was Damon Sinclair, a recent college graduate. To add to the piece, Sinclair remembers that Jessica borrowed her baby nephew, Stephanie's child.

"She was standing there by the water's edge, holding this

infant in her arms and doing the stand-up," he says, "when a kid came up from behind and whacked her on the rear with a surfboard. She put that baby down and tore out after this kid, chasing him one hundred feet or so until she got him. She yelled, 'Look, you little motherfucker! Don't mess with *me!*' It was absolutely hilarious," he says. "I wish we'd filmed it."

Before long, Sinclair became a soundman for WPVI, and ran into Jessica several times when the two were covering the same events. He found that, like Jessica's colleagues in Houston, some of the Philadelphia reporters admired her aggressive technique while others resented her ambition—not just her upward mobility, but what some considered exhibitionism. She sometimes wore leather pants that were so tight, as one reporter remembers it, "that if she had a nickel in her back pocket, you could see Jefferson's portrait."

"There was a certain amount of arrogance to her," says Sinclair, "and while I had seen that sweet, shy side of her, I recognized that she didn't make an effort to be friendly with people. I remember one story everybody covered, about a woman in Chester, Pennsylvania, who had a statue of Jesus that supposedly bled—you know, the stigmata effect. People were lined up around the block to see this thing. Well, all the reporters were standing there joking about it, and Jessica went in and got the real interview and left. She was more focused, and she didn't care anything about being social with the other reporters. A lot of people thought that wasn't nice. But television news is an awful business, really. And you've got to be extremely well-adjusted to survive."

In June 1973, Ron Kershaw got on the train for the infamous Metroliner Run, familiar to every unemployed TV reporter, producer, and director on the East Coast. The idea was to ride the train into town, cab over to a station to talk about a job, and then get back on the Metroliner and do it all over again in the next city. In Washington, Kershaw was finally offered a job as a reporter, and he would have accepted on the spot had he not, while waiting for his appointment, read a news item in *Broadcasting.* It noted that Dick Williams had recently been named news director at WBAL, the Hearst Corporation–owned NBC affiliate in Baltimore. Kershaw thought he'd stop off and see him on his way back to Philadelphia.

The two had met on only one occasion, and four years before,

143

but Kershaw and Dick Williams had a bond. Williams had been Walt Hawver's protegé in Albany, New York, before Hawver had moved on to KTRK in Houston, where he had inherited Ron Kershaw. Kershaw so resembled Williams in looks, in instincts, and in writing skills that Hawver had called his old friend and said, "You won't believe this, but I've got your twin down here!" And the two were, for all practical purposes, each other's alter ego, with the same outlook on how to do television news.

In Baltimore, Dick Williams told Kershaw he couldn't give him a reporter's job, but that he desperately needed an assistant. He was up against WJZ, the exceedingly strong local Westinghouse station, and nobody thought there was a prayer of turning things around. If Kershaw took the job, he would be working in the nineteenth market—far from the top-ten market prestige of Washington. But Kershaw liked the challenge, and accepted. The station's June 5, 1973, press release announced that Kershaw was joining WBAL as the producer of the seven o'clock news; in October, he would be officially named assistant news director.

Now Kershaw moved his belongings from Gypsy Lane into a modern, shag-carpeted apartment at 1811 Rambling Ridge Road, in the sprawling Twin Ridge complex on the north side of Baltimore. Jessica made frequent use of the swimming pool, lying out in the sun in her bright green bikini, but she considered the complex ugly, tacky, and totally without character. And so, because she wanted it to be true, she told both Bill Mandel and Bob Morse that on the weekends, she and Ron lived in a lovely old farmhouse halfway between Philadelphia and Baltimore. At times, she went into great detail, describing the pastoral beauty outside their front window.

With Kershaw now gainfully employed and living in another city, Carl Cochran thought that Ron and Jessica might have a chance at making their relationship work. Instead, Jessica began to return from her weekends in Baltimore with all the old signs of physical assault. On more than one occasion, says Dave Neal, producers would look up a half-hour before airtime to see her walk in with a black eye or a large cut on her face.

Cochran found it was even worse when Kershaw came to Philadelphia.

"The real near-fractures and the major abrasions and hematomas started during this period," says Cochran. "There were many weekends in a row where Ron would come up and they would battle all day Saturday and Sunday. Then he would storm out to catch a train back to Baltimore, and she would spend Monday and Tuesday in a blue fog. Finally, they would apologize to each other on the phone, and then it would just be repeated when Friday rolled around. It was really like 'Weekend at the Fights.' "

Cochran spent a lot of time analyzing the situation. He understood, as Kershaw had said, that fighting was a way to bring them close, to give them contact, to prove that they could arouse passion in each other. He also saw that the beatings had a sort of narcotic effect on Jessica—that she almost welcomed them, and that she seemed somehow disappointed when Cochran would stop the fighting when he was around, preferring instead that he simply be there afterwards for the prop-up. Finally, it dawned on him what was happening.

"This was when the emergency room visits started," he says. "Although at times things got very serious, in most cases, the beatings would be just slightly over the line—a particle in the eye, or an abrasion of some sort—and she would seek medical attention primarily as an excuse to get a prescription for pain pills. We were always running off to a different emergency room—instead of a regular physican—because she thought that was the only way she'd be able to get the pills. And because Jessica was becoming well-known around town, she was also afraid of drawing undue attention and suspicion from visits to the same physician. But medical attention for Kershaw abuse would not be uncommon once a month."

Jessica was not particularly afraid of what Kershaw did to her physically, Cochran says. "But she was incredibly afraid of what he did to her emotionally."

After such encounters, Dave Neal would often find Jessica scribbling long love letters to Kershaw on yellow legal pads— "Moonlight and roses and dreams shit," he says, "stuff that real people don't do." Neal knew she had supported him financially while he was out of work—paying for his car repairs, taking him on expensive ski trips—and Neal tried to reason with her. But Jessica would tell him the same thing she told everybody else: If she left Kershaw, a part of her would die.

In the fall of 1973, Dave Salzman, the young program director who had hired Jessica from Houston, left KYW to return to KDKA in Pittsburgh. His replacement was Bob Sutton. Together, Sutton,

Jim Topping, and Alan Bell talked about their plans for the station and, in particular, for Jessica Savitch. By the following summer, they hoped to pair her with Mort Crim on the daily "Newswatch 5:30." But before that could happen, Bell told Topping to come up with a vehicle that would create a presence for her—something that would make an indelible mark on the perception of the viewers, and establish a "star" position for her in Philadelphia. Whatever it was, Bell didn't want Jessica minimized as a ball of fluff. The idea was to give her credibility.

As recently as 1971, Reuven Frank, then president of NBC News, had told *Newsweek,* "I have the strong feeling that audiences are less prepared to accept news from a woman's voice than a man's." Bell didn't believe this, and he didn't go along with the opinion that women's voices were harsh, or that they didn't project authority. "But," he says, "I didn't want to have the slightest possibility of it with Jessica, so we leaned very hard in the other direction."

Topping, respected as a journalist who cared, and not just about the show business aspect of TV news but about the content of stories, set his mind on building the Savitch image. He began by reviewing what it was that had drawn him to her in Houston, the fact that she was an aggressive reporter, and that she took direct ownership of her stories—"that she was the person in charge of the material, and you were going to see it through her eyes." And since Jessica's arrival in Philadelphia, Topping had seen something else in her—a "marvelous" sense of vulnerability.

"She was perfectly believable, and she carried lots of authority," says Topping, now the news director at KTRK, Kershaw's old station in Houston. "But this vulnerability gave her great femininity. It wasn't a sensual or sexy quality. You simply identified with her first as a woman, because of the way she related to the subjects in the stories. Of course, she could bare her teeth and drag you right down onto the pavement if you weren't going to give her an answer, but she was always very gentle with people in the most intricate of situations."

Recently, the station had sent Mort Crim to report on the American draft resisters exiled in Canada. Because Crim had to file the story piece by piece, it ended up being a multipart series entitled "The Boys Who Can't Come Home." Viewer response was heavy; many people phoned to complain that the young men

146

were "yellow-bellied commies" who had refused to serve their country. Topping liked the attention they were getting, and he also saw that the pieces blended easily into the half-hour newscast. Several stations around the country were already doing five-part series for prime time broadcast—these were really just short documentaries divided up into digestible portions—but no one was doing them in Philadelphia. He thought they could create an identity for the station.

Bell suggested a series that would put Jessica under duress, a situation that would show her to be courageous and plucky—as brave as any man—yet also underscore that obvious vulnerability. Topping bandied the idea around with Dave Neal, and they came up with both a subject and a title: "Rape . . . The Ultimate Violation." Rape was still a taboo topic in the early 1970s, but the news director and his assistant sat down and outlined two especially dramatic segments, one in which Jessica, in voice-over narration, acted out the part of a rape victim, cornered in a basement laundry room at night. The piece was the real-life story of a local woman who, while she pledged her help, refused to go on camera.

Jessica had learned in Houston that for an assignment of any consequence, a good crew was almost everything. The best crew at KYW was the documentary unit: a clear-eyed, aggressive young photographer named Joe Vandergast; an affable soundman named Paul Dowie; and a whiz of a film editor named Allen Kohler. They were a tight, experienced team, three men who could communicate without speaking. Someone around the station had dubbed them "The Philadelphia Foreskins."

Soon, Vandergast found himself the recipient of a good deal of attention from Jessica Savitch. He liked her, and he admired the way she put a little different spin on her stories. It wasn't until years later that he realized she had "courted" him for her rape series. He was flattered: "She was the sharpest lady I ever met."

Topping talked Jessica through it: "Give me the sense of what it would be like in a musty little room with only one window looking out on the street level. Show me the desperation of being trapped by a rapist, with nowhere to run and nowhere to hide. Project it as the stuff of a woman's nightmare," he told her, and Joe Vandergast followed suit, employing a jostled, hand-held camera technique to convey the victim's point of view.

The most memorable segment of the series placed Jessica in

a desolate warehouse district near 4th Street and Washington Avenue, one of Philadelphia's seamier neighborhoods. City police had lately used decoys in the area, a high-crime district where a number of rapes had occurred. With the permission of then-Mayor Frank Rizzo, Jessica, wearing a belted, brown wool coat and carrying a shoulderbag, took the place of the plainclothes police officer on patrol. While police were stationed at both ends of the street in case of an actual attack, Jessica had nevertheless placed herself in a measure of real jeopardy. She insisted that the scene be shot at midnight, for mood, and that there be no artificial lighting—only the hazy glow from the streetlights. The crew would shoot her from a van parked on the opposite end of the block, with Vandergast using a long, night-vision lens, and soundman Paul Dowie a wireless microphone. No one would be closer to her than six hundred feet. That way, as she talked about her fear and apprehension, her vulnerability would be real. Afterward, the police gave Jessica a silver whistle with her name and the date engraved on the side.

The five-part series, which aired on the eleven o'clock news the week of October 29–November 2, 1973, was enormously successful. "She just bowled the market over, and set the standard for what that genre ought to be," Topping remembers. And there were even bigger rewards. First, "Rape . . . The Ultimate Violation" would win the 1974 Clarion Award from Women in Communications. And later, representatives of local and state governments would credit the series as having generated new legislation concerning the rights and the treatment of rape victims and the prosecution of rapists in Pennsylvania, Delaware, and New Jersey.

At the time the series ran, what most people commented on was how convincing Jessica had been in her fear and vulnerability. There was a reason for that, she told Jim Topping: She had been raped herself as a teenager in Atlantic City. A date had taken her to a party, where he drank heavily, and later forced himself on her.

But Jessica could never seem to recall the facts the same way twice. To the Rands, she said she had been attacked at radio station WOND when she was sixteen, something she had never mentioned to anyone in her youth. To Carl Cochran, she intimated that she had been sexually assaulted by a family member as a child, although she apparently never related such an event to any of her psychiatrists. And now, during the filming of the rape series, she told Joe Vandergast that a man had grabbed her in Central Park during her gofer days at CBS.

"One day we went to interview somebody for the rape series," Vandergast says, "and we had to wait for him in his office. Jessica had already told me this story about a guy grabbing her in Central Park. I said, 'There's really not much a woman can do if a man wants to rape her.' And she said, 'Sure there is.' I said, 'It's a matter of mathematics—a matter of poundage.' She looked at me and she said, 'There's no way you could take me down.' I said, 'I'm going to take you down right now.'

"So here we were in this big corporate office, and I jumped on her and took her to the floor hard. I said, 'I'm sorry, but I think you'd better come back to reality. If I'd really wanted to hurt you, I could have.' And she had the most amazed look on her face. She just said, 'Jesus Christ!' "

In the years before she left Philadelphia for NBC, Jessica would go on to do some eight multipart series in all, usually scheduled to air during periods when the station was scheduled to be rated by A. C. Nielsen. The subjects included divorce, the singles life, abortion, the Philly Sound in rock and roll, and Philadelphians who had made it big in Hollywood. They ranged from being superficial to innovative.

From her limited editing experience in Houston, Jessica knew that the film editor (the "cutter") had the real control over a story, and that even with the best footage imaginable, it was the editor who could make or break the piece. Kershaw had drilled it into her time and again. Now she wanted to be in the editing room whenever Allen Kohler cut her series. According to Dave Neal, management said no. Nobody else got to edit with Kohler—the station couldn't afford the overtime. But Neal went to bat for her upstairs, and soon he was bragging that Jessica was sleeping on the editing room floor.

Neal didn't know that Jessica was using amphetamines and cocaine to stay awake. Others, meanwhile, couldn't figure out how she'd suddenly developed a remarkable skill for matching words and pictures. Although Lonnie Reed had watched her cut and write a number of stories on deadline—"and they were fabulous"—the truth was that whenever she did a five-part series, she would go to a private telephone and call Ron Kershaw, who would write and edit the pieces for her long distance.

"We're not just talking about general ideas," says Dick Williams. "We're talking about, 'Which sound bite should I use here?' Now, *that's* insecurity. And it would go on for days, for hours at a time. He was her producer. In life, and in work. That's where they were inextricably wound."

Because the rape series was such a hit, Alan Bell immediately called for another such showcase. By this time, Topping had become a new father. He and his wife had attended natural childbirth classes, and he was taken not only with the emotional quality of the sessions, but with how the couples involved cut across all socioeconomic boundaries: "Here's a woman and her husband who owns a gas station in South Philly, and they're right next to the debutante from one of the Seven Sisters colleges and *her* husband," Topping says. "And we're all down on the floor huffing and puffing and learning how to do all this stuff." Topping thought it was a real slice of Americana. And in 1973, at the forefront of the feminist movement, with women fighting for the right to control their own bodies, it was a perfect, contemporary, cutting-edge topic for Alan Bell's new protegé.

Jessica balked. "It's women's magazine journalism!" she complained. But because childbirth still was generally considered too graphic a subject for television, Topping was able to convince her that the series could be so powerful and compelling that she'd have every eye in Philadelphia.

In preparing the series, for several weeks, Jessica and her crew practically lived with John and Ellen Condello, the young couple who had been chosen to exemplify the natural childbirth experience. The Condellos had consented to let the news team follow them through every step, including the actual birth of their baby. As the weeks passed and the Condellos placed more and more trust in the strangers who would document one of the most intimate moments of their lives, the crew became emotionally involved with the story.

"You have to understand," says Jim Topping, "that for the entire time I worked with Jessica, she was always in one of three places—either on the peak, on the way up or down, or at the bottom. That was almost a daily routine. So she would get excited about the series, and then as she was going out on the street, she'd

150

say, 'Oh, I just don't know what to do!' And she'd shake her head and mope, and we'd outline it, and she'd get excited again. Then she'd go out and hit it during the day, and come back in and we'd all say, 'Fabulous stuff!' And then she wouldn't know what to do for part two, and we'd go through all that again. It was exhausting, but exhilarating."

This time, after Topping had performed his usual function and Jessica was beginning to plot exactly how she would handle the birth scene, the station began buying promotional ads for the series in the regional edition of *TV Guide*. There was only one problem: Ellen Condello was past her due date, and everyone was frantic that the baby would not appear in time for the scheduled birth segment.

Jessica recalled in *Anchorwoman* that immediately before the series was scheduled to air, she began compiling a list of every woman in the Delaware Valley who was due to deliver by natural childbirth. That way, even if she had to substitute a stranger for the mother, at least they'd have a birth and a going-home scene. Joe Vandergast remembers that he, Jessica, and Paul Dowie were eating dinner at a Chinese restaurant when John Condello had them paged: Ellen had gone into labor.

When the series finally aired on the eleven o'clock news that November of 1973, the viewing audience saw Jessica, wearing a blue surgical gown and mask, holding Ellen Condello's hand and wiping her brow as she was rolled into the delivery room. Topping had been right. The sight of Sarah Margaret Condello emerging into the world was a riveting emotional experience, made even more so by Jessica's controlled but passionate stand-up, delivered with the surgical mask now hanging around her chin.

Afterwards, Topping reviewed it with her. "Look at the imagery that's involved as the camera pushes in to your face," he told her. "See the theater of that, the framing, and how it plays to your words, the look in your eyes." The news director smiled. "It's magic."

The day after the birth segment aired, everybody in town talked about it—commuters coming in from the suburbs, disc jockeys, newspaper columnists. "It instantly defined Jessica exactly as we wanted, without Machiavellian intent," Topping says. "She was a 'partner in experience.' She became not a voice, but a mega-

151

phone for extending television into human lives." The series launched Jessica as Philadelphia's first true female news star.

Jessica was certain it was her ticket to the network. In December 1973, she sent a copy of the eleven o'clock newscast to Martin Haag at WCBS-TV, and copies of the rape and natural childbirth series to the network news division, hoping to set the wheels in motion toward going back to New York. The tapes made the rounds, and at last, in what would come to be the first in a series of such abortive moves, Jessica received a firm offer to come to the network as a reporter.

Kershaw told Jessica she was crazy for chasing the network, that Westinghouse would never let her out of her contract. Jessica reminded him that Dave Salzman had given her a verbal agreement to release her should a network job come along. But Salzman was no longer at the station. Apprised of the offer, Alan Bell put his foot down, firing off a blistering letter to Richard Salant, the president of CBS news. Bell had spent "a ton of dough" researching Jessica's potential popularity with viewers, and with the two special series, a considerable amount of time building her into a star. He wasn't about to let her go. "We're flattered," Bell told the newspapers at the time, "but that's why we have people under contract. If other stations or networks want our talent, it proves that we must have a good news team here."

Jessica was enraged—and frantic. Instead of accepting that she'd simply made a bad deal, or realizing that she still had much to learn before going to the network, she saw only that she had worked night and day since she was a teenager to achieve her goal. It was owed to her. And since Dave Salzman had given his word, the station should honor it. "She was just obsessed with getting out of Philadelphia and getting to a network," remembers Dave Neal, "and every time an opportunity came and somebody else filled the job, she was a wreck. She'd just go crazy."

Ron Kershaw spent days battling with her about it. "She was so obsessed with going to New York that it seemed like a disease," he says. "I thought if she forced the obsession to the surface, like with that first attempt with CBS, it would dissolve in the light of day. But the more I tried to make her see this, the more determined she became, and the more enraged I became." So, because "She wanted to be lied to—she wanted the fantasy," as Kershaw puts it, several months later, in early 1974, Jessica would try again, this time with ABC. As before, there was interest, but it cooled when the network learned that she was under contract to Westinghouse. As Dean Borba—and even Bill Schwing—had warned her before she signed, the Group W contract was hopelessly ironclad, and everyone in the industry knew it.

Dave Neal also told Jessica that trying to get out of it was useless, but he saw how she might be able to get something else. "I'd say, 'Look, you're crying, your face is all broken out in blotches. Go home and get some sleep, and in the morning pick up the phone and say, I'm not coming in.' She'd say, 'Oh, I can't do that. It's not professional.' I'd say, 'It's being smart. So you don't come in one day. The second day you don't come in. The third day you don't come in. The management will say, Jessica, what can we do for you?' And you'll say, 'Well, I don't know.' And they'll say, 'Maybe if we gave you more money, you'll feel better.' And you'll say, 'You know, I'm starting to feel better already.' *That's* the way to handle these guys."

And so Topping tore up her contract, rewriting it for $26,000 a year. "I'm not sure exactly which period this was," Topping says, laughing, "but I never will forget how we're in the middle of this classic labor-management dispute, where she's not working, and she calls me up to ask how she can fix something on her expense account!"

With her salary increase, Jessica decided to move into Hopkinson House, a luxurious cream-colored high-rise on Washington Square, near 7th and Spruce. She liked its being near the station, but also that it had a security desk and underground parking; she had learned that the underside of fame was celebrity—that people would stop her on the street and want her autograph, want to claim a small part of her. Her popularity was turning into a cult, as if she were a movie star, helped along by the constant features about her in *Philadelphia* magazine and other local press notices. Occasionally, she got strange phone calls at the station from men who had seen the rape series and wanted to know if she'd been really scared out there on the street. It made her fearful for her safety, and at times she would ask Vince Leonard to drive her home and watch her until she was inside the building.

Carl Cochran did not make the move with her, returning instead to Houston, and then moving on to San Francisco. "The turmoil between Jessica and Ron was getting so great that I couldn't take it anymore," he says. "There were always seven or eight plateaus that we all worked on, and just when one conflict would be in remission, there would be a countervailing influence, be it drugs or whatever, that would drive us all the other way. It was just a major whirlwind at all times."

Indeed, Kershaw and Jessica now consciously tried to have a "double" relationship, separating the personal from the professional. They agreed that it was better for themselves and everyone around them to break off their engagement offically. They could still use Jessica's work as a way to talk on the phone every day—"to get their fix," as Josh Howell, then a WBAL reporter, puts it. Whenever Jessica felt that Ron wasn't paying enough attention to her, she would find what seemed to her to be a very real crisis—a situation from which she was desperate to be rescued.

"She was always looking for somebody to make her feel important, to give her a sense of worth," says Sharon Sakson, the WBAL producer who became close to both Jessica and Ron. "One day I was working the six o'clock news, and I saw her come into the newsroom. I went over to say hi, and she was so upset. She was wearing curlers, and a yellow scarf tied over her hair. She said, 'My car broke down, and the station is upset with me! I'm going to be taken off the air!'

"I was holding her arm, and she looked over and saw that Ron's door was closed. She said, 'He's here, he's here, isn't he?' Then the door opened, and Ron came out, and she just ran to him, and they went back in the office and closed the door. Of course, none of it was true—they did want her on the air. She was just frightened, and she wanted him to comfort her. That was always a symbol to me of how the relationship was."

But if the weekend started out in a loving and supportive way, it usually ended differently. Kershaw was becoming increasingly remote and inaccessible, because, as he says, "I was turned inward on my pain."

By now, he and Jessica spent much of their free time with Dick Williams and his girlfriend, Lonnie Reed, a smart and attractive former newspaper reporter who was then handling press for Senator Henry "Scoop" Jackson in Washington. Reed wanted to make the transition to TV news. Although she was fully aware that Jessica didn't extend herself to everybody, and that she could be brittle and prickly, Reed realized that Jessica's behavior stemmed almost wholly from her insecurity. When she did take someone in as a friend, Reed found, Jessica could be "the best"—spending a generous amount of time with her in the preparation of a good TV audition tape, giving her advice on how to market it, and showing her how to translate her print experience into the broadcast medium. In return, Reed listened sympathetically when Jessica called in the middle of the night "in hysterics" about her problems with Kershaw.

On a typical weekend—"and this must have happened ten times," says Williams—the four would plan to gather for a leisurely dinner at one of Baltimore's favorite seafood houses. The women would arrive in town on the Metroliners and the couples would meet at the TV station. But then Kershaw would become obstinate, as if demanding, one of them remembers, "Does this experience involve social graces and having to be polite to strangers? Does it mean eating foods that don't have gravy on them?" A quarrel would ensue. Kershaw always wanted Jessica to fix the Southern food of his youth—chicken-fried steak, vegetables cooked soft and seasoned with pork grease. Jessica, who was afraid to go to a restaurant in Philadelphia because she was always approached, wanted desperately to eat out, to do something nice in the anonymity of Baltimore. Eventually, Dick and Lonnie would leave them arguing at the station, with a promise to meet them later at Kershaw's apartment.

"When we'd get to Ron's place," says Williams, "it was obvious that they'd just had a two-hour, tumultuous, knock-down, drag-out fight." They knew that Kershaw drank far too much alcohol, but because "all the signs were there," Dick and Lonnie suspected that the two of them had also been using drugs. Kershaw was only a moderate user of cocaine, then commonly consumed in the WBAL newsroom, but he was a heavy user of marijuana, amphetamines, and Quaaludes.

From there, the four would go through what Williams calls "a typical, bizarre, Mr. Media evening." Kershaw would switch the radio on full-tilt, put the sound down on the TV, and then sit with the channel flipper, trying to come up with surreal matches of audio and video—mating a radio spot for headache tablets, for example, with a car commercial on TV.

"If you were screwed up enough," says Williams, who enjoyed drinking alcohol but, like Reed, abhorred drug use, "it was very funny. But this would go on for hours, until finally Lonnie and I would elbow each other and leave. It was a very complicated relationship. Jessica would use Kersh for a soft landing place, and then blow him off whenever it was convenient for her—cancel when she'd planned to come down, for example. But even if they loved each other the way Mary loved Joseph, he had to be resentful of her success. I'll never forget the sight of this woman, who was making money that seemed stratospheric to both of us, standing in the kitchen cooking this stupid Southern food. That was the way Kersh exacted his revenge."

To some of their other friends, this was also a way for both Ron and Jessica to act out certain roles. She would at first refuse his requests because it led to his getting the upper hand. And he would force the situation to exorcise all sorts of demons, including a mother who had given him away. Aside from the times they attended rock concerts—Kershaw was especially fond of Elton John—whenever Jessica was in Baltimore, Ron insisted that they never leave the apartment. There, he would put her in her place, to be his wife, to be what she would have been had she not abandoned him in Houston and shamed him in Philadelphia. Then he would begin to call her names and explode in anger. As one of her psychiatrists would later say, Jessica almost welcomed the cruelty of his ways because it substantiated her own negative self-image.

When she was back in Philadelphia, Jessica would tell friends that she worried about Kershaw, that she wanted to help him, but, as she would say, "Either I never could, or he'd never let me." If she and Kershaw were too estranged to speak directly, she would telephone Josh Howell and Sharon Sakson to check on his well-being. Kershaw had begun to see numbers of other women, but after a single bout of all-night drinking and all-night sex, never would want to see them again.

Jessica, too, now had other companions. Lonnie Reed had introduced her to an attorney, a man who "thought she was adorable," as Reed says, "but she was terrified of him because she thought he was going to think she was stupid—that she wouldn't measure up." For a long time, off and on, she would see a local writer, a married man who would come by the station for her in his Mercedes, because, as one of her bosses says, "She wanted publicity, and he was obviously smitten with an incredible crush on her." There were also many casual dates—an architect, for one,

NFL film producer Steve Sabol, for another, as well as "a couple of balding, pinky ring, thug guys," in the words of one of Jessica's producers.

One man she did continue to see for a time was Bill Mandel, the *Philadelphia Bulletin* staff writer. Mandel suspected that Jessica was interested in him partly because she was fascinated with print journalists. From the time she was a teenager, she had been haunted by the idea of being a writer herself, telling Barry Swartz, "I do so fervently wish that I could write with some degree of depth and beauty." She thought that newspapers and magazines were somehow more "real" than television, which she had once defined to Kershaw as "half truths in the pleasant illusion of reality," a reworking of a line from one of her favorite plays, Tennessee Williams's *The Glass Menagerie*. But Mandel also saw that most of the time Jessica really wanted only company—any company—because she could not stand to be alone.

"Basically, I was in love with her," says Mandel, now a general news columnist for the *San Francisco Examiner*. "I felt very lucky to catch her attention, because she was obviously a person with an unlimited future. She was 'on' a lot, but when she was relaxed, she was the most incredibly charming, intelligent person. It was always a surprise to me how much she had read, how much she knew about current events."

The first time Mandel visited Jessica's small, one-bedroom apartment in Hopkinson House, he was stunned to find that she had almost no furniture, and that what was there, including a nubby, tan tweed couch, looked rented, as if she had no interest in making a real home. Instead, everything was in the service of her career—a mammoth television, a professional format video tape machine for critiquing her newscasts, a stereo, an étagère to hold her videotapes, and even a "soap-on-a-rope" microphone so she could practice her stand-ups in the shower.

"She wanted nothing to come between her and her work, no possessions, no personal involvements, and no decisions on what to wear," he says. Her closet contained only jeans and a dozen silk blouses in all colors, and she wore a gold "#1" on a chain around her neck.

Mandel worried about her eating habits—how she could make an apple last a week, and how, left to her own devices, she would subsist on tuna fish and Jamoca Almond Fudge ice cream from

Baskin Robbins. Usually, she was on some kind of screwball diet, explaining she was hypoglycemic, and carried a bottle of high-protein liquid in her bag. But Mandel was especially concerned that, "There was no 'her.' She was like a mirror turned inside out. She had no real center. She just had a nice package." Before they would go out the door, he recalls, she would stop, adjust her hair and makeup and ask, "How are my visuals?"

Mostly, because Mandel wanted to fatten her up, their dates consisted of going to dinner. By this time, Jessica had taken to disguising herself in a rainbonnet or white bandanna, or sometimes a bouffant hairpiece and dark glasses. She would always ask for a table where she could face the wall, and in what Mandel found a poignant example of her insecurity, she apologized to the waiters for her lisp, afraid her speech impediment was so severe that they couldn't understand what she was saying. More than once, Mandel drove Jessica up to Bucks County, Pennsylvania, to the picturesque town of New Hope, where they would dine at a country inn called Chez Odette, named for one of the restaurant's earlier owners, Odette Myrtil, a Broadway actress who at one time portrayed "Bloody Mary" in the musical *South Pacific*.

Whatever activity the two pursued, however, Mandel never had the sense that she did anything because she enjoyed it, not even sex. He found her to be not a languorous person, and not a sensual person, but quick and abrupt, perfunctory, as if she were taking part only because it was expected. It was important that her partner achieve a climax, but she didn't seem concerned about experiencing one herself. He thought it was her way of establishing control.

"It wasn't particularly satisfying," Mandel says, "but I saw that she really just wanted warmth and acceptance. And, of course, the more clothes you took off, the less attractive she was. In one way, she was just a skinny little girl. But in another way, she was like an old Slavic woman, because her skin was not soft and powdery, but leathery, almost lizardlike.

"We kind of kidded about getting together," he remembers. "I thought it was interesting that she didn't say, how would you like to be Mr. Jessica Savitch? but *Mrs.* Jessica Savitch. But I knew nothing was really going to happen with us. Number one, her star was rising a lot faster than mine. And number two, she was, as she put it, 'addicted' to Ron, and I was only the weekday boyfriend."

There were many times, Mandel says, when he and Jessica would be "literally in bed together—sometimes just watching TV or eating pizza" when Kershaw would call. "He would treat her like a bad dog," he says. And because she needed Ron's total approval, she would never cut the conversation short or apologize to Mandel for ignoring him.

Jessica and Bill would continue to be friends until the end of her life. Their romance cooled down in the summer of 1974, when Mandel became seriously interested in another woman. By that time, his evenings with Jessica consisted mainly of sitting around and smoking marijuana. "But she told a lot of stories about cocaine," he says. "One time she was in New York, at a network correspondent's party, and this very famous reporter snorted so much coke that he took his clothes off and tried to jump over a glass coffee table. She said it was scary, because he missed, and fell on top of the table, where the glass shattered under him."

Mandel often thought that Jessica made up a past, present, and future to meet what she thought was everyone's expectation of her. He had no way of knowing that the cocaine and coffee table story was simply transposition, her own episode from Houston, redone.

For a time, Jessica had been seeing a gynecologist, Dr. Joel Polin, for what she believed was a recurrence of the blocked fallopian tube she had suffered in college. Polin discovered she had florid endometriosis, a condition in which the lining cells of the uterus migrate to abnormal locations in the abdominal cavity. She would complain about her discomfort long distance to Carl Cochran, who would send her enormous bottles of pain pills he got from friends. But now she was having different sensations, and her periods had stopped. At first, it never dawned on her what might be wrong, but the test was conclusive: She was pregnant. And she was certain the baby was Kershaw's.

Only a few months before, Jessica had told Paul Dowie, her soundman on the special series, that "before it was too late, she wanted to quit the business, get married and have babies, and live in a little white house with a picket fence out front," a variation of her farmhouse fantasy. But she hadn't meant quite so soon, and it was becoming increasingly obvious that marriage to Kershaw would never work out. She worried about being pregnant on camera, about how long it would take to get her figure back in shape.

159

And she was sure that an infant would hamper her chances of going to the network. Still, for a while, she tried to find a way to go ahead with the pregnancy, to risk the disapproval of her family and her audience and to rear the baby on her own.

Finally, one day she went to Jim Topping and tearfully asked if they could talk. The two went to the little alcove on the second floor overlooking the KYW lobby. "It was the ultimate depressed Jessica," he remembers. "She cried until I didn't think she could have any tears left." For three hours, she told him of her desire to love something of her own, about the effect the natural childbirth series had had on her, and about her "almost Catholic guilt." But in the end, the decision was made. Carl Cochran, who would come running back to Philadelphia whenever Jessica's problems overwhelmed her, arranged for an abortion out of town.

In the weeks after the abortion, Jessica was filled with regret, unable to shake her shame. The mere sight of a small child would dissolve her to tears. She began to see a stress management counselor, a man who helped her not only with the aftereffects of the experience, but in other ways, showing her that her hypoglycemia had roots that were psychophysiological. He also taught her techniques for reducing the anxiety in her on-air delivery. On one occasion she inadvertently paid him twice for a session, and he returned her second check with a note, explaining the confusion. Jessica scribbled a thank you, saying, "It's probably the only time anybody ever gave me anything back."

Despite the counselor's help, Jessica would occasionally dwell on the abortion and search for emotional justification for the act, something beyond the cold and clinical assessment of what a child would have done to her career. Drawing on one of her favorite fantasies, she would tell Bob Morse that she had terminated the pregnancy because she had been raped.

But to Kershaw himself, Jessica said nothing—not that she was pregnant, and not that she planned an abortion or had one. Only months after the fact did she finally bring herself to tell him what she'd done. Then he was inconsolable, for despite his firm belief that they were "star-crossed," and that he would die before Jessica in some self-destructive fashion, he had often envisioned that they would spend their last years "rocking away together in some old-age home," surrounded by their children. He told her he felt the loss of their child as deeply as if it had been born and then died.

160

Finally, he broke down at the thought of her having endured such an agonized time alone, promising that he never would have hurt their baby the way he hurt her.

In years to come, Kershaw would continue to be haunted by these events, writing Jessica bitter, poignant letters. These would throw Jessica into whirlpools of emotion. Later, before she left Philadelphia for NBC, she would have a second abortion. This time, according to Carl Cochran and others, the decision was not so difficult. She had been able to pinpoint the conception to a one-night stand with an executive in the broadcast industry. It was a meaningless fluke, and nothing more. By 1975, she was sufficiently at ease with the topic to do a five-part series on abortion and euthanasia, "Moment of Life/Moment of Death."

Now, in the summer of 1974, Jessica again tried to concentrate on matters other than her painful relationship with Kershaw. Instead of going to Baltimore every weekend, she began spending more time in Margate with her mother, and in Wilmington with Ben and Lil, who were preparing to retire to California. Jim Topping could always tell when she'd been home, or even when she'd spoken with her family on the phone.

"There would always be a big, emotional wave that rocked through, and she'd always be wrung out. She approached those weekends and holiday dinners like she was going to the dentist. She didn't talk about it much, but the implication was that she was out there running amok instead of settling down and marrying a doctor or an attorney, having two children, and going to the club. Whatever it was, it made her very depressed." In lighter moments, Jessica referred to the confrontations as "the family Olympics."

Meanwhile, Jessica was spending so much time with Joe Vandergast and Paul Dowie in the field that they had become as intimate as a family, and perhaps more supportive. Dowie, who was older than Jessica and Joe, acted as something of a father, automatically giving her neck and back rubs at the end of a long day's shoot; Jessica often feel asleep in his lap in the car. He also would insist that they stop each day to get her a vanilla milkshake with an egg in it, a protein drink to build her strength.

Vandergast, who had become like a brother, knew not to shoot her in profile because, as Dick John had told her, "Your nose is all wrong." The cameraman also took pains to hide her bad skin and thinness, to "protect her from the public," softening his lights with diffusion and using a Number 1 fog filter on his lens. Shooting film, a warm medium that often enhances natural colors, helped to make her look prettier than she really was, and prettier than she would ever look on the cooler, highly resolved videotape. "Film took the hard edge off," Vandergast says. "And she had a very hard edge all around her.

"We established a trust among ourselves," he says, "and she knew that we were never going to hurt her." As time went on, they came to appreciate, as Alan Bell did, that, "She had a silly streak a mile wide," and that she possessed a marvelous sense of humor as well as a genuine sense of caring about the people who helped her achieve her goals—remembering birthdays and anniversaries, bringing in a giant toy box for Jim Topping's baby son, and throwing a surprise fiftieth birthday party for Dave Neal.

But the film crew also saw her crying jags and drastic mood swings, and her frantic cravings to get to the network. To Vandergast, especially, who sensed a streak of tragedy in her, she would talk of her fear that the industry was passing her by: In the spring of 1971, veteran correspondent Marlene Sanders had broken through the masculine preserve to anchor temporarily the "ABC Weekend News." It was only a matter of time before a female got the job permanently, Jessica said. The problem was that there were others in line ahead of her. In 1972, Catherine Mackin had become the first female network television floor reporter at a national political convention, going on to make her reputation covering Capitol Hill for NBC. Two years later, Ann Compton of ABC was recognized as the first television newswoman appointed full-time White House correspondent—the most prestigious beat in network reporting. Now Pauline Frederick was retiring from NBC. Who would take *her* place? All together, there were some twelve women reporters—including Marya McLaughlin, Liz Trotta, and Betty Rollin—at ABC, NBC, and CBS. How many more competent women would be hired at the networks before Jessica fulfilled her Westinghouse contract?

In July 1974, KYW management announced its plan to pair Jessica with Mort Crim as co-host of the daily "Newswatch 5:30." Crim, who co-anchored with Vince Leonard at eleven, would now also co-anchor at six, pulling triple duty. The extra shift did not especially trouble him, but sharing his solo anchor spot did. Even though Channel 6 planned to put Larry Kane on opposite him at

5:30 later that month, he saw no reason for adding Jessica; the current ratings were good enough, he thought.

"I took her out to dinner and said, 'Jess, I like you. I think you've got talent, and you're going to go places in this business,' " Crim remembers. " 'But I want you to be aware that I'm not real happy about this decision, and I don't want to go into it with false pretenses and built-up resentments. Having said that, I'm going to do absolutely nothing but cooperate with you. If you're going to be on the show, I want it to be the best show that we can do.' "

Jessica was taken aback, but she knew being matched with Crim, then in his late thirties, was a most fortuitous event. She had watched him closely since she first came to the station, standing in the studio with her hand on her chin, mesmerized by the way he took command of the camera. She saw how he could be gentle and affectionate with it, how he teased with it in a quietly humorous way, without sacrificing his dignity. Now he would become a role model for Jessica, a mentor. She would blossom as an anchor with him and would strive to emulate his clear, concise, and sometimes eloquent writing. Off-camera, she would come to lean on him almost as much as she had on Ron Kershaw, going to him for emotional solace and career advice. And on-camera, they would have a chemistry that would prove unstoppable, even when WPVI challenged them in September 1975 with the new pairing of Larry Kane and an attractive, blonde woman named Gwen Scott, whom everyone considered merely a Savitch clone.

Structurally, "Newswatch 5:30" was lighter than the six o'-clock report, with more emphasis on local news and special features. The six o'clock newscast offered the major local news stories in greater detail, covering the metro and tri-state areas, as well as the national and international news. When communications consultants McHugh and Hoffman, Inc., were brought in to analyze newscast appeals, John Bowen, the account executive (now president) of the company, found the home audience tended toward a "viewing consolidation," watching both half hours as a satisfying balance of information and personalities. The audience perceived the three newscasters as a family, working in an atmosphere of warmth, friendliness, and naturalness, using the right balance of seriousness and relaxed humor when interacting with one another and with effusive sports director Al Meltzer and folksy weatherman Bill Kuster.

"This whole team was coalescing around here, and suddenly we found ourselves up to our armpits in a series of well-defined television personalities," says Jim Topping.

By early 1975, KYW had pulled ahead in the Nielsen ratings, reaching a comfortable number one at six o'clock and eleven, and a runaway at 5:30. In October, they were still ahead in the Neilsens at 5:30 and six, but WPVI was up by a single percentage point at eleven. For a time, the stations would be neck and neck, one winning by a point in the Nielsens, and the other winning by a point in the Arbitron ratings. "But we felt like we were on top of the hill," Topping recalls. And the feeling in the industry was that Topping and Alan Bell had turned around an impossible situation, triumphing against WPVI's furiously paced, shotgun "Action News" with the advent of a "dream team" that still is referred to by television professionals today. For the next three years, the station would be "sitting pretty in the local ratings war," as Gail Shister of the *Philadelphia Inquirer* put it, and KYW would have its last, great shining. They would call those idyllic years the Camelot days.

5
Famous

If Mort Crim was seen as calming and quick-witted, and Vince Leonard, then in his mid-forties, as stable and serious, Jessica's KYW image was more complicated. The over-fifty viewers perceived her as "human, caring, and interested in populist concerns," as Jim Topping told *Philadelphia* magazine. But the younger audience always knew she wasn't as straight as she appeared to be, that while she exuded intelligence and knowledge, her jauntiness on the set hinted at a much freer spirit underneath.

The upshot was that Jessica was now the true toast of the town, a major celebrity. Men wrote in to say they turned down the sound on their televisions just to watch her face. They sent her gifts of intimate clothing, money to pamper herself at Christmas, and so many proposals of marriage that Jim Topping said, "Why don't we just station somebody in the lobby who can take them as they come through the door?" Women liked her, too: Their groups and clubs bestowed awards on her, and even the local Bloomingdale's decorated a Jessica Savitch room. Ida McGinniss, of the Speakers Bureau, was flooded with requests for Jessica to appear before local organizations. And, says someone who worked in the newsroom, "You can't imagine how much mail she got. She was a *star.*"

To her friends and co-workers, Jessica would refer to "Newswatch 5:30" as "the horror show." But "the Philadelphia years were the closest she ever really got to being happy," says Bob Morse. "There was nothing on this earth that was going to make her truly happy—not a job, not a person. But the recognition she got in Philadelphia brought some very up times. She had a role, and she knew what it was, and she was good at it."

Philadelphia gave her confidence, and the right partners to achieve her potential. Mort Crim hooked Jessica up with his attorney and agent, Donald Hamburg, in New York and, with Hamburg negotiating, Topping again tore up her contract and rewrote it, according to one source, for $60,000, then a staggering sum of money for a local female talent. Two years later, Ann Compton would make $55,000 covering the White House for ABC, and Margaret Osmer $50,000 for reading the news on "Good Morning America."

In September 1974, a month after debuting on "Newswatch 5:30," Jessica decided to celebrate her good fortune and borrowed $6,870.96 from the Frankford Trust Company to buy a yellow, 1974 Jensen-Healey sports car. It was sleek and sexy, a two-door stick shift, with a removable hardtop, and it fit the image she'd always wanted. Vince Leonard remembers rolling along the Schuylkill Expressway at sixty-five miles per hour when Jessica and her sister Lori came roaring past him, the little Jensen disappearing into a tiny blip on the horizon. "Jessica had automobile wrecks regularly," says Jim Topping. "Twice when I was there, she all but totaled the cars, and she fairly much beat up the Jensen. She seemed to always reach an intersection simultaneously with someone else."

Now on the weekends, Jessica would tool down to Baltimore with the top off, her hair flapping about her face. But Kershaw hardly had time to see her. Three months earlier, in June, Dick Williams had left WBAL for WPLG in Miami, and Kershaw had become the news director. His ego was on the line. He had boasted that he could raise WBAL to number one, ahead of the monstrous WJZ, and this was the moment of truth.

On his small operating budget, Kershaw hired rookies Lloyd Kramer and Jennifer Siebens straight out of Columbia journalism school, and matched them with his talented but near neophyte staff—Josh Howell, Sue Simmons, a young black reporter Dick Williams had found in New Haven, and Sharon Sakson, who would prove to be a brilliant producer. Don Harrison and Ron Smith temporarily held down the anchor desk, and when Harrison left for Minneapolis, Kershaw would try the revolutionary idea of putting two women—Amanda Arnold and Sue Simmons—on as co-anchors. Because they were renegades, up against the impossible, Kershaw's people bonded together with tremendous camaraderie.

"I had total fear of failure at work," Kershaw remembers. "I just dove into my job and stayed there, scurrying like a motherfucker." Sometimes Jessica would tear him away for a day to go up to Bucks County, where Kershaw, the history buff, would poke around where Washington crossed the Delaware. Once they visited David Savitch's grave in Wilmington, and sometimes they'd go to the trotter track. There, Jessica would bet on horses with such names as "Russian Spy" or "White Russian," hoping for a cultural connection.

Mostly, though, Kershaw was simply consumed by work, and Jessica would spend time with his visiting children or sit out by the pool and talk with Sharon Sakson, who lived around the corner. Jessica knew she and Ron could no longer communicate the way they had. She was hurt to see he now looked to Amanda Arnold or Jennifer Siebens for the conversations about television he used to have with her.

"The loss is that we grew apart and I never knew it," says Kershaw. "It had become such a bitter thing with me to win in Baltimore, and a bitter thing with her to be a star in Philadelphia, that we never met anymore. She wanted me to be proud of her, and I *was* proud of her, *but I never let her know.* Everybody was kissing her ass because she was a star on TV, and everybody loved her, *except me!* I didn't love her for that very reason! It was small of me, and it was shitty, but I did that. Even when she was so precious to me."

Now, aside from her exchanges with Sharon Sakson, nothing was the same for Jessica in Baltimore. Dick Williams was gone, and Lonnie Reed, who had listened so patiently to her frightful, 3 A.M. panic attacks, had moved to Palm Beach for her first TV job.

Back in Philadelphia, Jessica began spending time with Carole Goldman Bell, the wife of Alan Bell, KYW's general manager. Carole was extraordinarily bright ("I'd guess her IQ was 180," says a mutual friend), proficient in several languages, and something of a *princesse éloignée,* a faraway princess, living in her own little world. The news staff saw her come into the station barefoot, in peasant dress, and while some considered her "a nice lady," more than one thought she was uncomfortably eccentric. Alan Bell, today divorced from Carole, says Jessica and Carole easily found common ground: Both had lost their fathers at an early age, both had grown up feeling excluded from the mainstream, both vowed to improve their stations in life, and both were attracted to older men, "papa types."

Jessica admired Carole's intelligence, but she especially appreciated her willingness to teach her about "the life-style that Carole enjoyed as a consequence of my labors," says Alan Bell. Among other matters, Carole taught Jessica about food—fine wines and cheeses—and "all kinds of places to visit in Europe," the pleasures that a young woman of money and breeding might be expected to enjoy, and the pleasures that Jessica could now afford. Now it was Carole who would get the frenzied telephone calls about Ron, and Carole who would hold Jessica together after the fights. They spoke, by Carole's account, five or six times a day.

"Carole just took over Jessica's life," says Dave Neal. But Alan Bell figured Jessica might have wanted it that way. "Jess may have been the star and the externally successful person," he says, "but Carole was married to the puppet master."

In January 1975, Jim Topping, the news director who had helped build the operation, left KYW for KNXT, the CBS owned-and-operated station in Los Angeles. His replacement was Joe Harris, an eager and abrasive twenty-six-year-old who had taken WABC's Bill Beutel and Roger Grimsby to number one in New York City. From the outset, the news team didn't like him—they considered him arrogant and inexperienced, and they were appalled at some of his ideas for "improving" the news. "My job in the afternoon," says Dave Neal, "was to go pick up Jessica at two o'clock to make sure she came to work, and then stand by the door at four o'clock to see that she and Vince and Mort didn't leave. They were all threatening to walk out every day. That guy was really bad."

The friction reached a head in February, when Harris approached the anchors with a proposal for a "news involvement" series. He wanted each of them to go out into the community and masquerade as an everyday citizen—Crim as a garbage collector, Leonard as a hardware store clerk, and Jessica as a waitress. All three anchors drew the line, but Harris went ahead with the series with other staffers. For Crim, it was the last straw; during a prime ratings week, he left the country, saying he was on a "medical leave of absence." Joe Harris lasted at KYW for exactly eight months.

Harris's successor was Ken Tiven, who'd come up to Philadelphia from WSB in Atlanta, where he'd been something of a boy wonder. Tiven was a product of the Columbia University Graduate School of Journalism, a former *Washington Post* editor, and a technology freak. At first, since Harris had so alienated the news staff and management, he was concerned with making peace and simply holding onto the ratings. But his real mission, as he saw it, was to switch the station to ENG, electronic news gathering. In essence, that meant converting the news department from film to videotape, which alleviated processing time and allowed stories to get on the air a lot faster. It also meant installing new hardware to achieve instantaneous, live "mini-cam" coverage in the field. ENG—which Tiven helped to create—was the vanguard of television news, but many of the KYW staff didn't care for it. Too often it led to "live for live's sake," where reporters covered almost anything—festivals at shopping malls, for example—for the pure sake of capturing the immediacy of the event.

The coming of ENG was particularly threatening to Jessica, who sensed that her painstaking and well-crafted series—shot on film, where she looked the best—might be perceived as old-fashioned. As far as she was concerned, Tiven was only a technocrat, to be barely tolerated.

"The day I met her," Tiven remembers, "she said, 'I'm Jessica Savitch, and I'm pleased to meet you.' Then she rattled off exactly how many years, months, and days she had to work for me." The news director, who thought she needed more exposure at the station, was put off by what he calls her "icy self-control," but he took her to lunch in an attempt to know her better and to establish a good working relationship.

"It left me unnerved," he says. "There were two or three distinct people operating there, with an enormous capacity to bal-

169

ance things that were contradictory. She was like the guy who appeared on the 'Mike Douglas Show' with nine poles and plates. That's what she perceived life was about—getting all the plates spinning on all the poles at once. And there were many, many things that did not ring true about the kind of existence she led."

In March 1975, Sam and Rita Rappaport, who owned the Blum Stores, the women's apparel shops that supplied Jessica's on-air clothing, invited her to be the guest of honor at a fund-raiser for research in children's colitis. Jessica liked Rita, a generous, friendly woman; she had survived the Holocaust, but her father had died at Auschwitz. Rita and Sam, who was known primarily as a real estate investor, often picked up Jessica for lunch in one of their several stretch limousines, depositing her back at the station in time to do the news. They also liked having her to their home in Cherry Hill, New Jersey, for parties. "We didn't want anything from her, and she didn't want anything from us," says Rita, "except trust."

Soon, Jessica had adopted the Rappaports, and their children, Tracy and Wil, as her third, and most important, surrogate family. Dave Neal was horrified. "I said, 'Jessica, when you're in the position you're in, you shouldn't be hanging around people like that.' " He told her they were "celebrity bangers," and interested in Jessica only as an ornament. She defended them, insisting that although Rita was only ten years older than she, the couple had taken the place of her parents. With their extravagant and super-visible life-style, the couple more aptly resembled Ben and Lil, but they were far wealthier. A decade later, in 1986, *Philadelphia* magazine would name Sam Rappaport as one of the forty richest Philadelphians, estimating his worth at $100 million, and citing him as "probably the largest individual landholder in the city. Sammy Rapp, as he used to be called back in the distant days when he knew Sylvan Skolnick (a/k/a Cherry Hill Fats, the 742-lb. criminal mastermind) has come a long way."

There was more. Rappaport, according to a 1977 *Philadelphia Inquirer* story, was also "the biggest landlord of adult bookstores and theatres in Philadelphia."

"My husband's in the paper every other day," says Rita Rappaport. "The more successful you become, the more someone tries to drag you down. But your friends are your friends, and Jessica was more than a friend. She was like my sister—'god-

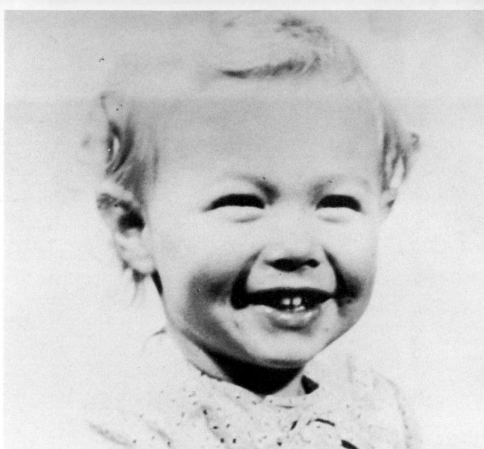

Jessica Beth.

A little Shirley Temple doll, with her father, David Savitch.

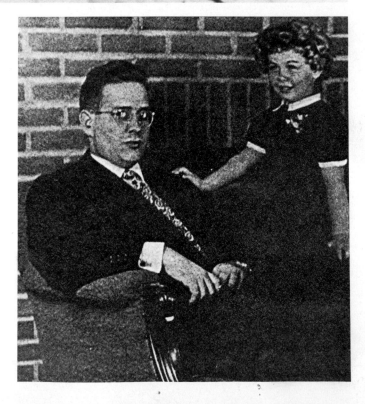

Darling— The happiness you have brought me is so great that I have one wish only— That this couple with their eyes on the stars will continue forever in Love, J. B.

Jessica and Barry Swartz, 1963. She inscribed this photograph: "Darling— The happiness you have brought me is so great that I have one wish only— That this couple with their eyes on the stars will continue forever in Love, J. B. [Jessica Beth]."

Future anchorwoman.

(ABOVE) With best girlfriend, Rusty Nicholl (left), New Year's Day 1964.
(ABOVE RIGHT) Mother and daughter, 1982.
(RIGHT) The high-achieving Savitches, 1979. Clockwise from top left: Leon Savitch, Rae Savitch Levin, Manny Savitch, Lil Savitch, Ben Savitch.

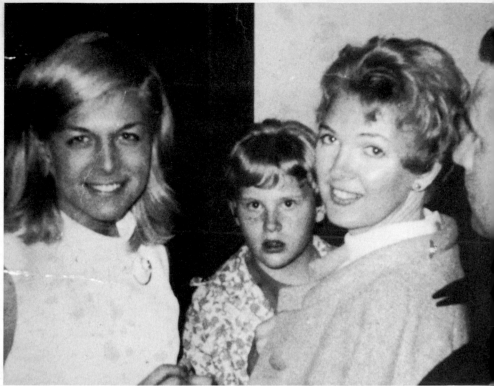

NEWS MEDIA

SAVITCH

Reporter-KHOU-TV

Expires: 4-4-73

NATIONAL AERONAUTICS
AND
SPACE ADMINISTRATION
MANNED
SPACECRAFT CENTER

JESSICA BETH SAVITCH

(JOAN BUSCH)

(OPPOSITE, TOP) With the Schwings, college graduation day, 1968.

(OPPOSITE, BOTTOM LEFT) Rookie reporter, KHOU, Houston, Texas, 1972.

(OPPOSITE, BOTTOM, RIGHT) "Dodge Girl," 1967.

(ABOVE) Tony Busch and "Beth," at the reception of her marriage to Mel Korn, January 1980.

(RIGHT) With longtime friend Ed Bradley, 1982.

(MARTA TABICKMAN)

(ABOVE) *KHOU All-Stars. From left: Carl Cochran, Judd McIlvain, Wally Athey, Jessica, Ron Cutchall, Bob Wolf.*
(BELOW) *In 1972, the idea of a female cameraman was so novel that when Jessica photographed Gus Mutscher arriving for his trial, the* Abilene Reporter-News *photographed* her *for page one.*

(ABOVE) *Jessica and Ron, with Dick Williams (top left) and Lonnie Reed, in Kershaw's Baltimore apartment, 1974.*
(BELOW LEFT) *With Sam and Rita Rappaport, 1975.*
(BELOW RIGHT) *Ron Kershaw in 1979, having just been named director of news at NBC-TV.*

(PHOTO BY ARTHUR SIRDOFSKY, COURTESY OF GAMMA-LIAISON)

(PHOTO BY DIANA WALKER, COURTESY OF GAMMA-LIAISON)

(PHOTO BY DIANA WALKER, COURTESY OF GAMMA-LIAISON)

(ABOVE) Primping on the set, June 1979.
(LEFT) Washington, May 1980.
(OPPOSITE, TOP LEFT) Chewy, woman's best friend.

(OPPOSITE, TOP RIGHT) With housekeeper Lelia Bright.

(OPPOSITE, BOTTOM) Anchorwoman, with weekend "Nightly News" producer Herb Dudnick.

(PHOTO BY DIANA WALKER, COURTESY OF GAMMA-LIAISON)

(COURTESY OF HERBERT J. DUDNICK)

(LEFT) *Jessica and Mel Korn, on the eve of their engagement, 1979.*
(BELOW) *At the DuPont-Columbia awards, with Hugh Downs, 1981.*
(OPPOSITE, TOP) *Jessica Savitch-Payne, with groom Donald Payne and his sister, Patricia Payne Mahlstedt, March 1981.*
(OPPOSITE, CENTER) *The newlyweds, March 1981.*
(OPPOSITE, BOTTOM) *At the Savitch-Payne wedding reception, March 1981: Florence Savitch and Stephanie Savitch-Newman, with her children David and Michael.*

With Roberta Spring, March 1981.

Jessica at the Kentucky Derby, Louisville, May 1982. Having undergone abdominal surgery two months before, she was still too weak to maneuver through the Derby crowd, but brightened up whenever photographers came around.

(RIGHT) *Jessica and Pat Garvey, October 1982.*

(BELOW LEFT) *David Buda and Chris Connal join Jessica at the Rappaports'* Anchorwoman *party, October 1982.*

(BELOW RIGHT) *With Marta Tabickman, October 1982.*

(MARTA TABICKMAN)

ARTA TABICKMAN)

(COURTESY OF MARTA TABICKMAN)

(*ABOVE*) Anchorwoman *author on PBS "Late Night" with Mort Crim and producer Bill Pace, 1982.*

(*LEFT*) *Jessica, 1982.*
(*OPPOSITE*) *One of Jessica's last public appearances, September 30, 1983, at the Philadelphia Emmy Awards. Earlier that month, Jessica had undergone nose surgery in Los Angeles.*

Martin Fischbein, 1982. An executive at the New York Post, *he was killed with Jessica the next year.*

The Delaware Canal in New Hope, though usually dry as shown here, was filled with four feet of water when Jessica's car plunged in during a rainy weekend in October 1983.

mother' to my children. And Sam just became her rock. She respected him, because she knew that whatever she asked him, he'd always tell her the truth. She was at peace with us, and she would confide the deepest stories of her life."

Apparently, Jessica would also confide some of the most evanescent. She told Rita that she, too, knew how horrible it was to lose a father at a young age, and how, instead of drawing families together, such a tragedy often split them apart. When her own father died, Jessica said, her mother had placed her in a Catholic boarding school, run by nuns in starched, crisp habits. The description was the very picture of the Holy Angels School for troubled girls in Rochester, New York, where she had volunteered as a college student.

In the spring of 1975, Jessica and the film crew flew to Hollywood to shoot their series on famous Philadelphians. Joe Vandergast was walking down the hall of the hotel one day when he heard Jessica screaming. Her door was ajar, and he bounded in to help. But she was merely talking on the phone to—he surmised by the language—Ron Kershaw. Vandergast simply backed out the door, but not before he saw her "jumping up and down, like she was bananas, like her body couldn't get the sound out hard enough."

Kershaw had grown increasingly critical of what he perceived as a change in Jessica's character, that she was buying into the star system, starting to believe her press, riding around in limos with Mort Crim, and hanging around with people who would perpetuate the network anchorwoman fantasy—"anchor-itis," as he called it. He saw that she'd now taken to wearing Gucci belts from the exclusive Nan Duskin shop, subscribing to such upscale publications as *Palm Beach Life,* and dropping references to béarnaise and Beaujolais. The first time she called Crim and Leonard her "colleagues," she and Ron had a ferocious fight, Kershaw erupting, "Hey, it's me! We're not acting now. These are the fuckin' guys you read the news with—they're not colleagues, they're shift workers, same as you!"

One weekend when Kershaw had finally begun to relax about the way his newsroom was shaping up, he and Jessica went to the Poconos to ski. Jessica had introduced him to the sport, and he was entranced with it. When they arrived at the lodge, the bellman took them to their room, and Kershaw was astonished to find that it "was bigger than our apartments." The bellman pointed out a generous arrangement of flowers, and a large fruit basket. For a moment, Ron thought they'd been given the wrong room. And when he tried to tip the bellman, he learned that, in fact, the room was complimentary, "for Miss Savitch," the Philadelphia TV star.

Kershaw told Jessica that they couldn't accept it. " 'You're a big to-do. This is a good indication of it, better than research or ratings. We'll just pay for the room, that's all.' "

Kershaw began to unpack. Suddenly he looked over to see Jessica loading up the fruit and flowers and shoving them toward the door. "I said, 'Jess, what the fuck are you doing?' She said, 'You told me to send it back!' I said, 'No, Jessica, we just can't take a big-ticket item like a room, because it will be perceived as a bribe.' "

Jessica realized then that it would be discourteous to return the fruit and flowers—no one would prejudice a story for a basket of fruit—but that they could not accept the room. For several minutes, neither of them spoke. "It's just like what Sissy [Farenthold] taught us," Jessica finally said. "It's not so important having an office, as how one gains that office."

"Jessica believed that until the day she died," says Kershaw, "but she tried to run away from it. She tried to lose herself through brutal fights with me, and through two marriages. She sold out along the way, and *she could not resolve it.* She worried about things like that, and she studied them, which is why she had integrity. But 'fruit-in-the-room' became a metaphor to us. Once you start *expecting* the fruit in the room, you're dead. You've crossed that line, and you're in television seriously and psychotically, because you don't see that the fruit's not there for *you*—it's there because of *TV.* That's the line everybody in television crosses, and you don't stop at a basket. You start referring to the people you work with as 'colleagues,' and you start sounding pompous and self-important. Jessica went on to consciously cross that line. *Knowingly.* "

Kershaw thought he was the final obstacle, her last attachment to reality: "She made a decision to go into the fantasy, even though it tortured her. It ate her up inside."

Shortly after the two returned from the mountains, Jessica made a speech before a local business organization. Afterward, a good-looking man in his middle forties approached her and introduced himself, saying he was a banker in town. Soon he began calling her for lunch, and then dinner, and then for picnics in the park. She loved to talk, he says, and he liked the way her face lit up when she went on about her dreams of network anchoring. But he was honest with her from the beginning, telling her he was married, that he wasn't in love with her, "but that I really wanted to take her to bed."

For several months, Jessica refused his sexual advances. Then she invited him up to her apartment in Hopkinson House. (She had moved from the twelfth to the thirtieth floor.) She was so thin, he remembers, that he could put his hands around her waist and still bring his fingertips together.

Almost immediately, the two began a ritual on Thursday nights. She would buy the food—usually steak, creamed spinach, and chocolate-covered strawberries—and he would cook. There would be candlelight, and music, and before bed, a couple of lines of cocaine. "That was the first time I'd ever seen it," he says.

Jessica had now begun using cocaine as a stimulant for love-making—the drug has a reputation as an aphrodisiac, although frequent users often experience diminished sex drive and interest. She would tell a psychiatrist that she had difficulty enjoying sex without it; it wasn't something she thought was very important. What she really wanted was simply to be held, but most men she knew would not be content with that. Cocaine made her feel like the perfect lover.

One night she and her banker had just finished dinner, when Jessica brought out the tiny plastic bag of cocaine. A heavy, grey thunderstorm had rolled across the city during the meal, and now the lightning was beginning to play against the handsome French doors that opened onto Jessica's tiny balcony.

"She turned out all the lights, and opened the doors and insisted that we get right where the wind and the rain were coming in," he says. "I thought it was so hilarious that at first I could barely function. But the lightning and the thunder just did something to her. She was really turned on, screaming."

Now, in contrast to her earlier, non-cocaine induced lovemaking, Jessica sought and achieved orgasm almost without fail. She thought she had found a miracle drug. Cocaine melted her inhibitions about nearly everything. She would get out the "soap-on-a-rope" microphone, slip Rod Stewart and Joe Cocker on the stereo, and act out her rock singer fantasy, putting on a whole show. The banker was amazed that she knew the words to all the songs. Sometimes, when she felt especially loose, she would strut around the living room as if it were a stage in a cavernous auditorium. The banker would fall on the floor from laughing, and Jessica would jump on him, straddling him, and ask if he had any idea what it was like to be seduced by a big-time rock star. Then they would lie on the thick, pile carpet, and she would adjust the lights so that they could watch their rhythmic gyrations in shadow on the wall.

Sometimes, in the afterglow, she would turn her face to his and softly ask, "What would happen if we got married?" But the banker told her he would not leave his family. "It wouldn't have had a snowball's chance in hell," he says. "She just wasn't the marrying kind. Besides, I was a father figure. She always denied it, but I knew that it was true."

On Sunday, June 1, 1975, forty-six-year-old Melvin Robert Korn lulled away the morning in bed, thumbing through *Today,* the *Philadelphia Inquirer* magazine. There the advertising executive came across a profile of twenty-eight-year-old Jessica Savitch by Maralyn Lois Polak. The article was headlined "Pretty People Are Suspect," part of a longer quotation in which Jessica expressed her fear that attractive women were perceived as poor journalists. The piece carried a comely photograph of her in a safari suit.

Korn was president of J. M. Korn & Son, Inc., Philadelphia's tenth largest advertising agency and a company he had inherited from his father, whose picture hung in a prominent spot in the office. He had seen Jessica a few times on TV, and he liked her. For that matter, Korn liked show business. As a boy, he had lined up fruit crates and made his own set of drums, cutting the top off a pretzel tin for a cymbal, and using whisk brooms to beat on a pail. Now he kept a professional trap set in his office, and as a former record promotion man, he subscribed to *Variety* to keep up with the goings-on in the entertainment field. His friends described him as "Mr. Show Biz."

Korn liked celebrities. He readily told strangers that one of the high points of his life had been getting to know Joan Crawford. He traveled around town in a chauffeur-driven Cadillac limousine, looking to all the world like a VIP.

"Mel was always the entrepreneur," says his friend John Sculley, the CEO of Apple Computer and former president and CEO of Pepsico. "Whenever I'd see him, he'd say, 'Hey, I got a new angle for you!' And he was just full of ideas. Mel is very resourceful, and very street smart. He could give something the sniff test and know if it was going to sell."

Korn also had lots of chutzpah, Sculley says. "If Mel saw somebody who was interesting, he would figure out a way to meet them. You'd always be amazed at the people Mel knew."

Until recently, Korn had been living with his second wife, Patti, and his four children, aged nine to seventeen. But now he and Patti had separated, and Korn was starting to see other women. Jessica Savitch, the new darling of Philadelphia, appealed to him on several levels. He wondered if the eighteen-year difference in their ages would bother her. He also wondered if it would bother him. Korn, whose firm did marketing, consulting, and public relations work for a number of food products, figured that he had "more baking time in the oven."

"Certain things jumped out of the story that just intrigued me," remembers Korn.

The following day, Korn picked up the telephone and dialed Harold Pannepacker, his sales representative at KYW.

"Harold, you know I don't normally do this, but I'd like to meet Jessica Savitch."

Pannepacker was stunned. Then the affable Korn heard a laugh in his ear. "You and about a thousand other guys, Mel!"

Korn reminded him that he was separated now, and added that if Jessica ever wanted to have a meal, he thought "We might be able to communicate well, and possibly develop some friendship." It took a few weeks, but Pannepacker called back.

"Jessica would be interested in having lunch or dinner," the sales rep said.

"Wow!" Korn exclaimed. "Why?"

"Don't ask me! Maybe you just hit it on the right day!"

Korn took Jessica to dinner. "That's when she told me she was living with a guy down in Maryland," he says. He was disappointed, but in the fall Jessica accepted his second invitation. Later, "I said, 'Well, jeez, let's go out to the country sometime and have dinner again.'" She said she would call him. "But that was it," he recalls. "I never heard from her."

Jessica now had increased demands on her time, partly because Ken Tiven was following through on his plan to put her on

additional shows. In September 1975, KYW management announced that on top of her regular duties, Jessica would soon
become the solo anchor for the noon news, which had been co-
anchored by Matt Quinn and Marciarose Shestack, the latter of
whom was moving on to WNBC-TV in New York. Jessica and
Quinn, a political journalist generally recognized as the best reporter at the station, were also named co-hosts of a new program
called "Meetinghouse," a live, one-hour, weekly public forum that
addressed such volatile local issues as runaway kids, illegal aliens,
the quality of the public schools, and the criminal justice system.

Airing in prime time—eight on Tuesday nights—the show
featured a panel of three or four experts and a vocal, sometimes
passionate studio audience, which sat on risers around the stage
and asked questions. Jessica and Quinn moderated the exchange.
The idea was to get things stirred up.

Bill Mandel, who had been noticing the same changes in Jessica that Kershaw had, often attended.

"This was a lot like 'Donahue,' or the Oprah Winfrey show,"
he says, "and a lot of times the people in the audience couldn't
express themselves properly in terms of getting out what they
wanted to say. Until I saw Ted Koppel, I thought Jessica had been
the best there was in taking a garbled statement by the expert, or
a question from someone in the audience, and translating it into
very clear English. She really had an uncanny ability to do that.

"When she first started at KYW," he goes on, "she felt a
responsibility to the public. People would wait for her in the lobby,
and she would speak to them. But by the time she was finishing her
contract, she was so frustrated with being forced to remain that she
became something else. On 'Meetinghouse,' for example, the format of the show dictated that the audience would come down off
the risers and talk to her as the credits rolled, and she'd give them
this incredibly empathetic expression. But the second they killed
the cameras, she just shot out of there in mid-sentence, and got
into her limo. The people were absolutely *aghast* that she went
from being this amazingly concerned person to this iceberg."

Mandel was so alarmed by Jessica's behavior that he confronted her with it.

"My job is to be empathetic during the hour," she told him.
"My job is not to hang around and be talked to by the public." And
then she would laugh. "Later, she started saying, 'Once you can

fake sincerity, you've got it made.' It became her favorite motto."

Nevertheless, "Meetinghouse" perpetuated the image of Jessica as a serious journalist. The month it debuted, the local educational station, WHYY, named her Philadelphia commercial TV'S "Person of the Year."

Afterward, Harry Harris, the *Philadelphia Inquirer* TV writer, asked her about her plans. Jessica informed him that she still had twenty-two months to go on her contract, and then she hoped to go to a network—but not to become "a commentator, quasi-news," like Barbara Walters, whom she did not consider a pacesetter. "In what I consider 'the top of my field,' there are no women," she said. "That's the across-the-board network anchor like [Walter] Cronkite and Harry Reasoner."

As another barometer of Jessica's rise in the industry, Ithaca College asked her to return to campus for one week each year as a visiting professor. It was a triumph she could not pass up, especially since Westinghouse allowed for education-oriented leaves of absence. She would teach a one-credit course called "Television News." The first time she went, in October 1975, she told her class of twenty-five students that the first requirement for a successful television journalist was stamina: "I would say it ranks above ability."

Jessica's return to Ithaca came one month after CBS's "On the Road" correspondent Charles Kuralt spoke before a Dallas convention of the Radio and Television News Directors Association and decried what he called "the continuing disgrace of this profession." After watching hundreds of hours of local anchormen throughout the country, he reported, his lingering impression was one of "hair. Anchormen's hair . . . neatly parted, hair abundant, and every hair in place . . . But I can't remember much that came out from beneath all that hair.

"I know [this profession] to be riddled with glib, highly paid poseurs who wouldn't last two weeks as $125-a-week cub reporters on the local newspaper," Kuralt said. "I am ashamed, I think we all ought to be ashamed, that twenty-five years into the television age, so many of our anchormen haven't any basis on which to make a news judgment, can't edit, can't write, and can't cover a story." The remarks would soon be quoted in the industry like a Bible.

In mid-November 1975, William Small, senior vice-president and director of news for CBS, came to Philadelphia for the national convention of the Society of Professional Journalists, of which he was president. Knowing that others at CBS had tried to hire Jessica at the outset of her Westinghouse contract, Small invited her to his suite in the Benjamin Franklin Hotel to talk about coming to the network as a reporter when she was free.

Only a few short years ago, such an offer would have made Jessica ecstatic. But now she no longer thought of herself as a correspondent. She was an anchor. She asked Small for a guarantee that if she accepted she would eventually assume anchor duties. Small, one of the staunchest of the old-time journalists, and a man who believed that anchorship was reserved for reporters who had labored many, many years in the field, made no promises.

"She didn't turn me down quite that night," remembers Small, now the director of the Center for Communications at the Fordham University school of business. But the eventual answer was no. She thought she could do better.

In early 1976, Jessica and Dave Neal went to New York. Neal had gotten a call from Ron Tindiglia, the news director at WABC, Channel 7. Tindiglia, who until recently had been the news director at WPVI in Philadelphia, and Al Ittleson, the vice-president of news for ABC's owned-and-operated stations, wanted to talk to Jessica about coming to work. Tindiglia knew how riveting Jessica could be on screen, and he was fully aware of what she did for ratings.

Jessica informed her New York luncheon companions that she was flattered by the offer, but that she was really only interested in a network job. She wanted to be the first major female anchor. Ittleson reportedly offered to try to set up a meeting for her with Bill Sheehan, head of the network news division.

ABC had always been a distant third in the network news race, and Sheehan never stopped searching for ways to change that. He, like executives at CBS and NBC, constantly looked around to see what techniques local stations were using to attract audiences, including the trend toward female co-anchors. For some time, he'd been thinking of pairing a woman with Ted Koppel on ABC's Saturday night news. He'd reportedly been looking at Pat Harper and Connie Chung, then in the CBS Washington bureau. Now there was Jessica Savitch to consider. Sheehan was interested.

By now, KYW was becoming increasingly reliant on electronic news gathering, with one "instant eye" van in operation from seven A.M. to midnight, and two more expected by July. But Ken Tiven needed another strategy to lure audiences for the eleven o'clock news. ABC's prime-time programming provided a huge lead-in for WPVI's local eleven o'clock newscast, but NBC wasn't doing the same for KYW. The perfect solution, as he saw it, was to assemble Philadelphia's first "anchor troika"—putting Jessica on with Vince and Mort at eleven, beginning in February 1976. She'd been after the eleven o'clock spot for months now anyway, even though it was obvious that neither Vince nor Mort was going to give up his seat.

Tiven had tried the tri-anchor situation before, in Washington, D.C., and he saw it could work if the duties were divided up in a way that distinguished each anchor from the other. On a rotating basis, one anchor would be an expert witness/reporter out in the field, beamed in by the instant eye. The other two would remain in the studio, and all would have parity. "If you had cooperating anchors, it was a godsend for getting all three luminaries on the program," says Tiven, who now runs the country's only independent public television station, WQEX, in Pittsburgh.

The luminaries disagreed. "We knew it wouldn't work," sighs Vince Leonard. "It was a dismal failure from the very start."

Suddenly, there was trouble in Camelot. Three people who genuinely regarded one another as family—Mort and Vince had even chipped in to buy an airplane together—now began to view the others as rivals. Tiven would come in to the station in the mornings and find separate notes from two of the team, complaining that the other members had more on-air time than he did.

The news director thought the same two anchors, including Jessica, were more interested in being on camera and giving speeches than they were in covering stories. For the most part, Alan Bell concurred. Jessica, especially, tended to be "a spoiled brat" about doing any reporting not involved with her special series. But Jessica wasn't the only member of the "Eyewitness News" team eager for his contract to expire. Crim was getting feelers to come to WBBM in Chicago, to replace Bill Kurtis, soon to depart for the "CBS Morning News." Now, during the commercial breaks on the 5:30 news, he and Jessica would whisper back and forth about their various negotiations for moving up and out, confident that since their offices were so small—even the new ones were a minuscule eight-by-seven feet—this was the only place they could talk. What they didn't know was that the audio men left their microphones open—and that Alan Bell and Ken Tiven were sitting in Bell's office, hovering around the studio line monitor, hanging on their every word.

The tri-anchor arrangement allowed Jessica to drop her stint at noon, but with the 5:30 news, "Meetinghouse," and her special series, she was still working far longer hours than her counterparts. Through her agent, Don Hamburg, she demanded yet another hefty salary increase. Both she and Hamburg knew that the more money she was getting at KYW, the bigger her leverage would be with the networks. Tiven and Bell didn't mind paying her more money to stay on past the expiration of her contract, but Jessica argued for compensation just to stay until the original expiration date. It was a never-ending battle.

Finally, one day, Tiven went to New York and met with Hamburg in the Palm Court at the Plaza. Hamburg, whom Tiven found to be a practiced artist at the laundry list approach to contract negotiation, "wanted Tuesdays and Thursdays off in months that end in *r,*" Tiven says, citing how far Hamburg would go to get the most for his client, and he wanted "to confuse us so that no one knew what was important anymore."

Tiven's job was to sit there for an hour and a half and say no. But by the time the two men shook hands, Jessica Savitch, who had come to KYW as a $17,000 a year reporter, was now taking home the magical sum of $100,000. Don Hamburg was very pleased with himself. Shortly, on the recommendation of Joel Chaseman, Jessica would have a New York financial manager, Robert Andrews, to help her handle it all.

Now, on Thursday nights, Jessica couldn't keep from gloating to her bemused banker. A hundred thousand dollars! "Jesus!" she would say to him. "I probably make more money than you do!" The banker was delighted for her. But now that she was doing the eleven o'clock news, their nights of lovemaking ended earlier than either of them liked. He was fascinated to watch her put on her makeup. He saw her body language change, heard her voice become authoritative—saw her go from the fragile little girl to the tough TV anchorwoman right in front of him. And then he would go home and lie next to his wife, turning his television to Channel 3. "Christ, to lie there and watch her after that," he says, "was really something."

In the middle of March, Mel Korn was out of town when his secretary told him he'd had a message from Jessica Savitch: She was ready for that dinner in the country. Korn was thrilled. He listened avidly to Jessica's stories about turning down CBS's Bill Small—"Bill Small, for goshsakes!"—and about holding out for an anchor job. ABC would be a wonderful place for her to go, he thought, even though "it was still half a network." But before Jessica went anywhere, he told her, she needed a little "packaging."

"First of all, this kid was gorgeous to me," says Korn, today president of Geographic Marketing Group in Philadelphia. "You know what I mean—you got a great product. Forget television. Just seeing her look great was wonderful, but then I realized she made her living by total imagery." Korn offered to help her succeed, to "put the finishing touches on her," as Dave Neal remembers, continuing the private tutoring that Carole Bell had begun with foods and wines, and picking out—and paying for—a new wardrobe, getting her out of blue jeans and into clothes of style and sophistication. Jessica was both eager and wary, anxious to improve her chances for the anchor spot, and yet afraid that she was giving up her aspirations of real journalism.

Korn pampered Jessica and indulged her whims. Soon his chauffeur-driven limo was showing up at Hopkinson House to collect her for work, to take her to New York, to take her shopping. Now, partly because Kershaw detested such events, Mel would escort her to her public speaking dates and award shows.

At first, Korn did not demand that she stop going to Baltimore on the weekends, and when he eventually found out about the drugs, he cautioned her, but did not immediately insist that she stop. He would do anything to win her, although he was beginning to sense how fragile she was—that she could not cope with her day-to-day problems. And he knew that she frequently complained of nightmares. She would call him in the pre-dawn hours of the morning, sobbing that she wasn't any good for anybody, and warning him that "anybody who's gotten involved with me has had nothing but trouble." She was now so disturbed about going into a restaurant that Korn would arrange for a private dining room so she would not be subjected to the public. One of the reasons she loved the limo was because it protected her from her fans, whose intrusions she'd come to fear and dread. The big Caddy was a luxurious, airtight safety chamber, whisking her through the streets of Philadelphia late at night in a surreal, impressionistic glow.

Bill Mandel remembers that Jessica "talked about Mel with this sort of tittered embarrassment, about how much older he was, and how he wore a toupee. She said, 'He treats me like a father.' I got the impression he had sort of adopted her."

But Ida McGinniss thought Korn was a perfect balance for Jessica, and others concurred. "Mel's a wonderful guy, and he deserves a tremendous amount of credit," says Dave Neal. "He just took over everything." That was precisely what concerned Joe Vandergast: "It was kind of strange. One day I work with her, and she's sensitive, and warm, and fun, and then all of a sudden, we're talking anchor, and every day this big limousine's picking her up, she's being wooed by the networks, and there's a third force pulling her away." Several other KYW staff members thought Jessica's new boyfriend was variously "weird," or "odd"—that he had a "Hollywood press agent" look.

By the spring of 1976, Jessica had heard nothing from Bill Sheehan about the ABC anchor job. Worse, the year was turning out to be one in which women reporters and anchors were being hired in record numbers at local stations throughout the country. Female reporters were getting increased airtime at the networks as well, including Jane Pauley, Judy Woodruff, and Marilyn Berger at NBC, and at CBS, Renee Poussaint and Lesley Stahl. According to Joe Vandergast, it was Stahl whom Jessica feared most. Not only had she proven her mettle as a reporter during Watergate, but she and Jessica were the same physical type. Jessica knew that could cause problems down the road.

Now she nervously scanned the television page every morning, fearful of what she'd find. The time they still talk about at Channel 3 was the day Bill Sheehan announced that Barbara Walters was moving to ABC to co-anchor its "Evening News" with Harry Reasoner at an annual salary of $1 million. Jessica's highly audible outrage lasted for a long time; then she went into a corner of the newsroom and cried. The signing made history, but not just for the money: Barbara Walters was the first woman to co-anchor a network evening newscast.

By the time Dave Neal caught up with her, it was obvious to him that Jessica needed professional help. "She's not even a news-

woman!" Jessica cried. "She's a goddamn *hostess!* A personality!"
There was no comforting her. Neal kept reminding her that she
was still young, but Jessica was beyond reasoning. She *couldn't* just
go to the network as a reporter! Anybody could do that. Even the
woman Dick John had hired to replace her in Houston, Linda
Veselka—by now Linda Ellerbee—was already at NBC. She *would
not* follow that woman to the network as a reporter! Jessica had to
go in as an anchor, with prestige and standing.

As usual during this period, Kershaw offered little consolation. He had worked long and hard to build WBAL into a station
of merit, and now his shop was finally reaping recognition; soon,
among other accolades, they would pick up two regional Emmy
awards. But in June, Kershaw would finally get his real reward,
when the Nielsen book would rate his six o'clock news number one
in the market. He had done it!

Now Kershaw asked Jessica who she was seeing during the
week.

She told him she had become friends with a man named Mel
Korn. He was good to her. He was in the marketing business; his
biggest accounts were soft-drink bottlers.

Kershaw let out a howl. "Root beer! Are you shittin' me?
You're seeing a guy in *root beer?*" Kershaw snorts. "She never had
a real relationship with Mel Korn," he says. "We had a huge argument about that." Soon Jessica began turning up with injuries
which, she told friends and the press, she'd received in a series of
minor accidents. Such accidents were possible, of course, but when
Carl Cochran and his lover visited her sometime that year, Cochran was alarmed to see that the Kershaw beatings had not diminished. Furthermore, it was now fully apparent to him that Jessica's
cocaine use had become a dependency: She was hooked.

So was he. "As before," says Cochran, "our level of drug
usage was exactly the same. By 1976, we entered a stage where
cocaine became not a recreational drug, but a multi-required daily
high. It was more expensive back then, but we'd buy it in bulk, and
we'd try to just buy two quarters [of a gram] a week each, so that
it was never more than a two or three hundred dollar a week habit.
But if we had a safe source to get a large amount, that precluded
having to worry about it for a while."

One of the problems of cocaine addiction is that once the
initial euphoria wears off, in about thirty minutes, users often feel

more depressed than they did before taking the drug. To avoid the awful "coke blues," they often get caught in "binge and crash" cycles, taking other drugs, such as Valium, to dull the effects of coming down.

In the spring of 1976, around the time Jessica received the devastating blow of Barbara Walters being hired at ABC, Dick Williams, Kershaw's old news director, got married in Miami. Jessica planned to fly down for the event, and then she, Kershaw, and Williams's ex-girlfriend, Lonnie Reed, would go on to the Bahamas for a few days of vacation.

"Jessica never made the wedding, but she flew into Nassau on Sunday," Reed remembers, "and I noticed she had a full bottle of Valium. She was popping them like crazy. I said, 'Jessica, why are you taking Valium on *vacation?* You're supposed to be relaxing.' And she said, 'I can't—I can't.' By Wednesday, that huge bottle of Valium was almost gone."

"In the beginning of her career," says Carl Cochran, "Jessica was motivated by delusions of grandeur. She had an outlook and a perception of herself, her world, and her place in it, that was unique. And in the early years, this worked in a very positive way, because all those fears and feelings of inferiority made her strive to be a hell of a fine reporter. But once drugs entered the picture, all those psychological factors that had pointed her toward the positive now began to point her toward the negative."

Sometime during the summer of 1976, Jessica attended a dinner party given by Ida McGinniss. There she met a professional psychic named Joan Durham. Unlike many such "party" mediums, Durham's success had been such that she was well known to law enforcement officials throughout the country, and was credited with helping to solve a number of difficult murder cases. Jessica, long attached to the notion of powerful psychic phenomena, arranged for a private reading from Durham at Ida McGinniss's home in the Dorchester in Rittenhouse Square. Durham says she knew nothing of Jessica's background.

"I took her into one of the back bedrooms," remembers Durham, a south Philadelphia native, "and when we began the reading, the first thing I told her was that I saw her father with her in spirit. I said, 'I see him with his arm over your shoulder. He's still looking after you.' And I glanced up, and the tears were just coming down from her eyes. She wanted to know if he was at peace, if he was happy."

Jessica went on to ask questions about the upcoming events in her life, and about her relationship with Kershaw, whose engagement ring she still occasionally wore. Durham told her she and Kershaw would go to New York, and that they would be together there, but not for long. Then Jessica asked about her death. Lately, she had been telling Mort Crim—who would also begin going to Durham—that she did not believe she would live much longer than her father, who had died at thirty-three. "I told her we're all only here on borrowed time, to work something out, and that we all write the time in the book," Durham says. "We may not write how we're going to die, but we do write the time." Joan Durham would become an indispensable part of Jessica's support network.

In July, Jessica began work on her most ambitious project yet. She had been toying with the idea of doing a special report on the increasing number of female police recruits. She identified with their struggle to gain acceptance among their male counterparts, and she likened it to her own starting-at-the-bottom days in Houston. But this time she wanted to do something bigger than a five-part series, something in the hour format. "Lady Law," as the award-winning documentary was to be called, was the perfect subject: Philadelphia had become a Justice Department test area for women in police work.

One member of the KYW viewing audience who paid special attention to Jessica's anchoring and showcase projects was a man by the name of Edgar Griffiths. Chairman of the board of RCA, the parent company of the NBC television network, Griffiths watched Jessica nightly from his home in Cherry Hill, New Jersey, where RCA was headquartered. His wife, says Alan Bell, was a greater admirer of Jessica than Griffiths.

One day, according to Kershaw and to E. Gregory Hookstratten, a California-based news talent agent, Griffiths mentioned to Herbert Schlosser, president of NBC, that he'd like to see Jessica brought into the ranks. Schlosser in turn told Richard C. Wald, head of the NBC news division. The word went around that the Philadelphia anchorwoman was one of Griffiths's favorites, and that soon the news division would be "forced" to take her. Today, there is some belief that the story was mythical, that while Griffiths was "very fond of her," according to Bill Small, eventually sending her a huge, china "Nipper," the RCA trademark pooch, Griffiths's influence on the news division was minimal. Others say this was precisely the time when higher management began increasing its whims on the once autonomous news. Whatever the veracity of the story, according to some perceptions at NBC, Jessica Savitch already had one strike against her before she ever set foot in 30 Rockefeller Plaza.

As 1976 was drawing to an end, the NBC-TV network, and particularly its news division, was in perpetual flux and deep trouble. The glory days of the Huntley-Brinkley era were long gone, and except for one thirteen-week period in 1974, John Chancellor, the stiff, professorial anchor of the "NBC Nightly News," had never been able to beat Walter Cronkite in the ratings, not even when the network brought in David Brinkley to co-anchor with him earlier that year. Now there was the Harry Reasoner–Barbara Walters team to contend with, of particular import because NBC was still second in the news race, but ABC had pushed NBC into third place for prime-time programming. If NBC fell to third in news as well, it would likely lose a sizable number of its affiliates. The consequences could be dire.

Chancellor's contract was up in 1977, and rumors flew around the building that he would be replaced by Tom Snyder, Tom Brokaw, or possibly both. Soon the newspapers would pick up the story, reporting that Chancellor, NBC's best-known news personality, was entertaining other offers, particularly one from CBS.

What was especially interesting about the Chancellor-Snyder-Brokaw triad, as Barbara Matusow pointed out in her engrossing book, *The Evening Stars: The Making of the Network News Anchor,* was that it became a symbol for a schism at NBC over the way the news division appeared to be heading. To the old guard, which was shrinking in numbers almost daily, the important goal was to continue producing a solid, journalistically sound evening newscast. To another group, "NBC Nightly News" was far too stodgy, and the only way to pull ahead was to forget prestige and go for ratings, perhaps borrowing some of the flashy, trend-setting techniques that had worked so well for local news management.

The majority opinion, however, was to liven the pace without compromising the network's integrity. Still, these proponents were uncertain about just how to do it—whether to keep Chancellor, whom most of the correspondents revered, but whom the producers regarded as too enmeshed in international politics for America's true taste, or whether to go for Brokaw or Snyder.

Should Chancellor decide to go elsewhere, most NBC correspondents and producers thought that Brokaw, then a "Today" show host and former White House correspondent, was generally acceptable as his replacement. There had been a time when his youthful good looks and his slight speech impediment had worked against him, but he was respected as a solid journalist—if somewhat resented for advancing so quickly in the ranks. On the other hand, certain of the management—including NBC President Herbert Schlosser, a former entertainment attorney—argued for Snyder, believing that his boisterous personality would draw new viewers and quickly boost ratings.

The idea of putting Tom Snyder on as the anchor of the "NBC Nightly News"—the figure who would represent the entire news division, and to some extent the network itself—was unthinkable to Richard C. Wald, head of the NBC news division, and to almost everyone on the news side of things, including Chancellor. "In his view," wrote Matusow, "Snyder was only in it for the money and the ego, using journalism purely to promote himself as a celebrity." Even if he could pull the lapels of the viewer through the screen in an active, involved performance, Snyder—who like Jessica had come out of KYW, but by way of California—was also anathema to the sanctity of the network evening newscast. He seemed a disturbing harbinger of the way the industry appeared to be changing, with the primacy of the performer over the journalist. And anyone vaguely of his ilk was perceived as poison among the old guard correspondents at NBC—as a charlatan, fraud, and poseur who would not be suffered long.

On September 23, 1976, President Gerald Ford and Democratic presidential nominee Jimmy Carter met in Philadelphia at the Walnut Street Theatre for the first of their nationally televised debates. NBC sent down a small crew headed by Bob Mulholland, one of Dick Wald's deputies, and a vice-president in charge of specials for news. The video for the ninety-minute event would be provided by a "pool" of cameras, and fed to all three networks in New York on one line, via the ABC remote truck. All three networks also sent an anchor and a reporter, and NBC produced that portion of their coverage out of a trailer and a truck parked outside the theatre. This video would be sent to New York on another line, and combined and switched with the pool video. To save money, Mulholland had opted not to buy a "return" video line, which meant that the only way he could see what was being aired on the network was by watching KYW.

Ken Tiven had several mini-cams spread around Philadelphia, including one outside the theatre, where Jessica was assigned as a reporter. She was nervous that night, and especially keen on impressing Mulholland. If he liked her, he would surely tell Wald. NBC was the one network she had yet to approach for an anchor job.

As it turned out, Bob Mulholland would see a lot more of Jessica Savitch that night than he'd planned. Some ten minutes before the debate was scheduled to end, the audio line blew. Ken Tiven got a call from one of his assistant producers, who told him, "I don't know what's going on, but everybody just ran out of the ABC pool truck, and they all went into the theatre." Tiven knew that "if it's more than one guy with a screwdriver, you can figure you're in deep shit." And indeed, John Chancellor, Walter Cronkite, and Harry Reasoner were now pressed into service to placate viewers for the next thirty minutes until the audio was restored.

With that, Tiven got the opportunity to prove what ENG was all about. The station abandoned the NBC coverage, alerted Jessica and Matt Quinn, who had been stationed inside the theatre, and switched to Mort Crim back in the KYW studio. A staff announcer broke in—"This is Eyewitness News, a special report"— and Crim was on. "As you can tell," the veteran newscaster began, "the audio's disappeared. There's a lot of confusion going on, and Jessica Savitch is outside the Walnut Street Theatre. Jessica, what do you know?"

Mulholland, without his return video line from New York, was now forced to watch the KYW coverage. At the outset of the debate, he had been furious with Jessica—she had run long on her remarks for the local audience. Instead of hearing, "From the Walnut Street Theatre in Philadelphia, this is an NBC News special presentation. Now here is John Chancellor," all the viewers heard was, "—or," the last syllable of the anchorman's name. Jessica would later claim in her book that her remarks had been pretaped, and that the KYW computers rolled her promo late. But Mulholland had come roaring out of the remote truck, accusing her of ruining Chancellor's opening.

Now Mulholland stared at the monitor to see Jessica take command of the situation, fielding live reports and interviews, and conversing intelligently with Crim and Matt Quinn. Mulholland was in the unique position of being able to see simultaneously a story unfold live in front of him and watch a reporter describe it on the air. That one half-hour told him almost everything he needed to know about Jessica Savitch. She was cool under pressure, she could scramble for the sources, and she could report a story fairly and accurately. That, combined with what he'd heard about her anchor skills, made her a most alluring talent.

"The next day," says Tiven, "Bob Mulholland was on the phone, playfully screaming at me for having stiffed him on the return video, and complimenting me on the wonderful job we had done. But the truth of it is he saw an awful lot of Jessica Savitch that night in his frustration, and he liked what he saw. And, of course, he knew that NBC was going into the tank so fast you couldn't even see the air bubbles."

For Mulholland, there was the problem of where to put a Jessica Savitch: NBC had only seven half-hours of network news a week. But Cassie Mackin had anchored some of the weekend editions of "Nightly News," and within a year, she would follow Barbara Walters to ABC. Mulholland did some checking. Jessica had precisely a year left on her Westinghouse contract. He would stay in touch with her, ask for her tapes. And he would show them to his boss, Dick Wald.

Meanwhile, sometime in the fall of 1976, Jessica learned that Don Hewitt, producer of CBS's "60 Minutes," was planning a spin-off show called "Who's Who." Jessica thought she might be able to parlay such a co-host spot into an anchor job, or failing that, into a slot on "60 Minutes." Don Hewitt was one of the most respected men in television. But there was another reason she wanted the job. The chief reporter was to be Dan Rather, whom she had tried to emulate since Houston.

She did well in the New York audition—along with Barbara Howar and Phyllis George—but was once again informed that if she were offered the job, it would be impossible for her to escape her Westinghouse contract.

Now Jessica turned again to Joel Chaseman.

"CBS was really still what Jessica called her 'network of choice,'" remembers Chaseman, "so we worked out a strategy. I remember having lunch at the Gloucester House with [CBS news head] Dick Salant, trying to sell him that the ideal replacement for

Walter Cronkite, when Cronkite decided to quit, would be a combination of Dan Rather and Jessica Savitch co-anchoring the 'CBS Evening News.' " Roger Mudd was the popular choice in those days, but Chaseman tried to convince Salant that the way to succeed Cronkite was not with yet another white, male anchor, but with a team—something different, something that wouldn't be compared with the man the industry affectionately referred to as "Uncle Walter."

Chaseman failed. Salant told him CBS had too many obligations to the senior staff members to consider such a plan. "He said, 'How can we talk about Jessica Savitch, when we have Lesley Stahl?' " Chaseman says. "But this was also a time when professional journalists were looking down their noses at attractive women who communicated well. You know, they had one. And if you had to weigh one against the other, Jessica was sixty-five percent communicator, and thirty-five percent journalist."

One night early in November 1976, Jessica was at KYW, talking on the phone to Ron Kershaw in Baltimore shortly before airtime. She excitedly told him that she'd been talking to Bob Mulholland, and that it looked like NBC was really interested in her, maybe even for a weekend anchor job. The words ate at Kershaw like acid. He believed that Jessica was the best on camera since Murrow, he says, but knew that if she went to New York and bought even further into the star trip, their relationship was hopeless. NBC would eat her alive. He knew what they were like, he told her. They would see her as not having paid her dues. They would see her as a female Tom Snyder, a performer. Now his tone grew hostile.

"NBC is the stodgiest, smuggest, most obnoxious of all the fuckin' networks," Kershaw told her. "It's the network of the empty, old grey suits. Who ever gave a fuck about what John Chancellor ever said, just once in his life? He's the blandest motherfucker on earth! And NBC is the *epitome* of John Chancellor. They're all like him! They'll go out of their *way* to torture you up there."

Now Kershaw was half crying, half screaming. "I hate you," he said into the phone. "I hate myself for following you up here." After a thousand threats of breaking up, a thousand pledges to stay together, it had come down to this. It was over. Jessica hung up the receiver, feeling her emotional balance beginning to slip away.

When someone finally found her, she was hiding under a desk, trembling, disoriented.

"It was an anxiety-panic response," says Mort Crim. "This was not a constant work mode, but there were two or three incidents of this kind. And it just became necessary to talk her through, and get her calmed down to go on the air."

But this time, Mel Korn says, Jessica could not go on the air. Crim went on alone. And Jessica was taken to Pennsylvania Hospital. Afterward, her gynecologist, Joel Polin, and Carole Bell recommended her to a local psychiatrist named Stephen Schwartz. Several times a week, Mel's car and driver would take her to Schwartz's office in the suburbs. Soon the visits grew less and less frequent; Korn was sorry, because he thought the sessions with Schwartz were helping to lessen her anxiety.

On November 19, David Savitch's birthday, Jessica flew to California to spend Thanksgiving with Ben and Lil, who had moved to Laguna Hills in retirement to be near their children. Mel and Carole Bell took her to the airport for the six P.M. flight. To Lonnie Reed, she would admit that she was going on a medical leave, a rest required by a period of psychological turmoil brought on by a host of worries, not the least of which was Kershaw's negative reaction to her growing success.

On Thanksgiving Day, Jessica flew to Marco Island, Florida, to meet Mel Korn. He was waiting for her with white roses, caviar, a gold pin, and a pigeon-blood star ruby ring. He had arranged for a penthouse. During the day, they enjoyed the sunshine. Still, Jessica ached for Ron. On December 1, she flew back to California and called him, asking if she could come east so they could start over. He told her no, it was finished. She vowed she would never call him again.

In early 1977, Dave Neal, who had moved over to WCAU, was getting pressure from his new news director, Eric Ober, to introduce him to his friend Jessica Savitch. Everyone was interested in her, especially the CBS owned-and-operated stations. In the spring of that year, Jessica got the nod from none other than Ed Joyce, the same man who had refused to give her a desk assistant's job during her pre-Houston gofer days. Now he wanted to talk with her about a co-anchor slot at WCBS-TV, the network's prestigious flagship station where he was news director. To Jessica, it was a world-class irony, worthy of O. Henry.

Joyce, whom Jessica would describe in *Anchorwoman* as "a country gentry type with his pipe and tweedy, patched-elbow look," invited her to lunch at an elegant New York restaurant. He was poised and proper, dressed in his executive suit and executive manners. Jim Cusick, the assistant news director who had been a news writer and editor during Jessica's WCBS radio days, came along. For every day of the last seven years, she had yearned to show Ed Joyce how wrong he'd been about her. She had lain awake at night and seen his face, had it loom up before her as she gathered her resources for the childbirth series, before she stepped before the camera for her WCBS audition tape, before she found the courage to anchor for Dick John in Houston. He was her personal, private devil, slapping her with his pointy tail every step of the way.

Now, ensconced in the handsome restaurant's surroundings, Jessica brought up the painful subject of her gofer days. She leaned across the table and managed a nervous smile. Before they went any further, she said, she had a question for him:

"Why didn't you hire me?"

Jessica wrote in her autobiography that Joyce studied his plate, arranged his tie, and clasped his hands.

"You want the truth?" he answered.

"Please."

"Jessica . . . I don't even remember you."

Before the lunch was over, Joyce offered her a contract in the $200,000 range. But Jessica no longer had any interest in Ed Joyce or any job he might offer. She thanked him for his interest, but explained she was in negotiation elsewhere. She had heard once again from Bob Mulholland. And before the year was out, Jessica Savitch planned to be the Golden Girl of NBC.

For the past several weeks, Dick Wald, president of the NBC news division, had been talking to Don Meaney about a woman named Jessica Savitch. Mulholland was high on her, he said. NBC talent scout Bill Slatter had mentioned her to Joe Bartelme, a network vice-president for news, and Bartelme also thought she had a certain electricity. Wald asked the Washington bureau chief to take a look at some of Jessica's tapes.

Meaney, a kind, "friendly uncle" sort whose surname belied his true personality, told his old friend Wald that he'd be glad to run them. He'd been thinking about bringing another woman into the bureau for some time now, but hadn't settled on any one candidate. Meaney was mindful of the multimillion-dollar antidiscrimination suit that NBC's female employees had filed in 1975, but he also enjoyed working with women. Most of all, he had been sent to Washington to "build up the place," as he says, "including people," and before long, he would be able to say he hired both Linda Ellerbee and Andrea Mitchell, a KYW Newsradio alumna. Now Meaney needed someone with exceptional spark on the air. "It was terribly important to have somebody good," he explains, sitting in the dining room of his Washington home, "because things were going down very badly at NBC in those days."

When Meaney got the tapes, he slipped the rape series into the playback machine and settled in his chair. It was well-written and well-edited, he thought, and Jessica handled herself nicely on camera. The same was true of "Lady Law," the documentary Jessica had done on the training of policewomen. But when the bureau chief put the anchor tape on, "It struck me immediately," he would tell journalist Judith Adler Hennessee, "she just *demanded* your attention. You got the feeling she was telling the news *to you.*"

Several days later, Meaney got on the Metroliner to Philadelphia. He had an appointment to meet Jessica at the 30th Street Station, from which the two would go to lunch. Arriving in the depot, Meaney looked up to see Jessica standing at the top of the escalator. It was still premature to make her an offer, but at that moment Meaney knew that he wanted her in Washington.

When he returned to the bureau, Meaney told both NBC President Herb Schlosser and Dick Wald, who had yet to be totally convinced that NBC needed Jessica Savitch, that of all the female candidates he'd reviewed, his thinking was running toward Jessica. "She knew what she wanted to do, she had the intelligence and the energy to pursue it, and she was absolutely eyecatching on the air."

Jessica made a trip to Washington for still more discussion—she wanted a prestigious reporting assignment such as Capitol Hill, the White House, or the Senate, as well as anchor duties. And Meaney would make yet another visit to Philadelphia. This time, Jessica would pick him up at the station in Mel's flashy limo.

As usual whenever Jessica was about to make a major career

move, she sought out her network of advisers. Joel Chaseman told her, as tactfully as possible, that the Senate beat would be a mistake, that she was much more of a "focused" performer—communicating with her eyes, with the way she leaned forward—than she was an intellectual journalist. He feared she would get a vivid story, and one the audience would remember, but that it would be only a surface account.

Jim Topping, with whom Jessica still kept in touch by phone, told her that going to the network was the most terrible decision she could make, that she hadn't developed enough self-confidence to handle network pressures. Ken Tiven agreed, and went on to say that she would be joining an operation in great disarray, an organization that did not know what it intended to do with its network newscast. NBC was "all chaos, all the time," he said.

Finally, Mort Crim sat her down and advised her to forget the anchoring and concentrate on being a correspondent for three years. "I said, 'You're a marathon runner, Jess. You're not in it just to do the hundred-yard dash and hang it up. You want to have a long career at the network, to grow and develop. But pay your dues and gain the experience. Don't let them push you to a point where it's counterproductive for you. You need to back off, because they're not going to pull you back. Remember, there are two dangers in life. One is not getting what you want. And the other is getting it.' "

But Jessica persisted. The weekend after her third meeting with Meaney, she and Korn retreated to Lancaster County, in scenic Pennsylvania Dutch country. There, not far from Kennett Square, they outlined the perks that Jessica, as an upcoming network star, should have in her contract. "As a marketing person," says Korn, "I knew we needed to lay out the whole concept." If Barbara Walters could demand a hairdresser in her ABC contract, why couldn't she? Walters also got an additional secretary, employed by ABC, a researcher, a makeup consultant, a wardrobe person, and first-class hotel accommodations whenever she traveled. Why should Jessica have any less, even if she was new at the network? That's how you show your worth, Korn believed. And what about a clothing allowance, and limousine service? Most important, Korn said, if the normal going price for a new correspondent hovered comfortably under $100,000, Jessica should certainly have more as an anchor, even if they just put her in on the weekends.

Now Donald Hamburg, Jessica's agent and attorney, began to meet with John E. Ghilain, NBC's contract negotiator. Jessica had been very specific about two points. While anchoring, she wanted written editorial control over her copy, and the assurance that she would be able to see both the monitor and the floor manager at all times. It was a hedge against what Jessica feared most—that she would look bad on the air. She saw it not as vanity, but as an attempt to force the network, as she would tell Kershaw, "to give out a better product."

"Hamburg rolled out the laundry list approach again," says Ken Tiven. "He went in and asked for four hundred and seventeen things, intending to give up two or three hundred, but figuring he'd come out with at least a hundred he'd like. And I remember him telling me that to his utter amazement, NBC rolled over and agreed to almost everything, giving her all sorts of things it had never given anybody else."

The final three-year contract, which called for Jessica to be based in Washington, stipulated that she would be paid $115,000 for the first year, $125,000 for the second, and $140,000 for the third. Jessica then wrote a follow-up letter which demanded, among other things, $15,000 for "personal relocation expenses," in addition to the customary moving expenses which NBC would also pay.

The idea of such Hollywood-styled perks as a hairdresser was still horrifying to the majority of the old-school correspondents. When Barbara Walters did it, she had set herself up as an object of much ridicule, resentment, and even hatred. Had Meaney in fact agreed to such a thing with Jessica? "I easily could have," replies the former bureau chief, who worked with Walters before she went to ABC. "Something like a hairdresser is a small thing to keep somebody important happy. And that's exactly the way we looked at it. By then, it had become a very soluble deal as far as NBC was concerned. And just before Jessica was hired, I talked with the president of NBC [Schlosser] about some of these things. The last conversation I had with him, he said, 'Whatever it is, go ahead.' "

The network needed a strong new presence in its news lineup. It needed someone who could vitalize old viewers and galvanize new ones. It needed another good reporter, someone who was engaging, authoritative, and articulate. And it needed another woman on staff.

But most of all, NBC desperately needed a major positive

announcement to drop on its affiliates at their May 1977 convention at the Century Plaza Hotel in Los Angeles—something that would keep them from losing hope and jumping ship. It needed a very big plug to fit a hole that seemed to grow larger by the day, a hole that leaked revenues and the very lifeblood of the network. And it hoped like hell that Jessica Savitch was a part of that stopple. Meaney and Schlosser were already at the convention, sweating bullets, when Hamburg and Ghilain finally came to terms.

"It was very important to be able to announce something important like, 'Hey, we have this new girl, Jessica Savitch, and she's really going to make it,' " says Meaney. "That was the extent of what effort there was toward getting her on the air. The president of the company was very anxious to have something good to say about *something*, for god's sake."

Joan Showalter had been right. Jessica was exactly thirty years old.

On May 24, 1977, NBC issued a press release announcing that Jessica would join the network in September as a correspondent "who also will do some anchor work." In the coming months, she and Meaney would hammer out the specific duties: She would start as a general assignment reporter, to learn the Washington news scene, and eventually be assigned to a specific beat—probably the Senate. She would also be called upon to make occasional appearances as a Washington interviewer on the "Today" show, and she would be among those correspondents who anchored and co-anchored news specials, particularly live coverage situations that occurred in the District. Finally, she would anchor or co-anchor regularly scheduled weekend news programs and "Updates," both evening and daytime, "as dictated by circumstances," as Meaney put it.

"Her dream was fulfilled," says Bill Mandel. "Now the nightmare began."

On Friday, May 27, 1977, Mort Crim made his final appearance on "Eyewitness News." He had gotten the plum position at WBBM in Chicago, and now he became the first of the Camelot team to leave. His last broadcast carried an air of poignancy, and at the end of the show, the producer ran a nostalgic montage of clips assembled from Crim's five-year stint.

Mel Korn knew that Jessica would be distraught over Mort's

leaving, so to brighten her mood over the Memorial Day weekend, he chartered a private plane to take them to the Hamptons. There, they would relax in a luxury resort; Korn promised to return Jessica to Philadelphia by midday Monday. She was set to begin her new KYW co-anchoring duties with the fresh-faced Roy Weissinger, who looked somewhat like a younger Mort Crim.

Now that Jessica was going to NBC, Alan Bell had decided that she should continue her duties at 5:30, but be pulled off the anchor desk at eleven. He asked Tiven to assign her to reportorial chores. "Jessica has asked to become more active as a reporter," Bell told the *Philadelphia Inquirer.* "It will make a very nice transition to her new assignment." Jessica bristled, telling the paper she'd have preferred anchoring both shows until she left. "I don't think I had to hone my reportorial skills. They were honed up enough to get a network job."

There were still some fascinating stories to cover in the KYW viewing area. Earlier that month, a man named Caron Ehehalt had drowned when his car fell into the Delaware Canal in nearby New Hope. Ehehalt had just eaten at Chez Odette—the restaurant Jessica had frequented with Bill Mandel—when he drove out of the parking lot in a thunderstorm, mistaking a narrow towpath at the back of the lot for an exit. Lawyers for the man's estate would file suit against the restaurant and the Commonwealth of Pennsylvania, contending that the state was negligent not to erect guardrails along the canal, and that the restaurant had failed to warn motorists that the towpath was not a way out.

"I'm not sure about this," says Joe Vandergast, "but I have a funny feeling that I covered that story, and that the reporter was Jessica Savitch."

On Memorial Day, May 30, Korn flew Jessica back to Philadelphia in time for her 5:30 newscast. She promised to call him afterward, and they would go to the movies. But when Jessica returned to Hopkinson House after the news, she found a surprise visitor: Ron Kershaw had come up from Baltimore to spend the holiday. As the night wore on, Mel Korn waited to hear from her. She didn't call. When he rang her apartment, she didn't answer.

The evening had started out well. Jessica told Kershaw she had gotten copy control at the network, so there would be no mention of "government bigwigs," no misplaced modifiers or sentences ending with prepositions—the things that drove Kershaw, an accomplished writer, up the wall. They made love, they forgave each other, and they promised never to put each other through such torment again.

But now, late at night, Kershaw grew melancholy. Her course was set, he said, but the Rabbit had no course. The Rabbit was drowning. Jessica told him she would not let him drown, that they would both survive. But things could not go on as they had. "This dime store tragedy we're living has to have a livable ending, or maybe a livable beginning," she said, smiling at her analogy. The relationship was simply no good for either of them the way it was. Kershaw became furious. "This *relationship*?" he exploded. "It isn't just a *relationship*. It's my *life.*" If it was only a relationship, he said, he would end it now to save Jessica the trouble. He would jump off the thirtieth-floor balcony. Jessica felt the blood come to her face. "Go ahead!" she said angrily. "Maybe that would be best for both of us!"

As Kershaw moved toward the French doors, Jessica ran to stop him. He pushed her aside, tore open the doors, and began to climb the small barricade. "Don't come near me!" he yelled. "I'll do it!" Jessica saw that he meant it. Frightened, she called Dave Neal. "Ron is here!" she cried into the phone. "He's standing on the balcony, threatening to jump!"

"I didn't want to hear about it," Neal says today, remembering. "She said, 'What should I do?' I said, 'Give him a shove! Push the son of a bitch, that's what you do! Get rid of him!'"

Jessica, now frantic, hung up and dialed Dr. Schwartz. By Korn's account, she told him Ron had been drinking, that he was threatening to kill himself. The psychiatrist said he would come over. By the time he arrived, Jessica had managed to get Kershaw off the balcony. Now he was sitting in the living room. The doctor talked with him for a while, and persuaded him to leave. He asked if she wanted to call Mel or Carole Bell to come over and stay with her. Jessica said she wanted to be alone.

But later, after the doctor left, Kershaw apparently came back. Now he was raving that she had humiliated him, that she always found somebody to fight her battles. First it had been Joan Showalter, then it was Dave Neal. "They both say the same thing—cut your losses, get rid of this Kershaw guy!" he shouted. "What the fuck do they know about anything?" And now she had the great Dr. Schwartz, he accused. He hated the doctor, hated anyone who might suggest they should not be together. Kershaw noticed that Jessica had turned on the radio. But she was not listening to their music, not listening to rock and roll. She had tuned in an easy-listening station—music that ran contrary to everything they both believed.

"Why are you listening to that shit?" he demanded.

Kershaw began to pace the room. He thought that he had lost her, that she had sacrificed her soul just to make it to the network.

Jessica got up to confront him. And then Kershaw evidently charged at her, leaving her bruised, black and blue, with scratches and welts over her entire body. When she came to, the police were there, asking questions. In the days to come, she would try to keep the incident quiet, but several people would find out varying bits and pieces—Mort, her secretary, Kathi Clarke, and her attorney, who dealt with the police. "Fortunately," says a friend, "they were able to keep it out of the papers. That would have finished them both off." It was their most violent fight. According to Korn, Jessica was unable to return to the air for a week.

In the following days, Jessica called Ron and told him she had been thinking about what she could do for him that would not destroy her in the process. It was as important to her that he be able to release the "magic"—that he be able to institute his ideas about television—as it was for her to get her shot at the network. But now, she said, her health was not the best, and she must not allow herself to be upset. She asked him to carry no guilt, just as she was trying to ease the guilt that had plagued her for the past five years. What happened on Memorial Day was the sum total of their childhoods and their other relationships, she said. It wasn't her, and it wasn't him. It wasn't even them. But they needed to be careful with each other, and with themselves.

"I would like to see you finish in Baltimore and then go home to North Carolina," she told him. She said she would come to him there, that she neither loved nor sought anyone else. "I will help you in all the tangible ways I can—be your friend, and your sounding board. You need not worry about money. You were there for me for the last five years. I will do the same for you."

Ron told her no. If they could not be together, they would make a clean break. He promised her he would never come after her.

Jessica cried softly into the phone. "I think maybe you're

crazy, Ron. I think perhaps I am, also." She told him she still loved him, but differently now.

"I will use the things you taught me," she said.

Kershaw said nothing.

"You're a winner, Bun. You were always the one with the realistic dream. And you were always the one with the magic."

On June 7, 1977, Kershaw wrote a letter to WBAL General Manager Lawrence M. Carino, tendering his resignation for "personal matters requiring my full attention." To friends such as Dick Williams, he would say he was leaving because Carino wouldn't give him the tools he needed to win in the market. Two days after Kershaw resigned, the Nielsen ratings came in. The station already owned the six o'clock spot. But now WBAL had also captured the eleven o'clock ratings, dramatically toppling WJZ, its powerful, longtime rival. Kershaw had gone out in style.

In the months before her departure for NBC, Jessica could barely hide her contempt for the station she now felt had thwarted her at every turn over the past five years. She knew she had offended her employers and colleagues by her demanding behavior—refusing to show up for an "Eyewitness News" group photo, for example, insisting that the temperature in the studio be turned down so low that the crew and producers complained bitterly to management—but she believed that even though many people at the station had come to despise her, the bottom line was that when the red light came on, she was in the studio, and the viewers loved her.

Now, despite Alan Bell consenting to cut three months off her contract, and that accumulated vacation time would allow her to leave KYW in August, Jessica still was furious and resentful. Whether she was frustrated at feeling like a "lame duck anchorperson," as she would say, or whether she was absorbed—or in Kershaw's view, repulsed—by having wholeheartedly embraced the star system, she told the *Philadelphia Inquirer* that "Now I'm going to a job I want." She spent more time giving lucrative speeches around town than she did at the station, breezing into KYW half an hour before airtime, glancing at the script—which she no longer cared about writing—throwing on her makeup, and returning phone calls. At six o'clock, the moment her newscast was over, she would leave.

Several of the producers thought she was trying to get fired.

But Alan Bell insisted, according to Ken Tiven, that "We put our best spin-polish on this whole endeavor, and take the most credit we could, like we were sending our daughter to the big city. As far as I was concerned, she was history, and a giant pain in the ass. I just wanted her to do the minimum we'd asked her to. And I said, 'Please don't do anything that's going to embarrass you or me or NBC,' because [with KYW an NBC affiliate] she was going to be coming right back at us."

Jessica and KYW continued to walk a delicate line until one day in the last weeks of her contract. The station recently had unveiled a strange, futuristic news set, based on a floor plan that had worked splendidly for WXYZ in Detroit. The staff had quickly dubbed it "The Starship Westinghouse," because of its modular desks and odd angles. It had a space behind the anchors that stationed reporters such as Trudy Haynes, who would come on to deliver her entertainment report, and then vacate the chair for someone else. The design dictated that when the anchor intro-duced the in-studio feature reporter—whom he could not see in his immediate peripheral vision—he would rotate in a 170 degree arc to face him, staying cognizant whether to turn left or right, depending on which of the chairs was currently occupied. Says Tiven, "It was not a set on which you could plunk yourself down and simply read the copy and not pay much attention."

On this particular day, Jessica came in late, picked up her script and walked on the set. Whether she'd forgotten her IFB earpiece that reporters wear to stay in touch with the control room (some say it stands for "interrupt for broadcast," and some say "interrupted fold back") or whether, as Tiven says, "She just didn't give a shit anymore," Jessica began reading, with no way to take direction other than by hand signals communicated by the floor manager.

Several minutes into the broadcast, Jessica was shocked to discover that her script didn't match what was on the Tele-PrompTer. The problem was simply that she had her pages out of order. But because Jessica assumed it was the TelePrompTer script that was out of order, she continued to read from her script.

Since Jessica was not wearing her IFB, there was no way to tell her to go to commercial. The floor director frantically waved his arms, but Jessica ignored him, blithely reading a lead-in to Diane Betzendahl. "Now," she said, "here's Diane to tell you all about it." But when Jessica swiveled to face the reporter behind her, there was no one in the chair. Betzendahl was scheduled for the next segment.

"Okay," Jessica said, facing the wrong camera and leading into a commercial break, "Delaware law could make you a profit if you keep your eyes open. That story up next on Eyewitness News."

The moment the newscast went to the commercial, Jessica flew into a tirade, throwing her hands up and screeching in fury. As the lights dimmed to keep the studio cool in the dead of summer, she continued to rant, acknowledging that her pages were out of order, but yelling that somebody else must have done it. She started to assail the floor crew.

After thirty seconds, Jessica was still berating the crew with such frenzied passion that the control room was mortified she had forgotten the mid-break bumper, a ten second "billboard," in which the director used a shot of the anchor person in semi-silhouette, over which he superimposed the coming stories: "*Tonight at 6:00:* Don Fair: STRIKE DEADLINE, Beverly Williams: FREEDOM WEEK, Orien Reid: DOG FOOD $$"—and so forth.

But in a most astonishing example of Jessica's ability to separate what she did in front of the camera from her emotional, off-camera personality, the moment the lights came back up for the bumper, she stopped in mid-rage and regained perfect composure, only to snap right back into her harangue—flailing her arms and bobbing her head back and forth—for the remainder of the break. "We're coming out," the floor manager announced. "Stand by, ten seconds . . . five . . ."

At the three-second mark, Jessica took a deep breath and blew the air out of her cheeks in a keen, angry motion. Then she settled her face into its usual comely demeanor. "The country's conversion to the metric system has been a slow one," she said, speaking in the perfectly modulated tones that had helped her gain such an adulatory following in the city of Brotherly Love.

"It became the Great Fly Act of all fly acts," says Tiven, likening the news team to a vaudeville troupe of performing insects. And to a staff that had finally come to regard Jessica as an insufferable prima donna, it was a chance to have fun. Since the commercials were rolled in from master control, and the station made its logger tape, or record of every show, from the studio line, the engineers had a copy of Jessica's entire raging exhibition. Before long, someone got the idea of stripping the audio off and dubbing in Aram Khachaturian's "Sabre Dance," the surgingly melodramatic music that has played under almost as many comedy routines as "Flight of the Bumblebee." Now when Jessica railed against the crew, she seemed to be almost directing the orchestra, her wild gyrations impelling the musicians to their frantic finish. It was amateur "Candid Camera," a prize new addition to the station's gag reel of memorable bloopers.

On August 19, 1977, Jessica delivered her last KYW broadcast. As it had done for Crim, the station produced a farewell reel, trotting out excerpts from the special series, and splicing in interviews with such "This Is Your Life" luminaries as Jessica's high school principal. Jessica took it all like a rising young starlet, looking into the camera and saying that since NBC was carried over KYW, she found herself in the unique position of leaving and staying at the same time. She went on to thank her audience for their loyalty over the last five years, and at the end, she teared up.

There were at least two going-away parties, one at Vince Leonard's house, at which the remaining Camelot team gave her a little gold anchor to wear around her neck so, as weatherman Bill Kuster said, "When we see it show up, we know you're thinking of us." And Mel Korn threw a dinner party at an elegant French restaurant on the wharf; Carole Bell invited Lilyan Wilder and her husband from New York. Wilder gave Jessica a *chai*, the Hebrew symbol of life.

Of the crew members who hated to see Jessica go, Joe Vandergast was particularly sad—not just because she was leaving, but because she was going to the network a different person than the one he'd known at the beginning of her KYW career. He wondered how much the drugs had played a part. "I think at that point the erosion had already started," he says in retrospect. "She had just set herself up so perfectly to fail."

And indeed, before Jessica ever arrived in Washington, a number of the organization had already formed an unshakable opinion of its new correspondent and weekend anchor. The wicked "Sabre Dance," dubbed off in an infinite number of copies, had winged its way to New York and Washington and countless NBC affiliates. One day when Jessica first got to the bureau—moving into Cassie Mackin's old office—she saw a group of veteran reporters crowded around a playback monitor, hooting in derision. When she moved to join them, one of the best-known of the correspondents stopped her, pulling her aside. Later, he showed her the tape himself. Jessica was horrified to learn of its existence, but under the circumstances, she tried to make the best of it. "In her four-year stay here," the correspondent says, "that was the only time I ever saw her laugh."

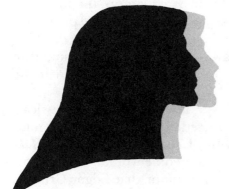

6

To The Network: NBC and Washington

The anchor must be credible to his own organization as well as to the public. To get the support he needs, he must be perceived as a man of credibility, experience—a man who has earned the job. There must be a belief in his character and stability. It is not just his appearance, but his whole history in TV. After all, the anchor is called on in time of national crisis. It's an important job, requiring literate, experienced journalists. They have to be perceived as the best you have.

—HERBERT SCHLOSSER, past president, NBC, in Barbara Matusow's *The Evening Stars: The Making of the Network News Anchor*

On Labor Day weekend, Mel Korn drove Jessica to Washington to begin her NBC career. The network put her up at the Watergate Hotel until she could find housing of her own. Jessica washed Mel's socks out in the sink, and when he returned to Philadelphia on Sunday, she sat on the edge of the bed and cried.

Jessica showed up for work at the bureau, housed in the same handsome complex with WRC, the local affiliate, knowing almost no one except Don Meaney. She had no web of friends to buoy her. Of the two bases—New York or Washington—the D.C. bureau was thought in some ways to be the favorable place to work. In New York, there were locked doors on every floor and nobody knew who worked around the corner. But in Washington, the local and network staffs shared one big newsroom, and there were picnics on the front lawn. Even though Ken Tiven would go on to describe it as "an antiseptic, green-tiled maw—I didn't find the Washington bureau a very happy place"—people were generally said to be friendly.

From her first day there, however, it was obvious that Jessica's reputation as a prima donna had preceded her. "The story I got," says writer Barbara Matusow, author of *The Evening Stars: The Making of the Network News Anchor,* "was that people wouldn't even show her the way to the ladies' room." The rumor that Edgar Griffiths had foisted her on the organization also hadn't helped, and neither had Jessica's friendship with Don Meaney, who was said to be her "guru." When the bureau chief was eventually shuffled out of his post to travel the country visiting affiliates, Jessica's co-workers smugly asked, "Who's going to hold her hand now?" Says Bill Mandel: "She finally hit a level where people were nastier than she was ambitious."

But Jessica would never really fit in at the bureau for a number of reasons, mostly because she was perceived as a local talent who hadn't worked her way up through the usual ranks. Not only was she being rewarded with a weekend anchor job—for which she would travel to New York each Sunday starting November 6—but the 60-second "Updates" *and* the Senate beat, long recognized as one of the choicest reporting jobs as well. As one of the most-respected NBC Washington correspondents puts it, "I came here after fifteen years with the network, working around the different bureaus, and I would have loved to have gotten the Senate."

The idea of putting Jessica on the Senate beat was a calculated move to establish her credentials as a journalist, to validate her as an anchor. Covering the Senate would almost guarantee her frequent exposure on "Nightly News," and the way the Senate stories were handled in those days—not demanding that the reporter be an expert on foreign, defense, economic, or even social affairs— they were manageable pieces for any solid generalist who had a good grasp of the workings of Washington. For Jessica, the latter would prove the stumbling block—covering the Senate meant cultivating sources, being social, scuffing the shoe leather. Nothing in her Philadelphia experience had prepared her for it. And very quickly, it would prove to be a fatal mistake in yet another way. Jessica simply wasn't ready.

"The real blame for that," says Paul Duke, moderator of PBS's "Washington Week in Review," and NBC's Congressional correspondent from 1969 to 1974, "belongs to the network. The Hill is an extraordinarily tough assignment for any rookie reporter. Think of it—she had been a local anchorwoman in Philadelphia, suddenly uprooted and brought to Washington and given a major assignment that would give her high visibility. She had no real background in Washington politics, much less how Congress operated. NBC obviously wanted her glamour more than her reporting."

When Duke was hired by NBC, he had covered Capitol Hill for five years for the *Wall Street Journal.* He knew his way around, and he knew it took two years for a good reporter to learn the Hill ropes. But NBC was now asking Jessica to cover the Senate— beginning with a report on the status of the Humphrey-Hawkins unemployment bill—part-time, only three days a week. It was impossible, especially with her other regular duties. And now they also had her occasionally co-anchoring the weekday "Nightly News," filling in for David Brinkley with John Chancellor, and filing reports for the "Today" show, where she had once been considered for the co-host job before Jane Pauley was hired in 1976. Jessica's debut on the network, in fact, had been on the "Today" show on September 9. To most people, it looked as if she were getting all the plums.

Compounding Jessica's problems with her co-workers was the fact that she hadn't just come to the bureau without fanfare. There was much advance billing—a full page story in *Us* magazine headlined "Barbara Walters, Move Over!" the month she got there, in which her salary was inflated to "between $150,000 and $200,000," an immediate source of rancor among the other correspondents in the bureau. Such magazine interviews—and there

207

would be many more to come—were set up by NBC's New York publicity department, along with appearances at numerous industry functions, such as affiliate meetings.

"You have to remember that at that time, NBC was not number one in entertainment, and the ratings were not that fantastic, so that Jessica was one of the up-front people," says Sid Davis, who would replace Don Meaney as bureau chief. All of that drew criticism from her colleagues, who were still cackling over the "Sabre Dance." And it took time away from her reportorial education. "She did try to learn the Senate," Davis asserts. "While she did not have the Washington background that was necessary for some of the high-powered stories she was given, she went at her work in earnest. She covered the Panama Canal vote and debate, and, to her, it was one of the highlights of her career on the Hill."

Aside from the other gripes some of the correspondents had with Jessica—the fact that she had not started out in print journalism, that she was not a particularly good writer, and that she had paraded the first personal hairdresser into the building—she personified one of the reporters' worst fears: the performers were taking over.

Only the year before, NBC correspondent Eric Burns had been talking with John Chancellor, when the anchorman asked Burns what he eventually wanted to do in his broadcast career. Burns, who was then in the network's Chicago bureau, replied that he'd like to anchor the "Today" show. Chancellor advised him to spend a few more years in Chicago, then go to a bigger domestic bureau, such as New York, then to an assignment abroad, then return to the United States for a second-string assignment in Washington, then work up to a major assignment in Washington, such as the White House, and then *perhaps* he'd be anchor material.

"Everyone who wanted to move up from reporting knew that this was the way you did it," says Burns, now with Fox Television. "But when NBC broke away from this in hiring Jessica [and other networks hired other "performer" journalists] you can't imagine the shock waves that went through the industry. It was a revolution. You didn't work your way up because of your journalistic skills and get rewarded for them *in combination* with your performance skills—you *started* at the top, strictly *because* of your performance skills.

"I admit that in principle I was jealous," says Burns. "And I remember people such as [then NBC White House correspondent] Judy Woodruff being just stunned by Jessica's hiring to be an anchor. Of course, in that sense, she was a tremendous choice. You know what kind of a celebrity she became."

Indeed, Jessica possessed one of the most riveting news faces in the history of television, viewer preference surveys scoring her high with both men and women, who found her movie star appeal tempered by what Jessica would call "an Iowa farm girl look." Her fan mail ran several hundred letters a day, many of them requesting autographed photos, some fifty others asking questions about Jessica's hair and clothes. The network treated her almost no differently from a starlet, and, in fact, used her as such, particularly on the "Updates," the enormously profitable capsule newscasts viewed by some fifteen million people nightly—a far larger number than watch the weekday evening news. When she delivered her trademark smile at the end of her broadcast, "I'm sure the dials fell off the meter," says Dean Thomas Bohn of Ithaca College. The cliché began to circulate that "No matter how bad the news is, if Jessica smiles at the end of the show, it seems better." Eventually, in 1982, Jessica's peers of one hundred anchormen and women from across the country would name her "the sexiest female anchor" in America, with Dan Rather her sexy male counterpart. Soon, Ida McGinniss would not be able to accommodate all the requests for Jessica's speaking engagements.

Such tangible proof of success would do wonders for the ailing NBC network, but the experience would only intensify Jessica's subversion of self. Now, when Jessica found the basket of fruit in the room she insisted on bringing it home with her. "The close-up camera became not only a symbol of her career but her identity and her reality," says Tom Bohn. "She didn't have the strength to retain her own personality in light of what the network wanted her to be, which was MGM. She started out as a working journalist, and they waved money in front of her and said, 'We don't want you as a stand-up reporter. You're a face, and a name, a close-up personality.' She bought into it, but she never lost sight of what she'd done."

In October, Jessica moved from the Watergate into the luxurious Foxhall Apartments, a hulking, modern building at 4200 Massachusetts Avenue, N.W., near the NBC complex on Nebraska Avenue. She was living there, in number 105, when she put in a

209

call to Ron Kershaw. Before he left Baltimore, Kershaw bought a van and a Siberian husky pup, planning to take a *Travels with Charlie* tour of America and "write something profound." He and Chewbacca, or "Chewy," as he named the blue-eyed female, would meet Jessica at various points on the road while she was covering stories. Finally, when he ran out of money back home in North Carolina, Ron and Chewy went to Washington to live with Jessica.

"She had just done this whole place in sort of Jean Harlow black and white," says Kershaw. "Lots of stark chrome, plants, and white carpet all over the house. You know, give me a break, but that was Jess, too. Well, Chewy had been out on the road with me, eating cheeseburgers at McDonald's, and Twinkies from 7-11, running in the Smoky Mountains, and being a wolf.

"Chewy and Jessica were a lot alike. They were both sly motherfuckers—cute, calculating, and manipulative. And they were both Siberians, both prima donnas. One night, Chewy shook all the plants out and pissed all over the place to set down territory—just terrorized poor Sveltie cat. Did everything to just rip that place apart. Jessica was paying like $1,400 a month rent for this place, and the dog *wrecked* it in one night. You had an animal *determined* to be destructive. After Jessica got through having a nervous breakdown over it, she got carpet samples and checked them against Chewy's urine, and then recreated the apartment around the dog. I think she became more attached to her than she was to me, or to anything she had ever known in her life."

In early 1978, Kershaw left Washington for ABC News in New York, becoming the senior producer of the network's weekend news programming, and quickly moved over to the nightly news operation as producer in charge of economic coverage. Because Chewy had become one of the few constants in Jessica's life—she now regarded her as their "child"—Kershaw left the dog behind. One night before he moved, they listened to Elton John records, to "Candle in the Wind," John's tribute to Marilyn Monroe. "That's just how I feel," she told him, "like a candle in the wind." Jessica had never failed at anything before. But she thought her luck might be running out now.

After Ron's departure, Jessica found she couldn't care for Chewy by herself. Through Kathi Clarke, her secretary from Philadelphia, who was now answering her fan mail and signing it—even personal notes to the Rappaports—with a rubber stamp,

Jessica met a Washington woman named Lelia M. Bright, whom she wanted to hire to walk the dog.

"I had no intention of walking no dog," says Bright, a short, round, cheerful woman. "But the minute you start talking to Jessica, you fall in love with her. So I walked Chewy for a day or two, and then Jessica was fixing to go out of town, and I packed her bags. All of a sudden, I became her personal maid! Jessica was my baby who never growed up," says the housekeeper, shaking her head. "This was a little girl who needed a mother to watch after her." Now, whenever Jessica would enter the Foxhall complex, she would start hollering, "Lelia!" all the way down the hall. "I'd have the door open most of the time for her," she says, "and she would run right in."

In New York, where Jessica would usurp John Hart—whom she had dated briefly during her CBS gofer days—as the anchor of the Sunday edition of "Nightly News," she would be forced to take part in several network "experiments." One was a brief co-anchoring stint with Gerald Harrington, a black, little-used correspondent for CBS who had moved over to NBC.

Harrington had a reputation for coming in late and reading copy that someone else had to write for him, and on the air, where he and Jessica called each other "Jessie" and "Gerry," Harrington frequently stumbled over the copy, unable even to say, "Goodnight from us at NBC News" without blowing the line.

To the old guard, it was another horrifying example of the start of the so-called personality cult of television news, and the lengths to which the network would go to win ratings. No one knew what was next. In October 1977, Herb Schlosser fired Dick Wald as president of the news division, and replaced him with Lester Crystal. Two months later, John Chancellor said that he intended to retire as anchor of the NBC "Nightly News" to become a commentator, at an unspecified date. And in January 1978, Edgar Griffiths would announce that Fred Silverman, the president of ABC, was coming to NBC as the head of the company. In taking his former network from number three to number one, Silverman had gained a reputation as "the man who was driving the quality of television down," as Barbara Matusow reports. It was a time of terrible unrest at the network, when no one was sure of his allies. And, as Jim Topping offers, Jessica got caught up in trying to figure out which executive she was supposed to impress.

The sports announcer on the Sunday edition of "Nightly News" was Dick Schaap, a congenial man who had come to TV from print, only to discover that "television is not for grown-ups."

"The first time Jessica and I did the show together," recalls Schaap, "I said, 'I suppose people have told you that you look like Lauren Bacall.' And she said, 'Yes, they have.' And I said, 'Are you as bitchy as she?' And Jessica gave that little half-smile and said, 'Bitchier.' I thought it was wonderful, and from then on, we got along great." Schaap and his wife would sometimes have dinner with Jessica and Mel Korn, who, on nights they hadn't planned on going out, would show up at the studio with soup or roast beef sandwiches.

Jessica also got along well with the show's new executive producer, Herb Dudnick, a much-respected television figure whom Jessica would call one of her best teachers. Dudnick, who also hailed from Atlantic City, knew that part of the resentment toward Jessica was simply that she happened to be a woman. He understood the psychological difference between anchoring in a market such as Philadelphia, where he'd also worked, and anchoring for network. He knew the insecurities that haunted her. But Dudnick, now the news director at KRON in San Francisco, thought Jessica was "one of the best, pure anchors that I've seen in the business. And she was a workhorse."

Dudnick and Jessica would often stay and talk after the broadcast, but since they saw each other only once a week, Dudnick would not become the kind of mentor or nurturer that Alan Bell and Jim Topping had in Philadelphia. Nor would he pamper and protect her as Dave Neal, Paul Dowie, and Joe Vandergast tried to do. But he realized that NBC had "shoved her into the Senate, and NBC always had a history of shoving people and then saying, Good-bye! I guess they would justify it in the old sink-or-swim tradition. But basically, there was a lack of help. They let her alone, and it didn't work."

Shortly after her arrival at NBC, Jessica was on the phone with Mort Crim. He had been right, she told him—she should have become a general assignment reporter first. They had moved her along too quickly, and the resentment on the part of her peers, especially the older correspondents, was sometimes more than she could take. Now the word had come down that the network brass was unhappy with her anchor work, specifically her delivery. They had hired her for her naturalness and her flamboyance, and then they said, as Jim Topping puts it, "Now you're at NBC—you don't have to do that anymore, child."

"NBC had a staccato style of delivery that they tried to instill in people," says Bob Morse, now general manager of KTTV, in Los Angeles. "It was well-known throughout the business. Jessica had worked for years to develop her style, and it really hurt her in terms of her emotional makeup when they tried to redo her. She was furious about it, and trying to please them at the same time, and it took away her confidence. She had gotten really, really good in Philadelphia, but after she'd been at NBC a while, she was never again as good as she had been the last couple of years at KYW."

Now Jessica was calling Jim Topping with desperation in her voice: "Did you see what I did tonight? It's just not right! I can't get it! I don't know what the hell they want me to be!"

Instead of the strong, authoritative personality with the undercurrent of vulnerability, Topping now saw an overly strong woman with a certain shrillness. He thought he could tune in one week and see one personality, and tune in again and see yet another one. Jessica would return to Lilyan Wilder's studio to try to rid the brittleness, the artificiality, and the mannered personality— to try to recapture what had been so winning and brilliant. "I've never spoken to Lilyan about it," says Topping, "but I suspect she would wait at the door each evening to see which Jessica walked through."

"I don't know what caused it," says Wilder, "but after she went to Washington, she veered away from that spontaneous use of herself, and became very patterned. She just gave up trying to be creative and original, trying to be herself. It was very difficult for me to work with her. When I would point out things that could be better, she would burst into tears and run into the bathroom."

"Eventually," says Joel Chaseman, "I got to where I couldn't watch the weekend news. She was too thin, too tense, trying much too hard."

As Jessica's confidence continued to slip, she asserted herself in various other ways, trying to show her standards for excellence. Too often, she chose the worst methods possible.

One night, in an episode that would become as famous as the "Sabre Dance," Jessica delivered an "Update" immediately after a Presidential speech. Because she was always well aware of how many people would be watching each night—she elected not to do the Friday "Updates" because the viewing audience was smaller then—Jessica knew she would have a bigger tune-in than usual. A commercial rolled wrong, making the program look sloppy, although it did not cut off any of her presentation. Jessica, who felt that the higher she rose in the industry, the more incompetent the technicians became, unleashed her usual barrage at the crew, including a line that would live on in infamy on "Tapes of Wrath," a hilarious blooper reel of outtakes and embarrassing moments: "This is prime-time television here, folks!"

Such outbursts were sometimes warranted, and Jessica was not the only anchorperson known to blow up whenever standards were compromised or talent was made to look bad on the air. Almost always, says one network executive, she had reason to complain, even if her tactics were not the best: "You tolerate the eccentricities of the people who are 'producers,' and she was." But Jessica did far more damage to herself in a different kind of incident that took place about the same time.

Linda Ellerbee recounts in her book, *And So it Goes,* that in April 1978, on the night the Senate was to vote on the adoption of the Panama Canal treaty, a woman Senate correspondent, recently arrived at NBC:

> was inside the Capitol, in the rotunda, at a desk, waiting to report the vote.
>
> It was raining. The hour got later and the rain harder. [National political correspondent] Tom [Pettit] and Senator Mathias stood there, Tom with a microphone in one hand and an umbrella sheltering the two of them in the other. Both men could hear in their earpieces everything that was being said in the rotunda. What they heard was a woman complaining that her hair didn't look right and this was network television, and if the network couldn't hire a hairdresser who knew what he was doing, well, they should hire another one right after they fired this one. . . .
>
> Neither man mentioned the scene inside. They were professionals.

"The worst thing about Jessica," says a female correspondent in the bureau, "is that she is the ultimate victim in television news. She behaved in ways that were bound to be destructive. She treated people badly, and in the end there was nothing for her. People didn't understand that it was not done out of meanness, but out of severe insecurity."

Jessica was not without female friends at the network, but they were seldom other correspondents. Instead, she found friendship with a pretty production assistant named Roberta Spring, who worked mostly out of New York, and with a Washington-based tape editor named Terri Verna. Both women were kind and supportive, and no threat to Jessica's on-air status. In time, there would be other girlfriends, and a retinue of secretaries and hairdressers. But these, too, were the subject of some ridicule among fellow reporters and crew, who called them "Jessica's groupies."

"I remember seeing them," says one woman, a former NBC correspondent, "and they looked pathetic. I kept thinking, she thinks she's Warner Brothers in the thirties and forties. Her notion of stardom is what people like Joan Crawford had—they arrive with an entourage, heels clicking, much hoopla. That didn't exist in television news, and she seemed anachronistic. Jessica lived a life she thought was the star fantasy. And, of course, the price of living a fantasy life is death."

The first week of September, Jessica entered Graduate Hospital in Philadelphia for surgical removal of her left ovary. One friend ascribes the problem to her recurring bout with endometriosis, another to a cyst. Afterward, according to Lelia Bright, she went home to Margate to recuperate for a week.

Ten days after the surgery, Jessica was back on the air. She wrote in *Anchorwoman* that she did not want the network to know the extent of her health problems, fearing she might lose the opportunity to cover the Senate race for the off-year election of 1978, her most critical assignment yet. Although her health was still shaky, she wrote, she went to the Senate and interviewed every incumbent running for reelection, did phone interviews with their opponents, and flew to several states to follow key races, including that between Senator William Hathaway and GOP Representative William Cohen in Maine. The gist of her piece, which ran on "Nightly News" on November 3, was that the race was one of style over substance, and that Cohen was running on issues, while Hathaway saw it as a personality contest. The field producer, Susan LaSalla, and the freelance cameraman, Dean Gaskill, leaked it around that when it came time for Jessica to do her stand-up, a "rock-bound coast of Maine" shot, with the waves crashing behind her, Jessica refused to get out of the car until the wind died down—she didn't want her hair to blow. Finally, and only when the crew was losing light, did she comply.

One of the people watching NBC that night was Pulitzer Prize–winner David Halberstam. The veteran political reporter was appalled to see an interesting Senate race "totally trivialized," and when he tuned in to the election coverage later that month, he was so shaken by the fact that all three networks featured their star performers over their knowledgeable political reporters that he wrote a piece about it for *TV Guide.* Halberstam singled out several journalists, including Harry Reasoner, for tweaking, and devoted eleven lines to Jessica, concluding that "she most assuredly was not there Election Night because she knew anything about national politics . . . NBC's two best political reporters, Douglas Kiker and Tom Pettit, were barely used."

Today, Halberstam says, "I gather that it upset her greatly that I said these things, but it was obvious that she was being brought along too quickly. I don't think it's a matter that she got 'lost.' I think they offered her a lot of bait, and that there are not many people who have the resistance for stuff like that. Of all the people who did, though, she least of all had it. Because with her almost manic ambition and hunger, and the network's system, which was bent on extracting the lesser qualities, she had no countervailing value system of her own."

Don Meaney told Jessica she was "excellent" that night, and today insists that "She did a remarkable job—had a remarkable sense of every Senator and what he was going to do, and it got on the air that way. I'm quite sure it was David Brinkley who said to her, 'You know, that turned out well.' " But later, according to another NBC correspondent, Brinkley would publicly call Jessica "the dumbest woman I ever met." Whichever of these described his truest feelings, perhaps he did not know that Jessica was on the phone constantly with close friends such as Mort Crim saying Brinkley—and John Chancellor too—ignored her even when she was anchoring with them. Whether indeed this was true, and whether they resented her "new girl on the block" status or had contempt for her lack of experience, part of it may have been because she represented the new trend in television broadcasting.

The same month as the election, Jessica would be called upon to deliver a live report that would help change the largely unflattering in-house perception of her journalistic skills. The occasion was the Jim Jones massacre in Jonestown, Guyana. Shortly after Jones ordered cult members to ambush Congressman Leo Ryan, NBC reporter Don Harris, cameraman Robert Brown, and two others at the Guyana airstrip, nine hundred and nine American followers of the fanatical California religious leader committed suicide drinking a concoction of Kool-Aid and cyanide. Late Saturday night, when Jessica got the call to come to New York early the next day, the mass suicide was not yet known. But as the anchor, Jessica would interview field producer Bob Flick, who had escaped the ambush and picked up footage of the killing of Ryan and Harris, photographed by Bob Brown just before he received a bullet to the head. Flick would script and narrate.

Shortly before airtime, it became obvious that Flick was in no emotional shape to look at footage of his colleagues' deaths, which left Jessica to narrate the raw, unscripted footage the staff had not even had time to screen. She would be looking at it for the first time along with the viewing audience, and her narration would need to be unemotional and factual. Dressed in a grey Ultrasuede suit and scarf, Jessica looked both glamorous and authoritative that night, describing with clarity and the correct level of concern and detached professionalism the scene of Don Harris throwing away his cigarette in preparation for boarding the plane, and the cult members arriving on a flatbed truck and opening fire on the congressman and newsmen. It was an excellent test of immediate response for a broadcast journalist, and she adapted herself well to a changing situation.

The broadcast aired on November 19, David Savitch's birthday. "I think that may have been her finest hour at NBC," says Herb Dudnick. But whatever new respect Jessica gained from the broadcast, she quickly lost—mainly because she continued to hold herself apart from her colleagues.

"There is a personality profile to news people that I nailed down early on," says one former NBC news reporter. "First of all, the news industry attracts immature people, because it allows you to be an adventurer, and to make a lot of money doing it. Second, it's a perfect world to hide out in, especially if you're one of the walking wounded, where something is wrong and you never quite grow up. And third, the news industry attracts antisocial people, because you can observe, rather than participate. Life is one big Halloween party, and you just keep changing costumes."

In her early days, in Houston and Philadelphia, Jessica asked for help when she didn't know something. But her ready-made star status apparently precluded that at NBC, especially with someone who covered a related beat. "She thought *they* thought she should already know those things," says one of her friends. "Especially since she was making so much more money than they were."

"If you walked down the hall and encountered her," remembers NBC Supreme Court reporter Carl Stern, "she wouldn't make eye contact. It was strange, because when she came in here, she had a marvelous reputation as having been a real tiger in Philadelphia. But then she went up on the Hill to cover the Senate and disappeared, as though she tumbled into a hole. The entire time she was up there, I don't recall one story that she dug up. I don't recall her going around talking to people, I don't recall crossing her tracks on the Hill, and I never heard a word from anybody reacting to a meeting or an on-air piece that she did. It was as though she wasn't here. She left no footprints in the sand."

By 1979, except for her broadcasts, Jessica wasn't even coming into the office regularly, and when she was there, she was often obstinate. "I asked her to do a couple of stories, and she just refused," says an assignment editor. "I thought, boy, this is a person who really has a problem with the news." Adds a veteran correspondent: "Her relationship with the news bureau had deteriorated something awful. I never saw her around the office. We all thought she was staying home, being busy with phone calls, with the hairdresser, with clothes, however busy you can get doing nothing."

As her insecurities deepened, Jessica's cocaine problem got worse. She never had to look far to find a source, or to find someone to do it with—cocaine use was common among many people who worked at the NBC Washington bureau. Says a staff director, "I think I know most of the people who were involved when coke was really heavy in this building, and most of them are gone now. But there was a lot of buying, selling, and using here, and there were lots of coke parties. I think it was the vogue, like penny loafers, and it just kind of petered out."

Jessica's growing cocaine use made her paranoid about coming to work, where she perceived, perhaps correctly at times, that people were out to get her. Ron Kershaw thought her real nemesis was Sid Davis, who worked under Don Meaney and would eventually take over as bureau chief in 1980.

Specifically, Kershaw says, Sid Davis wanted Jessica to go to early morning breakfasts with Congressional leaders, to make contacts—something Kershaw thought producers should do.

"Jessica didn't give a fuck about the Senate," Kershaw says. "She did people stories. All those guys—they screwed her, and they made her crazy. They led her to believe she was too shallow to belong. She kept trying to be accepted by them, and no matter how much she adhered to their standards, she could not win. She tried to seek their approval so much that she sold herself out. She was a victim in many respects. I said, 'Don't play their games! Don't jump through those fuckin' hoops!' But all she wanted to do was please. And she got bumped around like somebody in a pinball machine. If they had just let her feel free to be herself, she would have been excellent. And Sid Davis was the guy who really did her the harm. He wanted to prove she was a blonde bimbo who didn't belong there, and was there only because Edgar Griffiths forced her in."

"Ron may be right, but I don't think Sid's a villain in this," says Joel Chaseman. "I think she just got no coaching." And Ken Tiven agrees. "I think they all mishandled her," he says. "But it sounds like Sid wanted her to get out and be a reporter, and that doesn't sound inconsistent with a Washington bureau chief." Don Meaney puts it best: "Television journalism has become a very different thing. Now the focus is on how good something is on the air. That isn't the same thing as running up and down the Senate knocking on doors, which I never felt was as important as being terrific on the air. Very openly, Sid Davis did not agree with that."

For his part, Sid Davis defends much of Jessica's journalistic reputation and talks repeatedly of her diligence in trying to learn about areas she had no background in when she came to Washington.

But on January 16, 1979, the day after *Newsweek* ran its full-page story about NBC's "Golden Girl," predicting that Jessica was "clearly NBC's reporter most likely to succeed," the network announced that Jessica was being taken off the Senate beat and put on general assignment "to broaden her reporting experience." Her replacement was Tom Pettit. It was clearly a demotion, and Jessica was humiliated. But she would continue to anchor the Sunday edition of "Nightly News" and to deliver the "Updates." And she would also occasionally appear on "Meet the Press," as she had in 1978—longtime producer Betty Dukert thought she asked good questions—and to contribute regularly to "Segment 3" (also called "Special Segment"), an in-depth showcase spot on "Nightly News" that was not unlike Jessica's old multipart series at KYW. Despite the demotion, jealousy was still high among Jessica's peers: Everyone wanted such choice assignments as "Segment 3."

On March 24, 1979, Jessica and Mel had dinner with John and Leezy Sculley to celebrate Mel's fiftieth birthday. Korn, who had recently vacationed with Jessica at the Half Moon Plantation outside Montego Bay, Jamaica, thought the relationship was almost finished. He had divorced his second wife in 1977, hoping to win Jessica, but she seemed to be beyond his grasp. Now Jessica invited him to go with her to California the following week to attend her grandfather's eightieth birthday party. "Never did I realize," he says, "that we were going to get engaged!"

The proposal, Korn recalls with some irony, came on April Fool's Day. But it was Jessica who popped the question—not Korn. "I don't know if it was being with family that did it or what," he says, "but we were having breakfast in the suite, and she literally got down on her knees and said, 'Will you marry me?' I said, 'Are you serious?' And she said, 'Yeah.' I said, 'Well, that's certainly music to my ears.' And that was it. She called her mother, and I called mine."

When they got back to New York, the couple would draw up a prenuptial agreement. Then Korn would go to Tiffany's and buy Jessica a ring, arranging to have a waiter deliver it with a bottle of champagne and a rose when they dined at the Palm Court at the Plaza. In California at the family reunion, when the couple announced their engagement, Saul Savitch looked at his brother Leonard and shook his head. "Another marriage like Sissy's," Saul said, remembering his cousin's annulled first marriage. Leonard told him not to judge too quickly. Then Leonard went up and shook hands with Jessica's fiancé and walked back to his brother. "Saul," he said, "you're right."

Korn later figured Jessica proposed because she realized "I was getting ready to fly the coop." But there may have been other factors. It was now heavily rumored around NBC that Jessica was hanging out with a lesbian crowd. And a newspaper reporter had gotten wind of Jessica's big fight with Kershaw on Memorial Day 1977.

"She thought she could put a lid on it by marrying this guy— somebody who had a life outside of television," is Kershaw's opinion. "That way, she figured she would just be interviewed about her professional life. She wanted *no past.* In other words, she was marrying him for PR reasons! Fuck you! I went nuts! Absolutely gone South bonkers. I went to see a psychiatrist. I was Thorazined out."

On Easter Sunday, April 15, 1979, Kershaw walked around crying in the rain in New York City. Jessica would beg him to get help. On Tuesday, April 17, Kershaw sat in his new psychiatrist's office and wrote to her, informing her that he was waiting to be taken to the Mensana Clinic in Stevenson, Maryland. She had asked him not to phone, so he also sent a telegram. Jessica told Mel she had to go see him. Korn drove her there himself.

After ten days, Kershaw was released. Since Jessica had changed her phone number, he immediately began sending more telegrams, begging her to go with him to a psychiatrist. Jessica didn't want to do it. She was already seeing one on her own, Brian B. Doyle.

"I thought maybe if we went to a shrink we could learn to grow apart," Kershaw says. "We'd tried to hate each other, and it didn't work. I had been through such humiliation, and it was *so* crazy, that I didn't want anything to do with her, but I needed to get away from her." When she didn't respond, he sent still more telegrams, with such messages as "Help," or "Time is short." Sometimes he sent two a day. Jessica hired a bodyguard.

Finally, after several months, Jessica relented, and agreed to go with Kershaw for joint counseling in New York. The doctor told them their problem was that they were both paranoid about their personal privacy and secrets, that they didn't want anyone to touch that inner place, but that both of them had the ability to touch it in the other. They could get together, get close, and love each other only up to a point. Then, like two magnets, they'd repel.

The therapy was a failure: They ended up falling in love again.

221

"I said, 'Good. Now you can get out of this marriage,' " Kershaw remembers. But Jessica informed him she could not.

"Why not?"

"I've already sent the invitations. I've told the Crims."

"So what?"

"There's another reason."

"What?"

"We're already married."

Jessica and Mel had gone down to Sanibel Island and gotten married secretly, she said. The upcoming wedding at the Plaza—Jessica no longer considered herself to be Jewish and did not want a religious ceremony—was just for show.

"I went off the deep end again," Kershaw says, running his hand through his hair. "But then she called me up and said, 'Rab, you've got to stay by me. I truly love you, but I've got to go through with this wedding. Then I'll get a divorce and we can be together.' " Kershaw told her she was incapable of being a friend to anyone anymore, including herself. And he'd appreciate it if she'd keep his dog out of her publicity pictures.

That night, around nine o'clock, Jessica called Lelia at home. "She told me she'd had an accident, and she wanted me to rush up to Foxhall," the housekeeper remembers. Jessica had slit her wrist. "I knew it was a sympathy thing," she says. "She'd been on the phone with Ron and had this argument. But she didn't do it enough to really hurt herself. All we had to do was put a little tourniquet on it, stop the bleeding, wrap it up."

Mel Korn says there was no elopement in Sanibel Island. The Florida bureau of vital statistics agrees. Jessica had simply lied to Kershaw again, to prevent their ever being together.

During October 1978, when she was still on the Senate beat and traveling to Maine, Texas, and Tennessee, Jessica leaned heavily on her field producer, Susan LaSalla. LaSalla, who had worked as a desk editor, was new at field producing, but her main problem on the road was not getting the story or the sources, but propping up Jessica Savitch.

"Susan had to play Mommy in a gargantuan way," says one of LaSalla's friends, a former NBC correspondent. "Finally, she just got so fed up with Jessica that she said, 'Would you goddammit grow up!' And when somebody paid attention to her, whether it was positive or negative, Jessica responded, so she got to like

Susan. One day, Jessica was supposed to do a piece on the Senate. Susan was involved with this, and Terri Verna, the tape editor. Terri told me that Jessica called her and said, 'I can't do it! I'm a nervous wreck!' She was shaking and incoherent, out of terror. And Susan had to go over to the apartment and pull her together. But Terri also knew about her cocaine habit. She said, 'Look, Jessica, you've got to stop this shit.' "

Both LaSalla and Verna would protect her in public. When feature writers approached LaSalla for quotes for the Savitch profiles, LaSalla would talk about how "fun" she was to work with, about her "gorgeous clothes," and how she liked to tease her, call her "Golden Girl."

But in May 1979, everyone's patience wore out, beginning with Lee McCarthy, a correspondent in the NBC Boston bureau. McCarthy had been covering Canada as part of his beat for three years, and he knew more about the Canadian political system than any other reporter in American TV. As time neared for the election of the prime minister, McCarthy wrote a memo to the foreign desk, saying he thought it was a good story: Joe Clark, the little-known leader of the Progressive Conservative Party, would probably oust Pierre Elliott Trudeau, who had served as Canada's chief executive for more than eleven years.

McCarthy got a call from weekend "Nightly News," asking him to go up to Canada and do a preview, and he assumed he would also do reports for "Today" and weekday "Nightly News." The correspondent was ready to leave when he got another call. McCarthy would not be doing the weekday "Nightly News" reports—Jessica Savitch would. He asked if something was wrong with his work. "Nothing wrong with your work," the bureau chief said. "We've got to showcase Jessica as a reporter." McCarthy was, he says, "beyond steamed," but went up to do his other pieces about the last days of the campaign, taking along a library of materials.

"I'll never forget this," says McCarthy, now anchorman at WTAF in Philadelphia. "My editor and I were crammed into a little rented Mustang—it wouldn't even hold all our luggage in the trunk—and Jessica pulled up to the hotel in a Lincoln Continental Town Car with Susan LaSalla and cameraman Chuck Fekete. Chuck is an old friend of mine, and we looked at each other and just laughed."

223

Suddenly, LaSalla bounded out of the car with a look that mingled apprehension and relief. "Oh, my God, I've got to talk to you!" The field producer knew that Jessica knew nothing about the election—in fact, nothing about Canadian politics. LaSalla knew she needed coaching.

After dinner, to be professionally obliging, McCarthy went up to Jessica's suite, taking along his files and notebooks, so that she and Susan could pick his brain. He was shocked to learn that Jessica had boned up for her coverage by reading about Canadian history—nothing that would have any impact on her story—and that the questions she asked him were "so basic that a reporter with a minimum level of experience would not bother. She didn't even know that people were not going out everywhere in Canada to vote." Not surprisingly, "Her preview piece out of Toronto was a disaster," McCarthy says. "I remember watching and going, oh, my God. I was embarrassed to be part of the program that aired the spot." New York agreed.

For the second-day story, "Nightly News" brought the team back into New York where they could oversee the production. Somehow, things got so botched that they hadn't even gotten some of the video they needed. Eric Burns got a frantic call to send in some of the tape he had shot there several months before.

But nothing could undo the damage. Paul Greenberg, executive producer for "Nightly News," who'd had to deal with shallow reporting from Jessica from the moment she hit the network, considered it the last straw. "The story goes," says Burns, with two other network sources confirming, "that he went into the president's office and said, 'Either you fire me, or this woman never appears on "Nightly News" again.' And he won. Jessica Savitch was never a reporter on [weekday] 'Nightly News' for the rest of the time she was at NBC."

At the end of 1979, Jessica was assigned to a magazine show called "Prime Time Sunday." Here, she would appear both in the studio, with host Tom Snyder, for whom she sometimes filled in on the "Tomorrow" show, and as a reporter on such stories as the rise of the Federal Express company, and a profile of Tom Hayden and Jane Fonda. The assignment took her further out of mainstream news, and her stories would be highly produced for her. But even here, there was trouble. The Hayden-Fonda profile, at a cost of some $220,000, was lacking in almost every respect and required "a lot of editing," Snyder says. Jessica would regret almost everything about the brief experience—the show did not last long—except meeting Tom Snyder's agent, E. Gregory Hookstratten. "The Hook," as he was often called, seemed to like her. And one day, she figured, she was bound to need a good agent.

Right now, Jessica thought her days at the network were numbered. The irony was that as David Brinkley retired from his co-anchor spot with Chancellor, Jessica was still getting heavy play in the press as Chancellor's "possible successor," along with Tom Brokaw and Tom Snyder. But in the spring and summer, NBC's "Nightly News" ratings had slipped to third, behind CBS and ABC. CBS's Bill Small had come over as president of NBC News, and Richard Salant, former CBS News president, had also moved over to the network.

Small was, of course, the same man Jessica had refused to go to CBS for as a reporter, and a man who believed that broadcast personalities should be journalists. And Salant was the man she had riled when she tried to get out of her KYW contract long ago. It had been their idea to send her to "Prime Time Sunday," allegedly to boost the program's poor ratings. She considered the assignment a demotion, and she was right. "The rap on Bill Small," says Joel Chaseman, "was that he didn't know how to use talent." Small would say there were a lot of good correspondents, but not enough places to use them.

"Those of us who worked under Salant and Small had the feeling that they both came over from CBS to *show* us how to run a news division," offers Tom Snyder. "They were the keepers of the Murrow flame, and they were going to teach us how real journalists acted and behaved. They really made us feel badly. I, especially, felt worthless, not competent. And I think Jess was caught in that same thing. Certainly David Brinkley was. And that can be really debilitating to talent. We used to call it the 'CBS-ization' of NBC News."

Even if Jessica had been the best reporter on "Nightly News," however, the truth of the matter was that she never would have replaced John Chancellor, or even David Brinkley.

"The story of Jessica's being in line as anchor is a myth," says Bill Small. "When I came to NBC, Jessica was never talked about that way, except in articles and gossip columns. I am not a Savitch detractor, and I think she had remarkable success. But I certainly never encouraged [the anchor idea]." And, it turns out, neither did Don Meaney when he hired her. "Oh, no," says the former bureau chief. "Never . . ."

And so the idea that Jessica Savitch would become the first woman anchor since Barbara Walters was only a fantasy—a fantasy that Jessica concocted with the connivance of the press.

"At one particular point," says Herb Dudnick, "I thought she could probably anchor the evening news, because she was very good, and she was very magnetic. But the real problem was with Jessica. After she got an awful lot of publicity and demands on her time, she hit a plateau, and then she deteriorated. I always place it at about the time of her first marriage. The person I saw before, and the person I saw afterward, were decidedly different."

On Sunday, January 6, 1980, Jessica Savitch married Mel Korn in the plush Terrace Room of the Plaza Hotel. The month before, she wrote out a check to the hotel for $12,000. She intended it to be a wedding fit for a princess, a wedding out of a fairy tale, with two matrons of honor, two ring bearers, a Bible bearer, a flower girl, ushers, groomsmen, and 173 family members, friends, and business associates—some of whom, like Tom Snyder, would buy her a full place setting from Tiffany's at $950. Before the ceremony, the guests gathered for cocktails and remarked about the beautiful blue spruces still left up from Christmas. "It looked like a coronation, that's how beautiful it was," Jessica's sister Lori said.

Almost everyone who had ever played a significant role in Jessica's life was invited—the Schwings, the Rands, Tony Busch, Faith Thomas, Dick John, Lilyan Wilder, Ida McGinniss, Herb Dudnick, Mort Crim, Vince Leonard, Joe Vandergast, and even Bill Small, who, like many others, found Mel Korn an "odd choice" of husband. Ron Kershaw, who was now the news director at WNBC in New York—where he would create the remarkably successful "Live at Five"—was not invited, and Korn hired guards to make sure he didn't get in if he showed up. Jessica would tell Larry Fields of the Philadelphia *Daily News* that she and Mel had been receiving death threats since they announced their engagement, "and she didn't want any nuts to know where they could reach her on her wedding day."

Mel and Jessica, who was breathtaking in a traditional white gown, were to exchange their wedding vows promptly at 12:30. But by noon, when the judge who was to marry them had not yet shown up, Jessica began to panic. At 1:30, she sent Dave Neal to find him, and Martin Rand—who was now a mail-order minister in the Universal Life Church—considered performing the ceremony. Rand was searching for Scripture when Neal found Hizzoner, who explained he'd wandered in on time but hadn't recognized anybody, and had just mingled with the guests, eating and drinking until someone notified him. Ben Savitch, who was to give the bride away—and who was to become ill with cancer before the year was out—tried to take it in stride. Lonnie Reed overheard the guests introducing themselves: "Hi, I'm Jessica's dentist," "Hello, I'm Jessica's gynecologist." "Everybody had his role," she says, "and they all became her family."

Finally, the ceremony began. "Jessica wrote something to be incorporated into the vows," Vandergast remembers, "and when the judge started reading it, he read it wrong. Jessica said, 'Stop right now, everybody stop. This is my wedding. I wrote this. You will read it the right way.' I just looked at my wife and I said, 'Here we go!' But it was a very cold ceremony." Tony Busch agreed. He knew that Jessica had always liked Kahlil Gibran's *The Prophet,* but when the judge read the stanzas on marriage—"Stand together yet not too near together, for the pillars of the temple stand apart"— Tony turned to Faith Thomas, sitting on his right. "Uh oh," he said. "This marriage is already in trouble."

Almost immediately after Jessica and Mel returned from their honeymoon in Jamaica, the new bride was off to try to rejuvenate her career during "Campaign 80" as NBC's podium correspondent at both national political conventions. She needed to do her best: Her contract was up in the fall. Korn understood that he would hardly see her. She would continue to be based in Washington, and he in Philadelphia. They would try to get together on weekends, with the idea of buying a town house in New York if Jessica could get her base of operations changed. She wanted to get out of Washington, out of that bureau.

As she had with the 1978 election, Jessica immediately began boning up on the politicians involved, copying every fact she thought she needed to know on three-by-five cards, and carrying them with her for quick reference. The podium correspondent in the frenzied pace of a convention—an assignment requiring a vast knowledge of politics—would be called on to explain complicated issues without much advance notice. And most assuredly she would be doing off-the-cuff interviews. Jessica was desperate to show she could handle it.

First, she called Lonnie Reed, who had worked for Senator Henry "Scoop" Jackson, and got a good briefing on what was likely to happen. Then she went to the Vanderbilt University videotape library and watched the coverage of the 1976 conventions. After that, she contacted the Parliamentarians of both parties and met with them privately. Now she would trail candidates through eight states. "I remember her studying volumes and volumes of paper, trying to prepare for those things," says NBC newswriter Richard Berman.

But there was much at risk. The podium producer was traditionally the Washington bureau chief. That meant Jessica would be working with Sid Davis. She had to impress him. According to Bill Small, Davis, too, was reluctant about the pairing. "But Sid became a believer, and Jessica did extremely well at those conventions," Small says. "They worked well together. Not easily at first, but by the time we got into the conventions proper, he was glad to have her."

In February and March, when Jessica was on the campaign trail, Mel Korn called her twice with distressing news. He had lost two of his biggest clients within thirty days. His business would suffer unprecedented losses. He would, in fact, be in trouble—one of the clients declared bankruptcy, owing him several hundred thousand dollars. It was the last thing he needed because when he and Jessica returned from their honeymoon, Korn's second wife, Patti, had had him served with an emergency support summons. She'd done the same thing in December, asking $21,000 "for back child support and other obligations." The news had made the papers. Korn had spent so much money keeping Jessica in high style that he'd run himself into the ground. He couldn't buy that New York town house any time soon, and until she found out for certain she would be transferred, it was foolish to even think about it.

"Everything revolved around Jessica so much," says John Sculley, "that Mel didn't have any time to spend on his business. At the same time, Jessica was just enraged that she had married this man who she felt was successful, and then suddenly here he is on the verge of bankruptcy. So she was angry because she didn't want anything to get in the way of her career, and because it looked as if she were going to have to carry Mel financially, too. That cooled the relationship pretty quickly."

Because Korn really loved Jessica, he assumed that she loved him, too, and that she would at least be sympathetic to his situation. But when they met at the Plaza in the spring to talk about their life together, he was shocked when Jessica told him, "This isn't the package that I bought! I sold out cheap!" The discussion turned into an argument, and Jessica told him he couldn't comprehend the pressure she was under. He was never sure whether she meant it, but at one point, she opened the window in the bathroom and looked as if she were going to jump. Korn grabbed her and threw her on the bed. He was worried about her, telling her she had to stop using cocaine. "Honey, look how little you weigh!" he would say. Jessica insisted it didn't affect her appetite.

The couple would go through another major upheaval in New York the first week of July. Korn again wanted to talk about the marriage, when NBC announced that Roger Mudd was coming over from CBS. Jessica knew she'd never get a shot at the anchor seat with Roger Mudd in the organization. "She went berserk," Korn remembers. "To her, that was the end of her career." The day after, Jessica got on the plane to go home to Washington. "Call your lawyer and find out what it takes to get a divorce," she told him. "I don't have time for this. I've got to focus on my work."

As the Republican National Convention got underway in Detroit's Cobo Hall in July, Jessica's attorney, Donald Hamburg, working in conjunction with the powerful news talent agent Richard Leibner, was negotiating Jessica's second NBC contract. They wanted $265,000 for the first year, $285,000 for the second, and $300,000 for the third. Jessica would move to New York and anchor one weekend "Nightly News" broadcast and five "Updates" each week. She also wanted a wardrobe allowance, first-class air travel, a private office and secretary, and a one million dollar life insurance policy.

Leibner was able to convince the network that Jessica had tremendous value at affiliate gatherings and meetings. But before he came aboard, Jessica worried she hadn't much bargaining power, so Korn suggested she pay a visit to her friend Edgar Griffiths. Korn believes she did so, but there is no reason to think Griffiths interfered in the negotiation one way or another. However, calling on him for help proved to be another of her tactical errors—it was one of the strategies her colleagues held against her.

"I remember sitting with her between rehearsals in the Joe Louis Arena in Detroit," says one of the NBC directors, "and she just kept saying she couldn't believe she'd been renewed. She didn't understand why they'd done it. She didn't understand what they wanted from her even, what contribution she could make. She was absolutely amazed."

Today, Sid Davis speaks well of Jessica's performance at the conventions, saying "she did an enormous amount of homework for them." David Halberstam might argue that any reporter who needed to do such research shouldn't have been there at all. But Davis points out that Jessica was the reporter who got Nevada Senator Paul Laxalt to say on camera that Ronald Reagan's running mate would not be Gerald Ford, as rumor had it. He doesn't mention, however, that it was Chris Wallace who got the real scoop—that George Bush would be Reagan's running mate—thus eclipsing Jessica's brightest moment. As her producer, it was Davis who lined up almost all of her interviews, including Laxalt.

"The floor reporters are the ones who are really the gutsy ones," says Davis. "But Jessica took that podium job and made it into something. I think she could have become as good as a lot of correspondents we see today who we think are first-rate. At the conventions, she was very aggressive and constantly feeding ideas to the control room, saying, 'I've got so-and-so, I can do this.' "

But a reporter for *U.S. News and World Report* says, "She simply didn't know what she was doing. I saw Sid there with her, and he was practically nursemaiding her—more or less sitting on her shoulder. She never would have made it without him." Especially, says Barbara Matusow, since Jessica had memorized her set pieces, feeding them into the tape recorder and playing them back through her earpiece—the old trick from Houston—only to get confused when the director simultaneously began giving her instructions in the other ear.

As it turned out, Jessica had several other distractions during the convention. Korn was there with his friend John Sculley. "Mel was almost like a business manager for her, looking after every detail of her life," Sculley says. And, because she resented anyone who valued her to that degree, Jessica seemed to loathe him for it, all the while remaining almost totally dependent on him for other things. When the convention was over, she would manage to slip off to southern Maryland with Kershaw. Korn, who had no idea of his wife's whereabouts, finally received a phone call from her one morning about four o'clock.

"She was like somebody drowning in water, jumping from one back, to the next back, to the next," Korn says today, "anything to keep feeding that emotional need."

In August, when she was covering the Democratic National Convention at Madison Square Garden in New York—where Ron was based—Jessica asked her husband not to come with her. Korn wrote her a letter, in which he laid his feelings on the line. He told her he loved her, and because of that, he had been devoting his life to her exclusively, asking in return only her understanding. He was hurt that she interpreted the reverses in his business as a cruel act committed against her, and that she could not see him as a man coping with a problem but only as someone who had "deceived" her. He was saddened to see that she regarded every attention he paid her as a birthright and entitlement.

"I am left with the feeling that our marriage is not an experience in which I happily share, but an experience in which I dutifully serve," he wrote. "I have been a whipping boy, a nuisance factor, and a place in which to dump all of your negativeness, resentment, and anger. You reveal to me a nature that is disspirited, frustrated, and neurotic. And your destructiveness is claiming both yourself and me. If we cannot be equal partners in love, trust, and devotion, then our relationship is worthless."

Over Labor Day weekend, the couple reconciled for a visit with the Sculleys in Camden, Maine. Jessica had again been plagued by gynecological pain during the conventions, partly, she thought, because she had returned to work too soon after her operation two years ago. Now, as the weekend began, she began to feel worse. Still, she wanted to go. She liked the Sculleys, and strangely enough, Sculley had been contacted about becoming a candidate for president of NBC.

"I wasn't terribly interested in it, but I mentioned it to Jessica, and she got all excited about it," Sculley remembers. "She was constantly trying to get me to go and actively pursue the job. She didn't like Bill Small—she thought he'd never give her a major anchor position, that he just wasn't in her camp."

When Jessica said she was having pain that weekend, Korn didn't have much sympathy for her. He was "suspicious that she

231

might be fooling around, or lying to me." And he knew that she avoided the sexual side of the marriage whenever possible. In fact, without cocaine, she couldn't enjoy a physical relationship at all anymore. He had tried to get her to quit using drugs altogether, saying, "My God, it's your career! Suppose you get caught! You're a dead duck!" She told him she didn't use as much as she used to. But he had never seen her so bad. Now she was going into the bathroom with her purse "from morning to night." He was afraid the Sculleys would figure it out, especially since she was spending more time with John than she was with him. "It was a horrendous visit," Korn says.

The couple was staying at the White Hall Inn. The establishment was excited to have such a celebrity staying there until, as Sculley remembers, "she demanded to have every possible service available." Then the guests began to complain: Mel and Jessica were up all night arguing. Jessica didn't want to hear about cocaine, she didn't want to hear about business problems, and she wanted her pain to stop. Korn didn't want to hear about NBC or anything else except when they were going to start living a normal life.

Suddenly, Jessica folded up like an accordion. Mel rushed her to the Camden Community Hospital, where he spent the next several days by her side.

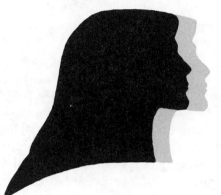

7

Jessica
Savitch-Payne

When Jessica returned to Washington after the 1980 Labor Day weekend, she was still almost doubled over with pain. While some of it was undoubtedly stress-related, her psychiatrist, Brian B. Doyle, suggested she see a new gynecologist. His wife was a patient of Donald Rollie Payne, and Doyle thought Payne, who seemed to have a magic touch with his patients, might be suited to Jessica's personality. Doyle dialed Payne's number and talked with the office manager, Jeanne McIntire. She remembers that he described Jessica's symptoms as abdominal pain and irregular bleeding, and made an appointment for her to come in on Friday, September 5. Payne's Washington office, in Foxhall Square, at 3301 New Mexico Avenue N.W., was just behind Jessica's apartment.

Donald Payne was forty-four and had been in private practice in obstetrics and gynecology for about ten years. In that time, he had built a steady practice among Washington's wealthy and well-known, and he had became friends with a number of the women who came to him professionally, reaching a level of platonic intimacy with them that far exceeded the usual doctor-patient norm. Most of his patients found him sweet, smart, funny, and utterly charming. But some of them also suspected there was more to him than met the eye.

"I thought he was neat, and a very cute and wonderful guy," says Rebecca Daugherty, who remembers he wore a T-shirt when he delivered her baby. "I was very fond of him. But I also thought he was a little bit of a scalawag. Two of my friends went to him, too, and I never could put my finger on anything definite, but we always thought he had a pretty good time, if you know what I mean."

To his office staff, which was devoted to him, Payne was exacting and demanding—a perfectionist—and not an easy man to work for. But he always showed appreciation for a job well done, and he could be extraordinarily caring and generous—paying for the wedding reception of his medical assistant, Gina O'Neal, who had grown up in foster homes, and arranging for a retirement pension for each member of the staff. "He was always there to be your friend and do anything he could to help you," recalls Jeanne McIntire, "and he just exuded laughter and humor. You couldn't help but like him."

Jessica Savitch liked him right off the bat. Nearly six feet tall, with an athletic body and infectious smile, Donald Payne cut an arresting figure when he entered the room. His reddish-brown hair had begun to recede, but it framed an open, friendly face with dark brown eyes and a slightly aquiline nose. The trim, blond moustache he had worn for several years somehow served to make him look more boyish. It would be a lasting irony that in this first, short visit to his office, Jessica thought Payne was one of the most seductive personalities she had ever met.

Payne, who had a patient in labor at the hospital, examined Jessica quickly and suspected she might have a pelvic mass, or that her remaining ovary might be enlarged. He told her he'd like to admit her to Sibley Memorial Hospital later in the month. There he would get a sonogram, a graphic record of the generative organs, and perform a laparoscopy, a surgical procedure in which he would make an incision below the navel, and insert a probe to explore the fallopian tube, ovary, and pelvic region.

When Jessica left, Payne hurried to get to the hospital. As he was going out the door, his staff teased him about having a beautiful celebrity in the office. "I'm not impressed, I'm not impressed, I'm not impressed," he shot back, and flashed what Jessica would later call his pirate's smile.

Jessica was terrified of what the tests would show. Despite her two abortions in Philadelphia, she had been telling friends such as Lonnie Reed how desperately she wanted a baby and feared the test results would put an end to that dream. She had no real intention of staying home and caring for an infant (that job would be left to a nanny) but she still coveted the idea of a secure home with a husband and child—the family unit that had been lost to her when her father died. And now it was more important than ever: If NBC finally did decide to fire her, she would say she quit to spend time with her family. "She needed someone to cling to when she broke down," as one friend puts it.

On September 6, she was in New York to anchor the Saturday edition of "NBC Nightly News," and at four A.M. on Sunday, she called Mel Korn from the Pierre Hotel, which she'd suddenly started favoring over the Plaza. Mel knew their relationship was almost over, and the change of hotels suggested further proof. In the three years Jessica had stayed at the Plaza, Mel had gotten to know the room service staff well; certainly they would notice if Jessica started having new guests or companions.

The reason she called, she said, was to let him know that she had just made out her will. Of the one million dollar life insurance policy NBC provided in her contract, she was bequeathing one quarter of the money to her mother, one quarter to Stephanie, one quarter to Lori, and the final quarter to Ron Kershaw's children. Although Mel's marketing and advertising agency was sweating out its terrible cash flow problem, Jessica informed him she was leaving him no money, as their prenuptial agreement had specified. At the mention of Ron Kershaw, Mel "wanted to hang up the goddamn phone," but listened as Jessica read him the entire will.

Jessica had prefaced reading the will by telling Mel she knew he wasn't going to like it. When she finished, Mel told her she was right, and he agreed with what she'd said several months before— that they might as well get divorced. Back in the summer, Mel had gotten an anonymous letter, telling him he ought to keep a closer watch on his wife. He had hired private detectives to check it out, and had recently gotten their report. His heart sank when he read it: Jessica was seeing Ron Kershaw again. Korn didn't know it yet, but there was already even another challenger to consider.

In the weeks to follow, Jessica and Donald Payne would begin to find excuses to talk on the phone, and by the time Payne admitted her to Sibley Hospital, the two were clearly smitten with each other. Jessica liked his good looks, his social position, and his apparent affluence. She also learned that he was the father of four boys, having only recently been divorced after nineteen years of marriage, and that he was still dealing with the trauma.

Meanwhile, Jessica had put in a call to Kershaw, and when she told him she was going into Sibley, he came running. He met Donald Payne in Jessica's hospital room, and already he knew what was happening. Kershaw had covered the medical beat in Houston and says that he pegged Payne at once as "another fucking society-climbing doctor—a dime a dozen guy. He just wanted to take Jessica to parties in Georgetown."

Kershaw had felt sorry for Mel Korn, because Jessica had used him—used him up—as he put it, and he'd never even really had her. Mel was a victim. But Kershaw's view of Payne was far bleaker: Both Korn and Payne had bought a TV star, "not knowing she's a fucking psychotic person," never bargaining for anything other than the celebrity, the glow, but Payne was a calculating person who deserved what he was in for.

In many ways, Jessica and Don were alike. He, too, was vaultingly ambitious, never willing to settle for second place. And like Jessica, he also had a tendency toward depression. In fact, Payne had been in psychotherapy for six years. But Jessica and Don shared another important secret: He, too, was heavily dependent on drugs.

Who was Donald Payne? Jessica was already involved with him before she knew much about him. Born January 23, 1936, the son of an insurance salesman, he had grown up in Wichita Falls, Texas, where he lived until he went away to Rice University in Houston in 1954. The significant influences of his youth were his mother, an English teacher at local Midwestern State University, his involvement with the Christian (Disciples of Christ) Church, and his desire to become a doctor.

According to Don's sister, Patricia Payne Mahlstedt, six years younger than her brother and now a Houston psychologist, both their parents were loving, responsible, stable adults whose primary focus was their children. They had high expectations for their children, but supported them in multiple ways to achieve their goals.

Don's father, Rollie, from whom he received his middle name, appears to have been personable, gregarious, and "very self-confident—one of the friendliest men I ever knew," according to the family minister, Rev. Dr. George R. Davis. For several years, Rollie Payne commuted to Beaumont for his job, and for a brief period he owned a luxurious white Buick convertible—an enormous status symbol in those days—although the family was not well to do. The father impressed one of Don's cousins as a colorful character, someone who liked the good life whether he had money or not. And, Don would tell friends in his adult years, his father was an accomplished philanderer. Don's sister, however, resolutely denies this, calling him a sweet, sensitive man who was always loyal to their mother.

In many ways, Eleanor Payne, an organized and energetic woman who took charge and got things done, seems to have been the head of the household. She also sacrificed for her children, making sure they had the things they needed to take part in school activities. When Don was sixteen, his mother opened the first travel agency in Wichita Falls, building it into a successful business while teaching and attending school events. Her students admired and respected her.

With her own children, though, things were often tense. Don complained in years to come that his mother was a domineering figure who dictated his every move. Patty only says that in her adult years she and her mother were good friends, having "resolved our differences before she died. We had enough distance between us emotionally that we could be close. She and Don did not. They were so close, so enmeshed, that they pushed each other's buttons, or at least she pushed his."

The most turbulent emotional battle between Don and his mother was to begin while he was at the University of Texas Southwestern Medical School in Dallas, when Eleanor Payne announced that she was divorcing her husband. Three years earlier, Rollie Payne had suffered a heart attack, and his wife had nursed him back to health. Patty says the reasons for the divorce were "very complicated," but insists that philandering was not one of them. Don later told friends that the divorce was the biggest trauma he had ever experienced. "Dr. Payne often talked about his father's running around," Jeanne McIntire remembers, "but he said he never thought his mother would divorce him for it." For the rest of her life, Eleanor Payne spoke of her former husband with contempt, leaving both her children hurt and angry.

In medical school, Donald Payne began dating Dee Anna Anderson, a student at Southern Methodist University. Dee had grown up one street over from the Paynes in Wichita Falls, and Don's mother wholeheartedly approved of her. But in Don's junior or senior year, Dee became pregnant, and they married in February 1961, while he was still in school. The Rev. Dr. Davis, whom Don had called upon for help when he applied to medical school, performed the ceremony.

From the beginning, there were problems. His wife, Don found, was as skilled as his mother at trying to run his life. "Dee was an attractive woman, but she was very demanding, and she wanted Don to walk the straight and narrow, which just wasn't his way," recalls one of his medical school friends.

Don's peers noticed that he and Dee lived in higher style than the rest of the medical student community; their place was always better furnished, and they drove a more expensive car. "It wasn't that Don wanted money more than anybody else, it's just that he seemed somehow to have it as if by magic," recalls his friend. "I always thought they lived beyond their means, and I never understood how they managed to do it. The trappings of things were very important to them."

The Donald Payne charm apparently worked wonders, even then. He impressed one of his fellow students as being "among the most engaging persons I've ever known. He and I could look at one another and have an understanding. No words had to pass." But most of his classmates didn't like him. And it was not insignificant that when he was graduated from medical school in 1962, Don Payne finished second from the bottom of the class.

In 1963, upon finishing his internship at the University of Iowa, Don once again called upon The Rev. Dr. George R. Davis for guidance. Davis had moved to Washington several years earlier to become the senior minister of National City Christian Church at Thomas Circle. Payne, who was about to enter the army, wanted a special assignment in Washington—something prestigious—and asked the minister to put in a word for him. Soon he had a cushy appointment as the Chief Medical Officer of the Military District of Washington. The post entailed tending to the medical arrangements of visiting dignitaries, and it put Don right in his element—making useful contacts and associating with celebrities.

"When I was in Washington," says Thomas H. McConnell, with whom Don had gone to both college and medical school, and who had also joined the army, "I lived in the sorriest kind of walk-up flat you can imagine, down in Arlington, off Columbia Pike. But Don lived over in Bethesda, in a nice little redbrick house on a tree-shaded street. And for the life of me, I never figured out how he managed to do that sort of thing."

Without ever changing houses, in 1965, Payne moved into a three-year residency at prestigious Georgetown University Hospital, calling still again upon the Rev. Dr. Davis, who was now known as President Lyndon B. Johnson's personal pastor, to help open doors. In time, Payne was elected to the position of Chief Resident. In December of that year, Ethel Kennedy was due to deliver her eleventh child, Rory Elizabeth Katherine Kennedy. Payne's closest friend from that period believes that Payne "very cleverly, and elaborately plotted" to be on call when Mrs. Kennedy needed ministration, and indeed he wound up delivering the 8 lb. 4 oz. child by cesarean section. Ethel Kennedy took a liking to him, and the following Fourth of July, she invited Don and Dee to the Kennedy compound in Hyannisport, Massachusetts. Dee was then pregnant with their third son, whom they named Joseph Patrick Payne, after the old Kennedy patriarch. Payne always kept a picture in his office of Ethel Kennedy leaving the hospital with her baby.

At the end of the 1960s, Payne went into private practice in Washington, setting up a professional association with another physician. According to Jeanne McIntire, the partner was not surprised when Payne quickly built up a successful practice, but added that one reason Payne was so in demand was because he performed abortions for Washington's high-ranking society women during the years when abortion was illegal. He found it easy to admit a patient for irregular bleeding, do a D and C, and then say he had discovered she was pregnant, since pregnancy tests then were often less than accurate. His partner was distressed, for not only was performing abortions against the law, but he was Catholic, and his faith did not condone such practices. After two years,

239

Payne and the physician parted ways, McIntire says. In years to come, Payne would lose his privileges at Georgetown, a Catholic hospital, when another obstetrician pointed out that he was performing abortions on request.

Apparently, Don Payne had been anxious about life in general for some time. In 1974 he began seeing a psychiatrist, Georges Zavitzianos, who, Payne told friends, diagnosed him as manic depressive with suicidal tendencies. For a while, Payne saw Zavitzianos as often as three times a week. As the years wore on, Don's sister, Patty, tried to help him herself, but realized his problems were beyond her, and believed that despite the therapy, he was deteriorating badly.

To compound things, in April 1975, Don began having severe stomach cramps and chronic diarrhea. He was admitted to Sibley Hospital, where he stayed a month. Tests revealed he was suffering from hepatitis B. Far more serious than hepatitis A, or infectious hepatitis, which is transmitted by food handlers via the fecal-oral route, hepatitis B, or serum hepatitis, is spread by contact or inoculation with human blood products, usually by needles or blood transfusions. Infection can be severe, and the disease frequently becomes chronic, lingering on, chewing up the liver. Fatalities are not uncommon.

Hepatitis is a risk that all physicians, particularly surgeons and obstetricians, face, because they come in such intimate contact with blood. The amniotic fluid contains viral particles as well, and an obstetrician working on an infected person can easily pick up the disease if he has a scratch on his hand or if he tears his glove while operating or delivering a child.

Donald Payne also could have contracted hepatitis B in two other ways. One is by shooting drugs intravenously, although there is no real evidence that his drug use was so advanced by then. Another is by having become infected through sexual transmission, as it can be spread the same way as the AIDS virus, even though it is not concentrated in semen. In any case, Payne was frightened. He asked The Rev. Dr. Davis, whose National City Christian Church he and Dee attended for a while, to visit him in the hospital.

Before long, however, Payne was back on his feet. By 1976, his medical practice was thriving, and he had an office in the suburbs and a new office—decorated in blinding, bright color schemes—at Foxhall Square. His marriage, on the other hand, was in deep trouble, and the atmosphere tempestuous. Dee, described by one of Don's colleagues as "the perfect doctor's wife—I remember her sweeping into our tenth medical school class reunion in her diamonds and jewels and magnificent, floor-length mink coat"—was always complaining that Don didn't make enough money. But as Don told Mrs. H. M. Papp, one of his patient/friends, it was a no-win situation. When he worked longer hours, Dee complained that he was never at home. At the office, he was often moody.

The Paynes were now living in a $208,000 house in Bethesda. But Don had also recently bought a $350,000 redbrick, four-story town house at 2023 Q Street N.W., in Dupont Circle near Connecticut Avenue. When it came time to furnish the house, he thought of Mrs. Papp, who worked at Garfinckel's downtown department store. Papp had told Payne that if he ever wanted to buy anything, she would be glad to let him in on her employee discount.

"He came into the store one day with a very immature young man," Papp remembers, "and said he was setting up housekeeping on Q Street. The boy looked to be sixteen, and I thought for a moment that he was one of Donald's sons. I said, 'And this is one of your handsome—?' And he stopped me and said, 'No, this is my friend.'

"So we went shopping, and Donald blew a nice amount of money on Waterford crystal and beautiful linens, and then on clothes for the boy. Dr. Payne obviously wanted to be super-magnanimous, and do things that would make this young guy happy. It was almost like buying things for your child, or your wife, or your girlfriend—someone you really want to impress. They were asking each other, 'Do you like this?' you know. But the sad thing was that Dr. Payne felt very much at home in the Waterford department, and the young boy felt very ill at ease. I kept thinking, 'What is an intelligent man like Donald doing with this kid?' Sex is over and done with in ten or fifteen minutes. What kind of conversation could they have?"

Papp, who had worked with many homosexuals when she managed a beauty shop, never suspected that Payne might be anything but heterosexual. To this day, she believes that Don wasn't a true homosexual, but a heterosexual who became disenchanted with the female species. "It really blew my mind," she continues, "and the next time I saw Donald, I said, 'My God, you're a faggot! I can't believe it!' And he just laughed."

If the young boy was the first of Payne's male lovers at Q

Street, he certainly was not the last. For a time, Payne was involved with a man who worked in computers. Friends say there was also another lover, who became difficult when Don's romance with Jessica made the papers. One of Don's attorneys remembers the day Don called and said the man was putting pressure on him for money, and wanted to stay in the Q Street house. "Don said, 'Help me on this!' And I said, 'Just stand up to the guy and tell him to get out!' "

In December 1976, Eleanor Payne died of emphysema. The following year, Don again became ill with chronic hepatitis. He entered Georgetown University Hospital, where his second bout with the disease proved to be much more severe than the previous one. He lost forty pounds.

On Labor Day of 1977, Don phoned his old friend Thomas McConnell in Dallas. McConnell was practicing pathology in partnership with the late Dr. Charles Ashworth, who had been their professor at Southwestern Medical School. Don said he was calling from his hospital bed.

"They're advising me this, and advising me that, and they want to biopsy my liver," Payne told him. McConnell told him to go ahead with the biopsy, and Payne called back in a panic. "I've really got to come down and see you. They're telling me all these terrible things about my liver."

The pathologist took a look at the biopsy, read the report, and sighed. "It was a grim-looking thing," he says. Don was on the verge of cirrhosis. "I really thought he was doomed."

But Dr. Ashworth, who was a legend in Texas pathology circles, studied the sliver of tissue for hours on end. He agreed it looked bad but thought the biopsy showed collapse fibrosis, instead of productive fibrosis—an inflammation or scarring that occurs in chronic hepatitis and can lead to cirrhosis. Ashworth didn't think the prognosis was as bad as everyone said.

So Payne packed up his slides and went to California, where he saw two doctors, one considered to be the foremost liver and chronic hepatitis expert in the world. The prognosis was not good: Payne had three to five years to live. He would either experience liver failure and go into a coma, or bleed from the big, dilated veins around the esophagus.

McConnell, who was godfather to Payne's second son, David, remembers the way Don took the news.

"There's obviously a difference of opinion on this," Payne said, and refused to take the prescribed steroids or undergo treatment, insisting that he felt fine. Payne wanted to listen to his body and make his own judgments.

McConnell was amazed at the ease with which his old friend shrugged off his worry. But Don had his own way of dealing with stress. Another of Don's physician friends in Texas was shocked when he showed up with "a fistful of marijuana," and explained that he'd been using drugs for quite a while. As matter of fact, Don told his friend, he had smoked so much marijuana at one point that he contracted gynecomastia—enlargement of the male breasts, a well-known complication of heavy marijuana use—and had to have a breast reduction. Later, that same doctor would come to suspect that Don, who Jeanne McIntire says routinely took diet pills and handed them out to his staff on occasion, had "fried his brain" on stronger drugs.

The time came when Don felt it was only fair to go to Dee and tell her the truth about his homosexual affairs. His admission was honorable, but friends say the wounded Dee saw it as carte blanche to get what she wanted in the divorce, for she reasoned, correctly, that Don would be frightened of the news becoming public. Payne had expected that his wife would be vindictive, but, according to friends, he was enraged when she told him she'd made sure the boys knew what kind of man their father was. Aside from the damage it would do to his relationship with his sons, he perceived it as a searing reminder of the way his mother had attempted to turn him and Patty against Rollie Payne.

Don was determined he wouldn't let that happen to him, and for a time he insisted that he live in Bethesda with the family, even though he and Dee barely spoke. But he confided to Mrs. Papp that whether he arrived early, late, or on time, Dee arranged it so that the children were never around when he got home. If the three eldest boys, in their late and early teens, were old enough to understand what their mother had told them, the youngest child, John, who was ten, only knew that he missed his father. Payne came close to weeping when he told a friend how he had driven past the intersection where John was a school traffic guard, and that father and son had waved to each other, powerless to do anything more.

"One time when I was going to see Dr. Payne, I took my older son with me so that he could hear my new baby's heartbeat,"

243

Rebecca Daugherty recalls. "And I sensed that Dr. Payne was very sad then, very lonesome for his own children, whom he adored. He had pictures of them all over the office. Even though there were long periods of time when he wasn't allowed to see them, he hadn't been able to break the bonds."

Dee Payne filed for divorce on April 9, 1979, citing *a mensa et thoro,* a divorce from bed and board, or a partial or qualified divorce, where the parties are forbidden to cohabit. Don came back from a weekend at Rehoboth Beach and found an order barring him from the house.

"He called me," Elizabeth Guhring, his divorce attorney, remembers, "and he said, 'What do I do now?' I said, 'We have to cope with it.' And he sighed, and he said in this tired, matter-of-fact voice, 'Well, I guess it's back to the baths.' "

The day Jessica Savitch walked into his office, Donald Payne had been divorced for exactly five weeks. With all the accusations about homosexuality, the case had been bitter and exhausting.

Don had come out of the whole thing feeling depressed, worthless, and vulnerable. And when Jessica started to flirt with him—sending him hard-to-get tickets to impressive functions—he couldn't quite believe it. "He expressed with utter amazement that, 'My God, this gorgeous woman, this charming woman *loves* me!' " his attorney remembers. " 'And more importantly, I think I'm in love with *her*!' " Even if Don was more attracted to Jessica's celebrity than he was to her feminine attributes, the end result was that he was deeply drawn to her. "It was just as if he had been in jail," says one of his friends, "and Jessica had let him out. He was desperate to prove to himself that he wasn't homosexual."

At first, Lelia Bright recalls, Payne was timid in his courtship. And then one day at about one o'clock, Jessica was at home when the front desk called to say she had a visitor. "Tell Miss Savitch that it's Dr. Payne."

Lelia was upstairs packing Jessica's bags for a trip when the doctor arrived. When she came down, the couple was "sitting right close to one another. I went on in the kitchen, and when I came out, Dr. Payne picked Jessica up, put her across his shoulder, and was going upstairs with her. And Jessica said, 'Oh, my God, oh, my God! Lelia, I am so embarrassed! I would *never* let you see me like this.' She knew that *I* knew what he was carrying her upstairs for."

Then, as the couple laughed together, the housekeeper was given a distinct dismissal. "Mrs. Bright," Payne said, "your mother called a little while ago, and said you should come right home."

In the beginning, Jessica liked everything about Payne, including their sexual relationship. If Payne was thrilled to be able to tell Mrs. Papp, "I never felt so good—I'm reborn!" she felt the same. Exhilarated when she talked about him, she snuggled in her chair and wrapped her arms around her waist, as if she were hugging herself.

"It was sort of like, 'Oh, aren't I a little dear?' and 'Doesn't he love me!' " says someone who knew her then. "It was almost as though someone were reading her a story. She obviously thought she had found the man who was going to pick her up and carry her piggyback through life. You got the feeling that she would be happy forever after."

For now, however, there was the problem of what to do about Korn. Jessica wasn't telling anyone that Mel was on his way out, but when she failed to go to Philadelphia for Tracy Rappaport's bat mitzvah on September 25, Rita knew that something was up. Jessica would miss her "goddaughter's" bat mitzvah for only one of two reasons: She was either in the hospital, or her marriage was dissolving.

A few weeks into the month, Korn had gotten a call from Jessica's attorney, Donald Hamburg. According to Korn, Hamburg asked him what he thought it would take to make the marriage work. Mel laid out six ground rules.

Number one was that Jessica had to stop using drugs. Korn was now confiding to friends that her habit had gotten "pretty bad" in the last few months. In fact, whenever he and Jessica had been together, "There weren't two of us there, there were three of us."

Second, Jessica had to keep seeing her psychiatrist, Brian Doyle, "to get a handle on herself, and find out whether she could love herself first, and then love another person."

Third, she had to decide that Korn—and not Ron Kershaw—was indeed the person she could trust with that love, "so that it can be nurtured and then grow right."

Fourth, Jessica had to be an equal partner in the marriage.

Fifth, to parallel Jessica's individual psychotherapy, Korn con-

245

sidered it vital for the couple to go together for marriage counseling.

And sixth, they had to live together. Korn said he knew he had agreed at the beginning of the marriage that they would see each other only on weekends, at least until Jessica moved her base of operations to New York. But now it was time to move forward.

Hamburg said he would talk to his client, and at the end of the day, Korn got an irate phone call from Jessica. She began to scream that no one understood her, that she had an election to prepare for, and that she couldn't possibly talk about any of this until after November 4.

"I said, 'My God,' " Korn remembers. " 'I know you're working hard, and you're traveling, and you've fought hard to make it at a young age, but you're not the only person who does this work!' "

Then he remembers stopping himself and telling her they'd get together after the election. "I wish we'd never gotten married, because at least then the friendship might have remained," he says.

With Jessica's new NBC contract, which went into effect in October, she had gotten her base of operations changed to New York, a goal she'd worked toward for some time. But now she wanted to stay in Washington with Don. Before long, he began going to New York with her when she did the Saturday edition of "NBC Nightly News" (which she now anchored regularly, instead of Sunday) and they'd make a weekend of it—buying gifts for each other at Gucci's and Tiffany's, and, on one occasion, roller skating like kids through the lobby of the Pierre. Jessica took pictures to show to her friends.

Lelia was worried. "Dr. Payne was a very sweet person," she says, "but I told Jessica, 'Dr. Payne is bad news! You leave him alone!' " But it was already too late.

Meanwhile, Jessica's acute abdominal pain had recurred. The tests Payne ran at Sibley Hospital had been inconclusive, and because Don was now too intimate with her to continue to be her doctor, she made an appointment with Dr. Bruce Ames. Believing that she had either an intestinal problem or a flare-up of the endometriosis that had plagued her in Philadelphia, Ames admitted her to the Columbia Hospital for Women, and ordered X-rays of the intestines, along with a pelvic sonogram. Both were normal, and the doctor wanted to do further exploration.

Jessica was frightened about the ramifications, but she was almost equally concerned about her election night performance, where she was slated to anchor the House and gubernatorial desk. She still didn't have the gut instinct about politics that would cover her lack of knowledge, and she was sure that sooner or later she was going to get into a situation she couldn't handle, and that the whole country would see it.

"The closest she came was election night, when she had to report on the governors' races," remembers an NBC director. "Sometimes the material would come in willy nilly and hysterically. And they would be throwing things at her, and she had no way to assimilate them, because she didn't understand the big picture of what she was doing. A couple of times she'd get asked a question, and it was like 'The Twilight Zone.' She'd make up one of those answers that isn't an answer. Like, 'Well, nobody knows for sure, Tom, but it looks like in the next few minutes, we'll have those results for you.' Pure coverup. But you can only bluff it so far. And I think she was always amazed at how far she got away with it."

Mel Korn, who still had no inkling about Jessica's affair with Donald Payne, loved to be with his wife on occasions such as election night. When Jessica hadn't said anything about his joining her to Lelia, the housekeeper asked if Korn was going to be there. Jessica said no.

"I said, 'Why not?' " Lelia remembers. "Jessica said, 'Because I'm going to be too busy to be bothered.'' Lelia eyes widened. "I said, 'You are never too busy to be bothered with your husband. What's going on here?' " Jessica told Lelia they'd talk about it later.

That night, Lelia was watching the coverage when the telephone rang.

"Mr. Korn said, 'Mrs. Bright, has Jessica come in?' I said, 'No, Mr. Korn, Jessica's not here yet.' " She told him there was an NBC party afterward, and that Jessica would not be home early.

Korn continued to call every half hour until 3:30 A.M. Finally, Jessica came in a little after four. At 7:30, Korn was on the phone again. Lelia woke Jessica and told her Korn wanted to know if she was ready to talk.

Jessica flopped over in the bed.

"Hell, no."

"Maybe I could have hung on for another month," Korn says.

"But I didn't see any indication that she wanted to do anything except get rid of her marriage. The career was an excuse. She kept me away during September, October, and through the election. What really capped it was when I read over that list of the six things that I felt should be done. I looked in the mirror and I said, 'I've got to be crazy! Where is she going to get the time?' "

Korn wasn't naïve enough to think that Jessica might still love him ("I think she had loved me as much as she was capable," he says), but he counted on a certain amount of reciprocal behavior. Ben Savitch had died while Jessica was in the hospital, and Korn had gone alone to the funeral, flying all night to California, attending the service, and flying back that night, because he thought one of them should be there.

"I thought in all the years that she might have learned something about dignity and respect for people and relationships," Korn says, looking back. "But in the end she hadn't."

On November 10, after ten months of marriage, Mel Korn filed for a "divorce by consent" in Philadelphia's Court of Common Pleas. He'd started seeing a psychiatrist himself. At fifty-one, he was facing his third divorce and the collapse of his family business. The week before, *People* magazine had run a profile of his wife. Jessica admitted that her work load had been hard on the marriage. "Mel and I went into it knowing this would be a transition year," she said. "It's been tough—tougher than I expected, because more was required of me than expected."

Sometime around Christmas, Jessica moved in with Don on Q Street. She insisted on bringing Lelia, whom she depended on not only to cook her meals but to buy everything from her suits to her shoes to her bras. Payne already had a housekeeper, Sarah Bailey. Both women were devoted to—and possessive of—their employers. Now they were two housekeepers with only one house to keep.

At first, Don's biggest problem was with Chewy. He didn't like dogs in general, but he hated this one for several reasons. He knew that Chewy had been a gift from Ron Kershaw, whom Don had met when Kershaw came to visit Jessica in the hospital. It was obvious that the two men hadn't liked each other on general principle, let alone because of their mutual interest in the same woman. Payne, who had no real idea of how much history Jessica shared with Kershaw, still disliked the way Jessica doted on the dog. And in her new surroundings, Chewy sometimes defecated on the rug or on the kitchen floor. It drove the doctor wild. To top it all off, Sveltie the cat didn't care for Payne's cat at all.

The arrangement was chaos from the beginning. Sarah would cook something special for dinner, for example, and Lelia would say she'd have to fix a different meal for Jessica, who was a finicky eater. Sarah also resented the disruption in her routine—she changed sheets on a certain day, and that was it. On occasion, a member of Payne's staff would drop by and find the two women bickering, stopping just short of a shouting match.

In a way, Payne, who had a fine sense of humor, could appreciate the comedy in that. But he complained about the way Jessica prowled around the house all night, or phoned him in the wee hours of the morning when she was out of town. He said often that he couldn't get enough rest to do his work.

Far more disturbing to the doctor, friends report, was the way Jessica demanded that he devote all his time and attention to her. At times, she could be surprisingly sweet, such as when she would pick four-leaf clovers and drive to Don's office with them in the middle of a trying day. But then she would turn around and make unrealistic demands, forbidding him to drive to his office when there was ice on the roads, even though he had twenty patients to see, and shouting to the point of frenzy when he refused to comply.

"I remember a real battle they had one day," says a member of Payne's staff. "Jessica was giving a speech in Chicago, and she wanted him to go with her. He told her he couldn't, he had office hours scheduled in his Gaithersburg [Maryland] office. Well, she just ranted and raved, and carried on something terrible. Before she left that day, she must have called our office fifteen times. Finally she said, 'Well, why don't you just give up your practice? I can support you.' " From suggestions such as that, Jessica would graduate to tears, or her usual screaming.

"I love her, but I can't live with her," Payne told his friends.

Meanwhile, Don was drawing his blood and mailing it down to Thomas McConnell to run the SGOT, or liver enzyme tests. McConnell was amazed to find the enzymes were only slightly elevated. "I *can't* be very sick," Don would tell him. "Look at this!" Aside from the turmoil he was experiencing with Jessica, Payne said he felt fine. Maybe 1981 would be a good year after all.

Along with her Saturday "Nightly News" broadcast, Jessica was still anchoring the weekday prime time news "Updates," and

249

serving as backup on the "Today" show, where producer Steve Friedman thought she was "very strong in pop culture," and good for the program. In the coming months, he would pair her with Jane Pauley for a rare two-female anchor combination and, over the length of her NBC career, use her on the show for some seventy-five co-host appearances. In addition, Jessica provided commentary on the NBC Radio Network, sometimes calling Mort Crim, who had spent four years at the ABC Radio Network before he got into TV, and running her script by him. With the presidential inauguration coming up on January 20, she would also anchor NBC's special programming on the inaugural balls.

The inauguration meant that a number of the influential friends Jessica had made through the years would be in town, and Jessica wanted to show off her new beau. She thought of John and Leezy Sculley. Sculley was really Mel's friend. But Jessica had gotten close to him over Labor Day, and she had a separate bond with him through Lilyan Wilder, who had helped Sculley with his public presentations.

Jessica got the Sculleys excellent seats for the inauguration and invited them over to the town house. There they met Don, but Sculley remembers that the atmosphere was strained.

"Leezy and I both sort of looked at each other," Sculley recalls, "because it seemed like a strange relationship. We couldn't figure out what they were doing together. It didn't seem to make any sense." Mel, Sculley thought, was at least in the circle of show business. But Don "just didn't look like the type of person who was going to follow Jessica around to her TV shows."

James Whalen, the president of Ithaca College, where Jessica now served on the board of trustees, remembers going by the NBC Washington studios to see her one night at around this time. He was in the lobby, trying to convince the security guard that he had a legitimate appointment, when "a nice-looking guy, wearing a sheepskin jacket," came in and asked the guard to tell Jessica he was there.

"By the way, I happen to be first," Whalen said. "I can't get to her." Don came in and punched a few buttons and got Jessica on the phone.

"She came running out," Whalen says, "and she introduced us, and the three of us went back into the office. Jessica and I finished whatever business I was after at the time, and then she went out to do her thing. So Don and I sat there and talked for a while, and we watched her on television. He had a nice smile, and a friendly way about him, and he seemed easygoing, sort of loose. There was something comfortable about the guy. When she came back, we teased her a little bit, and then I had to go. She saw me out, and as we were walking down the hall together, I said, 'Gee, I like him, Jessica.' And she got excited. She said, 'Do you?' And I looked at her again and I said, 'I *really* like him. I *really* do.' And she was going down the hallway as I was walking out, but she turned around and came back, all full of smiles, and threw her arms around me. She said, 'Thanks a lot! I really, really appreciate that!' "

Among the few physician colleagues Don socialized with was Carl Sylvester, an anesthesiologist at Sibley. Jessica liked Carl's wife, Jean, and the couples went to dinner together often, and were frequently in each other's home. For Don's forty-fifth birthday, on January 23, they decided to celebrate together. Jessica had arranged to buy a special piece of jewelry for him in New York, and when a friend brought it down to Washington in the middle of the night, she put her coat on over her gown and went to NBC to get it.

The night of the birthday, Jessica brought a Polaroid to capture the event. The pictures show a jubilant Donald Payne, surrounded by his friends, opening his presents, and kissing the woman who now dominated his life. "Happy Birthday," the wrapping paper said. "And many more."

In the coming weeks, Jessica was to learn about some of Don's other friends. The first piece of real information about his homosexual past came from one of his acquaintances, a gay man who lived in the Dupont Circle neighborhood and thought at the time that Payne's infatuation with Jessica was a passing fancy. From there, she sought out other of his friends.

Had she and Don discussed his sexuality? Did he ever confess to her, the way he had to Dee? His attorney says she would not be surprised if Don spoke candidly to her at the beginning. "Don couldn't keep something from you if he felt you needed to be told." What she told him of *her* own sexual relationships is unknown. But Payne confided to a member of his staff that, "He thought all her female friends were lesbians," and he particularly disliked the way she encouraged one young woman, who "followed her around like a puppy dog." One of the women he referred to then will say only that "Jessica looked for love anywhere she could find it, because she perceived that as affirmation of self."

Less than two months after Jessica moved to Don's home on Q Street, she packed up and went home to Foxhall. Says Jeanne McIntire, "It was a case of one about to kill the other if somebody didn't get out."

Soon they were back together again, but briefly. "I moved Jessica four times within three months," says Lelia. "I never did turn in the form that said she'd actually moved out of Foxhall, because I was afraid to." For at least one of the moves, Payne's medical assistant, Gina O'Neal, helped Jessica pack her things. She was astonished to find the presents from the marriage to Korn still in their boxes. But another friend found more than that. "Every time I'd go to move something, I'd find a pack of drugs"—behind the furniture, in the bookcases, anyplace. "Everywhere you looked, there was a stash of marijuana and coke, just lying around open."

For a few weeks, the couple tried seeing each other, without living together. Often, Jeanne McIntire says, the staff had trouble keeping track of where the doctor was. "We used to laugh and say, 'Are you at "his" or "hers" tonight?' " Finally, they settled on the arrangement Jessica had had with Kershaw and Korn: They would spend the work week in their respective houses, and the weekends together. But that really meant they had only one day to share. When Jessica did the Saturday night news from New York, she often stayed over to visit her friend, WNBC anchor Sue Simmons—whom she had first met when Simmons worked for Kershaw in Baltimore—catching the shuttle back on Sunday mornings.

Even that proved problematic.

"One weekend, Jessica thought she was alone in a string of inner offices here," says a member of the production crew on "Nightly News." "She was famous for throwing fits, of course, and for screaming at people over the telephone, especially. Well, this one day, she was on the phone, and it was obvious from the conversation that she was yelling at Payne about not picking her up at the airport. I don't think I've ever heard anyone scream so loud. It wasn't made clear whether there was an arrangement, but she was screaming that he had destroyed their relationship, and that she could never depend on him. I don't see how anybody could have come out of that and not be hoarse, but she did. She came out just as smooth as anything, and went on the air. It was just two *totally* different sides to her."

Finally, in February, Don said he wanted out. Jessica told Lelia she was glad, that she thought he was "a mental case."

A couple of weeks later, Payne called Jeanne McIntire and asked her to come into his office.

"I went upstairs and he said, 'Jeanne, I'm in an awful mess,' " she remembers. "I looked at him and laughed, and I said, 'What have you done now?'

"He said, 'Jessica's pregnant.' "

"She wanted a baby *so* bad," Lelia says, "and she was determined that she was going to have this one, regardless of what it cost her. She said she just wanted something of her own to love."

But by now Don was reluctant to marry her. At his age, he didn't want another child, and certainly not with Jessica. There was another complication. The standard provisions to Jessica's contract contained a morals clause.

Lelia remembers reminding her that she couldn't keep a job with NBC and be pregnant and not married. "She said, 'Well, then I'll take a leave of absence, go out of the country and have it, and then I'll come back and say I adopted it.' "

That's what Lelia thought she was going to do, until one day after Jessica had moved back to Q Street. When Lelia came in, Jessica was on the telephone downstairs in her office, screaming.

"It made you shiver. We'd never used those words in our household." Jessica got up and closed the door so Lelia wouldn't hear. Lelia thought they probably heard her in Wyoming.

Sarah came in and rolled her eyes.

"This has been going on since I got here at seven," she told Lelia. "When he left for the office, she got on the telephone."

Payne was pushing for an abortion. Jessica had said absolutely not. Payne wanted to know how it would look for a well-known doctor to have impregnated a well-known TV newswoman. Jessica wanted to know "who gave a fuck."

"She really just made him go through with this marriage," Lelia says.

One colleague remembers Jessica with sympathy at this time. "I certainly wouldn't call us deep personal friends, but we were friends," says Lea Thompson, a consumer reporter who works out of WRC, the NBC Washington affiliate. "I had two children by then, and Jessica was always very interested in how I was managing to have a balance between a family and a career. It was obvious to me that she was envious of that, and that she felt a great sense of regret. Because she saw that the tremendous amount of attention that had been paid to her earlier in her career had dropped off, and she was reaching for something. But she was very frustrated and confused about what she wanted in her personal life."

As the weeks went on, Don finally decided that if Jessica was so intent on having the baby, he owed her the respect of marrying her. He talked it over with The Rev. Dr. George Davis, and then went to his attorney, Elizabeth Guhring, and asked her to draft a prenuptial agreement.

"He said, 'It's got to be the tightest thing you've ever written,' " Guhring remembers. "He didn't have any intention of living one day with her, or of having anything to do with this child. He said, 'I'm not even sure it's mine.' "

Guhring went to work. "We were hard as nails," she says. "[The Agreement] recited, 'This is *just because* of her pregnancy. This is *just because* of her morals clause.' I lightened up on a few of the provisions, upon the pleading of Jessica's attorney, but I budged only about one-ninth of an inch. It was one of the toughest premarital agreements in the world."

Essentially, says Jeanne McIntire, who witnessed the signing, the agreement specified that there was no exchange of money between the two parties, since each party was self-supporting. If one of them died, the other would renounce all interest and right in the property and the estate, including family allowance.

Now there was only one thing standing in the way of a wedding. Jessica was not yet divorced from Mel Korn.

In the interim—and after the turmoil had subsided a bit—Don and Jessica decided to see if they could patch things up. They began taking trips together, to Vail, Colorado, to ski, to Hawaii, and to New York.

"I was at NBC doing a report one day," says one of the network's female correspondents, "and somebody said, 'Have you met Jessica's fiancé?' I looked, and here was this very thin, nervous-looking guy sitting on a couch toward the side of the newsroom. They introduced me, and I thought, 'Oh, boy, this is trouble.' Because he didn't seem like a strong, stable fellow, and she was a nervous, uptight dame. Before long, she was telling everybody that she was pregnant, and saying that when she told him the news, he said, 'I'm not ready to marry you. I'm in therapy three or four times a week.' And I remember thinking, 'God, Jessica, that's not something you tell anybody if you're a national figure!' I knew that couple was headed for terrible things. There was nobody playing grown-up.''

With the pregnancy and the swirl of the wedding plans, Jessica found it increasingly difficult to keep her life in order. She was beginning to have anxiety attacks again—although none as severe as the one which had sent her to Dr. Schwartz in Philadelphia—and according to Lelia, she was now phoning Dr. Doyle, her psychiatrist, as often as three times a day.

One day—they were then back at Foxhall—Jessica called Lelia in and said she'd been thinking. Maybe if she and Don had a house that had never been "his," or "hers"—a new house—they might be able to live together. They were building new town houses just behind Foxhall. If they moved there, Don would be within walking distance of his office. And she would still be right around the corner from NBC. It was already a fashionable address—Jessica had heard that James Watt, the secretary of the interior, and a couple of ambassadors had moved in.

"So she said, 'Lelia, I want you to go over there and pick out two houses, and out of the two I'll choose one of them.' And that's what I did," the housekeeper recounts. "I went through *all* of them, and I picked out two that I liked. The man was so astonished. I don't think he believed that anyone would send her maid over to pick out her house—much less, two of 'em!''

Jessica was thrilled. From the way Lelia described the house toward the back of the complex, Jessica could have the second floor for herself, and make the third floor into a nursery—there were even accommodations for a person who would take care of the baby.

As March rolled around, there was no denying that the baby was starting to show. With Jessica's divorce from Korn now final, the couple decided to marry on March 21, at National City Christian Church. Jessica would be fifteen weeks pregnant then. There was no time to have invitations printed, so Jean Sylvester was asked to get on the phone and invite the guests. Jean also arranged the reception at the Madison Hotel, just down from the church.

Don called The Rev. Dr. Davis, who was now retired from full-time ministry, and asked him to officiate. The pastor had performed Don's first wedding, and still felt some allegiance to Dee. But he agreed to be the primary figure in the ceremony, and phoned Dr. Earl M. Caudill, Jr., National City's associate minister, to assist.

By now, Don either had a change of heart about the relationship or had talked himself into thinking it might work after all. Suddenly he was telling friends that he loved Jessica more than he'd ever loved anyone in his life, and that he hoped the baby would be a girl. His sons had started to come around again, too.

The day before the wedding, Payne was in his office seeing patients. Mrs. H. M. Papp had recently been to him for a tubal ligation, and today she was in for her check-up.

"Usually the day before your wedding, you have a big question mark about whether you're doing the right thing," says Papp. "Especially if you've had a bad marriage before. But Donald was just shining. He was aglow, he was so happy, and he certainly didn't look like a man who was having a shotgun wedding."

In contrast to the circus atmosphere of the Savitch-Korn nuptials, Jessica's wedding to Don Payne was simple, and as she had done at her first wedding, the bride wore white, this time not a traditional wedding gown, but a high-necked dress with sheer, puffed sleeves. At her neck, she wore a circle pin of diamonds and sapphires—a gift from Don that would later be appraised at $1,500. Stephen Payne, Don's eldest son, acted as his father's best man, and Jean Sylvester was Jessica's attendant. Florence Savitch was there, and so were Lelia and her family and Mary Manilla, Jessica's old friend from her CBS days, with whom she had become reacquainted when they both attended a luncheon in New York. Most of the forty to sixty guests, however, were friends and family of the groom.

"Jessica had been telling me, 'I've met this wonderful man, he's so handsome, he's so wonderful, and on top of things, he's the Kennedys' doctor,'" Manilla remembers. "I said, 'Fine, Jessica, fine,' because I knew she romanticized things. But the next thing I knew, a woman I have never heard of called and said, 'Jessica is getting married, and she would like you to be at the wedding.'"

"I walked into this huge cathedral, and somebody showed me the groom,' she continues. "The minute I saw him, I went, 'Oh, shit.' His eyes! He was spaced out. He wasn't there. I said, 'Hi, I'm Mary Manilla, Jessica's friend.' And it didn't register. Then I saw Jessica, and I went up and said very insincerely, 'Isn't this wonderful? I'm so happy.' And she looked up at me and she whispered, 'Mary, I think I'm making a terrible mistake.' "

In the coming months, Jessica would tell friends that Don had tricked her, that the prenuptial agreement he presented the night before the wedding was different from what they had agreed on.

At the reception afterwards, however, all seemed well. Jessica signed an autograph for the associate minister's eight-year-old son—"To Cricket: I'm so happy you could be at our wedding. Jessica Savitch-Payne"—and several of the guests remarked on what a lavish affair it was. "Next to an Arab reception I went to once, with strolling everything and a sit-down dinner for four hundred, Jessica's was the most elegant of the thousands of receptions I've been to," says Lon Schreiber, National City's music director. "Everything was done superbly, top quality."

The pictures taken that evening show a tired but jubilant Donald Payne, raising a glass of champagne with his bride. In some of the photos, he looks both radiant and resolved. But in others he looks strangely hollow-eyed, sick of spirit and soul. He appears happiest in a family shot, with Jessica and his four boys.

Seventeen years earlier, Jessica had told Barry Swartz, then a pre-med student, about a fantasy she'd had.

"Last night, when I went to bed, I dreamed that we were married and had three boys. You worked in a hospital in San Francisco, and I worked at a television station near there and had an evening show. The boys all looked exactly like you—hair soft and dark and brushed to the side, and eyes dark with fires in the center. It was so wonderful, and we were so happy."

There was no honeymoon. In the days following the ceremony, Don would take his sons to Florida, and Jessica would stay home and work. When Payne returned to the city, he went to live in his house on Q Street. Jessica remained at Foxhall.

Elizabeth Guhring, the attorney who prepared the prenuptial agreement, turned to her secretary one day. "You watch," she said, "there's going to be a 'miscarriage.' " Guhring suspected that Jessica planned to abort.

Meanwhile, Jessica's oldest friends were learning about the marriage for the first time in the newspaper.

Tony Busch couldn't believe it. "That was the first any of us had heard about it," he says. "I'm not sure whether Faith Thomas called me, or I called her, but she was as taken by it as I was. Jessica had at least discussed Mel with us, but we didn't know anything about this guy. Nobody from the old group was even invited to the wedding. And Faith lived right there in Washington. She was worried."

Mary Manilla was worried, too. As the weeks went by, she couldn't get Donald Payne's eyes out of her mind. Finally she asked Jessica why he'd looked so strange. At first, Jessica told her she could only guess—that she'd been in his closet one day and had found a large bottle of amphetamines. Later she confessed that Don had given them to her, too. "He was forever handing them out to her when she was tired," Manilla says. "Finally it got to the point where I said, 'You're going to stop it.' She looked like a stick. They affected her badly—she started getting paranoid about everything."

In April, Jessica was on the road again, giving speeches. But the new bride was lonely. And now, barely two weeks after her wedding, she telephoned Ron Kershaw. The Payne months had been the longest she had gone without him.

"She said, 'What am I going to do, Rab? It's the worst mistake I ever made. He doesn't love me. He just wanted me because I'm on TV.' "

"I said, 'No shit, Brat. You just stubbed your toe, that's all. Next time, marry your podiatrist.' "

Kershaw laughs in the retelling. "It was cruel, and stupid and flip, but that's the way I felt. Who falls in love with their gynecologist, for Christ's sake? It's the most insulting thing of all. And she was like bumper pool, bouncing off this one and that. But it didn't matter. We were back together. And we didn't back-door anybody. We just loved each other. It was a continuum with us. It never stopped."

But Jessica was also spending more time with Don. On Easter, April 19, they attended church services at National City, and after lunch, Lon Schreiber, the church music director who'd played for their wedding, saw them come back to their car in the church parking lot. "They were just as happy as they could be," he says. But Jessica had to leave for New York that afternoon. She would be filling in on the "Today" show all the next week.

When Jessica got to New York, she went through her mail. She was used to bizarre notes from weirdos—men who sent her underwear with the days of the week embroidered on it, and men who said they had her in their bedrooms every Saturday night and wanted to make it permanent. But today she found a letter that stopped her cold. The Reagan shooting had occurred only a month before, and now she read: "Crazy what a woman can provoke a man to do," the note began, "but in my attempt to win your love, I'm going to murder John Swearman [sic] . . . I realize that as I mull my duty in the luxury of this Hilton hotel room, I only hope my historical deed will win your love and your respect." The note concluded with a twenty-five-line handwritten poem and was signed "M.B." Jessica checked the postmark: Elwood, Nebraska, April 9. She planned to show it to Marty Wall, the deputy head of security.

Early the following morning, Jessica was alone in her office when she heard a voice behind her. She turned around to see a man in his early twenties, staring at her with a haunted look. "I just want to see you, talk to you, touch you," he said, and started moving toward her.

Jessica lunged at him and shoved him outside, managing to lock the door. Frantic, she dialed Marty Wall. But her office was on the fourteenth floor of the west side of the building—on Sixth Avenue, away from the "Nightly News" section on the east side. By the time Wall got there, Jessica was nearly hysterical. The man had vanished.

On Tuesday, she called the FBI and showed them the note. Wednesday night, federal authorities arrested twenty-two-year-old Michael Berke at the Hotel Seton on West 40th Street. Berke admitted that "John Swearman," the man he said he would murder to win Jessica's love, was fictitious. But authorities found other letters the Nebraska farmer had written—to Dan Rather, John Chancellor, and Jane Pauley, threatening to kill President Reagan, Vice-President George Bush, and Secretary of State Alexander Haig. They also found photographs of the White House in his wallet.

By now, the story had broken in the press, and on Thursday, April 23, Jessica mentioned the incident on the "Today" show, thanking the Secret Service and the FBI.

To close the investigation, the U.S. Attorney's office asked

259

Jessica to come in for questioning on Friday. That morning, she was padding around her office with her shoes off and somehow banged her big toe. The toe began to throb, and by that afternoon she couldn't wear her shoe. When Marty Wall arrived to take her downtown, Jessica couldn't walk. William T. Abbott, Jr., an NBC attorney who usually handled such cases, offered to support her as she limped to and from the limousine.

"Jessica was very concerned about the publicity over this," Abbott recalls, "so she wanted to avoid the cameramen from the TV stations, and certainly any of the photographers for the newspapers."

At one point, pursued by photographers as the trio came out of the U.S. Attorney's office, she hopped toward the nearest building, a Catholic church next to the police complex.

"Once we got inside," Abbott continues, "I waited at the door to see whether Marty was coming, and Jessica began wandering around the church by herself. I turned around and saw her hobbling toward the candle stand in the back. I looked away for a minute, and when I turned back again, she was lighting candles with the little taper, and writing notes on small pieces of paper and leaving them in the pews. What was in the notes, I don't know. But this went on for ten or fifteen minutes, and the interplay of her emotional frailty, her celebrity, and the craziness of it all was really quite extraordinary. She was so terribly vulnerable, limping around doing crazy things, with lunatics after her."

In the days immediately afterward, Lelia worried about how the trauma would affect Jessica's pregnancy. But soon she was joking about it to her friends. "Jesus," she told one, "first I marry a psychopath, and then I've got them crawling around in my office!"

By the time she recounted the incident to talk show host Nancy Merrill in 1982, she had embellished the story for higher drama. "I felt cold metal on the back of my neck," she told Merrill. "I'll never forget it. I turned around, and he had a knife."

At the end of April, Jessica and Don were set to go to Acapulco on vacation. Payne had been there several times before, and he loved the beaches. When he returned, Jeanne McIntire asked if he'd had a nice time.

"Oh, Jeanne, it was terrible," he said. "We hardly ever left the hotel room!"

Jessica had spent the whole time on cocaine, he told her. A one point, they were out somewhere when she went into the bathroom, staying a long time. When she came back, he told McIntire, "She had white powder on her lip. I said, 'What's that powder on your face, Jessica?' and she flew back to the bathroom to get it off."

Now Don complained to several of his friends that he didn't know what to do about his wife's drug problem.

"She was flying around to all these different places, making speeches," one woman says, "and sometimes Don would go with her. They'd be identified as 'Jessica Savitch and Guest,' you know, and arrive at all these glorious functions in a chauffeured car. At first, Don said, 'Gee, lousy, rotten, horrible me, how do I deserve this?' But then he got to where he hated to go—her habit was so bad that he just had to pour her on the plane. He said he pleaded and preached to her against it, but it didn't do any good."

But according to Lelia, Don was also behaving erratically. "Dr. Payne would call her up one minute and say, 'Jessica, I don't want anything more to do with you. Don't come see me, and don't call me,'" Lelia says. "It really tore her apart. Then in an hour or so the phone would ring. I'd pick it up, and he'd be just as nice as he was when he first met her. His personality changed just like that. I said, 'Jessica, nobody acts like that who's got good sense.'"

Jessica agonized over what to do. In the last month, she had told Mort Crim that with her many gynecological problems, she was terrified she might lose the child. To someone else, she confessed that she was worried about how her drug use might damage the fetus. Finally, there seemed no alternative: She decided to have an abortion. "She was afraid the child would be as crazy as its father," says Lonnie Reed. "But I think Jessica also thought *she* was losing it. She was tortured about her ability to choose and make decisions." Now Jessica arranged for a money order for $350, using a fake name and Roberta Spring's address. Without telling Don, she would have the abortion done secretly on her next trip to New York.

When it came time to have it done, "Roberta went with her," says a friend.

Before she left the hotel for the procedure, Jessica called Don and told him she was bleeding, and that she was going to a doctor. Afterward, she phoned to deliver the rest of the story: she had lost the child.

As with the first Philadelphia abortion, the experience was deeply upsetting. "I remember how hysterical she got," says Mary Manilla, who never questioned that it was anything but a miscarriage. "She was crying, and begging Don to come up to New York to be with her. She tried to say things like, 'Well, of course, he's very busy.' But she just kept crying and saying, 'It was a boy! You could see it. It was a boy.'"

According to his office staff, Don knew what had happened, but he let Jessica think he'd believed her story. In a way, Don said, he felt sorry for Jessica. But his office manager could also see that the news was a relief. For the past month, he had been telling friends he planned on divorce.

Now, without the pressure of pregnancy, he suddenly changed his mind again. "He wanted the opportunity to really see if the marriage could work out," says Elizabeth Guhring. "Because he was not a divorcing kind of man, really."

Although Carl Cochran and others knew the truth, Jessica stuck to her miscarriage story, even to close friends such as Mort Crim and Lonnie Reed. In 1982, she told the *Houston Chronicle*, "I really wanted that baby I lost."

By late spring, Jessica had finally decided to buy the larger town house that Lelia had picked out for her on Embassy Park Drive. According to the Deed of Trust, she arranged to borrow $165,600 from Perpetual American Federal Savings and Loan on May 29.

In early June, Don began spending more time with her, but he didn't like the style of the town house—attached on both sides— with the residences arranged by courts. He preferred his rambling old house, and he wanted to hold on to Q Street as a retreat. Lelia was glad. She and Jessica had begun finding scalpels stuck up under things, stashed in odd places. "I'd go to move the linen, and I'd find one," Lelia says. "It chilled me to the bone."

Meanwhile, Don was still sending his blood to Thomas McConnell, checking his liver enzymes. And he began asking his staff if they thought he was capable of practicing. Jeanne McIntire wondered if his psychiatrist kept him coming only for the money. "Clearly, he was starting to lose ground," says McIntire. "I honestly believe he thought he was losing his mind."

Jessica's friends thought the same. Mary Manilla was down in Washington one day just after Jessica had moved to Embassy Park

Drive. She told Manilla she was fixing dinner for Don that night in an effort to get him to move into the town house permanently. Since Jessica couldn't cook, Manilla planned the dinner.

"Lelia was there, but she was leaving," Manilla says. "So I decided I would make it simple—roast beef, potatoes, and string beans—and I put the roast in the oven and told her how long to cook it. Then I had to go wait in her empty apartment at Foxhall, because she said, 'You've got to stay here in case something goes wrong.' Well, I was only there for about an hour and a half, when the phone rang. Jessica was hysterical."

"He left!"

"What happened?"

"I don't know. He won't tell me."

By now, Jessica had exhausted her ideas for making the marriage work, and from time to time she phoned The Rev. Dr. Davis for advice. Dr. Davis had made it clear that he cared about Jessica as an individual, and not just because she was married to a man he had baptized and sponsored through every important stage of his life. Often, when he telephoned and found her gone, the minister would talk with Lelia about the state of the marriage, as well as Jessica's overall well-being. He worried about the demands of her work and the strain of her private life. The minister had suffered a breakdown five years earlier, which coincided with his retirement from National City. He knew what stress could do.

On June 8, Dr. Davis sent Don a lengthy mailgram. He referred to Jessica's complaint that Don had waited until the night before the wedding to present the final prenuptial agreement, and that it had differed from what he and Jessica had orally agreed upon. He went on to suggest that Don had not only deceived his wife, but the clergyman who had performed his wedding ceremony—an act as serious as deceiving a government official.

Who knows how such castigation settled in a troubled mind? But to Don it may have looked as if his oldest ally, and the prime religious and moral figure of his life, had sided with the woman he told Thomas McConnell was "so harsh and cruel that he could not stand it." Jeanne McIntire adds, "He said over and over, 'She just wants to ruin me.'"

On the afternoon of Thursday, June 11, Jessica was upstairs taking a shower when the doorbell rang "as if someone was sitting on it," Lelia says. Jessica put on her robe and went downstairs, and when she opened the door, Payne nearly fell in on her.

"He said, 'Just hold me tight, Jessica, don't let me go,' and he sobbed so hard."

For the next two hours, Jessica sat on the sofa with her sad husband, holding him and stroking his head.

Finally, when he had become calm, she fixed them some tea and a sandwich. "I have to go to the studio now," Jessica told him. "Would you like to go with me?" Payne said yes.

"After that, he acted normal," Lelia says. "When they came back from the studio, she fixed some bacon and eggs for them. And she thought he was fine."

The following night, Don was back at Q Street. Sometime during the evening, he slipped into despair. At first, he tried to slash his wrists. But he lacked enough Xylocaine to numb the skin, and stopped with the first small scratches. Then he shook out a massive—though not fatal—dosage of Valium, and swallowed.

Next, he picked up the phone and called his medical assistant, Gina O'Neal. As they began to talk, Gina realized that some of his conversation didn't make sense, and that he wasn't responding to her questions. Indeed, Payne was preoccupied. He had now filled a syringe, and was attempting to inject a lethal dosage into a vein. But in his shaky state, the doctor failed. "Dammit!" he said. "I can't even do that!"

Gina hung up and called Carl Sylvester, Don's friend and physician colleague.

In the days afterward, Jessica and Carl moved Don to Embassy Park Drive, so that someone could watch him at all times. Dr. Zavitzianos, his therapist, recommended that he be admitted for treatment, and Jessica and Carl began to check out psychiatric hospitals. They decided to get him out of town, to try to protect his privacy. Jessica worried about the impact the situation would have on her career.

Thomas McConnell, meanwhile, was sitting at his desk in Dallas, and began thinking about his old friend.

"It was one of those strange kind of sixth senses," he says. "I hadn't heard from Don in a while, and he'd been calling me fairly regularly. So I picked up the phone and called his office, and Jeanne McIntire answered. I said, 'I'm just calling to see about Don.' And I can't remember what my clue was, but she hesitated a little bit, and said something about him not being in a hospital.

And I said, 'Has he tried to commit suicide?' Something just told me."

In a little while, Jessica called McConnell and told him that Carl Sylvester had suggested taking Don to the New York Hospital–Cornell Medical Center in White Plains, New York. She wanted his opinion.

The following Monday, Payne phoned Jeanne McIntire and asked her to come over to the town house. When McIntire got there, Jessica left the two alone. They talked for about an hour and a half, and Jeanne was surprised at how rational he was.

"He said, 'Jeanne, I'm going into the hospital,' " she recounts. " 'How long do you think we can keep the practice going?' I told him I could run it for three months on the income that we had, but that then we'd have to think about it. Dr. Payne had an excellent practice, but he had bought so much real estate that he'd made himself house poor, paying the mortgages. I asked him to sign some checks so that I could cover the expenses and pay the girls.

"And then he said, 'Jeannie, I'm not coming home, I know.' I said, 'Don't talk that way. I'll keep it together as best I can for you. You just get well, and come back so we can carry on.' And he said, 'No, if she gets me in that place, I'll never get out.'

"I tried to tell him it was best that he go get some concentrated treatment, and I said, 'You'll be back in no time.' He shook his head, and he said, 'I hate to do this to you, but you'd better start looking for another job.'

"I got up and went over to him and gave him a hug and a kiss, and I said, 'Just get well. We'll take care of everything.' And then I was crying, and he was, too."

At one o'clock in the afternoon, Lelia told Jessica it was time to leave for the plane. Don did not want to go.

"Jessica did everything to get him in that car, but he wouldn't do it," Lelia recalls. "Finally, she remembered that he liked candy and chewing gum, so we coaxed him in there with Baby Ruths and Lifesavers. He was just like a child. I said, 'Dr. Payne, when you come back—' And he said, 'No, Mrs. Bright, I'll never get back.' "

In the weeks to come, Jessica would cry as if she were broken. For a time, she sobbed for days on end, and Lelia tried to comfort her. "And then I'd go home, and I'd cry *for* her. But we would have our little Bible sessions, and I would tell her what the Word said, and she would read it with me."

But after a while, Jessica grew angry. Mel had been a disappointing husband, going nearly bankrupt on her, but Payne, she said now, had deceived her. At first, he had seemed to offer her security, social position, a home, and a baby. But Don didn't have the ready financial resources she thought he had, and he did not want their child. He didn't even want her. And now he had not only shamed and humiliated her, but he had abandoned her. She decided she would leave him when he got well.

For the next few weeks, however, Jessica would do something that she had never done in a male-female relationship. She would be the nurturer, the caretaker. She visited Don twice a week, dressing in disguise, staying at the White Plains Hotel. Jeanne McIntire recalls that when another woman on Payne's staff went to see him on visitors' day, Jessica became offended, as if she were giving him all the emotional support he could need, that only she could restore him. Don told Elizabeth Guhring how often Jessica came to see him, "And there was nothing from him like, 'She stuck me up here,'" Guhring says. "It was all, 'Thank God for Jessica!'"

After their sessions together, Jessica would go back to the hotel and get on the phone. One of the people she called was Ed Hookstratten, the California news talent agent. The relationship with agent Richard Leibner wasn't working out, she said. She thought he was dropping the ball on her career—when, in fact, everyone knew she didn't have a clear picture of how others saw her. They talked for hours, and Jessica told him the intimate details of her problems with Don. Hookstratten, who had a soft spot in his heart for her, didn't want to complicate things with a business relationship.

While Don was being hospitalized, Jessica began spending more time with the circle of friends that had sparked so many of the rumors about her. In essence, they were a coterie of women who engaged in lesbian activities. They also used cocaine. According to Lelia and others, one of the people who supplied cocaine to Jessica was a woman who worked at NBC. A list of Jessica's expenditures from that year shows that she wrote the woman—who refused to be interviewed for this book—four checks totaling $1,200 in one twenty-six-day period. Later, Lelia would also find three of Jessica's coke spoons—two with Coca-Cola motifs, and the third with an enameled Indian design, she recalled. One day, a black woman who lived in New York arrived at the house on Embassy Park Drive with the woman who was obviously her lover.

Lelia was shocked. "I said, 'Jessica, what on earth is going on here?' And she said, 'Let's go upstairs in the office,' which was on the third floor. So we went up there, and she told me what they were. I was never so astonished. I said, 'No, I can't see this!' I'm just plain and old-fashioned, and I've never been around people like this.

"So I said, 'Jessica, you've got to be more careful of your friends.' I couldn't believe that she would even allow someone like that to the house. And she said, 'I might have friends like that, but that's one thing that I would never do myself, Lelia.' And I told her again, 'You cannot do this!' But they were always wanting to talk to Jessica about their love life problems. And she would listen, because she was kindhearted."

To Jessica, the events of the past few weeks compounded her view that things were closing in on her. In two years, her contract would be up for renewal, and now she was certain the network would not pick it up. Somehow she needed to make herself look like a valuable property, the way it had been in her first years at NBC. She decided that if she came out with a best-seller, she might be able to recapture the glamour at another network. She had been making notes about such an idea since her CBS gofer days.

On June 12, Jessica signed a contract with the writer Barbara King to collaborate with her on what would eventually be called *Anchorwoman,* published by G. P. Putnam's Sons. Jessica received a $50,000 advance, out of which she would pay King $17,000 for her work. Jessica's contract with King called for "a biography/autobiography . . . from small town to anchorwoman." But the final product would bypass her private life to concentrate on her rapid rise in the world of broadcast journalism, and her status as a role model for young women. She and King would begin work that summer.

In the middle of June, Joan Durham, Jessica's psychic, walked into her house in south Jersey and glimpsed Jessica on television.

"I looked at it, and I said, 'Oh, my God,' " Durham recounts. "Her aura was black. I immediately got her on the phone, and I said, 'Jesus, what the hell is going on in your life?' And she started to cry. I began telling her things I could feel, and she was silent. Finally, I said, 'Who is Don?' And she said, 'He's my husband.' " Durham was shocked. Like the rest of Jessica's old friends, she had never even heard of him.

After they talked for a few minutes, Durham asked Jessica to send her Don's picture.

"I told Jessica I saw serious emotional problems, as well as tremendous instability," Durham says. "I also went so far as to relate Don's homosexual situations. I even 'had' the name of a man he was involved with. Jessica sort of gasped, and she said, 'Oh, my God, that's his close friend.' " When the psychic learned that Don had attempted suicide and was being hospitalized, "I told her that if he wanted to commit suicide, he'd find a way, even with constant supervision. I said, 'Honey, you'd better be prepared.' "

In mid-July, the doctors at Cornell Medical Center decided that Don was ready to go home. Jessica told Lelia she thought it was premature, that he was only pretending to be well. In retrospect, Thomas McConnell thought the same. Don had called him after his first few weeks at the hospital, and then they spoke again. "I knew he was in deep, deep trouble when I talked to him that last time, because he had lost that ability [to laugh]. He seemed flat emotionally. He kept telling me that it was costing a lot of money to be in the hospital—there's no professional courtesy with psychiatric patients—and he had to get out and go back to work to earn enough money to pay his bills.

"Oftentimes, people with mental illness come out of the hospital and get back into the same construct," McConnell continues, "where every force conspires to reproduce the problem. I tried to get him to come down here to Dallas and stay with me for a while, but he just wouldn't hear of it. Looking back, I think he had already made up his mind to kill himself."

8
Nightmare

The doctors at Cornell Medical Center insisted that Don could not go back to Q Street alone, so sometime during the third week of July, Jessica brought him home to Embassy Park Drive. According to Lelia, Jessica was frightened of what he might do, and wanted him out of the house as soon as possible. Then she would see about ending the marriage.

For now, though, everyone was pretending that things would work out. Lelia introduced him to the next-door neighbors, and Don began treatment with another psychiatrist in nearby Falls Church, Virginia. On July 21, the therapist prescribed 150 milligrams of amitriptyline hcl, an antidepressant.

According to Jeanne McIntire, Don was to have two weeks of rest and relaxation before he returned to the office. But he couldn't rest; he had always grown anxious when he wasn't working, and now he told Jessica he was afraid he wouldn't have enough money to send all the boys to college. He was spending a lot of time brooding and sitting around the house, where Chewy was constantly underfoot. Don asked Jessica to put the dog in the kennel, and finally she complied.

At the end of the month, Don went back to work. He held hours at his Gaithersburg office on Thursday, July 30, moving over to the Foxhall office on Friday. Jeanne McIntire remembers that "the patients were so happy to see him, you couldn't believe it. They just wanted to put their arms around him and hug him. We didn't schedule a real heavy day. If everybody had known he was back, it would have been a madhouse." Sometime during the day, Payne slipped away to see his psychiatrist, who gave him a prescription for 25 milligrams of Elavil.

Late that afternoon, Payne and McIntire went over the finances. There was "something like $40,000 or $50,000" in the corporate checkbook, "with $79,000 outstanding." Payne treated himself as a salaried employee. He sat down and wrote out a series of checks: $1,380.00 to Dee Anderson Payne for alimony and child support for August, and $2,057 to New York Hospital–Cornell Medical Center. That left a balance of $4,105.47 in his personal checking account, and $1,334.12 in savings.

"We talked for a few minutes," McIntire says, "and I asked him if he had any plans for the weekend. He said he and a friend were supposed to play tennis on Saturday, but he didn't know if he felt like it. So I said, 'Well, I'm going to be home this weekend. If you don't have anything better to do, give me a call and we'll go up the street for lunch.' And he said, 'I might do that!' I can see him yet, standing in the door waving his hand. He said, 'Goodnight, Jeanne, have a nice weekend.'

On Saturday, August 1, Jessica was scheduled to do "Nightly News" in New York. She had asked the network if she might do the broadcast from Washington that night, but the answer was no: the weekend news was always done from New York. Don told her not to worry about it. He was fine, he said; he would have dinner with his son David and David's girlfriend. It would give them a chance to catch up.

Now, before she left for the plane, Jessica asked Don if he wanted her to stay home. "I noticed the two of them standing in the courtyard in front of the house for some time, embracing and talking very privately, in a serious tone," their next-door neighbor Doris Foster says. "Then they sat on our front steps for a while.

They had their arms around each other, and I assumed they were working something out. It was a very loving conversation. I guess she was trying to cheer him up."

After Jessica left, Don got on the phone and canceled his tennis date, saying he just didn't feel like playing. His friend asked if Payne would like him to come over to talk. "No," Don said, "I've got some things I want to think out. I'd like to be by myself." That night, Payne went to dinner in Alexandria with his son and his girlfriend. "David said Dr. Payne smoked an awful lot of cigarettes," Jeanne McIntire remembers, "but otherwise, he seemed fine." They capped the evening with a banana split from Jeffrey's, an ice cream parlor near Don's office on New Mexico Avenue. The party broke up early. It had been the first anniversary of Don's divorce from Dee.

About 12:30 or 1:00 A.M., Jessica phoned from New York. She was glad to find Don in good spirits. They talked about her broadcast, and the news of the day. After about forty-five minutes, Jessica told Don she could come back that night if he thought he needed her. He said that was silly. He'd see her about the usual time, 10:15 A.M. He'd have the coffee on, and the coffee cake in the oven. It was a custom with them.

On Sunday morning, August 2, Payne rose early. He showered and shaved, and put on blue jogging shorts and a yellow short-sleeved shirt. Then he went downstairs to make the coffee, poured himself a cup, and scanned the Sunday papers. After that, he picked up Jessica's paperback copy of *I'm Dancing as Fast as I Can*, TV producer Barbara Gordon's harrowing account of her addiction to Valium, and her subsequent treatment in a mental hospital. Don sat back down in the chair in the living room, propping his feet on the ottoman.

> After each session with Julie [Gordon's psychologist], the symptoms always returned—the numbness, the hollowness, the unreality, the terrible thoughts . . . This was depression, Julie told me. I had thought depression meant simply sadness. I didn't know one felt crazed, insane, dumb, dead, numb, enraged, hysterical, all at once. Depression is a killer . . . I was not prepared for being oppressed, for being victimized, for being in a mental hospital.

271

Payne turned the book face down on the table. He stood up and pulled the ottoman off to the side, leaving his coffee. He reached for Chewy's long leash, an olive drab strap about one-half-inch across. Then he put the coffee cake in the oven to warm. Jessica would be home soon.

At about 9:00 A.M., Pat Garvey and Donna Fitzpatrick stepped onto the Embassy Park tennis courts for their usual Sunday morning match. Garvey, a bearded social worker in his late thirties, had taken a year off in his career and was intent on improving his game. He played tennis there as often as eight times a week, usually with his friend Fitzpatrick, an attorney who lived in the complex. In a little while, a young woman would show up on the court next to them and wait for her partner.

A little past 10:00 A.M., Jessica arrived at the complex and walked toward her town house, directly in front of the tennis courts. Garvey and Fitzpatrick noticed her come up—they saw her every week at the same time. Garvey, who watched CBS news and had never even heard Jessica's name, knew the thin blonde as just another attractive woman. There were a lot of them at Embassy Park.

Jessica had bought in New York some of Don's favorite croissants, and she put the little bakery box down as she unlocked the front door. Now inside, she put the box in the kitchen, and looked for Don in the living room, calling his name. When he didn't answer, she shouted up the stairs, and then began to climb the fourteen steps to the second floor. But Don was not in the master bedroom to the left of the landing, nor in the sitting area or bath. She began to yell his name so loudly now that Schuyler Foster heard it next door. Jessica would later say that her heart began to pound when she could not find Don on the second floor, and she ran up to the third level so noisily that Foster could hear that, too. Don was not upstairs in the office or the spare room.

Frantic, Jessica flew down the stairs and ran out the back to see if the car was there. It was. Then she thought maybe Don had walked over to his office, so she dialed the number. No answer. By now she was nauseated with fear, and she walked down to the tennis court, where Garvey and Fitzpatrick were still playing, and on farther to the swimming pool. But Don was in neither place. Jessica began to tremble as she walked back up to the house, but she tried to think where else he might be. She decided to call Carl Sylvester. Maybe Don was with him.

Back inside, she reached for the telephone and sat down on the top step of the stairway leading to the cellar. She was halfway through Carl's number when she noticed the light on in the basement. "Don?" she called. "Are you down there?" She began to walk the fourteen steps down.

The basement, which was unfinished, with concrete floor and walls, was really one large room, divided into laundry and storage areas, and accessible by two doors at the bottom of the landing. She first tried the door on the right, which led to the washer and dryer area. It was locked. She then walked a few feet down the hall to the other door. Jessica opened it and began walking around to the other side, partially hidden by a wall.

There she found her husband, hanging from the neck, Chewy's leash suspending him from a two-by-four cross beam. His left foot was still resting on a bar stool, as if he had knelt on the cushion and simply slid off. The body was cold to the touch. Don's hands were black.

At first, Jessica could not comprehend that her husband was dead, only that he was hanging from the ceiling and needed to get down. The leash was wrapped repeatedly around the cross beam, and knotted on the left side of his head. Jessica picked up a broom, thinking that if she could free the knots, everything would be all right. Up to now, the body had been facing the washer and dryer, so that Jessica saw only Don's back. But as she began batting the leash, he twisted around to face her. Both eyes had hemorrhaged.

Jessica began to scream. She ran up the steps and out into the courtyard. In the weeks to come, she would say that she could hear someone screaming, but that she didn't know who it was, and could not find the source.

Pat Garvey and Donna Fitzpatrick dropped their tennis racquets and ran up to see what was wrong. The woman on the second court followed suit. Jessica, who was now flailing her arms, was so agitated that Garvey was afraid to touch her.

"Donna just stopped and said, sort of sternly, 'What are you trying to say?'" Garvey remembers. "But we couldn't make hide nor hair out of it, and Donna asked her again. Finally, Donna just went 'Boom!' and slapped her hard across the face. She got meek as a lamb. She said, very softly, 'Something's gone wrong. Someone's in the basement.'"

Garvey thought she meant there was a burglar in the cellar, and went into the house and grabbed a knife from the kitchen.

Jessica, Fitzpatrick, and the other woman followed him inside. Sveltie, the cat, nearly as distraught as Jessica, came screeching between their legs, and ran out of the house.

Garvey made his way downstairs and saw the body. Shaken, he went upstairs and told Fitzpatrick what he'd found. "Is he dead?" she asked. Garvey had seen enough dead people to know that Don was gone.

"Don't touch him," Fitzpatrick said.

Jessica went into a fury. "No," she screamed, "Cut him down! Cut him down!"

"He's dead," Garvey said. "I'm sorry, he's dead." Fitzpatrick dialed 911 and handed the phone to Garvey, who had Jessica pinned down on the kitchen floor. Meanwhile, the woman from the second court did what she could to calm Jessica. "We couldn't keep her seated," Garvey says. "She was just so limp, and she was crying and screaming, and trying to grab the phone." Finally, the police answered.

"We've found a body in a basement, hung," Garvey said into the phone. "It appears to be dead." The police dispatcher asked for the address. Garvey put Donna on.

"We're at Embassy Park," she said, and gave the house number. The police asked the name of the decedent. Donna looked blank. Garvey turned to Jessica. "Who are you?"

"I'm Jessica Savitch."

Garvey turned back to his friend. "I guess it's Mr. Savitch."

"Jessica began to shriek like a crazy person," Garvey recalls. "She said, 'No, it's *not*! It's *not*!' And I remember getting down on my knees and holding her face in front of mine and saying, 'Jessica, who is it then?' And she said, 'It's my husband, Donald Payne.'"

The woman from the second court stood up. "Donald Payne? Donald Payne, my *gynecologist*? I can't handle this."

"And she split," Garvey says. "None of us ever saw her again."

The ambulance, dispatched at 10:25, arrived soon after. With the police and the paramedics, Garvey says, "there were fifteen or twenty people"—a mobile crime unit, a fire engine, an ambulance, two sergeants, two homicide detectives, a fire captain, several officers, and a deputy chief.

Officer Dean L. McKnight had some questions for Jessica. No, she told him, she didn't know why he did it. She hadn't found a note. McKnight began checking off his form. "Was he an alcoholic?" he asked. Jessica said no. "Was he a drug addict?" Jessica hesitated. "I don't know." McKnight checked "unknown."

Donna continued talking to the police and making phone calls, using both of Jessica's two lines, and going next door to use the Fosters' phone. Garvey asked Jessica if there was someplace she wanted to go, a friend's house perhaps. Jessica had him get Jean Sylvester on the phone and arranged that they would go over there. Then, Jessica called her psychiatrist, Brian Doyle. They talked for about ten minutes, and Doyle said he would meet Jessica at the Sylvesters'. When Jessica hung up, she told Garvey she wanted to go upstairs, to get away from all the people in the house.

"I wanted to just lie her down in bed," Garvey says. "But then she had to go to the bathroom. I took a precaution. Because by this time I had figured out that she was some name personality, and that she had a psychiatrist as well. So I just wasn't going to let her be alone. I said, 'Jessie, I'm just coming in with you, hon. Let's go to the bathroom.' " Garvey shakes his head. "You're dealing with a child at that point," he says.

The two stayed upstairs for about an hour. Garvey had done shock therapy as a social worker, and he held Jessica's face between his hands and talked to her.

"She'd fall onto the floor from crying, or she'd be on the bed and she'd sag over and she'd say, 'He's dead! He's dead!' Then the next minute she'd say, 'Go down and save him! He's alive!' And I kept grabbing her and sitting her up, and saying, 'Jessica, he's dead. You can't do anything about it. He's gone.' I think she was already having a lot of guilt about leaving him alone that day."

By this time, the police had taken Don's body down, marking a slash on the beam where he had hung. Reporters, who had picked up the call on the police scanner, were wandering all over the grounds. Carl Sylvester had heard the news from his wife, and now he, too, was at the door.

Sometime after 11:00, while Carl was viewing the body, Jeanne McIntire and Gina O'Neal were talking on the phone. Gina had been away on vacation when Payne returned to the office, and she wanted to know how he seemed. Jeanne told her she was worried about him, and Gina said she was going to give him a call at home.

Carl Sylvester answered the phone. "You're too late, Gina," he said. "He's hung himself." The medical assistant, who had saved Payne from himself once before, was frenzied with grief. She called McIntire and told her the news. They wondered why Payne had chosen to hang himself with the dog's leash when, as a physician, so many other methods were available to him. McIntire, like Jessica, later, took the leash as a symbol, a final, malevolent message for his wife.

Garvey, meanwhile, worried about how to get Jessica to the Sylvesters' with reporters milling around. He packed some of her personal belongings—"I've got to have my hair dryer!"—and went with Donna to get Fitzpatrick's blue Toyota, pulling around to the entrance to the court. Then they directed the media to the small backyard where the ambulance was, and sneaked Jessica out the front. By now, the police had already taken Don's body out on a stretcher. As the trio went out the door, Garvey noticed what was left of Chewy's leash on the ledge overlooking the tennis courts.

Shortly after they got to the Sylvesters', Brian Doyle arrived and gave Jessica a shot. He handed Garvey a packet of pills. "Keep her calm," he said. Then he left.

Garvey took Jessica upstairs to one of the Sylvester girls' bedrooms. For the next three hours, he sat on the bed with her, rocking her, and stroking her head. As she had at the town house, Jessica alternated between hysteria and calm. "She'd say, very softly, 'He's dead. I can't do any more about it. I don't know why he did it,' " Garvey recalls. "And then she'd flare up again and get crazy and agitated, and say, 'Can we go see him? Please! He might still be alive!' "

When she became more rational, Jessica told Garvey that she was fearful of what the police might find at Embassy Park Drive, and asked him to drive over to the town house to look for drugs. He did, going through all the drawers and checking every place Jessica told him. He found no drugs.

Garvey then returned to the Sylvesters', and he and Donna helped Jessica make phone calls. Donna called NBC for her, and then Jessica phoned Lil in California. According to Garvey, Jessica's second or third call was to her mother.

"I was afraid to leave her alone, so I just stayed on the second floor with her," Garvey says. "And when she got her mother on the phone, she was crying. She said, 'I need you, Mom.' And from the conversation, I could tell that Mrs. Savitch was saying something like, 'I could get there maybe Tuesday or Wednesday.'

"I got on the phone and said, 'Goddamn it, Mrs. Savitch, she needs you right now!' Because I was worried about who was going to be with her that night. As it turned out, her mother *didn't* come for a while, because she had her elderly mother to take care of. Stephanie came down."

Now Jessica sent Garvey for her address book, and calmly figured out exactly who needed to be notified. The calls went to a mixture of professional associates and friends.

"She had a little spiel," Garvey says. "It was very blunt, very curt, and to the point. She said, 'I have something to tell you. Donald is dead. I'll let you know what the arrangements are.' Bam. Next one. Right down the line. She was a woman who knew what had to be done, and she could do it. I admired her for it. She spent a couple of hours saying, 'Okay, I need to do this, this, and this. Can you help me do it, Pat?' She was amazing."

Later that afternoon, when Jessica finished her calling, Garvey was afraid she would lapse back into her hysterical state.

"I just kept on probing her, asking questions, because I wanted her to talk about anything but Donald Payne," he says. "We discussed everything from weight, to what you eat, to where you ski. I was really shocked at how terrible her skin was, and I asked her about a scar on her forehead. It was so noticeable that I said, 'How do you go on TV with that?' And she said, 'Makeup does wonders.' "

The scar had started out as a pimple. But just as she would pick her cuticles and even her earlobes until they bled, she repeatedly picked the pimple until it became infected. Finally, she changed her hairstyle to hide it, resorting to bangs instead of the trademark sweep across her face.

After Don's death, she would tell people—including agent Ed Hookstratten—that she got the scar when she tried to cut her husband down with a butcher knife. But Pat Garvey, who spent hours holding her and wiping her tears that day, says there was never any blood on Jessica's face, and certainly nothing resembling a cut from a large knife.

That evening, according to Ed Thomas, Jessica called her old friend Faith, who came and stayed with her Sunday night.

On August 3, Donald Payne's obituary ran on the national wire services. It did not refer to his status as a physican, but to the fact that he was the husband of Jessica Savitch. Throughout the country, Jessica's friends and viewers picked up their newspapers to read:

> WASHINGTON—Dr. Donald Payne, 45, husband of NBC television journalist Jessica Savitch, was found dead in the basement of the couple's home here yesterday by his wife, police said.
>
> Dr. Payne, a gynecologist, apparently had committed suicide, investigators said. "The tentative cause of death is strangulation due to hanging," said Lt. William Ritchie. "Foul play is not suspected at this time."

Lonnie Reed put down her newspaper. "Oh, Christ!" she said out loud. "What a 'Jessica' thing to happen."

But Ron Kershaw took a more caustic view. "I knew what was wrong with that guy," Kershaw says. "I felt his frustration. He thought he was hustling Jessica, and Jessica hustled him. He hung himself in Washington while she was in New York, right? He was dying for attention. That's all it was. He was fucking hanging there *dying* for attention. With my dog's leash. But of course my first concern was for Jessica. I knew she was wondering, 'How can I sell this? What can I tell the papers?' "

Indeed, on August 4, UPI ran the following item:

> Dr. Donald Rollie Payne, the husband of Jessica Savitch, an NBC News correspondent, may have committed suicide by hanging because he suffered from acute depression caused by a chronic liver disease, the city medical examiner ruled today. Dr. Douglas Dixon said that Dr. Payne died of asphyxiation by hanging, and that depression caused by a liver illness was a possible cause.

But as it turned out, Donald Payne had one last secret. At the time of his death, his liver disease was nonexistent.

"When Don died," says Thomas McConnell, "I called the coroner in Washington who had autopsied him. I got a copy of the report, and it didn't say a word about anything being wrong with his liver. I thought, 'Is this the right body?' So I called the coroner, and he sent me a copy of his autopsy protocol and all of the slides. I looked at those slides, and that liver disease was just *gone*. It was the damndest thing, absolutely unaccountable! If Don was mentally deranged," says McConnell, "his liver had absolutely nothing to do with it."

The autopsy, as Dixon would tell Mary Walton of the *Philadelphia Inquirer* in 1982, showed that Payne's liver was "resolved," or cured. But according to Jeanne McIntire, the toxicology showed something else. The morning he died, Donald Payne had a cocaine level of 12 percent in his blood.

Jessica wanted to move out of the Embassy Park Drive town house immediately, but Brian Doyle insisted that she stay for at least a month. He also offered free counseling to Lelia and to Payne's office staff; he was not unmindful of the fact that it was he who had referred Jessica to Don in the beginning.

Jessica seemed to be taking it as well as could be expected.

"I called her two days after Don died," says James Whalen of Ithaca College, "and we talked for about an hour. "She was hurting, but she was still lucid, and she talked about the future. She said, 'I'm going to put one foot right in front of the other for as long as it takes.' "

To Jessica, there was also something prophetic about the events. Now there had been suicide in both families: first her grandfather, Eddie, and now Donald. In the next year, she would read everything she could find about the subject, telling Gael Love of *Interview* magazine that she wanted to write a book about it.

The funeral was held at St. Columba's Episcopal Church. Jessica sat in the front row with Don's sons, according to Thomas McConnell, and insisted that Dee, with whom she'd argued about the final disposition of the body, sit in the back of the room. The service was well-attended, and afterward, Jean and Carl Sylvester held a reception at their home.

Ellen Ehrlich, NBC's director of communications, remembers how tense Jessica was. At one point, she recalls, Jessica was sitting on a love seat with her mother, when suddenly she broke down. "Jessica was crying so hard, heaving almost," Ehrlich says. "And her mother just sat there with her arms in front of her. I wanted to scream across the room and say, 'Mrs. Savitch, can't you put your arms around your daughter?' " But the nurse, who had spent a lifetime comforting strangers, apparently could not.

A short while later, Sam and Rita Rappaport arrived.

"It was sort of crazy there," Rita says, "because you had two wives, and you had two mothers-in-law. Jessica didn't know what to do, or even who to talk to, besides Lelia and Roberta Spring. Then all of a sudden she spotted us. I'll tell you," she continues, "if I were a child, I would have been crushed. That's the way she held on to us. Her body was shaking from top to bottom."

Roberta Spring's presence was recalled with resentment in some quarters. "The day of the service," Jeanne McIntire recounts, "Roger Ohlrich and William Poist, Dr. Payne's attorney and accountant, came back with me to the office, because we had to make a decision as to what we were going to do with the practice.

"We were making an outline of plans," she continues, "when we heard a knock at the door. Roberta came rushing in, and Jessica was right behind her. Jessica demanded, 'Why are you here? Why wasn't I included? I'm his widow!' And Roberta wanted to know how dare we treat Jessica in this manner."

The trio tried to explain to Jessica that the matter involved the corporation and had nothing to do with her as the widow. "But there was no way that we could reason with her," McIntire says. "She ranted and carried on for well over an hour, tearing her hair, and throwing her hands in the air. In fact, she dismissed Mr. Ohlrich and made him leave the room. If she had been a child, you would have spanked her. She was totally out of control."

Studies show that people who lose a loved one to suicide not only feel more isolated, but *are* more isolated, because friends and co-workers feel uneasy being around the suicide survivor. Jessica knew that Don's death would only make the office politics even more strained. Indeed, NBC personnel joked that the reason Don took his life was because he came home and caught Jessica in bed with another woman. Jessica asked Bill Small and Sid Davis to transfer her to New York, effective in September—exactly a year after she first met Donald Payne.

In the meantime, Jessica accepted Mort and Nicki Crim's invitation to come to Grosse Pointe to recuperate. By now, she had already received hundreds of letters of sympathy, and she gathered a handful of them to read on the plane. There, she turned to a lengthy, handwritten letter from a sixty-two-year-old woman named Gerry McNabb, who wrote to say she knew the guilt she must be experiencing. "Two years ago," McNabb wrote, "my husband took his life in the same way." McNabb, a paralegal, gave

Jessica her phone number in case she wanted to talk. Jessica checked the return address: Orchard Lake, Michigan, not all that far from the Crims.

Four days later, McNabb got a call from Crim, whom she sensed was feeling her out to make sure that she wasn't a troubled celebrity hound. Jessica was at his house, he told McNabb, and would like to talk with her. The next day, Jessica phoned McNabb directly, and said Mort had offered to fly her to Pontiac in his private plane if McNabb would be willing to drive the few miles from Orchard Lake to pick her up.

McNabb thought they would probably spend the twenty-five minutes en route to her home getting to know each other and exchanging pleasantries. But from almost the moment she stepped off the plane, Jessica, dressed in a halter top and shorts, leveled with McNabb about her need to work through the tragedy emotionally and intellectually.

"It was a very intense four or five hours," McNabb says. "We laughed together, and we cried together, and I held her, because she really needed holding, and she responded to it. But despite the difference in our ages, I felt that we talked as contemporaries, sharing a common grief." McNabb told Jessica that her husband had had a drinking problem, and Jessica told her Don "had a dependency, too." McNabb assumed it was alcohol.

"I remember her expressing some bitterness in the fact that he had to know she was the only one who would find him," McNabb says. "And she talked some about the effect the death might have on her career. I remember she speculated that maybe she should go back into radio for a while, and then return to TV."

After ten days at the Crims', Jessica felt ready to go home. "The day she was getting ready to leave," Crim recalls, "she was hugging Nicki and crying, and she said, 'You two have really been wonderful. I don't know how I would have made it through this period. I'm going to put you in my will.' And I said, 'I don't even want to hear you talk like that. Number one, I'd be offended. I don't want anything from you except your health and your happiness. And number two, I'll be long gone before you'll ever have to worry about that.' And I never gave it another moment's thought."

On August 22, Jessica returned to NBC for her first "Nightly News" broadcast since Payne's death. Wearing a handsome white blazer, with a red blouse that revealed more decolletage than usual, a handkerchief billowing out of her breast pocket, a gold chain encircling her throat, and with Payne's sapphire and diamond circle pin placed like a badge on her lapel, she had never seemed more compelling—or more vulnerable. If her despair seemed "invisible," as the *Washington Post* was to write, she projected both extreme personal fragility and unassailable professional courage. The combination implied the potential for an on-air trauma of major proportions, as if she might do something irrefutably crazy at any minute—something no amount of explaining could ever cover up.

It was a performance, yes. But a brilliant one. Jessica knew that millions of people would tune in just to see how well she had borne up under her tragedy. They would be looking for the quiver of the lip, the knitting of the eyebrows. They wanted to see her crack and crumble before them, and they wanted to see her stoic and strong.

At the end of the broadcast, Jessica did something out of character for a professional newsperson, but almost predictable for the Jessica Savitch persona she had created for public consumption—she thanked the viewers for their thoughtfulness.

"And finally tonight," she began, "my professional relationship with you was overshadowed recently by a personal tragedy. I believe it bears mention here because of the thousands of letters and the phone calls and the kind expressions of sympathy which I have received. Please know, they are a great comfort. And I sincerely thank you.

"That's our report tonight," she concluded. "Good night from all of us at NBC News." The trademark smile then dissolved into sadness, and as the camera pulled back, Jessica bit her lip and stared down at the desk.

When Donald Payne's lawyers began to try to settle the estate, they discovered that the doctor's affairs were in great disarray. Jessica, who had signed away any claim in her prenuptial agreement, was nonetheless now acutely aware of the importance of a meticulous last will and testament. Almost immediately after she returned from Michigan, she began to arrange for a new will of her own. Again, she named her mother and sisters as her principal beneficiaries, but deleted Ron Kershaw's children.

On August 24 or 25, Robert Andrews, Jessica's business manager, told attorney Richard Blumenthal that Jessica had come to his office to execute her will and trust agreement, but that she wanted to make some changes—most notably to eliminate her sister Lori as a beneficiary. Florence Savitch would now receive a third of the estate, Stephanie Savitch-Newman, now divorced, would receive a third, and the final third would be divided among the seven people who had been the most supportive to Jessica in the aftermath of Don's death: Mort Crim, Roberta Spring, Lelia Bright, Jean Sylvester, Mary Manilla, Faith Thomas, and Don's sister, Patricia Payne Mahlstedt. Andrews, who under the new will was the executor of the estate, explained to Blumenthal, the draftsman of the will, that there had been a personal incident between Jessica and Lori, "which apparently was the cause of some animosity."

Just why Jessica cut her favorite sister out of her will is unclear. "The negative energy came from Lori's side," says one of Jessica's male friends. "And Jessica was reluctant to give in when Lori was hostile. Once Jessica was rebuffed, that was it."

"I tried very hard to talk Jess out of that," Mort Crim says. "I never understood it. I've done a fair amount of reading on sibling rivalry and relationships, and I guess I have a few insights into how that developed. Jess was very protective of and helpful to Lori. But at a certain point, I think the problem of being Jessica Savitch's sister—especially if you were somebody who wanted to go into the business—became more than Lori could deal with. And I think that there were certain areas where Jess could have, had her personality been different, made it easier for Lori."

Jessica, who felt she had almost reared Lori, had paid her tuition to Ohio University, where Lori majored in broadcast journalism. After college, Lori followed in Jessica's footsteps, doing radio news at WOND, Jessica's old station near Atlantic City.

Eventually she took her skills to another station where the Savitch name continued to spell magic—KYW in Philadelphia— settling on the radio side of the operation. There, Jessica's old friend, Dave Neal, immediately took her under his wing. "Lori's a very bright girl," he says. "They never gave that kid credit. I took a special interest in her, because I saw the problem that she was having as Jessica's sister, of always being compared to her. Lori's got a great amount of talent on her own."

But somewhere the sisters' mentor-student relationship became embittered. When Lori eventually married—she divorced soon after—Jessica did not attend her wedding. And when Jessica married Don, Lori stayed away. But Lori was to make a career in broadcasting, and events seemed to come full circle in a way when, early in 1988, it was announced that she had been hired as a general assignment reporter at WTAF-TV in Philadelphia. Interviewed by a local reporter about "comparisons with her famous sister," Lori responded with candor: "It's inevitable," she told *Philadelphia Inquirer* columnist Gail Shister. "I've been Jessica Savitch's sister for a long time. Somewhere along the line, you develop a sense of self. I'm me. I'll keep this job on my own merits. I'm also very proud of my sister. When people remember her, it keeps her alive for me."

By the time Jessica moved out of the Washington town house in September 1981, she was able to joke about the events of August 2, telling Bob Morse, "Don *ruined* my beam in the basement. Why couldn't he have just blown his brains out like everybody else?" But it had been twelve months of nightmare—a divorce, a potential murderer in her office, an abortion, a deeply troubled marriage, a suicide, and the dreadful business of discovering the body. In 1982, when Jessica appeared as a guest on Sonya Friedman's cable TV talk show, "Sonya!" she looked pale and drawn.

"You've had a very difficult year," Friedman said, and asked her how she was managing. "Do you say something to yourself that allows you to close it out, and just go on?

"I think about the stories that I'm doing," Jessica answered. "That's what I'm there for. How does the plumber who has eight kids and has just lost his wife go to work? He knows that if he doesn't do a good job, he's going to be fired. So he does what he has to do.

"What I do is a public job," she continued. "I chose it. I knew about it. I knew its shortcomings, its great strengths, its rewards, and I knew its drawbacks. Taking that all into consideration, I went ahead. And so, when the going got tough, just like the plumber with the eight kids, I had no choice."

"After she walked in that cellar and found Don hanging there, that's all she talked about," says Mary Manilla. "Jessica was a very different person before that marriage. It destroyed her. She was never the same after that."

9

The Spiral: New York

In New York, Jessica moved into a cooperative apartment at 400 East 56th Street, known as Plaza 400. An elegant, white brick building, with a magnificent French chandelier dominating the sleek lobby, it was perfect for Jessica's high-rolling anchorwoman image. The security was tight. A uniformed doorman carried women's packages for them as they stepped out of their limos in the circular driveway, and the man on the reception desk, in front of the well-tended plants and designer sofas, was properly snooty. Betty Furness lived here, as did Robert Andrews, Jessica's business manager. And partly because the building was near Sutton Place, one of the wealthiest residential areas in New York, most of the one-bedroom apartments cost at least $500,000. Jessica rented one of the two units Andrews owned in the twelve-year old, forty-floor building, first the larger 33-L, and later 31-F. The concierge knew the resident as Jessica Payne.

Jessica was now so dependent on Lelia that she was terrified to be without her. The housekeeper refused to leave her family to move to New York, but Jessica begged her to drive up on Tuesdays and stay until Thursday. She would furnish her a Cadillac for the trips. Lelia gave in, but immediately, Jessica was pressing her to come on Mondays, and then finding reasons why she had to stay until the weekend. Lelia, who was frightened to drive the interstates by herself, was now getting home at one A.M. On two occasions, she was so physically and emotionally exhausted that she could not take her hands off the steering wheel once she maneuvered the Cadillac into the backyard. Her husband would pry them loose, and then cut her out of her dress because she could not raise her arms.

One Saturday morning after such an incident, only a week or two after Jessica moved to New York, Jessica phoned one of her Washington friends around seven. She sounded strange—her voice was weak. She said, "You've got to take the nine o'clock shuttle back up here. Please."

"I said, 'What's wrong?' " the woman recalls. "She said, 'I'm sick. Call Dr. Doyle and get a prescription for Percodan for me. I'll tell you about it when you get here.' " The woman told her the drugstores weren't open yet; she couldn't make the nine o'clock shuttle. Jessica started to cry. "Please, I need it so badly! I've got to be at the studio at eleven!"

By the time the woman drove to the psychiatrist's home in Virginia, got the prescription filled, and drove to the airport, it was already eleven o'clock. In New York, she took a cab to Rockefeller Plaza.

"She looked like death warmed over," she remembers, "just as white and pale as she could be. I said, 'Come on back to the powder room.' We got in there and I asked her what happened. She said, 'Last night, I started having these pains, and I went on in the bathroom.' " She passed out, she told the woman, and when she woke up, she discovered she'd had a miscarriage. "She said, 'I was pregnant again. I didn't even know.' "

The woman was furious. "How did you get pregnant?" she demanded. Jessica told her that she and Don had slept together during her visits to White Plains. "I said, 'You had no right to get pregnant again, with Donald so sick! You just had an abortion!' I was actually mad at her for being that stupid and careless."

Jessica was numbed by the event. She sought out NBC's Ellen

Ehrlich. A Jew who had converted to Christianity, Ehrlich often discussed religion with Jessica. "I lost my husband last month, and I lost my baby this week," she said. But the story would change over the next few days: Jessica would tell Mary Manilla she'd simply awakened to find her bed covered with blood.

Dr. Doyle, too, was getting his fill. The last time Lelia had gone to him to pick up a prescription for Jessica, he told her he wanted Jessica to start seeing a psychiatrist in New York. Jessica was still calling him for hourly sessions, sometimes twice a day, sitting humped up on the radiator with the phone in her hand. Eventually she would find another doctor, in Manhattan, and still another, a woman, in Philadelphia, but the sessions would be short and infrequent.

A few weeks after the episode, Jessica got a call from NBC documentary producer Bob Rogers. Rogers had also worked on "Prime Time Sunday," and initially when he learned that Jessica was assigned to the show, he was distressed, fearing she would be too troublesome. According to Bill Small, Rogers had been surprised at Jessica's hard work and diligence, and now that he had finally been given the go-ahead on one of his pet projects—a documentary on the extent of Soviet spy activity in the United States—he wanted Jessica as his reporter. Small approved the choice—he wasn't quite sure what to do with her at the network, and this would be a prestige assignment.

"The Spies Among Us," as the documentary was called, turned out to be one of Jessica's best efforts. She looked silly walking around in her Burberry raincoat—like every Hollywood spy of the forties. But she was convincing in her grasp of the material, and the script, for which she received writer's credit— however dubious—was solid. The production necessitated her return to Washington, and when the crew drove down Embassy Row—near the town house where Donald Payne had killed himself—Jessica held on to her composure. Once inside the Soviet Embassy, she broke down, field producer Patricia Creaghan comforting her in the ladies room.

Jessica's assistant on the project was Jered Dawaliby, her new secretary in New York. A handsome man in the style of a matinee idol, Dawaliby, then thirty-three, sometimes sported a cigarette holder, prompting Jessica to give him a gold lighter from Cartier monogrammed with his initials. In the early months of their rela-

287

tionship, they got along well together, Dawaliby offering Jessica the perfect combination of professional strength and personal compassion.

Dawaliby was, by his own account, thrilled to be working for a woman he considered a star—he signed her "autographed" pictures for her with the inscription "Gratefully," because his aunt had a photo of Joan Crawford signed the same way—and he would cook for Jessica when he saw that her refrigerator contained only frozen Milky Ways and shriveled white bread. His wife, Alise, understood his attachment to both his job and his boss, and she enjoyed long conversations with Jessica about the occult and metaphysics.

There were other new people in Jessica's life now, including Alan D'Angerio, an NBC hairdresser, and his longtime housemate David Buda, an intelligent man who worked in word processing for a large firm. They would often be in the apartment when Lelia arrived, as would Roberta Spring, who Lelia says moved in with Jessica for several months. Lelia thought some of Jessica's friends had too much power over her—that they could persuade her to do whatever they wanted—and she was distressed to see that some of the female couples who had visited Jessica in Washington were making frequent visits to the New York apartment and smoking marijuana there. Jered thought the whole group was something like the lamprey—the fish that attaches itself to the side of another, rasps a hole in its flesh, and sucks.

Jessica hoped that the move to New York would restore some of her confidence, now that she was away from the people in the Washington bureau. But she continued to be haunted by the sight of Donald hanging in the laundry room—so very still—and she would wake up at night, shaking, and see his face. *Why had she left him alone?* Now, she would write him long letters and beg his forgiveness.

"One day she thought she'd lost that circle pin he gave her," says Lelia. "She was going to jump off the balcony!" The maid managed to wrestle her down. But soon, she would "accidentally" leave the gas on in the kitchen, going to sleep and forgetting it until Chewy barked so that the neighbors complained.

Sharon Sakson, Jessica's old friend from Baltimore, came through New York about this time on her way back from England. The two women went to dinner. "She had a huge plate of food in front of her, and I remember she just ate a carrot stick. This was a person who used to wear a bright green bikini out at the swimming pool and make jokes about men. Back then, even when she was unhappy, I could still make her laugh. But there wasn't any way to cheer her up now. The depths of her unhappiness were something that I knew I could not experience." Sakson, who had become a much-lauded network producer for ABC, wanted to put her arms around her and say, "Jess, please just hang on. It will be okay."

"She was completely falling apart," says Sakson. "And there wasn't anything anyone could do."

Despite Jessica's visits to her new psychiatrist, as the year 1981 drew to a close, Lelia saw that Jessica was deteriorating badly. She was like a planet pulled off course. She had no continuity, no center, no anchor. She didn't really live anywhere—her apartment was like all the others, no charm, no collectibles, all rented furniture—and she didn't really belong to anyone. Her relationship with Kershaw was still so tense that they barely spoke, and even though he worked for NBC, she hadn't seen him now for several months. Only two things held any significance for her anymore: Chewy, and her credibility on the air.

One day before Christmas, Jered stopped by Jessica's apartment to give her a present, and to show her what he'd bought his wife. "She had candles lit, and everything all Christmasy," he remembers. "I was in a rush, and she said, 'Won't you stay for a Christmas drink?' I said, 'Oh, Jessica, I'd love to, but I have to get home—Alise is waiting.' And she looked at Chewy, and she said, 'Jered has to go now. He doesn't want to stay and have a drink with us.' So I said, 'Oh, Jess, okay,' because I realized she was lonely. It struck me that everyone was buzzing about, people were happy, it was Christmas week, but that there were no connections for her at all." Finally, Jessica decided to go home to Atlantic City. She asked Jered to order a limo.

By the beginning of the year, Jessica often did not want to go in to NBC. She had convinced herself that if she encountered any of her superiors, she would be fired. The horror of the last months had aged her ten years, and she began to dwell on the idea of how long a woman could stay in the business. She would talk about it to Jered, who would come over to the apartment, where they would conduct her business.

"I'd say, 'You have to make an appearance in the office,'" Jered remembers. "'You have to look like you're doing something.' But Jessica was in no shape to do more than the minimum: her broadcasts. She rarely went in to do anything else as in earlier times. She was too weak to pursue the very politics that had been the destructive spine of her life. On some days, Jered and Lelia would spend most of their time trying to calm her: Wearing her nightgown and jewelry, she would put on her high heels and run from room to room, threatening to jump out the window. On other days, she was fine, coming in to NBC as if it were the first day of a new job.

Lelia told Jered she couldn't understand it. Jered asked her how much cocaine Jessica was doing. Lelia said not very much, only when those girls came over. Jered asked if Jessica almost always took a small beige case with her into the bathroom. Lelia said yes, but it was just body powder. Jered started to laugh. "Look closer, Lelia!"

The housekeeper didn't think more about it until one morning when Jessica was changing her nightgown. By now, she had reached the peak of her abuse. Often at that stage, cocaine users hallucinate that there are thousands of tiny insects—known as "coke bugs," or "cokeroaches"—crawling under the skin. The user scratches at the imaginary bugs until he bleeds.

Now Lelia looked over at Jessica to see claw marks all up and down her legs, her thighs, and her back. "When she would pull off her gown in the mornings," she says, "it would be just bloody from where she would scratch in her sleep. And her arms . . . for a while, she'd have to wear a long-sleeve blouse all the time, because she was just so clawed up."

Another friend, a man who worked at NBC, realized how severe the problem was in early 1982. One day Jessica told him she couldn't get Robert Andrews to give her a check, and she asked him to go over and pick up a parcel of money for her from a friend. As the man came back in the cab, he thought the package felt "like a pin cushion. I said, 'Oh, I know what this is!'" he says. He opened it to find "what must have been $75,000 worth of cocaine.

"I went into the office and I threw it at her," he remembers. "I said, 'Here! Here's your money.' She said, 'Oh, I didn't know! This is terrible!' I said, 'What if I got caught? Were you going to bail me out of jail?' She said, 'Honestly, I didn't know!'"

He was furious. "You're really crazy!" he said. "Go to hell!" But the next time she saw him, Jessica just wafted down the hall as if nothing had happened, leaving a scent of Shalimar in the air.

Now Jered began to wonder about such things, and asked Lelia if Jessica ever had her pick up a package for her around town. Lelia said yes, a couple of times, and that sometimes she'd have her pick one up and take part of it over to a friend's house. "Next time that happens," Jered said, "you'd better find out what's in it."

Lelia confronted her. "She apologized, and told me she'd never send me anymore." But the maid was horrified. "I said, 'Jessica! If the police had been there I would have been the one to take the blame! You would not have said that package was being picked up for you!'"

That would not be the last time Jessica arranged such transfers, however. There would be several conducted on train trips, an aborted effort to smuggle coke in the binding of a book, and, in the most reckless abuse of a friendship, the attempt to trick a woman into transporting a box Jessica described as a "bathing suit." When the woman became suspicious, she opened it to find a package wrapped in plastic, and then again in tissue. "It was enough cocaine for a pusher—not something for a weekend fling," she says. "I thought I would die. If I'd been caught with that, I'd still be in prison."

"You know, I really kind of lost respect for her then," Lelia says. "I was losing it all the time, but I kept hoping she was going to straighten herself up. And she promised me she would. She said, 'Lelia, I'm going to get involved in my work. There's going to be nobody coming into this house to stay but me, Chewy, and you.'"

But the next week, the maid came in and found Jessica with a young man named Ken Bastian. Bastian, a graduate student at Harvard, had interviewed Jessica several weeks before for a paper on media ethics. Tall—6' 8"—blond, and remarkably handsome, Bastian had impressed Jessica with his intelligence and his good manners. She liked the fact that he went to Harvard, where she still told people her father had gone, and she liked their discussions on religion and philosophy. Bastian, along with Ellen Ehrlich, had started Jessica going to the Episcopal church—they went together to St. Bartholomew's on East 50th—and now she declared in interviews that she was an Episcopalian. In some ways, Bastian reminded her of Payne. He'd even contracted hepatitis in the Peace

Corps. She wrote Don another letter, telling him she'd found someone he would like.

Jessica and Bastian, today a headmaster at an Episcopal day school in Texas, would talk almost every day in person or on the phone. And when he would come to New York for the weekend, "We had some romance there, obviously, but it was more like someone's crying, so you go hold them. It was a really heavy time. It took every bit of energy, every ounce of courage and determination she had to get through the day. And I mean, *every* day. It was very, very moving. She had such a core of goodness that no one ever saw."

In January 1982, Jessica flew to Phoenix for one of her many speaking engagements. Of late, whenever she was in a higher altitude—even in an elevator in a tall building—she suffered acute abdominal pain. The flight to Arizona was excruciating, and once she was on the ground, the pain did not subside. She ended up spending her thirty-fifth birthday in the emergency room at Scottsdale Memorial Hospital. Bob Morse, who had been in town for a meeting, stayed with her: "She was just screaming in pain."

When Jessica got home, she was so weak that Jered Dawaliby had to help her on and off the toilet. "Jessica was always bruised black and blue, but now I noticed that she had two or three ulcerated sores," he says. "They were the size of a nickel, or a dime. I don't know if they were skin abscesses, or what. But they looked like the kind of pustules a person gets with malnutrition.

"Let's face it," Jered says. "She was an addict." But addict or no, and despite the terrible condition she was in, Jessica still managed to get to work and to make her public relations appearances around the country, usually preparing her own material. Often, at such functions, she was too ill to be the gracious guest at cocktail parties held in her honor after the speech. There were bad feelings all around, and Jered would try to mediate.

About this time, Jessica began to speak increasingly of death. Several times in the past she'd told both Mel Korn and Jered that she wished her airplane would crash, that it would just all be over. Korn had called it a "death wish." But in the next breath, she would say all she really wanted to do was have children. Now Jessica told Lelia she was making out a new will.

"I was packing her bags one day," says the housekeeper, "and she said, 'Lelia, what do I have that you want when I die?'" The maid told her to stop talking that way, that Jessica would long outlive her. "No, I won't, Lelia," she said. "Tell me what you'd like." The two sat down on the bed together, and Jessica wrote it down: Lelia would have the diamond and sapphire circle pin that Don gave her, and one of her mink coats. "She looked up at me with this beautiful, sweet smile on her face, and she said, 'Thank you, Lelia.' "

Jessica then left town for Texas. Again, she was seized with terrible abdominal pain. Now she was frightened. She telephoned Sam and Rita Rappaport. Sam told her to fly into Philadelphia, and they'd get her into Hahnemann Hospital. On March 15, she was admitted for tests. Jessica had recently begun wearing a thin, gold "body chain" around her abdomen, the links soldered so it could not be removed. The hospital taped it down. People have different interpretations about what it was for: a drug spoon holder, a sexual aid, a reminder for her not to gain weight, or merely an ornament. She had given a matching one to a girlfriend and offered one to Tracy Rappaport who declined, finding it "really strange."

The following day, Thomas Sedlacek, who describes himself as primarily a cancer surgeon, took her into the operating room. Before she went in, Jessica made Rita promise she would tell her the truth about whether she'd be able to have children. Rita knew that Jessica wanted a baby so much that she would have given her Sam if it had helped.

"When she woke up," Rita says, "she looked at me, and I knew what she wanted to know. She couldn't talk, she was so dry, but I asked her if she understood me, and she nodded her head. I told her she could have all the kids she wanted. And we both started to cry." President Reagan sent a dispenser of Jelly Bellies. Jessica's family did not come.

There was no malignancy. Jessica would tell friends that the problem was adhesions to the intestines, a result of her previous operations. She blamed her condition for her lack of appetite and for the general deterioration of her health. For the past months, friends had asked her why her hair had looked so dull and straw-like, her nails ragged and malnourished, the skin around them red and torn. Her entire body seemed starved of nutrients.

Dr. Sedlacek refuses to comment on the specifics of her condition, but suggests the malady was indeed gynecological. He told Jessica that for some women, the pelvic organs become stress centers. He asked her to take a close look at the priorities in her life, to see a specialist in behavior modification. Then, he says, he prescribed "some fairly strong pain medication, including some narcotics, some hypnotics, and I believe some Valium, which I never saw her use or abuse.

"We talked a little bit about John Belushi, whom she knew somehow," he says. "She thought it was a terribly tragic waste that he died of a drug overdose. And she said that she just couldn't understand why some people did that."

Jessica told the doctor she would now get several weeks of rest. She was going to the Rappaports' condominium in Puerto Rico. There she would finish her book, *Anchorwoman*. She'd already started another one, she said. It was a children's book, called "After Ever After." The premise was that fairy tales were wrong— they set up a fairy tale in a child's mind forever.

For a time, until Rita could come down to join her, Jessica stayed in Puerto Rico alone, with only the caretakers of the condominium nearby, and the occasional guests she invited down. Recently, Jessica had begun to talk about seeing Colorado Senator Gary Hart in the months since she moved to New York. The relationship was not serious on either side—she had even mentioned him to Ken Bastian and Bob Morse—although Lelia says she had gone with Hart to Colorado, and he had visited her once in Philadelphia, where she introduced him to Sam Rappaport. But now in Puerto Rico, as she strolled the beach with a platonic male friend, Jessica talked a different story.

"She was at a point now where she couldn't keep her fantasies straight from minute to minute," says her friend. "Within one conversation, she said, 'When Ken [Bastian] and I were walking along the beach, we said such and such.' And then in a little while she said, 'Well, as I said, Gary told me on the beach that—' And I said, 'Gary who?' She said, 'Gary Hart.' I said, 'Senator Gary Hart from Colorado?' 'Uh-huh.' I said, 'Senator Hart came down *here*? I thought you said it was Ken.' And she said, 'I didn't say that.'

"This happened again in the same conversation, but, of course, I didn't pursue it, because it was too embarrassing. But I said, 'Well, why was Senator Hart here?' She said, 'He was interviewing me for First Lady.' I said, 'First Lady? Is he running for president?' She said, 'Uh-huh.' I said, 'Isn't he married?' She said, 'Well, that's over. It's just not public yet. We're not going public yet, either.'

"I don't know whether he was ever down there," says the man, "but I doubt it. You know, I'd known her for a while, and we had been friends, but I got to where I was afraid of her. I could see that the fantasies were so out of hand that I was afraid she'd imagine I was Dracula, or something, and shoot me." At one point during her weeks in Puerto Rico, when her drug supply didn't come in as planned, Jessica called a local physician. She identified herself, said she was there recuperating from an operation, and that she was in tremendous pain. "And then," says an intimate, "she went over and got shot up with some kind of painkiller. She was absolutely high as a kite."

One person she did not call during her trip to Puerto Rico was Lelia Bright. Jessica had decided she no longer needed Lelia to run her life, and she was retaining David Buda as her personal manager. He and Alan understood her needs better than anyone. She had Robert Andrews call and ask Lelia if she could find work in Washington since she didn't need her anymore.

In April, when Jered picked Jessica up at the airport from Puerto Rico, he was shocked at her appearance. Instead of the Gucci shoes, mink coat, and the beautiful hairstyle of old, Jessica had degenerated to halter tops, Spandex pants, and Chiquita slippers—cheap, filigree net shoes with metallic spike heels. Her hair was piled high on her head and wrapped in a turban, and her pants were so tight they revealed the outline of her vulva. Jered thought she looked like a hooker on Eighth Avenue, and by the time they got out of the airport, men were whistling and yelling catcalls. To Jered's astonishment, Jessica had a whole suitcase full of such ghastly outfits. One day while she was gone, he gave them to a church charity.

Since she was still on medical leave of a month to six weeks, Jessica began spending most of her free time with the Rappaports. She continued to work, but now on an increasingly limited basis. Several years before, the Rappaports had moved from Cherry Hill to the tony Philadelphia Main Line suburb of Haverford, buying a five and one-half acre estate with tennis court and pool. The couple fixed a suite for her on the third floor of the massive Tudor house, painting it an eerie iridescent blue. Jessica hung her framed awards on the wall, displayed her needlepoint around the room, and began calling the Rappaports "family" in public. Sam would accompany her to the Kentucky Derby, where she was the guest of then-Lieutenant Governor Martha Layne Collins. Jessica was still so weak that when Bob Morse, then with Louisville's WHAS, wanted to introduce her to his wife, she could not maneuver through the Derby crowd. Morse took her back to her box.

Now Jessica and Chewy would hole up at the Rappaports' for days or even weeks at a time, Jessica telling dirty jokes with Sam and reading Rita's library of romance novels, rating the sex quotient ("I wish he would rape her already!") on the inside covers. The Rappaports were amused at how childlike she could be, wanting to take one of the Rolls-Royce limos to the Wawa convenience store to buy peanut butter or Tastykake lemon pies—the kind of junk food she liked and was able to get down. When the family was in bed at night, she would roam around the house, leaving cold cuts unwrapped on the kitchen counter and trailing cracker crumbs up the wide staircase.

By now, Sam was buying Jessica elaborate gifts. One in particular was an immense diamond and gold coin ring, with a matching one for Rita. He also gave her "tens of thousands of dollars," because, as he says, she needed it, and he loved her. Robert Andrews sent Jessica a weekly allowance of only $350—he would say later that her bills were forwarded directly to him and that he would invest the remainder of her salary—and if the check arrived on Friday, she would have it spent by Monday. Because she could not handle credit cards responsibly, she was now limited to one, Jered says, for American Express. Sam and Rita say they never knew Jessica to have more than fifteen dollars in her wallet, and when she and Rita went shopping, Rita would often give her ten, knowing if she gave her any more, she'd lose the rest once she broke the bill.

A list of the checks Jessica wrote in the last years of her life, however, reveals a staggering number made out for large amounts of cash. Where this money—which was obviously outside her allowance—came from nobody knows, perhaps her speeches or gifts of the kind Sam Rappaport gave her. One day, Jered was mortified to find Jessica walking around with $5,000 in her purse. He chastised her for doing such a thing, and she became irrational, throwing the money in the air in the hallway of her apartment and leaving him to pick it up. When he tried to fill out her expense reports for NBC, she would often be missing thousands of dollars worth of receipts, and he and his wife would stay up all night trying to make the numbers come out. Soon, he would find himself in a squeeze play between Jessica and the NBC accounting office.

The Rappaports were undeniably good to her, becoming the people Jessica had long ago told Louise Schwing she wanted to pay her way in life. But their house, where she was always the center of attention—Rita frequently inviting friends in to show her off— was also a haven away from NBC, where she was viewed with mounting suspicion and concern. She was now just a reader who came in to appear on camera. Although she would always say otherwise in her print interviews, long gone were the days when she would write any more than the open or close of a weekend newscast. Once when a photographer from a magazine came to shoot pictures of Jessica for a "typical day in the life" story, she explained away the presence of Richard Berman—who had been hired in 1979 specifically to write copy—by saying, "I've asked Richard to come in today to help me write the script, because you were coming and I didn't think I'd have a chance to do it all myself."

Berman was actually one of the few people at the network who cared about Jessica and who understood the fierce insecurity that drove her to do such things. But other than Berman, she now had almost no friends at NBC. At the insistence of several other women, she was in the process of dropping Roberta Spring, who would walk around NBC crying and trying to figure out what she'd done wrong. Jessica's closest buddy at the moment was the Rappaports' chauffeur, a sweet-natured woman named Marta Tabickman who was also an amateur photographer. Jessica would pose for her camera whenever Marta asked, even doing a mock striptease for her in the Rappaports' cabana. One time, Jessica lost the screw from her Cartier bracelet in the back of the limo, and immediately flew into a panic, informing Marta that only a person she cared about deeply could replace it. Marta felt around on the floorboard until she found it, and then tightened the bracelet on Jessica's arm with a tiny gold screwdriver. "You know, Marta," Jessica said, "this means I'll always love you."

Soon the chauffeur was frequently going to New York to spend the weekend with her, Jessica sometimes also inviting another woman, Chris Connal, an NBC tape editor. At other times, Jessica telephoned Marta at 2:30 in the morning and asked her to come to New York to get her, Marta revving up the grey Lincoln limo and tearing out up the highway. Sometimes they returned to Philadelphia, or just drove aimlessly in the thin, tight hours of the night. Jessica brought her favorite pillow and blanket, and lay on the floor of the limo and watched television, clutching a small teddy bear she always took with her on her travels.

"She was never alone, but she was always lonely," Marta says. "She'd have a fistful of Valium because she couldn't sleep, or she'd be so wound up that she'd need some pot." If there was cocaine, "She'd do it, but she'd say, 'Please don't let me do this again.'" Suddenly tears spring to Marta's eyes. "I don't mean this maliciously," she says, choking out the words, "but it's a good thing she died when she did. If there hadn't been an accident, she would have died of an overdose."

In 1982, Bill Small resigned from NBC to become president of United Press International. Jessica was ecstatic. Now she thought she might finally get her shot at anchoring "Nightly News." But in April, nothing would keep Reuven Frank, the twice-told president of NBC News (he'd served previously from 1968 to 1973), from pairing Roger Mudd and Tom Brokaw. Although Frank had virtually no respect for Jessica's journalistic abilities, the anchor tandem really had nothing to do with Jessica's status at NBC—in recruiting Mudd from CBS, Bill Small had promised him the "Nightly News" chair on Chancellor's retirement. Mudd had generously offered to let Brokaw share the spot rather than see the younger newsman go to ABC when his contract was up. But Jessica saw only that she was being shut out again. It was another demoralizing defeat. The job was *owed* to her! She'd told the whole world that she would eventually get it! Surely someone, someplace, would give her the chance to show what she could do. It was clear that despite the shape Jessica was in, her eyes were still on the golden ring.

In the early months of 1982, David Fanning, the thirty-six-year-old producer of the eclectic PBS documentary series "World," had just been handed $6 million to make what was to be called "the most ambitious current affairs series ever produced for public television." The show was "Frontline." A weekly, hour-long, prime-time program, it would ostensibly breathe new life into the dying documentary form and examine a host of controversial topics, including an alleged tie between professional football and organized gambling and a police informer's role in the shooting of demonstrators by Klansmen and Nazis. It had a "heat shield" advisory board, including Richard Salant, the former president of CBS News who had gone over to NBC, and would eventually head the National News Council, and Ellen Goodman, syndicated columnist with the *Boston Globe*. The series would contain twenty-six documentaries, produced at a cost of about $200,000 each, by WGBH, of Boston, where Fanning was based, in conjunction with four other PBS stations: WNET/New York, WTVS/Detroit, KCTS/Seattle, and WPBT/Miami.

Fanning now had everything he needed except a host. For a time, he considered Charles Kuralt and Daniel Schorr. But, "We needed more than a host," Fanning would say in his crisp British accent. "We needed an anchor . . . someone with the expertise to handle the related [question-and-answer] segments at the end of some of the documentaries." More important, Fanning needed an audience-getter, a popular figure who could convince mainstream viewers to turn their channels to public broadcasting. David Fanning wanted Jessica Savitch. He got together with her agent, Richard Leibner. Fanning would later say "no one as good" had been in the running. His staff thought Fanning was "smitten" with her.

When Leibner called Jessica to tell her about the offer, she could hardly believe it. She wrapped her arms around her chest and hugged herself with joy. It would mean she would anchor the program—not co-anchor it with a man. It would mean that network executives and regular viewers would see "a serious newswoman in full charge of a significant news program," as Sandra Earley of the *Miami Herald* put it. And, Jessica figured, it would make it easier for a solo woman to chair an evening network newscast. Basically, it meant she had another chance.

Leibner approached NBC. Bob Mulholland was now president of the company, Fred Silverman having left in 1981. The agent asked for a nine-week partial leave of absence, from November 1982 through January 1983. Essentially, Jessica would be gone four days a week. She would continue to anchor the Saturday edition of "Nightly News" but would relinquish the "NBC News Capsules," formerly called the "Updates." Then, during production, the middle of January through July 1983, Jessica would spend Sunday, Monday, and perhaps part of Tuesday in Boston, poised for day-of-air update. It was a substantial investment of her time.

For face saving, Jessica told Mort Crim that Leibner had to go in "and fight hard—their nose was really out of joint" about it.

"It took a few weeks to persuade them," Leibner says. "Really, it was a question of me selling them on the fact that it would add to her notoriety." But Barbara Matusow, echoing others, says the release was "very out of character for NBC—a mark of how little they thought of her at the time." Judy Woodruff, who took over Jessica's duties at "Frontline" after her death, contests the statement, saying it shows nothing of the kind.

Jessica would introduce the series, serve as narrator on six programs, and occasionally conduct brief, in-studio interviews at the show's close. She would do some on- and off-camera reporting on the programs produced by the "Frontline" unit itself—as opposed to those purchased from independent producers—and she would do some writing. Her salary would be $4,500 per week during pre-production, for a total of $40,500, and $3,500 per program during production, or $91,000. In addition, Jessica wanted a full-time secretary-liaison-researcher—that is, David Buda—a credit card, prepaid expenses, first-class accommodations, and cash advances.

"We were tickled pink," says a member of Fanning's staff. "We thought she was a real catch."

In May 1982, executive producer Herb Dudnick left the weekend "Nightly News" to begin "Overnight" with Linda Ellerbee and Lloyd Dobyns. His replacement was Tom Wolzien. The thirty-five-year-old Wolzien knew that Jessica's career had dead-ended around 1980 or 1981, and that despite the quality of "The Spies Among Us," no producer other than Bob Rogers would work with her. She was generally seen as being more trouble than she was worth.

Wolzien thought Jessica was a tremendous talent, but he knew he had to "keep her on a tight leash." He had no patience with people who flew off the handle at the slightest provocation. It occurred to him that maybe no one had ever told her that wasn't the way to do things. The first time she went into a snit—when the chain for her microphone disappeared, and she thought someone had deliberately stolen it to make her wear the ugly pin-on variety—Wolzien called her in for a private talk.

In the following months, there would be other discussions, all essentially along the lines of, "Jessica, you don't do that. If you've got a problem, you come to me and keep your mouth shut." Jessica would tell him she had been in horrendous pain over her gynecological problems, that she had injured her incision in Puerto Rico, but that she had not stayed out longer for fear people would think she couldn't do the work. Wolzien sympathized with her, but he also made her understand that he was looking out for her best interests. In time, Jessica came to respect him, and Wolzien was regarded in the building as a wunderkind, the man who had tamed Jessica Savitch.

As the summer began, Jessica was in relatively good spirits. She was looking forward to the "Frontline" work, and to the publication of her book in October. To top it off, Reuven Frank had named her the principal correspondent for "A-News Capsules." Beginning July 5, she would broadcast the capsule news reports to the NBC affiliates. These were supplementary reports that the affiliates could insert in their programming whenever they chose, and which would serve as a parallel to NBC News. She would do three a day, Tuesday through Friday, at 4:30, 5:00, and 5:28.

Jessica thought her star might be on the rise again at NBC. The truth, says Art Kent, who was then managing director of Affiliate News Service, is that "Nobody really knew what to do with her, so they sort of said, 'She's yours. You take care of her.'"

Kent had been a correspondent overseas for a while and hadn't seen Jessica's work since she first came to NBC. Now he was surprised at what he found. "I could see that she was reading and communicating beautifully, but that she didn't know a damn thing about what she was talking about," he says. "It started to be obvious to a lot of us in New York. She had replaced what had been her good journalistic skills with the personality of an anchorwoman."

In the meantime, Jessica had heard from her banker friend in Philadelphia. His wife had left him, and he called Jessica and told her he was going through hard times. The first time he phoned, Jessica said for him to come up, that she would meet him at NBC. He watched her do the news that night, and when they went downstairs and discovered her limousine wasn't waiting, Jessica called the service. "How dare you do this to a star of my caliber!" she screamed into the phone. The banker was shocked and surprised even more when Jessica ordered the car to stop at an address on Central Park West. There, she told him to wait in the car while she went up to "an all-girl party." When she returned, she brought one of her friends to meet him. She also had a small bag of cocaine.

The banker would make several trips to see Jessica in New York, staying for the weekend each time. "But we never made love anymore after Philadelphia," he says. "She was just in no shape for it, physically or emotionally." The reality of it hit him one day when he and Jessica went out to walk the dog. As they strolled past a doorway, another dog jumped out and grabbed Chewy by the fur of the neck. The dogs tumbled over each other and moved into the street, still snarling and biting. As the banker moved to separate them, Jessica, wearing dark glasses and a cap so she wouldn't be recognized, went into a crouch.

"It was over in ten seconds," he says, "because those dogs have that thick fur to protect them. But Jessica was destroyed. She wrapped her arms around the dog, and began to sob hysterically, just completely out of control. We were almost in the middle of the street, and I could not get her up. I said, 'Look, Jessica, Chewy is fine! Look! She's really fine!' But it didn't make any difference. I had to pick her up and take her over to the curb. We sat there for a while, and she cried and cried, saying, 'We've got to get Chewy to the hospital! Please! She's hurt!' I did everything—ran my hand through the dog's fur to show her, had Chewy lick my face and jump up on my chest—but I couldn't get through to her."

Finally, the banker took Jessica back to the apartment, and put her down on the bed. "She must have slept ten hours, something she normally wouldn't do," he says. "But Chewy was everything—she'd transferred all the affection from the failed marriages and the love affairs into that dog. That was the one love affair that didn't fail."

The anchorwoman often took Chewy in to work, where the dog was well-known, well-loved, and considered by some to be "more human than Jessica." But at other times, Chewy was cared for by Gregg Smith, a twelve-year-old boy who lived in the building. Lelia had approached him one day about walking the dog while she was down in Washington. Soon Jessica became friends with Gregg's mother, Rose, a smart, friendly woman who worked in the fashion industry. She and her husband, an investment banker, knew a variety of influential people, and Rose offered to introduce Jessica to some of their friends. One was Richard Weisman, also an investment banker, and another was hotel owner John B. Coleman. Both Weisman and Coleman frequently gave lavish parties costing tens of thousands of dollars and counted a multitude of celebrities among their friends.

Weisman would squire Jessica around town, but their dating never really grew past the friendship stage. They liked each other's sense of humor. One day Weisman told Jessica he'd love to bring his daughter down to NBC some Saturday to watch her do the news. Jessica set it up.

"There was mass confusion going on that day," Weisman remembers, sitting in his summer home in Southampton, New York. "It was about five minutes to air, and Jessica was sitting at the desk saying, 'I don't have pages 2, 4, and 7. I *need* 2, 4, and 7.' Everybody's running around, and the TelePrompTer is off. It's not working. And it's three minutes to go, two minutes to go, and I'm beginning to think this is not normal. And Jessica looks at some guy on the floor and says, 'Look, I want *you* to go to the other side of the room, so that I don't even *see* you. You're not doing anybody any good.' And then she says to someone else, very firmly, 'I need pages 2, 4, and 7. And I need them now.' It's ten seconds to air, a guy comes running across the room and puts a paper down at her desk, and she looks up and says, 'Good evening . . . ' and goes right into it.

"Each time they'd go to a break, somebody would rush in with the very next page she needed. Finally, she says, 'And now a story from Australia. Maybe there's more to dolphins than we think. A boy fell off a fishing boat off the coast of southern Australia yesterday, and a school of dolphins circled the lad for over an hour, protecting him from sharks until the boat returned.' And then they went to break, and she said, 'Boy, I could use some fuckin' dolphins around *here* today.' And the place just cracked up."

By now, Jessica was sharing her New York apartment with Sue Simmons, the WNBC anchorwoman. The two lived together for a period of months, and Weisman let them come up and use his Southampton cottage while he was away. Rita Rappaport says Simmons moved in after a fight with her lover. Their relationship was based in part on humor and provocative wordplay. Says one of Jessica's co-workers: "The feeling you would get in their presence was as if there was a joke being played on you." One of Jessica's male friends says the pair had nicknames for each other: Trash and Flash. Jessica was Flash.

In the time between Lelia's leaving and Simmons's moving in, friends were shocked to see the way Jessica lived—dirty clothes piled in big mountains around the apartment, dog excrement on the floor, plants dying, sandwiches left in deli bags and strewn about the furniture, depressing food in the refrigerator—all grim conditions Simmons set about changing. By several accounts, Simmons was good for Jessica in other ways, trying to help her with her drug problem and going to bat for her with the network executives.

"Sue is a person you can really lean on," says Sharon Sakson. "She's a very strong person, and she's not judgmental, because she's seen everything from the time she was twelve years old. At NBC, she would go downstairs about six times a day to check on Jessica. Even other people would call her—like the producer—and say, 'I think you should come down here,' because Jessica would get so upset about just everything. She'd say, 'The prompter is going too fast!' for example, and she'd take it out on a floor person, just a little nobody she didn't like. At this point, you wouldn't recognize Jessica as the person I used to know. And Sue would go put her arm around her and talk to her, and calm her down. She was wonderful."

On August 2, 1982, the first anniversary of Donald Payne's suicide, Jessica's friends—Richard Weisman, Rose Smith, Rita and Tracy Rappaport, David Buda, and Alan D'Angerio—met in the apartment to take part in what Rose calls "a vigil." "We just sat there, like in a ceremony, half the night," says Smith. "She didn't want to be alone."

On September 20, the friends gathered again when Weisman and Smith threw a pre-publication party for Jessica's memoir, *Anchorwoman,* at Xenon, a glitzy disco on West 43rd Street. Rose would say, "We had it draped like Fantasyland." The menu, prepared by a White House caterer, featured such delectables as "hand-carved standing steamship round," and "sesame chicken-prune sauce."

Working with Jessica, Rose and Richard drew up a guest list of four hundred. Richard invited his friends—model Cheryl Tiegs, artist Andy Warhol, and New York Yankees owner George Steinbrenner—and Jessica invited hers—the Rands, Lonnie Reed, Mary Manilla, David Fanning, her mother, and Yvette Montilla, who was one of her friends from Puerto Rico. When it came time to pick out a dress, Rose, who was astonished to open Jessica's closet and find "mostly stuff from Lerner Shops," took her to visit designers John Anthony and Calvin Klein, finally settling on a white, beaded Halston original for $1,920.

The night of the party, Jessica was so nervous that Rose thought she was going to fly apart in a million pieces. "We had taken her clothes to NBC," Rose remembers, "because she worked that day. Alan did her hair, and she was so freaked out she just paced the floor. I said, 'Jessica, relax!' " By the time Rose got her to the disco, the author was two hours late for her own party, and, "We had to practically pull her from the car." Half the guests had left. Sue Simmons got up to say a few words, but when it was Jessica's turn to speak, "She could hardly do it," Rose remembers.

Afterward, Jessica spotted Lonnie Reed, and came running over. She was shaking. The Rands wanted to put their arms around her and protect her. Mary Manilla couldn't get near her and left. It would alienate the old friends for a year.

Jessica ran upstairs. There, she found Maria Pallais, a free-lance writer and researcher-producer. Pallais, whom Jessica had met through their mutual friend Sue Simmons, had often talked with Jessica about the horror of television, about how it sucked people in and bled them dry.

"Jessica looked absolutely gorgeous that night," Pallais remembers, "but I saw her getting more and more upset, because there were so many people there that she couldn't communicate with. She wanted to be for them what she was for everybody on television, and she couldn't do it." When a man approached Jessica and handed her a parcel of drugs, Pallais grabbed it and went into the ladies room, flushing it down the toilet.

"She followed me in, and she started crying," Pallais says. "Her makeup streaked and ran down and stained her beautiful dress. She said, 'I can't take it. All these people—these women, these men—they're all on top of me!' " Soon, Pallais left with Sue Simmons to do her eleven o'clock newscast. When the women returned to the apartment at 12:30, they found a trail of crumpled tissues leading from the door into the bedroom.

"Jessica had left the party, and nobody even knew it," Pallais says. "She was just completely smashed and crying. She said someone had been nasty to her [allegedly a tiff over Fanning's dancing with Yvette Montilla], but really she was just upset at being who she was." The women spent several hours trying to comfort her, but Jessica wanted to talk only about suicide. "She said she didn't have any children, she didn't have a love life, that her everyday existence was a nightmare," Pallais continues. "I said, 'Jessica, television is destroying you! You have to quit doing this! You're killing yourself!' But," the writer says sadly, "I think she really wanted to die."

Soon after, the weekend "Nightly News" staff noticed that Jessica came in with "a cut neck—fairly deep abrasions." Nobody ever asked her about it, or learned the cause.

In the next several months, there would be other *Anchorwoman* parties, one given by the hotel owner John Coleman, who was in love with Jessica, according to his friends, and bought her expensive gifts—an antique gold and jade ring, a Bulgari watch worth thousands of dollars. The Rappaports also gave Jessica a book party, since she had dedicated the book to them, as well as to her parents, to Donald Payne, and to her former psychiatrist, Brian Doyle. The guest list cut across all the years and aspects of Jessica's life, including Faith Thomas, the Schwings' daughter Tracey, Paul Dowie and Allen Kohler from KYW, Chris Connal, Elizabeth Guhring—the attorney had gone on to help Jessica after Donald Payne's death—and Pat Garvey, who had calmed her on that awful morning. Florence also came, and Marta Tabickman posed the mother and daughter with her camera.

If Jessica had been undone by the celebrities at the Xenon party, she was equally nervous now, but for another reason. Everyone there knew a different Jessica, a different person. They had all been tucked into separate drawers, fed conflicting misinformation, given different road maps to the same territory. In the hour before the guests started arriving at the Rappaport estate, Jessica knelt in front of the toilet, "heaving her guts out," Marta says. The chauffeur went into the bathroom to find Jessica lying on the floor. Marta put Jessica's head in her lap and laid a cold cloth across her brow.

When the short, breezy book came out that fall, reviews were mixed, generally negative. *TV Guide* summed up most evaluations, saying it "gives little insight into the industry, the broadcaster, or the woman." After *The New York Times* ran an unfavorable notice, Jessica complained to associate editor Clifton Daniel, who suggested she write a letter to the editor. She did not. In all the reviews, no one bothered to check the validity of Jessica's anecdotes, going on the strength that she was, after all, a professional truth teller. But down in Houston, Judd McIlvain thought, "It was like it was written by the Mad Hatter, because it just wasn't true."

And Steve Berger, Jessica's high school boyfriend who had introduced her to radio, fired off a quick letter to her, saying, "It's really
incredible that someone who claims to be a reporter can't remember what happened in her own life." Berger received a one-line
reply: "My memory's as good as yours—Jessica."

The day the book hit NBC, the staff in the New York and
Washington bureaus split off into little groups, reading it aloud
and laughing. "It was real hoot 'n' holler time," says one director,
"especially whenever we read a paragraph about something we
were supposed to be involved with. A lot of it was just made up,
or the roles were reversed, so that it looked like she had been the
hero when someone else really was." When Susan LaSalla read it,
a former NBC employee recalls, "She went around showing it to
people, saying, 'Am I crazy, or did this never happen?' " Barbara
King, the original co-writer, directed that her name be removed
from the book in May, disagreeing with Jessica over its content.

Nonetheless, because of Jessica's immense popularity with
viewers, *Anchorwoman* went into several printings, although not
ten, as she frequently claimed. It also generated an avalanche of
creamy feature articles and numerous television talk show appearances. Several writers wanted to know the truth about a rumor that
had not been covered in the book—that Jessica was dating Warren
Beatty. To Mary Walton of the *Philadelphia Inquirer,* Jessica responded, "Why would anybody want to know this stuff?" To Steve
Sonsky of the *Miami Herald,* she was testier: "Whom I date, what
I have for breakfast, what I wear, where I go on vacations—this
does not affect what goes out on the public airwaves. This is mine,
and mine alone."

Rose Smith had seen Beatty leaving their building on one
occasion. Tracy Rappaport had talked to him on the phone when
he called Jessica's apartment. Richard Leibner believed that Jessica
made several cross-country trips to see him. Jessica would tell
Jered that she and Beatty had gone to dinner with Jack Nicholson.
She would tell the Rappaports it was with his parents and Shirley
MacLaine. She would tell Mary Manilla that Beatty helped her get
over Donald's death in countless late-night, long-distance calls.
And she would tell a member of the "Frontline" staff that she had
spent Thanksgiving of 1982 with him, even though she had told
"Today" show producer Steve Friedman she was going to Atlantic

City. The Rappaports recall that she was in Puerto Rico with them the day after.

"I liked her very much, but I think it would be inaccurate to say that I knew her terribly well," Beatty replies. "We did *not* spend a Thanksgiving together. As for dinners, Jack Nicholson may have had dinner with her at some point, but certainly not when I was there. Lots of phone calls, and endless talks . . . I don't know where that comes from. She asked me for advice on something, and I helped her with that, and I think that did occur in a long-distance telephone call."

When asked if, as rumored, the advice concerned a drug rehabilitation clinic, he responds, "I wouldn't want to comment on things like that. I wouldn't want to say anything negative."

But whether Jessica ever sought professional help for her drug use, it became increasingly clear to some of her old associates that she was retreating further into fantasy, and that her grandiosity had gotten out of hand. Ida McGinniss, who had booked her speaking engagements since her early Philadelphia days, had had enough. Jessica grossed more than $200,000 from the Speakers Bureau in 1979 through 1981 alone, and her last check, for the Phoenix appearance, had been for $10,000. But the agent, who had regarded Jessica like a daughter, found her too difficult to warrant continuing the association.

Now Ithaca College faced the same dilemma—Jessica wanted a private plane to fly her the 240-mile distance to teach her seminars, which she no longer conducted on a regular basis. When the college explained that it could not afford the expense, Jessica, who had received an honorary degree from the school in 1979, no longer had time to return to campus. Furthermore, although she declared on several television talk shows that the proceeds from *Anchorwoman* would go to those worthy Ithaca College students who had lost their government loans, President James Whalen says the college never saw a dime.

In November, Jessica told a friend that she was planning to sit down and write a long letter to her mother, in which she wanted to unleash a lifetime of hostilities. She was angry at David Savitch for dying, and at her mother for inviting her to holiday dinners when she knew she had to work. She would ask the friend to send the letter after her death. The newswoman was certain it would not be far off. Jessica Savitch, one of the most recognizable women in America, was now scoring cocaine on the street.

On December 22, 1982, Jessica sat in the studio at WGBH, Boston, and recorded promos for "Frontline." She stared into the camera with a look that one staff member would correctly liken to a laser. "When you turned that camera on her, it was just fucking scary," he says. "She had a nut streak in her, definitely, but she also had some kind of an energy force behind her eyes. We used to talk about it that way. It was like she put on her little custom suit, shot a beam across the room, and zapped you."

In between takes, Jessica sat playing with her hands, squirming in her chair, running through emotions like a computer on Search. She looked maniacal. Her voice changed as quickly as her personality—dramatic and intense one moment, natural, then abnormally girlish the next. She fumed when the director asked for second takes. She sat with her chin in her hand and closed her eyes, menacing, threatening, promising to explode. Then she cooled out, nodded her okay, lolled her head on the back of her neck, made exaggerated, wavy hand movements, and smiled strangely. She was riveting, disturbing. She was wired.

"Frontline" debuted on January 16, 1983. Its premiere show, "An Unauthorized History of the NFL," would set the tone of the series and leave a lasting impression as to the quality and integrity of its journalism. The premise of the opening show—that gambling, organized crime, and professional football have long enjoyed a cozy relationship, was red hot and wide open to criticism. It would strongly insinuate—to dramatic theme music—that the mob had murdered Carroll Rosenbloom, the one-time owner of the Los Angeles Rams, off Golden Beach, Florida, in April 1979. And, twice, it would show a grisly close-up of Rosenbloom's drowned body, his eyes open, his face bloated and grotesque. "Carroll Rosenbloom," Jessica would pronounce in voice-over, "perhaps the first NFL owner whose underworld ties led to his death."

The "Frontline" staff had worked on the show for eight months, Jessica coming in to do an on-camera interview with NFL Commissioner Pete Rozelle, attempting to nail him on a double standard to players and club owners regarding the league's no-gambling-associations policy. The majority of the investigative reporting was being done by Scott Malone, and the bulk of the writing by the program's producer-director, William Crann. After much "fighting and screaming," according to a source, Jessica would also receive writing credit. To someone who didn't know how television fit together, it looked as if she were doing most of the work herself.

On Thursday, before the show was set to air on Monday, Jessica and David Fanning showed an incomplete preview version of the program to reviewers in closed-circuit screening. They were still wrestling with the dilemma of how far to go with the murder theory, and whether to air an interview with a Mafia figure who would name names, a figure who had been paid for his on-camera interview. Howard Rosenberg, television critic for the *Los Angeles Times,* basing his review on the incomplete version, still found much of the reporting "appallingly shoddy."

"That weekend was incredibly scary," says Malone, also an associate producer on the film. "After that press screening, the shit hit the fan. We'd felt what the reaction in the NFL was going to be, and their minions in the sports press all over the country. There was a campaign, orchestrated primarily by the NFL, to bombard us with attacks. On top of it all, I was out all weekend, still investigating the thing, sitting in a dingy little motel, having to get the operator to make the calls for me so nobody would know where I was. Here I was, trying to get the key football player to confess, so we could run the hard version naming names, and then I was hanging out with gangsters. I was more scared in Boston than anyplace I've ever been on any story."

When Malone got back to WGBH, he was told that the staff had gotten death threats—"or maybe just Jessica received them. When I came in, the whole 'Frontline' office was under police protection, guards everywhere."

Nobody was ever sure if the threats were real, or if Jessica just knew how to milk publicity. Whichever, now there were interviews about the threats as well as the program. She told anybody who would listen that they had nothing to worry about should there be an investigation of the "Frontline" reporters' own ethics, at least where cocaine use was concerned: "I've told my staff to clean up their acts," she said, straight-faced. "Nothing like that is going on anymore." And it may well be that she had cut back on her drug use, although it did not appear to be so.

At the outset of Jessica's involvement in the program, Malone had watched two producers brief her on what turned out to be a remarkably complex story, requiring a background on twenty-eight teams, playing fourteen games a year—1,500 players and a forty-year span. "They drove each other crazy," he says. She had trouble absorbing vast amounts of material, there would be screaming on both sides, and Jessica would stomp off in a flash of temper—"She could bend a spoon if she had to."

Over the past months, she and Fanning had exchanged words in a number of pressure-cooker situations—to the point, as one eyewitness reported, that he could "hardly even bear to be in her presence." The confrontation, Jessica would say, was over Fanning's controversial mingling of "cinematic" and journalistic values. But if she walked out, she always came back quickly. She knew that for this situation, it was do or die.

After the press showing, Jessica and Malone would get on the phone for two days of solid journalism. He had been disappointed in the "goddess" of Saturday night news—sorry to see the lovely vision was in reality a "horribly skinny" little girl with pockmarked skin. She looked frightful at times—one staffer telling another he was shocked at how disheveled she had been one day on a couch in the lounge. She seemed like "one of the street people," her clothes crumpled as if she'd slept in them for days, her hair stuck to her face. But he was never sure if she'd just been sick, or whether the drug rumors were true. And when the mood swings ran their course, she would be magnificent. Malone watched her lift the telephone receiver and summon almost anyone at will, including the Attorney General of the United States.

Malone was impressed. But he was also surprised when he saw that "she had great contacts with the underworld in Philadelphia. She made no attempt to hide it. In fact, she boasted that she could get us to one guy. She told me she'd gone running around in limousines with him."

When the associate producer finally saw the show on the air, he told Jessica he was proud of her. "We were having a party," he says, "and I went to her afterward. I said, 'You're fucking crazy, but you're wonderful.' I felt that, courtesy of Jessica Savitch, we did actual, physical, monetary damage to organized crime in America. For two years, gambling in America went down. There was something very powerful about Jessica Savitch taking on the NFL."

311

Not everyone saw it that way. Even with its last minute changes and substantiations, the program came under a cloud for its reporting, its handling of the Rosenbloom "evidence," and the ethics of the "checkbook journalism" used in gathering information. Jessica's interview with Commissioner Rozelle was described "as a clash of marshmallows." Several members of the advisory board were embarrassed. "We stand by the program," Jessica said, and surely most of what was wrong was not her fault. But her brilliant new showcase was tarnished. After that, she would narrate several programs, but she would not do much real reporting. Her main duty was to record the scripted fronts and closes in the studio each week.

Friends such as Jim Topping would call to tell Jessica her PBS work was the best she had done in three years; now that she was out of the milieu of NBC, she seemed relaxed and more herself again. But when he ran into her in New York around that time, Topping, who always knew "There was no real Jessica—she was someone we all made up, an empty vessel into which we put our desires for her," thought she looked "extraordinarily tired."

Topping was not the only one concerned. At one point, Mort Crim was not able to reach her for a period of months, when they had never gone longer than a week or two without speaking. Finally, she sent what he considered to be a "very formal, typewritten note, like she had dictated maybe twenty of these to her secretary—'Dear Mort, Sorry I haven't been in touch with you lately. I've been extremely busy at NBC,' et cetera, et cetera. It was," he says, "very strange."

Faith Thomas was also worried. After she saw Jessica at the Rappaports' book party, she called Tony Busch and told him that Jessica had surrounded herself with "users," with "people who always had their hands out." She made a trip to New York and came back depressed. Jessica didn't seem to have anybody who cared for her as a person. Like Mary Manilla, she believed they were "containing" Jessica, that they had begun to run her very life. Jessica said she was making out a new will. Roberta Spring would be removed, as would Donald Payne's sister, Patricia Mahlstedt. Jessica had new friends now, and they deserved to get her jewelry, her fur coats, and her car. She would see Donald Hamburg soon about drawing up the papers.

In March, Jessica and David Buda would have a major falling

out with Jered Dawaliby, who as her secretary, friend, and NBC employee, had spent the year and a half soothing ruffled feathers for her at the network. Several times, the NBC brass had approached him, asking about Jessica's alleged drug use, and he'd kept silent, but he would plead with Jessica to get help for her habit—NBC had a detoxification program—only to incur her wrath. She had fired him for it time and again, only to rehire him almost immediately. This time, when Jessica told him she no longer needed his services, he knew she meant it. She left a message on his answering machine that was so nasty he gave the tape to Marty Wall in security, fearing that Jessica might try to harm him. But to friends Jessica moaned, "Oh, Jered left me at the worst time!" And now it was David Buda, Jessica's personal employee, who called Tom Wolzien to convey her demands. The producer refused to deal with him. "We deal with Jessica," the producer said. "Jessica works for us."

For the past six months, Art Kent, the managing director of Affiliate News Service, had found that when Jessica showed up to do her afternoon "A-News Capsules," he would need to go in and coddle her, "to hold her hand," and help settle her down. The network was under pressure to see that what they did for the affiliates was perfect, and even though his job was "sort of like being a trainer of thoroughbred horses—you spend half your time with a whip, and half your time with a curry comb," Jessica was too mercurial for his taste.

"I saw my responsibility at that point as just making sure that she would perform, that she got on the air, that she did a decent job, and that she didn't blow it. Things had to be just so around her, and it was always a crapshoot whether she was going to make it that day. There were several occasions when she was very much on the edge and about to kick the whole thing."

If it ever happened, Kent didn't want it to occur on his air. Chances are it wouldn't—from June 1982 until June 1983, she would miss some forty of the capsules, partly because she was promoting her book, and partly because she was doing "Frontline." But Kent knew there were "a lot of days when she just didn't show up for bizarre and inexplicable reasons—a headache, a hangnail, or something as miminal as that." She would have David Buda phone Ed Planer, a vice-president, or someone else at the network. But she never called Kent directly, "even though she knew she should have. I wouldn't characterize the situation as, 'How are we going to get rid of her,' " he says, "as much as, 'Oh, my God, what are we going to do with this woman?' "

Even though rumors about Jessica's drug use had been rife in the building for some time now, the news executive never thought he saw her when she was "on something," but rather that her personality was simply so fragile. At times, during the day, and not at night when it might be called for, she would ask for a bodyguard to escort her through the building. "Working with her was like taking a slender crystal champagne glass and hoping to God it didn't shatter," Kent says.

While almost everyone at NBC was making bets about what would happen to her, Jessica wavered between trying to face up to her criticism—reportedly going in to talk with Tom Pettit, then the executive vice-president, and asking what she could do to deflect such hateful, unfounded rumors about drugs—and staying home, awash in fear and desperation. David Buda remembers Jessica making a call to her mother, in which "She was obviously asking her for love, saying, 'Please, I'm desperate, I can't go on,' but her mother was apparently not saying what she wanted to hear." The drug talk at work was "just knives to her," and he hoped someone in the company would take her under his wing.

But Jessica would only deny the real problem, Buda knew. When Bill Small was at the network, Jessica had made a point of opening her purse for him to show that all she carried were bottles of prescription medicine. She had finally called Mort Crim and tearfully told him that people were saying terrible things about her, spreading stories about drugs. "Are they true?" Crim asked. Jessica said no. Crim said if she knew there was no basis for it, to forget about it. But if there were a basis, he said, they should talk about it. Jessica told him he knew her better than that.

In the last eight months of Jessica's life, Carl Cochran, living in San Francisco, had begun receiving letters from her that both alarmed and saddened him. Since he'd last seen Jessica in 1976, Cochran had been through drug rehabilitation, and now he knew from her "horrible" correspondence that "she was not coming to grips with the rational world." He was never sure if the degree of animosity she said she was experiencing at the network was real, but he was certain that "She wrote to me from the depths of paranoic despair.

"She said, 'I went to my desk, and I found a little note that said, "We hate you, druggie!" Oh, Carl, I don't know what I'm going to do! They're out to get me! Who's behind all this? I don't know which way to turn! Don't they realize I'm doing the best I can? I have a professional career! Why is this happening to me?' " Her handwriting was shaky.

Cochran told Jessica that she must seek help. If she didn't, she would die. "Don't lecture me!" she said. "We've been there together! Just because you've taken your life in a different direction doesn't mean I'm ready to do that! You're not under the pressure I'm under!"

"This is a terrible thing to say," offers Cochran, "but I don't think she could ever have worked her way back. From the letters, it was obvious that she had undeniable, permanent brain damage. And knowing her, with the importance that she put on her 'place in broadcast history,' her death was a good thing. It was preferable to the way she was living."

In early 1983, Steve Friedman, the executive producer of "Today," offered Jessica a new show, one that might very well rejuvenate her career. Eventually called "Sunrise," it would air before "Today," and give her a chance to display the fine conversational skills she had shown while substituting for Jane Pauley. Friedman thought Jessica had a good linear interview technique and that she belonged on a "near-news" show, where she could rely on her personality and intelligence to converse with newsmakers. In his view, NBC had misused her, just as they had misused Tom Snyder. He saw that she was someone who never had a chance to find her spot in television, and he was excited to help her find it.

Jessica waffled. One minute she thought the opportunity sounded ideal, and the next, she feared she'd end up stuck in an early morning talk show. Besides, if she took "Sunrise," they might make her give up her weekend anchor chair, or the "Digests," as the evening news capsules were now called. Jessica no longer saw Ron Kershaw, but now she called him and asked his advice.

"They want to put you on at five-thirty in the morning?" he asked. Kershaw was incredulous. "Don't do it," he said. "You'll just be a warm-up for Jane Pauley. You're a *star*. Don't let 'em deemphasize that." The "Digests" might not demand a lot of the reader, he reminded her, but the audiences were huge. Everybody saw them. Everybody knew that's what Jessica Savitch did best.

Jessica told Richard Leibner, her agent, she would pass on "Sunrise." He encouraged her to go to the bargaining table anyway, to discuss her options in a spirit of cooperation with management. Rumor had it that thirty-seven-year-old Connie Chung was coming to NBC from KNXT, the CBS owned-and-operated station in Los Angeles, where she'd been since 1976. According to those close to him, Leibner saw that Chung could usurp her—that Jessica could be a dedicated journalist when she wanted, but who, too often, got caught up in being a star. Jessica didn't want to hear about such things. She informed Leibner she was paying off her contract with him and moving on.

However, in April, Jessica was panicked to learn that Friedman had not simply passed "Sunrise" along to another woman correspondent, but, as Leibner had predicted, Chung was coming to the network. Jessica got on the phone to her friends. The consensus was that Chung was a good reporter, a good news reader, and that she played politics well, getting along with management, staff, and crew. Jessica tried to keep from splintering. So what? Who'd see her at 5:30 in the morning? But the thought gnawed away at her. Jessica's contract was coming up in August. What if Connie Chung were NBC's new golden girl?

On May 2, Jessica was on location for "Frontline" when she telephoned New York during a break in the shooting. She learned that Reuven Frank, president of NBC News, was announcing that Connie Chung would join NBC August 1. Now, Jessica got the jolt of her life. Chung would replace her as the Saturday anchor of "Nightly News."

Jessica felt her stomach constrict. For a moment, she thought she would vomit. Then she burst into tears. She could not draw her breath. Her head began to spin, then to pound. What had happened! What did it mean? It was the end. "She knew she was in deep trouble at NBC," says Ellen Ehrlich. "Now she was positive that her contract wouldn't be renewed."

For the last two years, Jessica had been telling the press that local news had changed a lot since she was in it. It was much more inviting now—local anchors were beginning to earn hundreds of thousands of dollars, and, "There was something to be said for being able to stay in one market, one town, have regular hours, raise your family without constant traveling." She had believed part of it when she said it, but it was really just a safety net in case she got booted out of the network.

Jessica began to tremble. She had to do something fast. She thought there was really only one person who could save her.

Ed Hookstratten, the California super agent, was thinking about sleep when the phone rang at eleven P.M. The woman crying on the other end was Jessica Savitch. For the last year, he had turned on his set and seen her age before his eyes. "The Hook," who represented Tom Brokaw and Bryant Gumbel, in addition to Tom Snyder, may have been loud and abrasive in the Hollywood tradition, but he could also be tender underneath. And since 1979, when Jessica began calling him periodically, he had worried about her.

"I'm in Portland," she said tearfully. "I just gave a speech about what it's like to be an anchorwoman."

Hookstratten asked her how she was.

"I'm really up shit creek. I'm terrible."

He said he'd heard the news.

"There's a plane leaving for New York in half an hour, and one leaving for Los Angeles in twenty minutes," she told him.

"What time does it get in?"

"Three-thirty A.M."

The agent laughed. "Yeah?"

"Could you pick me up?"

The man Jessica was to call "Mr. Improbable" thought about it for a minute and agreed. She seemed so unhappy.

"When she got off the plane," he says, sitting in his penthouse suite above Van Cleef and Arpels in Beverly Hills, "she had on a white suit. She looked *fantastic.*" He smiles, remembering. "We had a very warm, loving relationship, so there wasn't any, 'Hello, how are you?' formality. She got in the car and she just said, 'Hold me.' And I held her, and that was it." Over the course of several days, she persuaded him to represent her. He asked her about the drug rumor. "It's bullshit," Jessica said.

The Hook called Bob Mulholland, president of NBC, and told him he now represented Jessica Savitch. He said he wanted a favor. Jessica's contract was up. He wanted her to stay at NBC for a year, and then he would take her someplace else, maybe to "60 Minutes."

317

"We're got to prove that they were wrong," Hook said to her.

In the next few days, Jessica roughed out what she wanted in her contract, first at NBC, and failing that, ABC. She told him she wanted a guarantee to be the next anchor if Mudd or Brokaw left, to be the principal back-up anchor on "Nightly News," and to be Sunday anchor immediately. She told him she wanted to contribute stories to "Nightly News" and "Today," and she had to have a research staff. She wanted to be floor correspondent at both conventions, she wanted limo transportation to and from all assignments, a full-time assistant, full-time hair, makeup, and wardrobe people, and a guard, mail screening, and phone protection.

She also said she owed NBC $2,000 in back expenses, for which she had no receipts. She said she wanted to continue doing "Frontline," and that she had been offered another PBS show as well. And, she wanted to write a newspaper column for the McNaught Syndicate, thinking it would give her, as she put it, "journalistic credentials, exposure, and enjoyment—I love writing." Besides, she said, "I need the money." The column only paid $500 per week.

The list went on, and on.

Ed Hookstratten told her not to worry. He would take care of her career. He would also give her a gold initial ring, and she would give him a gold money clip. Before she left his house, she wrote him a letter on the yellow legal pads she carried with her everywhere: "Please don't leave me."

Today, Hookstratten says Jessica's problem was simply bad management. She should have been groomed for the "Today" show. She should have been built as a star, the way Tom Brokaw was, with prestige assignments—in Brokaw's case, White House correspondent, then "Today" co-host, then "Nightly News" co-anchor. Jessica's detractors say there was certainly an attempt: Senate beat, "Special Segment" correspondent, major pieces for "Nightly News," major roles at the 1980 political conventions. She just hadn't established herself as a first-rate journalist. Hook says it didn't matter. "There was a *magnetism* to her. She was absolutely the best reader that television news has ever had."

In the weeks after her visit to Los Angeles, Jessica went on a sailing trip with Chris Connal and a man she had met at a Christmas party in 1981. Of the three, he was the only one who didn't know how to sail. He was also the only one who didn't know about

Jessica's drug problem. Before they left for the seven-day trip to Tortola, in the Virgin Islands, "there was some concern about getting something from an NBC locker," he remembers. He also recalls that while they were on the ocean, the sailboat boom struck Jessica in the nose. In later years, he would say, "She didn't bleed, nor was she bruised. We didn't think she was hurt at all."

At the week's end, Jessica and the man went to the Rappaports' condominium in Puerto Rico. There, Jessica spoke of nothing except her new contract, spending most of her time on the phone with Ed Hookstratten. "He's going to get me a million dollars, just like Barbara Walters!" she told her new boyfriend, fading off with a dreamy look. After a while, he thought she actually believed it.

When Jessica returned to New York in June, she began calling her psychic, Joan Durham, asking just when the contract would come through. Durham told her not until the very last moment—the end of August. But the psychic was also seeing other things in her readings. She warned her of bad road conditions, of problems with driving. She said, "I see Mort, with a long black robe, standing in a pulpit, and everyone there is holding hands. You aren't there. But you will always be with them in spirit." The anchorwoman captured the psychic's words on tape, and then sent them on to Crim in Detroit. Neither Crim nor Durham thought they made sense at the time. But earlier in the year, Jessica had gotten back in touch with the stockbroker in Philadelphia, the lover with whom she'd had her talks on the occult and metaphysics. Now she requested all of his *Seth* books, and information on mystical experience. He thought she was "drowning" in her career, and that she seemed "zombie-ish, as if part of her consciousness were already in another reality."

In the next few months, Jessica would make two appearances that would take her back to the settings of her first success. At the end of June, she returned to Rochester, where she worked during college, to speak at the first annual "Tribute to Women in Industry and Service" dinner at the YWCA. While there, she appeared on a local television show, hosted by Don Alhart, who had been president of Alpha Epsilon Rho when the chapter blackballed her.

Ann Rogers, who had started Jessica's modeling career, came over to see her, as did Tony Busch. Rogers was shocked to see her "completely drained of blood." Tony was alarmed at her disheveled appearance, and the way she mechanically picked at her fingernails, the cuticle torn and bleeding. In an observation that would haunt him for weeks, he found that, "She was a shell of the woman that I had known. Mentally, she was just gone. I could not reach her." And now, Joan Durham would begin to be plagued by nightmares. She saw a dark blue car, a shattered windshield, and the face of a blonde woman pressed up against it.

Later in the summer, Ron Kershaw, who had left "Live at Five" to produce NBC network sports programs, went to Saratoga Springs, New York. There, he and a group of friends made a day of the races and the famed Fasig-Tipton thoroughbred auction. Kershaw had not seen Jessica since Donald Payne's death. He had led his life exactly as before—propelling a second-rate news operation to the top, leaving the operation at the height of its glory, but spiraling downward in a thoroughly self-destructive personal life. All the while, he never stopped thinking of Jessica, brooding around the house to Jackson Browne and Neil Young records, finding himself and Jessica in every desperate lyric, drinking and drugging himself into balmy dreams of Houston. His friends worried about his fixation—told him it had gone on too long, that it was pathological—and that day in Saratoga they had coaxed him out to look at the horses and the women he and his friends would refer to as "tweeties."

It was evening. Kershaw stood on the upper tier of the Humphrey S. Finney sales pavilion, surveying the festive crowd, the crackle of celebration in the air. Down below—the distance of first to third base on a baseball diamond—his eyes locked on the back of a petite blonde, and he began to make his way down to introduce himself. Kershaw was halfway there when the figure turned and gazed in his direction.

"I was *struck dead,*" he says. *"I could not fucking believe it!"* She was there, in one of her rare attempts at reporting, to do a celebrity feature on Mrs. Cornelius Vanderbilt Whitney, scheduled for the Saturday "Nightly News." "It was like I was a guppy—towed in again!" Kershaw says. "It was so intense it hurt, like electricity." He could not bring himself to approach her. When he got home, he wrote her a letter, saying he couldn't pretend anymore. He still loved her, and he had always loved her, in spite of everything. She telephoned, and in typical fashion, denied being at the auction, but admitted to being in town. Kershaw only laughed. That was his Brat.

Jessica was seeing an attorney now, a Cherry Hill, New Jersey, man named Lewis Katz. Handsome and intuitively smart, he was recently separated from his wife and hoping to reconcile. But he was drawn to Jessica in a way he knew could not be good for him. She was obviously ill, talking of the "evil" that was out to get her. When they first met, she told him it would not bother her if he had other girlfriends. "It wouldn't even bother me if you were gay," she said. "You could have your life, and I could have mine." Katz was shocked.

Now the attorney saw that Jessica never woke up in the same room she went to sleep in. When friends told him they were envious he was dating such an alluring woman, he would wince, remembering how, like a child, she now took her small teddy bear wherever she went. Once, at breakfast, he had looked up to see her in the middle of "the saddest crying, for no reason I ever knew." Eventually, her behavior would drive him away, Jessica telephoning nine times in the middle of the night to start arguments. One evening, she had shown up at his beach house in a limousine— ranting that he had not picked her up at the airport, even though they had made no plans to meet—and then storming out to spend the night on the beach, returning at four A.M. At other times, she talked of her million-dollar contract.

Jessica spent most of August in California, going to the dentist, going to the gynecologist, getting herself in shape. She was stung on August 9, when a story hit the wire service quoting Roone Arledge, head of ABC News and Sports, as saying he was "not a fan" of Jessica Savitch. By then, she was ensconced at a new health spa, the Sonoma Mission Inn, just north of San Francisco. The spa was not set up for drug rehabilitation, only exercise, and every day, Jessica took her front-row place in aerobics class, wearing her bright green leotard and tights. On the hiking trail, the other women could barely keep up with her. She had told Lew Katz that her stay there was a gift, and had hinted to friends that Warren Beatty had graciously picked up the tab. But in September, she wrote the spa a check for $3,439.88.

Among the other celebrity patrons were writers Kitty Kelley and Blair Sabol, whose brother Steve had dated Jessica in Philadelphia. Both women remember how nervous Jessica seemed, Kelley saying she spoke so fast "It was like she was on five hundred milligrams of Preludin." After the third day, Kelley commented on how different Jessica acted from the woman on TV. "She laughed and said her sister told her she was so controlled that somebody could put a sword through her foot and she wouldn't budge," Kelley says. Sabol looked at it differently: "She rattled off the events of her life, including her husband's suicide, like she was reading the news. All those women in TV news—I think they make a deal with the devil."

Finally, at the end of August, Jessica's contract was renewed at NBC. With a salary increase to $315,000, she would remain at the network for a year, anchoring two "Digests" three nights a week, starting in September, and the afternoon "Digests," Monday through Friday, beginning October 10. In January, she would be restored to anchoring the Sunday edition of "Nightly News." The contract talked about "good faith efforts" to use her as substitute anchor, and about a "significant assignment" during the 1984 political conventions. Hookstratten had arranged for Jessica to fill in on the "Today" show during Jane Pauley's pregnancy, and she would return to "Frontline," where she told Ken Bastian she "had found herself and liked herself in her profession for the first time." Still, Jessica worried that the public would think she suffered a demotion.

On September 6, at Midway Hospital in Los Angeles, Jessica underwent her final medical improvement, an operation on her nose. Dr. Jack Sheen, who performed the surgery, says he repaired a deviated septum caused by "trauma." Jessica told him she had been hit in the nose by a sailboat boom earlier in the year and that she had suffered a broken nose in the baseball bat incident as a child. The doctor could not determine which accident had caused the problem, but says when he first saw her on September 1, "she was a chronic user of Afrin," a commercial nasal spray used to clear the air passages. He also performed minor cosmetic surgery, correcting her "slightly convex dorsum," or "hook" nose, excising her forehead scar—which had come to resemble "a third eye," as a friend remembers—and repairing a severely torn earlobe, the result of a still-mysterious injury. Afterward, he prescribed a "codeine medication," the antibiotic Keflex, and some sleeping pills.

The talk at NBC was that Jessica underwent surgery because her nose had collapsed from cocaine, and that, like many addicts, she had carried the nasal spray to counter the effects of cocaine vapor. But the surgeon insists that he saw "no evidence whatsoever" of cocaine abuse in Jessica's nasal passages. "And generally speaking," says the doctor, "when someone's on cocaine, they react very differently to medication. You have to give them much more than usual. She reacted just like I would expect a normal person to react."

The weekend of September 17, Jessica returned to New York. The following day, she wrote thank you letters to every physician she saw in California and every social and business contact she made. Then, according to Jo Rand, she telephoned her mother and told her, "I finally have my life back in order. I finally know where I'm going. I'm goal-directed again." She was upbeat. "Things are going to be okay."

On Monday, September 26, Jessica resumed her "Digests." That Friday, September 30, she traveled to Philadelphia to host the regional Emmy awards. Her appearance was a majestic homecoming. She had not seen Rita Rappaport for several months, or the KYW staff for years. Everyone talked about what a splendid job she did, how gracious and professional she had been. But the group was shocked at how old she looked, how hard, even with her new face, which was still puffy and strange. She appeared to be the mother of the woman who had once taken Philadelphia by storm. In a conference room before the ceremony, someone told Jessica she was the consummate role model for young women. A look of irony crossed her face. "If I'm a role model," she said, "we're in trouble."

During the first two days of October, Jessica appeared disconnected, uneasy. Much of the media was not reporting that she would be restored to the weekend anchor chair after New Year's, and the stories looked as if she had been relegated purely to the "Digests." She asked Ed Hookstratten to see what he could do about getting the press corrected. Now the word was out that the "Frontline" advisory board was unhappy with her performance, and had arranged it so Jessica could make a small contribution from New York, and not even have to go to Boston. A member of the board, Maynard E. Orme, general manager of San Jose's KTEH, criticized her dramatic intensity, saying, "Every issue is important, everything is a matter of life and death." Martin Carr, executive producer of WETA's "Smithsonian World," and also a member of the committee, said, "She doesn't have the gravity. She's very mannered, very Barbie doll."

But John Felton, of the "Frontline" consortium, made it

clearer: "We need to replace her with someone of stature who can attract that [same] kind of audience." Jessica's "Frontline" work was being cut down to next to nothing.

On Monday evening, October 3, fifteen million people sat in their homes watching NBC-TV. At 8:58, Jessica Savitch was scheduled to present the "NBC News Digest," the one-minute, "live" headline capsules that the blonde anchorwoman had made her stock in trade. When time for the "Digest" drew near and Jessica still hadn't arrived in studio 3K, producer Bill O'Connell asked correspondent Bill Schechner to get "painted up." Schechner, who appeared on "Overnight," broadcast from the same studio, often rotated the "Digests" with Jessica, Chuck Scarborough, and Linda Ellerbee. He had watched her come in night after night and do them, and he knew she did not regard them as fluff. She read them through several times, and she composed herself with a small gesture—a clenching of the air with her right hand, and then a semi-circular motion, ending with her hand coming down in an arc.

It was obvious that Jessica concentrated on the "Digests" as if they were important assignments. Timing was everything: If she read the copy too fast, she would have to draw it out and fill the hole at the close. But if she were too slow, there was no time to recover. When her 43 seconds were up, the computer would return the air to regular programming. With a ten-second commercial in the middle, it was trickier than it looked. There was no time to do anything but read, go away for ten seconds, come back, and get off gracefully—"I'm Jessica Savitch in New York. More news later on this NBC station and NBC 'News Overnight.' " Schechner liked to watch her do them. He thought she was one of the most engaging news readers ever.

Schechner was preparing to go on when Jessica entered the studio. She was in no shape to perform. She was not up, and she was not clearheaded. She insisted, as director Jerry Policoff and producer O'Connell readied the spot, that she was. Someone had to make the call. If Jessica were yanked off the air when she had been perfectly fine after all, there would be trouble. But at 8:58 P.M., October 3, 1983, Jessica Savitch went on NBC and showed the viewing public something it had never seen before. That night, the tough, professional newswoman collided with her fragile alter ego. That night, Jessica Savitch fell apart on network TV.

Her performance would be described in several ways: as excessive, woozy, slurring; as serious, massive brain fade; as merely simple faltering. But at NBC, most people saw it as the final, tangible evidence of the ravages of cocaine addiction. She slurred her words so wildly that even the most inattentive viewer realized something was dreadfully wrong. The proof came when the anchorwoman hit the word "constitutional," stopping between syllables. The pause was only a millisecond, but on television, that is an eternity. It is exactly how long it takes to destroy a career.

"The October third incident was prophetic in a way," says David Buda, "but it was the proverbial cry for help. It could have happened then, or many other times."

Jessica would blame the TelePrompTer. Jessica would say she'd had a glass of wine. She would say she hadn't eaten, that the lights had been hot. Later, after Tom Wolzien quizzed her repeatedly, she would say it had been both wine and Percodan. She would show Wolzien the bottles. Maybe, she said, she would throw all her possessions in the car and head out for a new job, a new life. Jessica Savitch had lost the only thing that mattered: her credibility on the air. And for a woman whose identity existed only on television, she had lost herself.

At 9:58, Jessica went on to do the second "Digest" without incident. Then, she went downstairs to Hurley's, where she met Mary Manilla. Jessica got down on her knees in the restaurant and cried. It wasn't what everybody thought, she said. Manilla told her she had to fight back. "You must get to the bottom of this!"

In days to come, everyone at NBC would try to find out what happened. Tom Pettit would call Terri Verna, who didn't know the answer. Bob Mulholland would call Ed Hookstratten, who insisted it was "nothing, a little flub." Jessica would repeat her bottom line: She had not been using drugs. Someone would remove all copies of the in-house tapes. And someone else at NBC would deface her photograph, taping a straw to her nose.

Lonnie Reed, then at WNEW, went over to Jessica's apartment during that time. The anchorwoman's hand shook so badly that she could not hold a glass. "She was decomposing in front of my eyes," says Reed. On October 14, she attended a reception at the Plaza Hotel for the NBC Press Tour, kicking off the fall season. Connie Chung was the center of attention, and Jessica now only a television curiosity. On the ride from 30 Rock, Jessica turned to Ellen Ehrlich in the limo. "I'm going to die in a car accident," she said. Later, at dinner with Ken Bastian, the topic turned to religion. He thought he saw a "real center"—one that hadn't been there before. "She understood what was going on," Bastian remembers. "She said, 'I really just want to go home.' "

Several days before, Jessica had her first date with Martin Fischbein. A former labor mediator who had once worked in President Nixon's Urban Affairs Council, Fischbein was now a vice-president at the *New York Post,* and an heir apparent to New York publishing power. The son of a herring vendor, he had been intrigued by the woman on TV, and asked Liz Callan, a mutual friend, for an introduction. Once, he had been engaged to a smart, pretty blonde named Merrie Spaeth. She, too, became an anchorwoman. On the morning after their engagement party, Spaeth awakened him to say she was marrying someone else.

Jessica liked the brash and brilliant Fischbein, who was two years her junior. At first, even though they attended *La Cage aux Folles,* he insisted on dating in the daytime. Dressing up at night added pretense—it got in the way of truth. Jessica told Lew Katz that she'd had a date to the theatre, and she giggled like a child. But when Fischbein called for Jessica at her apartment the following weekend, for a trip to Rhinebeck, New York, Jessica was so nervous she threw up in the bathroom. "Go on!" Mary Manilla told her. "It's time you had some fun!" Manilla put them in the car, and waved good-bye.

On Saturday, Jessica told Tom Wolzien, "I finally found somebody." She called Ed Hookstratten and said they were going to look at a farmhouse.

The night before, on Friday, October 21, Ron Kershaw visited Jessica's apartment. The two went out for dinner, and then came back to talk. "I got to the top of the mountain, and it's a hollow pile," she told him. Jessica was tired. Kershaw said they'd leave the network, go off and do the projects they'd always planned. "Rab," she said, "I'm dying. You'll have to do it for me." Kershaw left early—he had a football game in Baltimore the next day. He hated the network for what they'd done to her, for how unhappy they had made her, when she'd done everything they'd asked. As he walked to the elevator, Jessica leaned out the door. "Whatever happens, Rab," she said, "don't let 'em whip us."

On Sunday, October 23, Jessica and Martin Fischbein planned

to drive to Bucks County. Jessica told him she hadn't been there since she was a little girl. At one o'clock, the weather was dreadful—it had rained hard and steadily since the couple returned from 11:15 services at Marble Collegiate Church, which they'd both begun attending. David Buda suggested they stay in New York. Jessica, who had changed into tan jeans and top, boots, and a brown suede jacket, slipped on her new gold initial ring from Ed Hookstratten. She said she thought the rain would blow over. They loaded Chewy in the rented, dark blue Oldsmobile station wagon.

In New Hope, the weather thwarted much of the couple's plans. They arrived early for their reservations at Chez Odette, and Jessica made the first of her two lengthy trips to the ladies room. When she returned, Angela Csaszar, who now owned the restaurant with her husband, Frank, seated them by the fireplace in the barroom, table 39. They ordered two house salads, two sole á la rose, broccoli with hollandaise on the side, two melons, one coffee, and a bottle of Sichel Blanc de Blanc white wine. Jessica paid for the meal—$48.84—with her American Express card. Fischbein asked the waitress, Oankyae Bowlby, how to get to Route 287. It was dark, and still raining when they walked out to the lot at about 7:15. The fog had begun to roll in, and the visibility was poor. Jessica apparently got in the backseat with Chewy. Fischbein, who was known to his friends as a slow, careful driver, backed out of the parking space, put the auto in gear, and inched the station wagon toward the incline that led to the Delaware Canal.

Shortly after 6:00 A.M., Florence Savitch awakened to police officers knocking at her door. A man named John Nyari had come home at 11:30 P.M. and found the car in the canal in front of his property. The woman they'd fished from the water had no real home address. She carried only a card in her wallet with instructions to notify the little house on North Essex Avenue.

Thirty minutes later, the news began to come in on CBS radio. Of the three television networks, NBC did not announce it first, Steve Friedman of the "Today" show wanting to be certain Florence had been notified. "Television is not more important than life itself," he would say. People said the Mafia had gotten her for the NFL show. People said the Russians had killed her for the spies documentary. People who knew her well had been expecting the news for years. And not everyone was devastated. One of Jessica's co-workers phoned another: "I have the worst news," he said. "Chewy's dead."

Ron Kershaw was still in Baltimore when he heard about it from New York. He rented a car and drove to Bucks County. There, he pulled out his NBC press card and walked the banks of the canal, "covering" the story as a way to deal with grief. The rescue squad had originally thought the husky in the back floorboard was a fur coat. Now Chewy lay in a body bag. Kershaw had saved the dog from the dump.

On Tuesday, a gloomy, drizzly afternoon, the newswoman and her dog were cremated together, their ashes later strewn along the Atlantic. Mort Crim read a eulogy, quoting *Charlotte's Web:* "It is not often that someone comes along who is a true friend and a good writer."

Roth Memorial Chapel, a squat, brick building in the rubble of Atlantic City's seediest section, had never seen so many limousines, especially for only twenty-five attendants: Dave Neal, Mary Manilla, Sue Simmons, Tom Wolzien, the Rands, Tony Busch, David Buda, the Rappaports, the family, who had kept the list short, excluding even Jessica's cousin Saul. Afterward, people stood talking. A reporter approached Ed Bradley, who walked from the tiny funeral parlor in tears, carrying a long-stemmed rose. "Not today, man," he said. Florence, inconsolable, turned to the Rands. "Who's going to keep the family together, now that Jess is gone?"

The funeral director spoke. "Excuse me, folks. There's another ceremony in ten minutes."

In the days to come, Bucks County Coroner Thomas Rosko would announce that death had not been instantaneous, and that despite a slight head injury Jessica sustained when the car flipped over, striking a log, which indented a "V" in the roof, the official cause was asphyxiation by drowning. Autopsy results reportedly showed no drugs and little alcohol.

About six hundred mourners showed up for Martin Fischbein's funeral service in Hewlett, Long Island. His friends were people of power—labor lawyer Theodore Kheel, Senator Daniel Patrick Moynihan, developer Samuel J. LeFrak—some of whom would start a foundation in his honor. How sad, people said—

never a Lothario, Marty had fallen in love. "No," said his friend Richard Edelman, "he was in love with the idea of who she was. It was a fantasy romance come true."

On November 9, the Savitch family held a public service at New York's St. Thomas's Episcopal Church. Four hundred people attended, including NBC's Chuck Scarborough and Jane Pauley, who was identified in a newspaper photo as "one of Jessica's closest friends." Reverend William Billow, of Washington, said her "unconditional love of God made even the Nielsens meaningless." Several people wondered if Jessica had ever changed her will. She had not.

Later, Florence and Stephanie went through the apartment, carting away the fur coats and the jewelry, and then inviting Jessica's friends to pick out something to keep. Gregg Smith, Rose's son, was given Jessica's manual typewriter. Mary Manilla selected a framed certificate that said a star in the constellation of Pegasus had been officially designated "the Jessica Savitch."

Down in Philadelphia, the Rappaports would leave her powder blue suite exactly as it was, removing only her nightgown and two lipsticks. Those they buried in the ground on a hill in their backyard, next to the graves of Parfait, a white albino toy poodle, and Dede, the family's pet cockatiel. The marker, for both Jessica and Chewy, is homemade. The Rappaports have a new parrot now, named Jessy—the spelling a combination of the names of their friend, and her most beloved companion.

Epilogue

In April 1984, the Savitch estate filed a wrongful death suit against eight parties, including News America Publishing, Inc., owner of the *New York Post;* the Commonwealth of Pennsylvania; and Chez Odette. It charged that the state, which had erected no guardrails on the site, was negligent in failing to protect cars from falling into the canal, and that the restaurant had failed to properly warn drivers of the danger. The station wagon had been leased by the *Post.*

Nearly four years later, a week before the suit was to go to trial in February 1988, the parties agreed to settle for an amount equal to Jessica's future lifetime earnings. The *Post* would pay more than $7 million, the restaurant $650,000, and the state $250,000, the legal limit of its liability, for a total of $8.15 million. Arthur G. Raynes, an attorney for the Savitch estate, declared that the settlement "established the principle of equality of salary and longevity for women in television news."

Several of the beneficiaries, including Mort Crim, planned to set up scholarships in Jessica's name at Temple University, the University of Pennsylvania, and Ithaca College.